The World's Richest Wrecks

A Wreck Diver's Guide To Gold And Silver Treasures Of The Seas

Robert F. Marx, with Jenifer Marx

All cover images courtesy of Robert F. Marx.

DEDICATION

"There is something in a treasure
that fastens upon a man's mind.
He will pray and blaspheme and still persevere,
and will curse the day when he first heard of it,
and let his last hours come upon him unawares,
still believing he missed it by only a foot.
He will see it every time he closes his eyes."
Joseph Conrad

To my grandsons, Jack Gregory and Hudson Gregory, who hopefully will follow in my footsteps.

ISBN 0-9818991-1-0

The World's Richest Shipwrecks:
A Wreck Diver's Guide to Gold and Silver Treasures of the Seas

Library of Congress Cataloging-in-Publication Data

Marx, Robert F., 1933-
The world's richest wrecks : a wreck diver's guide to gold and silver treasures of the seas / Robert F. Marx, with Jenifer Marx.
p. cm.
Includes bibliographical references.
ISBN-13: 978-0-9818991-1-4 (soft : alk. paper)
ISBN-13: 978-0-9818991-3-8 (cloth : alk. paper)
ISBN-10: 0-9818991-1-0
1. Shipwrecks. 2. Treasure troves. 3. Underwater archaeology.
I. Marx, Jenifer. II. Title.
G525.M2253 2009
910.4'52--dc22

2008050976

Published by RAM Books
A Division of Garrett Metal Detectors

CONTENTS

Author's Note

"Treasure fever" is an acute and incurable condition. Nothing in this world is more thrilling than descending to the sea floor and finding it carpeted with shimmering gold. Those of us who have had this rare experience recall it vividly and often. We crave more—not so much the gold as the hunt—and then the rush that comes with discovery. Of course, the gold is very nice too. Once you get "treasure fever," it stays with you forever and I have it so bad after all these years that when I'm not searching for treasure at sea, I search for and find coins and other "treasure" during my early morning walks. I'm so superstitious that I won't take a flight without first finding a coin.

But nothing compares with searching for sunken treasure. The quest is at least 4,000 years old and has never been more popular or possible. In today's stressful, hectic world, the lure of sunken treasure offers a fascinating change of pace. Even novice sports divers fantasize about coming across a sunken ship, beckoning like a siren from the ocean floor and crammed with riches.

When I started searching for sunken treasure over 50 years ago, I was generally regarded as a romantic crackpot. People thought I had a better chance of finding the proverbial pot-of-gold at the rainbow's end. However, I've proven them wrong. I've spent my life in this adventurous business, working in over 60 countries on more than 3,000 shipwrecks and finding more treasure than anyone else ever has.

Spanish galleon under sail.

Most of the successful people in this business, including Art McKee, Mel Fisher, Teddy Tucker, Robert Stenuit, Burt Webber, and myself, caught "treasure fever" at an early age. Two factors were largely responsible for the onset of our obsession: *Wake of the Red Witch,* starring John Wayne and Harry Reiseberg's book *I Dive for Treasure. Wake of the Red Witch* fired our imaginations. I must have watched John Wayne plumb the Pacific to find an enormous golden treasure on an intact Manila galleon at least 25 times. Reiseberg inspired us with gripping tales about his adventures in recovering sunken treasures around the world, tales that were to my dismay largely fictitious. Several equally fanciful books also whetted our appetites with vivid descriptions of shipwrecks, lying intact in the deep with gleaming chests of treasure in their holds and skeletons at the wheel. An important feature of these volumes was the inclusion of "authentic treasure charts" pinpointing the locations of wrecks "containing millions in treasure." It looked simple, but I was to learn the hard way that all that glitters on an "authentic treasure chart" is not gold, and that no sunken galleons are intact.

(*Above*) Co-author Jenifer Marx holding a gold scabbard tip next to an iron cannon recovered off a French warship near the Turks and Caicos islands.

(*Below*) Spanish gold doubloons and silver pieces of eight.

Author's Note

The start of my diving career was not propitious. I had two near fatal accidents from homemade diving helmets I built when I was eight and nine. At the age of thirteen I ran away from home and went to Atlantic City, New Jersey, where I spent over a year working for a commercial helmet diver, who took me into his family and taught me all the tricks of the trade. It was on one of those dives in the frigid Atlantic that I found my first gold—a beautiful pocket watch.

I am still excited today about my second gold find. I moved from Atlantic City to California and was diving for lobsters off Santa Barbara near an old wreck, when I found over 400 shiny round objects that I thought were buttons. Not knowing that gold retains its bright luster no matter how long it has been submerged, I assumed the buttons were brass. Only after giving away most of them did I discover that my "buttons" were gold coins from the California Gold Rush era.

I then spent four globetrotting years in the Marine Corps, including two six-month tours on ships of the Sixth Fleet, showing the flag all over the Mediterranean where I got to dive on dozens of ships. They were of many types from many nations and spanned the ages and I found lots of artifacts and some treasure. It was intoxicating. I had dreamed of sunken treasure since I was a young boy; now I was determined to devote my life to shipwrecks. Despite great frustration and frequent danger, I have never had regrets.

After the Marine Corps I lived for four years on Mexico's Cozumel Island where I started the island's first hotel and the first diving resort in the world. These were the happiest years of my life. I explored the jungles and the seas, discovering hidden Mayan ruins and countless shipwrecks. I recovered extensive amounts of treasure and artifacts, only to have most of it seized by the Mexi-

(Upper left image) Dolores Fisher holding a gold disk and Mel Fisher with a clump of Spanish silver coins.
(Upper right image) Beautiful French bronze cannon recovered from a French wreck off Martinique Island in the Caribbean.
(Lower image) Spanish gold doubloons, also called gold escudo coins.

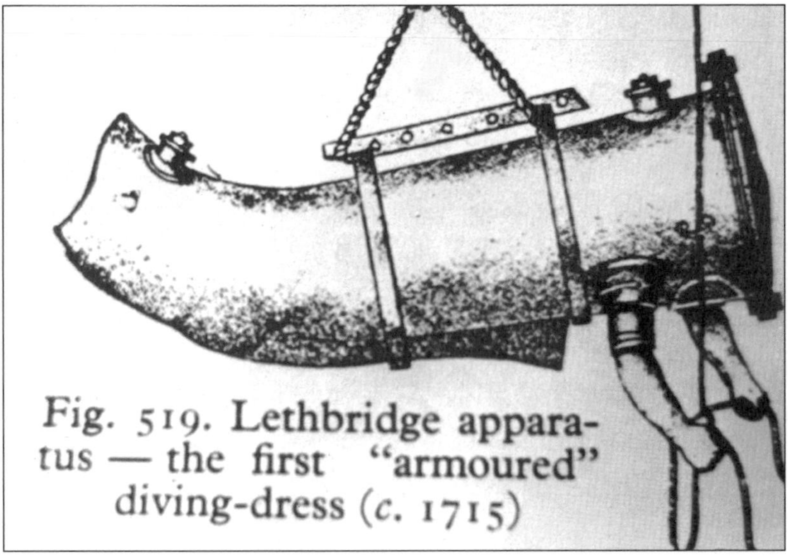

Fig. 519. Lethbridge apparatus — the first "armoured" diving-dress (c. 1715)

The diving invention of John Lethbridge, which he used in salvaging shipwrecks.

can government despite an agreement with them that I would own half of my finds. Not deterred by this experience, I decided to find greener pastures.

From Reiseberg's book and several others I selected 100 shipwrecks to go after in the Caribbean. I was convinced I would strike it rich, but I had a lot to learn. Fifteen months later, having searched from the Gulf of Honduras to the San Blas Islands off Panama, along the north coast of South America and adjacent islands as well as exploring every island in the West Indies and most of the larger ones in the Bahamas, I had found only two of the 100 "authentic" shipwrecks, and neither had anything of value on them. This was not surprising as I was to learn later when I researched original documents in European archives. Out of the 100 "authentic" wrecks, 74 existed only in the fertile imaginations of the authors upon whose information I had based my searches. Those that did exist were hundreds of miles from where the books placed them, or had no treasure on board. I call these "ghost wrecks" and laugh when I hear of professional treasure hunting groups going after them today. Those months were not ill spent. I

Small fleet of Dutch warships, mid-seventeenth century.

learned that success depended on accurate research and I set out to educate myself. Fortunately, the sale of treasure I found on several wrecks gave me the means to head for Spain and its archives and later to work in the archives of other nations. Since then, I have spent more than six years reading ancient manuscripts and amassing an unparalleled amount of authentic information on more than 80,000 shipwrecks worldwide.

Everywhere I go I am constantly asked how much treasure I have found. It is extremely difficult to answer this question since it's impossible to say what a treasure I found in 1960 would be worth today. For example, we found three identical gold and emerald crucifixes on the Spanish galleon *Maravillas,* which was lost in 1656 off the Bahamas. The first sold for $75,000 in 1974, the second for $250,000 in 1979, and the third for $450,000 in 1995. The late Mel Fisher said "Treasure is worth what you can sell it for," and he was unsurpassed in selling treasure. In 1973 I sold Fisher several hundred silver coins for $10 each. They were unattractive coins that I called "razor blades" because they were so thin that few of their markings were visible. Fisher, with his flair for salesmanship, managed to resell them for $250 each. Prior to Fisher's discovery of the galleon *Atocha* in 1985, those of us in the business had been selling Spanish silver pieces of eight for $50 to $150, depending on their condition and if they had dates. Fisher and his divers recovered over 150,000 pieces of eight from the *Atocha* and started selling them for $1,000 or more. Today some of the rare varieties sell for as much as $6,000.

Every time a new shipwreck is discovered, the media hypes it as "the richest ship ever lost" or the "richest ship ever found." When the *Atocha* was found, Fisher himself declared she was worth over $400 million, but the figure should have been more like $40 or $50 million as evidenced by the amount realized to date from sales of the *Atocha*'s recovered treasure and artifacts. This exaggerated claim gave birth to what we call "the Fisher factor" whereby finds are multiplied by ten to hype them and attract investors. Journalists, unfortunately, tend *not* to question these figures and do not investigate their plausibility. The most outrageous and irresponsible "Fisher factor" figure ever appeared in a 1998 *New York Times* article announcing the discovery, by a Tampa-based treasure-hunting company, of the HMS *Sussex,* lost in 1694 off Gibraltar. The author of that article, well known for previously exaggerated claims of shipwreck values, trumpeted the value of the *Sussex* as $4.5 billion. No shipwreck exists with even $1 billion in treasure. The richest ship ever lost was the Portuguese *Flor do Mar,* lost in 1511 off Sumatra Island, Indonesia. At the most, her cargo is valued at $100 million.

I'm sometimes asked if we are running out of "rich wrecks." Absolutely not; probably less than 1 percent of all ships ever lost with treasure aboard have been found, so there are many yet to be discovered.

(Upper image) Diver John Debry holding Spanish gold doubloons he found on a wreck.

(Lower image) Using a prop-wash, also called a blaster, to remove sand covering a wreck site. The wash of the boat's propeller is deflected downwards and blows away the sand.

Spanish silver piece of eight. This type of coin was minted from 1732 onwards. This one is dated 1742.

(Right) This drawing illustrates the method by which intact shipwrecks in water depths to 2,000 feet can be salvaged today using saturation diving techniques.

(Lower left) A man preparing the use a magnetometer, which detects the presence of large ferrous objects such as anchors and cannon. *(Lower right)* Dragging the sensor head of the magnetometer while the operator monitors the anomaly indicator chart.

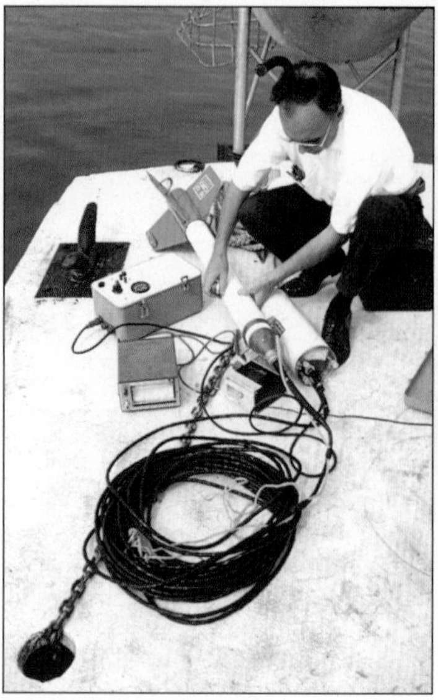

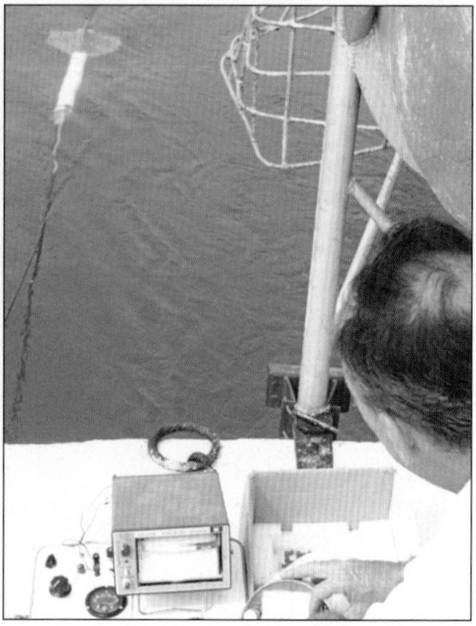

The majority of treasure recoveries made since the advent of scuba-diving gear have been on Spanish galleons lost in the New World. A few of these finds have received tremendous publicity, fueling the perception that galleons are the only desirable targets. This is not so. Less than 10 percent of treasure ships lost during the Age of Sail went down in the waters of the New World. A huge part of the globe has barely been explored for shipwrecks in modern times. During the past fifty years there have been some 200 major shipwreck explorations in the Western Hemisphere. In contrast, there have been fewer than twenty-five major expeditions elsewhere, even though there are so many more wrecks and huge amounts of treasure to be found in other parts of the world.

Until now accurate, detailed information on Old World shipwrecks has not been accessible to the public, thus eliminating them as targets for exploration. In addition, 95 percent of shipwreck explorers have been Americans who have concentrated on targets closer to home because of the logistics involved and the cost of such undertakings. Also, until recently it was far easier to obtain permission for shipwreck exploration and excavation in the Western Hemisphere than elsewhere.

My book, *Shipwrecks of the Western Hemisphere: 1492 to 1825*, was published in 1971 and later republished as *Shipwrecks of the Americas* and *New World Shipwrecks*. These books contain shipwreck data that I researched prior to 1968. Since then I have continued researching Western Hemisphere shipwrecks in primary sources, and this volume will include many shipwrecks not mentioned in my earlier books. I have never published any of my research on Old World ship losses, but have used it to locate wrecks, primarily in the Mediterranean, Atlantic Ocean, Indian Ocean, Far East, Australia, and the Philippines.

This book contains comprehensive information about the richest ships lost during the Age of Sail. The losses span the globe and range from single vessels attacked by pirates to entire fleets sunk in storms. From the many thousands of shipwrecks I have studied, I have decided to include in this book only vessels whose cargo is valued at a minimum of $10 million. This includes not only gold and silver specie and bullion, jewelry, precious stones, pearls, and porcelain,; but also objects such as bronze cannons, which today fetch between $20,000 and $40,000 and brass navigational astrolabes, some of which have sold recently for $400,000 each. I have selected targets that have a reasonable chance of being located. Consequently, I omit some well-known shipwrecks because their locations are too vague, as well as those that despite their fame do not exist. I intend this volume to be a starting point for the would-be salvor who will use it to select a target and then undertake further research to enhance his or her chances of success.

Information on search and salvage techniques, identification and dating of finds, and preservation methods can be found in my books *The Underwater Dig* and *Sunken Treasure: How to Find It*, and in books by other authors. In the interests of keeping the bibliography manageable, I have excluded works referring to "ghost wrecks."

FOREWORD

by Charles Garrett

What a pleasure it is to publish another book by Sir Robert Marx, particularly the one that is the culmination of his lifetime of research on the richest shipwrecks of the world. It was a true joy for me—a fellow treasure hunter—to read this manuscript for a number of reasons.

First of all, I consider Bob to be a great, honest, trustworthy friend. I've known him for several decades and have always had a great respect for his abilities as a seeker of underwater treasures and for him personally as a metal detectorist of the first order. He has been described by another shipwreck diver, E. Lee Spence, as "the true father of underwater archaeology." He is also a great storyteller and his books always include an element of exciting adventure mixed within the historical data he presents.

Bob has logged countless thousands of dives on Old World and New World shipwrecks off the coasts of every continent and has successfully retrieved great riches of gold, silver, jewelry and artifacts which date back hundreds and even thousands of years. His numerous accolades, which include being knighted by the rulers of three European countries, prove that his work is significant to many people. In addition to founding and serving on the boards of a number of marine archaeological societies, he has also authored more than 800 articles and reports and 60 books on history, archaeology, shipwrecks and exploration.

I have been thrilled to publish through our RAM Books publishing company several nonfiction treasure recovery books written by Bob and his wife Jenifer. The first was in 1981, *Quest for Adventure,* which chronicled his successful efforts to locate the lost 1656 treasure galleon *la Nuestra Señora de la Maravilla.* This was followed in 1986 with *Buried Treasure of the United States* and *Sunken Treasure: How to Find It* in 1990. In 1993, RAM Books published Bob's *Buried Treasure You Can Find,* a guide to thousands of treasure locations throughout the United States. We published Jenifer Marx's *Gold of the Americas* in 1996. She compiled a tremendous history and fact-filled book. As with all of Bob's books, I also recommend that all treasure hunters read it.

Jenifer and Bob Marx co-wrote *New World Shipwrecks: 1492–1825,* published by RAM Books in 1996. This volume touched on *all* documented shipwrecks of North America, South America and the Caribbean. As you can well imagine, the lists of ships were quite extensive for each area.

I was excited when Bob contacted me to say that he was finally ready to publish his most definitive book regarding the world's richest shipwrecks—the result of a lifetime of research and wreck diving. In this new book he departs the Spanish Main—his familiar treasure realms of the Caribbean and the Bahamas—to take us around the globe into new and exciting areas of exploration. He discusses enormous lost treasures of which most of us have never even heard about. You'll be amazed, as I was, at the intriguing possibilities for fame and fortune that he offers to the neophyte underwater salvor as well as the accomplished professional.

Bob is quick to point out that the famed Spanish treasure galleons which were lost as they sailed to the New World account for less than 10 percent of the ocean's richest wrecks. Considerable attention is paid to the most important ships lost off the British Isles, Africa, India, Europe, the Philippines, the Far East, Australia, the Antilles and other Old World shipping lanes. Most important to anyone who desires to make a fortune in diving a shipwreck is

(Upper) Charles Garrett searches for ancient artifacts in the Red Sea with one of his Sea Hunter metal detectors. *(Lower left and right)* Garrett with Bob Marx at the Garrett headquarters in 2008 posing with a cannon discovered by Bob and discussing metal detector use.

GARRETT

that this text covers only the lost ships whose cargoes held treasures worth at least $10 million!

Bob's marine archaeology is important to me because of the validity he has brought to the use of metal detectors in undersea treasure recovery. The abilities of Garrett's submersible detector, the *Sea Hunter*, became widely recognized in the diving community following the pioneering discoveries made with it by Bob and other successful treasure recovery teams, such as those of Mel Fisher. Not so well known is the fact that Bob Marx continues to serve as a consultant to me in the ongoing development of our underseas instruments, including the more recent *Infinium LS* land and sea pulse-induction metal detector. His advice and active support over the years have certainly contributed to the current technology housed within both current models of the *Infinium* and *Sea Hunter*.

Bob and I both caught "treasure fever" at young ages, served in the military and then ended up making careers out of our treasure hunting passion. His resume of successfully working shipwrecks could fill this volume. My pride stems from the satisfaction of having helped such adventurous souls in their quests by providing them with the best underseas detection gear to pinpoint those great hordes of silver, gold and antiques.

What makes *Fleets of Fortune* stand out among treasure hunting literature is that the author has certainly "done it." Bob can speak on wreck diving with great authority. Among his notary discoveries were his locating a *Monitor*-class Civil War ironclad off Cape Hatteras, NC, in 1955 and directing the archeological excavation of the sunken city of Port Royal in Jamaica from 1965 through 1968. At the invitation of the Lebanese Department of Antiquities, Marx explored ancient Phoenician seaports during 1973–74 and discovered shipwrecks dating from the Fifth Century B.C. He has discovered more than 3,000 shipwrecks in 62 countries, including a 17th Century Spanish merchant ship lost near Puerto Madryn,

Garrett's *Sea Hunter* and *Infinium LS* model detectors are ideally suited for sport divers working shipwrecks at ocean depths to 200 feet.

Argentina, which he found in February 2000. Two heart attacks have since slowed Bob's diving efforts, but he remains heavily involved in maritime archaeology as he directs the efforts of treasure recovery teams around the world.

The quest for sunken treasure is thousands of years old and is one that will never die. The world's oceans hold more gold, silver and priceless artifacts than can be harvested. The fury of Mother Nature's storms constantly changes the bed on which the ancient wrecks are scattered. This research on the Old World wrecks presented here will hopefully spur treasure-seekers the world over to make more glorious discoveries.

Charles Garrett

INTRODUCTION

We were taught in school that the Portuguese explorer Magellan, in 1522, was the first person to circumnavigate the globe. In fact, Chinese documents that have recently come to light show that a Chinese expedition sailed around the world a century earlier.

In March 1421 the Chinese emperor Zhu Di dispatched an enormous fleet of teakwood junks under the command of four loyal eunuch admirals: Yang Quig, Zhou Wenn, Zhou Man and Hong Bao. Their lofty mission was "to proceed all the way to the end of the earth to collect tribute from the barbarians beyond the seas and unite the whole world in harmony."

Few details have survived of this two-and-a-half-year epic voyage, but we do know that they discovered Antarctica, Australia, New Zealand and Greenland and visited all of major ports in the Indian Ocean, explored all of the African east coast and the bottom half of the west coast. Amazingly, they also explored the entire east and west coasts of North and South America. The fleet returned home to find the emperor deposed and the country torn by political and economic chaos. The new ruler was not interested in far-flung exploration and ordered that all records of this voyage be destroyed. If it weren't for the painstaking research of one man—Gavin Menzies—we would never know of this fantastic Chinese accomplishment.

The key to success in any maritime shipwreck project is exhaustive research, using primary source material whenever possible. Failure to prepare properly generally results in a great waste of time, effort and money. Rarely can a specific site be found without thorough research, as many have learned. One professional salvage firm spent over $100,000 fruitlessly searching for a galleon wreck in the Florida Keys. They came to me for help and I had to tell them their target was a "ghost wreck" and that the wreck was actually lost in the Bahamas. They had depended on information from a book by a writer who also invented a wreck he called the *Mercedes*. He claimed that it carried five times as much treasure as the *Atocha*, and was lost at the same time in 1622. A professional salvage company found one of the other missing 1622 ships and without doing proper research decided that they had found the non-existent *Mercedes*. In a lawsuit filed by the United States Security and Exchange Commission, the salvage company was severely chastised for raising funds by claiming that they had found the *Mercedes* when they had found a small ship of the fleet instead. The author of the book should have been sued for writing such false information.

Some people think that with today's sophisticated underwater electronic detection equipment it's no longer necessary to do extensive research as long as the general area of a wreck is known. I absolutely disagree with this concept. The more you know about a shipwreck the easier it is to locate and identify. Around 1990 a well-known inventor of submersibles and remote-operated-vehicles told me he was going into the shipwreck business, and I offered to provide him with research for a small percentage of his finds. He declined, stating that if he searched areas where he suspected rich wrecks lay, he would easily find a good one. Two years and over $200,000 later, he was knocking on my door for assistance and soon afterwards began finding rich targets using my historical data.

I had a similar experience with the Indonesia dictator Suharto in 1991 when he approached my company to locate and excavate the *Flor do Mar*, the richest shipwreck in the world. At the last minute, Suharto got greedy and decided that he could find the *Flor* on his own. He searched for two years and spent over $5 million without finding the wreck. He had based his search on information gleaned from an article in an airline's in-flight magazine, which erroneously placed the wreck 200 miles (322 kilometers) from where it was lost. I was brought in again and, armed with archival research and a copy of a chart showing the wreck's location drawn by the ship's pilot at the time of its loss in 1511, I found the wreck in two days.

Actually, a few significant underwater treasure recoveries have been made by lucky souls who never did a bit of research. Bermuda's Teddy Tucker, one of the world's most successful treasure hunters on whom the protagonist of the movie *The Deep* is based, started off by exploring the reefs surrounding Bermuda, using a glass-bottom bucket. When he sighted what appeared to be a human-made object, he would dive to inspect it. But for the few who have been successful, there have been hundreds who failed miserably. Most professionals agree that it is best to have the odds in one's favor, which means carrying out intensive research and planning before embarking on a shipwreck project.

Some years ago *Forbes* magazine ran an article on investing in treasure hunting and quoted me as saying: "The best way to invest in a treasure hunt is to go out on a yacht and stack the amount of money you want to invest on the open deck and enjoy a good stiff drink while you watch the wind blow the money into the sea." This infuriated friends in the salvage business. It upset me too. *Forbes* left out the end of my quote, which continued: "...unless you deal with the best people in the business, who have a legitimate target backed by impeccable historical research and a first-class operating plan."

Some people not only fail to research a potential target, but even lack the savvy to investigate locally available knowledge about a wreck. Some years ago a group of brash Texans asked me to lead a salvage operation off the north coast of Jamaica. They were quite secretive and wouldn't give me even a vague location of the site, which they claimed to have already found. When I reached Jamaica and they took me to the site, I almost died of laughter. I knew it well because in 1966 when the Playboy Club opened a hotel at Ocho Rios, the Jamaican government enlisted my services in creating a shipwreck attraction for the tourists. We dumped a boatload of ballast rock, some cannons, and anchors, delighting hotel guests who happily snorkeled around a "Spanish galleon."

The Belgian treasure hunter Robert Stenuit learned the value of scrupulous research the hard way. He launched his shipwreck career by going after Spanish galleons sunk in 1702 by an Anglo-Dutch fleet in Vigo Bay, Spain. He spent several years locating and salvaging them before he encountered documents revealing that the Spaniards had removed all treasure before the ships sank. Later, he went after the *Girona*, one of many ships lost off the British Isles during the ill-fated invasion attempt by the Spanish Armada in 1588. When the *Girona* was dashed to pieces on rocks off Northern Ireland, she was carrying the survivors and treasures from four other Spanish galleons, so that finding her would be the equivalent of finding five shipwrecks. Many had tried to locate this wreck, but until Stenuit, no one had succeeded. He spent 650 hours in pinpointing her location in several archives. The tedious work paid off when he found her in less than an hour of visual search and eventually recovered enough treasure and artifacts to fill a museum.

Stenuit again showed his research skills with the discovery of the Dutch East Indiaman *Slot ter Hoge*, lost in 1724 between Holland and the Far East with a large cargo of silver specie and bullion. Soon after the ship sank off the small island of Porto Santo, close to Madeira, the famous British diver John Lethbridge, using a wooden barrel full of air as a primitive breathing apparatus, recovered about half of the silver. Historic documents gave a vague location of the wreck, but Stenuit was fortunate to find a silver tankard once owned by Lethbridge. It bore an unusual design showing the precise location of the wreck, and Stenuit was able to recover some of the silver that Lethbridge had missed.

At the conclusion of my youthful wild-goose chase after "ghost wrecks" in the Caribbean, I realized so little was known about actual ship losses that I would have to commit myself to an intense program of original research. I didn't know then that I would spend over six years researching shipwrecks in some forty countries. In addition, I have employed dozens of professional researchers worldwide, either because I could not read the language or because I needed assistance in depositories that had overwhelming amounts of documentation. A word of caution: when hiring a researcher, make certain the person is ethical. On two occasions researchers working for me sold my research to other shipwreck salvors. Make sure the researcher is professional. I once spent four months chasing after a shipwreck in vain because the researcher I had hired confused the word "east" (*este*) for "west" (*oeste*), so I ended up searching the wrong area.

Because my original interest was in Spanish galleons, I started my research in the Archives of the Indies in Seville, Spain. This amazing depository of documents, related to the conquest and colonizing of Spanish America, contains over 250,000 daunting bundles of mixed maps, letters, orders, edicts, etc., called *legajos*. Each of these bundles is 2 to 3 feet (.5 to 1 meter) thick and most bear generalized titles such as "Papers from Peru: 16th century,"—which may cover a wide range of topics from mining to church matters. Before going to Seville, I spent twelve hours a day for two months studying old Spanish. I holed up in a remote cabin in Ontario with several thousand pages of microfilmed manuscripts from various times during the Colonial Period (1492 to 1830). It was hard work. The script initially looked like chicken scratches and there was a jumble of words in Castilian, Catalan, Basque, Portuguese, Latin and Moorish. Fortunately, I have a feel for languages and made satisfying progress. When I got to the Seville archives, the challenge I faced was not deciphering the ancient documents but finding the information I needed. This vast depository is very poorly cataloged and I often felt I was looking for the proverbial needle in the haystack. I couldn't do it all myself, so I hired researchers to assist me. The Spanish were meticulous record keepers, so persistent research in the Archives of the Indies will yield about 95 percent of the pertinent data on all New World shipwrecks, not just Spain's. I also found invaluable information in other Spanish archives: Simancas, Museo Naval, Archivo Histórico Nacional, Biblioteca Nacional, and the Real Academia de la Historia.

Unfortunately, most New World archives are bereft of useful shipwreck information. All the documentation predating Old Panama City was destroyed by fire when Henry Morgan and his pirates burned the city to the ground in 1670, and most of the documents postdating 1670 have been destroyed by Panama's humid, corrosive climate. Complete archives in Bogotá and Cartagena, Colombia, were destroyed during the War of Independence. Archives in Acapulco, Mexico City, and Veracruz didn't survive the Mexican War of Independence. Earthquakes destroyed the principal archive in Lima, Peru, in the seventeenth century and again in the eighteenth. Even in Spain, many documents were lost, particularly in 1551 when the House of Trade, where most of the documents dealing with the New World were stored, burned to the ground, and recently, in 1962, when a flash flood destroyed many more, which had been stored in the basement.

Documents concerning countless ship losses were often lost when the ships carrying them were themselves lost. In most cases three copies of a ship's manifest were made. One was carried on the ship itself, one on the flagship of the fleet, and the third was kept in the port from which the ship sailed. If the first two copies were lost, duplicate copies were made of the copy in port and sent to Spain. Other circumstances led to the loss of archival data. For example, British archives lost many historical records during the Great Fire of London in 1666 and during World War II bombing. Holland lost a vast amount of data on her East Indiamen during World War II, and France suffered great losses during the French Revolution when rioters destroyed various archives. The worst loss of historical documents in World War II occurred during the bombing of Manila, one of the last Japanese strongholds in the Philippines, when the entire archives were destroyed. In 1985 I decided to build a replica of an authentic Manila galleon. There

Author Bob Marx examines Spanish silver coins as they come up from the site of the 1656 *La Nuestra Señora de la Maravilla* shipwreck.

was no information on how these great ships were constructed, so I had to try to find relatively intact galleons in deep water. Fortunately, I located several in anaerobic areas of deep water where the lack of oxygen has protected them from voracious shipworms.

In 1755 Portugal suffered the greatest loss of historical documents of all European nations when what is still known as the Great Lisbon Earthquake tumbled the *Casa da India,* Portugal's principal archive, into the Tagus River and set off fires that destroyed other archives throughout the city. In 1746 a Portuguese fleet of twenty ships, including some returning from the Orient, was sailing from Brazil to Lisbon. A fierce storm forced the fleet into the Caribbean, where people on Barbados sighted it just before hurricane winds widely dispersed the vessels. Thirteen ships sank without a trace.

Survivors wrote about the disaster, but their accounts perished in the Lisbon earthquake. We know of it only from a London broadside, the newspaper of those days, which mentions the fleet appearing off Barbados during the storm.

Primary research is always preferable for obtaining the best information on ship losses covered in this book, but when it is not possible, careful research in secondary sources is often fruitful. Books and newspapers published before 1800 are generally found only in large libraries such as the British Library in London, the Bibliothèque nationale de France in Paris, the Library of Congress in Washington, D.C., and the Fifth Avenue New York Public Library in New York City. For New World shipwrecks, the best place to start is by consulting *Incunabula and Americana 1450–1800*, by Margaret B. Stillwell. It lists over 11,000 documents and books and gives the libraries that have them. For the Old World, consult the four-volume work by Robert A. Peddie, *Subject Index of Books*. It has an alphabetically arranged subject list of over 50,000 books written in many languages and has helped me immensely over the years.

Old newspaper accounts are also a valuable source of shipwreck information. More than once I've been able to identify or learn more about a shipwreck from newspapers. In 1959 I identified a merchantman I discovered off Yucatán by finding an article in *La Gazeta de Mexico*, published in Mexico City. Once I had her name, *Nuestra Señora del Milagros* (alias *El Matancero*), I was able to unearth her whole history in the Archives of the Indies.

Newspapers, first printed in the American colonies in 1690, were the only medium for public dissemination of news. An excellent source to consult is the two-volume work by Clarence S. Brigham, *History and Bibliography of American Newspapers, 1690 to 1820*. Newspapers listed the movements of ships, both American and foreign, and also published information on ship losses throughout the world. Unfortunately, the information was not always accurate, so it is important to cross-reference multiple sources of information. When Kip Wagner discovered several shipwrecks from

Author Bob Marx, using an early Garrett model XS500 metal detector, happily displays a gold escudo Spanish coin. While silver coins tarnish after only a short exposure to salt water, gold does not tarnish—although it can become encrusted with coral.

the 1715 treasure fleet off the coast of central Florida, he consulted Mendel Peterson, then the leading expert on shipwrecks at the Smithsonian Institution in Washington, D.C. Peterson's claim that the wrecks could not be from the 1715 fleet was based on a Charleston, South Carolina, newspaper article from the time, which stated that the entire fleet had been lost in the Florida Keys.

Most major European cities had newspapers (broadsides) from the mid-seventeenth century onwards. Some broadsides printed a paragraph or two on a ship loss; others, notably in Portugal, devoted as many as twenty pages to a single shipwreck. I found wonderful information on Portuguese East Indiamen losses in private collections of broadsides. *Lloyd's List*, published in England since 1734, records ship movements of both British and foreign ships, as well as ship losses and is a valuable source of information. Until recently it was necessary to go to London to consult these "lists," but they have been printed in a multi-volume work, available in many metropolitan libraries.

An important factor to consider when researching in primary source material is that there was no standardized calendar followed by all countries. In 1582 Pope Gregory XIII ordered that ten days of that year be omitted to bring the calendar and the sun into correspondence, thus creating the Gregorian calendar we use today. Protestant countries, however, clung to the Roman-era Julian calendar for many years. Until England adopted the Gregorian calendar in 1752, the new year began on March 25, so that a date of February 11, 1733 to the English was February 21, 1734, to Catholic European nations.

Charts and maps are often sources for locating shipwrecks. Over the years I have found hundreds pinpointing—with astonishing accuracy in some cases, and equally astonishing inaccuracy in others—shipwreck locations. Three cartographers drew three different charts showing the exact positions of the 21 ships of a fleet of treasure galleons lost in 1733 in the Florida Keys. On the other hand, a chart showing the locations of a number of galleons lost in 1622 in the same area was so inaccurate that it was useless. It would be foolhardy to mount a shipwreck expedition based solely on a charted location. The most accurate shipwreck charts were generally drawn by contemporary salvors.

A number of factors should be considered in referring to old charts and maps. Over the centuries, shorelines have receded in some areas and expanded in others. Many small islands and cays, especially in the Indian Ocean, that existed years ago have disappeared. New islands have appeared; some are human-made. The mouths of rivers and streams have often meandered considerable distances, and some have been closed by natural forces and humans. Place names change over the centuries and it is not always easy to determine the new name of a place from an old one mentioned in a document or other source.

Most depositories of primary source material have good collections of charts and maps. The most extensive collections, covering the whole world, are in the Map Room of the British Library in London, as well as the Library of Congress and the main branch of the New York Public Library in the United States. Some European libraries and archives have made both old documents and charts available for researchers on the Internet, which is a far cry from the days when I first started doing primary research. In those days many depositories barely had sufficient lighting.

Wherever I go I consult fishermen for shipwreck locations. They are usually very familiar with the surrounding sea bottom and often snag objects from wrecks in their nets. For example, in a one-week period, fishermen off Corsica took me to 26 ancient shipwrecks. Fishermen led me to all but six of the more than fifty shipwrecks I explored off Bahía, Brazil. The two major treasure finds made in the Gulf of Mexico in recent years, resulted from shrimp nets snagging chests of old Spanish gold and silver coins.

I learned the folly of lack of preparation the hard way. Many years ago I was confident that I could locate a fourteenth-century French shipwreck laden with 100,000 gold coins lost off Rye, England, because I had found excellent documentary historical information pinpointing the wreck. The information was so detailed that it gave the compass bearings of the wreck in relation to three buildings in the town that still stand today. After mounting a major expedition, without ever visiting Rye first, I arrived to find that there were cows and sheep grazing atop the wreck site. Over the centuries the land built out seaward, sealing the port from access to the sea and covering the wreck in the process. I never made that mistake again.

This book should be a guide for the reader interested in finding a treasure ship. I don't expect anyone to run off to search for any of the shipwrecks covered in this book without additional research and careful planning. After selecting a target in a specific area, the reader should devote time to further research, which must include learning about the regulations governing shipwreck work in the area of interest. Don't forget to visit the area to determine if it is even possible to find the target. Many shipwrecks close to shore have been covered over by landfill, destroyed by dredging, or lie in a forbidden military zone. Don't spend a lot of money before obtaining government permission and creating an organizational and financial plan.

Happy treasure hunting!

New World

CHAPTER 1

INTRODUCTION TO NEW WORLD SHIPWRECKS

Until Columbus's 1492 voyage to the New World, the economies of the European nations were stagnant due to a severe lack of precious metals, which were critical for expanding mercantile trade. It was the search for gold that led to the discovery of the New World. Columbus had read of Marco Polo's thirteenth-century travels in which he described a land called Zipango (Japan) so filled with gold that even the roof tiles were made of it.

Columbus was convinced that by sailing westward from Europe, he would reach Zipango and satisfy Europe's hunger for gold and silver. As it turned out, treasure was obtained not from Zipango but from the mines of Mexico and South America.

During the Colonial Period, about 90 percent of the precious metals mined in the entire world came from the New World. The Spaniards mined over half a million ounces of gold and more than 5 billion ounces of silver. This was the official tally, but these figures may well be doubled if we take into account the amount of unregistered gold and silver that was mined. Some was smuggled back to Spain and some used in the New World to purchase contraband goods from other European nations, which undersold the merchants in Seville who had a monopoly on trade with the New World colonists.

The importance of the New World treasure to Spain is evidenced in the following dispatch sent to the Doge by the Venetian ambassador to Spain in September 1567:

At the time of my last letter to you, I wrote that there was great anxiety all over Spain over the delay of the arrival of the annual treasure fleets, when the Genoese bankers informed the king that unless the fleets reached port shortly, they would be unable to negotiate any further loans for him, Philip II fell into such a state of shock that he had to be confined to bed by his physicians. The king then ordered that some ten thousand pesos, which was about all the money remaining in the royal coffers, to be used in various churches for the saying of masses for the safe arrival of the fleets. I am happy to inform you that the fleets have made port safely and there is now great rejoicing not only in the Royal Court, but throughout the land.

New World treasure was critical to the other nations of Europe as well, since it furnished nearly 95 percent of the precious metals on which their monetary systems were based. There is a popular misconception that only Spain benefited when in fact she benefited less than the rest of Europe. The reason is there was virtually no industry of any kind in Spain, which was totally dependent on

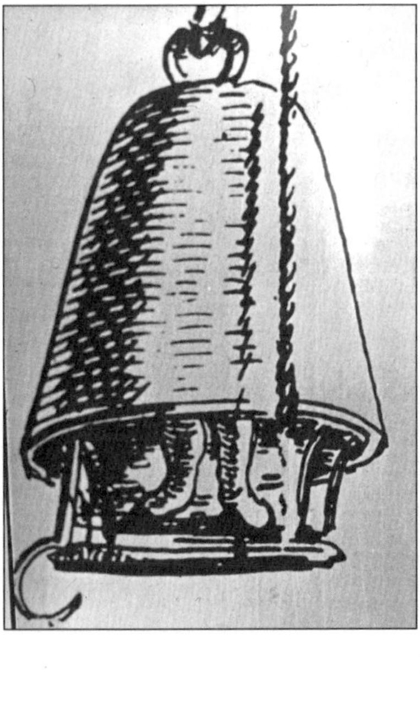

Diving bells such as this one were used to salvage wrecks worldwide. A diver would take a full breath of air in the bell and then swim on the bottom until he needed more air, which he obtained again in the bell.

The fabulously rich mine of Potosí in Peru (today in Bolivia), where over 60 percent of the gold and silver mined in the entire world in the sixteenth and seventeenth centuries was produced.

other nations for manufactured goods, both for export to the New World and for domestic consumption. Therefore, nearly all of the New World treasure was used to pay for goods from other nations, which used much of the silver and gold in expanding trade with the Orient.

During the first few decades of Spanish rule in the New World, the conquistadors obtained most of their treasure by plundering temples where generations-worth of treasure and tribute were stored. When they exhausted this source, they enslaved the Amerindians and forced them to work the mines that they had been digging in for centuries and set them to panning for gold in riverbeds. In 1545, about the time these two sources began to run out, a breakthrough occurred in Peru with the discovery of the prodigious silver mountain of Potosí (today located in Bolivia). Three years later, other rich silver and gold mines were discovered in Chile, Ecuador, Colombia, Guatemala, and Mexico.

Another boost in the amount of precious metals reaching Spain came in 1555 when a German alchemist introduced the use of quicksilver (mercury) in refining precious metals. This process, first used by the Phoenicians around 1,000 B.C., fell out of use during the European so-called Dark Ages when little precious metal was mined. The Spaniards discovered the Huancavelica mercury mine in Peru that supplied all the mercury needed by the South American mines. Mercury for refining in Mexico came chiefly from Hungary, with some coming from the Almadén mine in southern Spain, first used by the Romans.

For over three centuries lumbering galleons plied the route between Spain and the New World. The precious cargoes they carried were the lifeblood of Spain and affected the economies of most of Europe. American gold caused such an increase in gold supplies that the metal depreciated, sparking horrendous inflation all over Europe. As early as 1503 commerce with Spain's American colonies was strictly organized. The merchants of Seville enjoyed a virtual monopoly. A royal order created the House of Trade to control all aspects of commerce and colonization in the Americas, and hundreds of ships began sailing between the Spain and the New World on a scheduled basis.

The vessels leaving Seville carried a broad array of items for Spanish colonies because colonists were forbidden to manufacture anything at all. They were even forbidden to produce wine or olive oil, the two staples of the Spanish diet. Spain herself manufactured very little so the ships were laden with goods from almost every nation in Europe: tools and weapons, cooking utensils, glassware and ceramics, cutlery, cloth and trimmings, hats, shoes, religious objects, furniture, window glass, and even dressed stone and bricks for buildings.

On the return voyage, in addition to gold and silver specie and bullion, which was the main cargo in value, the galleons carried

(Facing, top image) The Bahama Channel is also called the Gulf of Florida. Note the islands off Cape Canaveral, which no longer exist. *(Facing, lower image)* Wooden remains of seventh century Byzantine merchant ship located off of Akko, Israel. Two meters of sand was removed which concealed the wreck when first found.

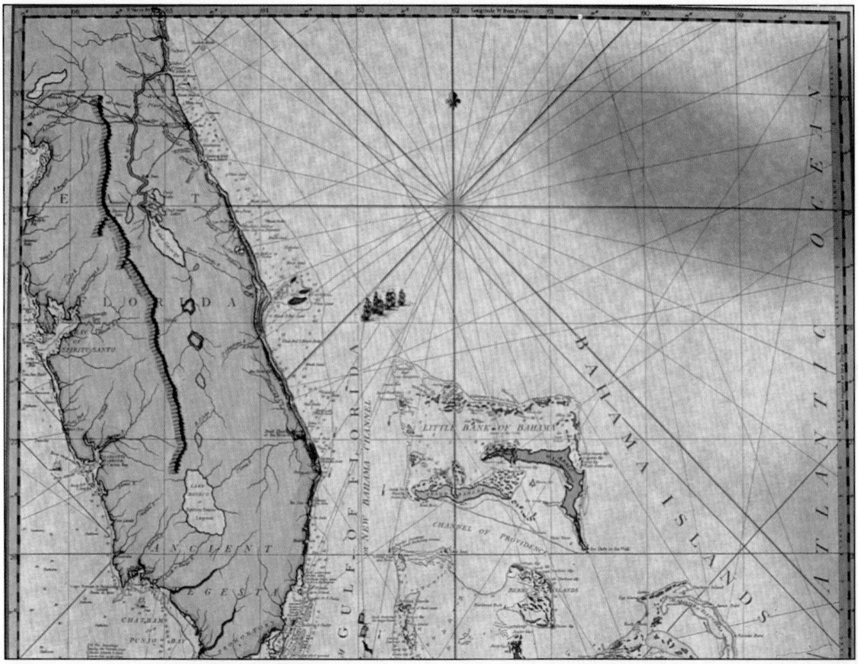
FLORIDA
BAHAMA ISLANDS
ATLANTIC OCEAN
GULF OF FLORIDA
NEW BAHAMA CHANNEL
LITTLE BANK OF BAHAMA
CHANNEL OF PROVIDENCE
ANCIENT
CHATHAM

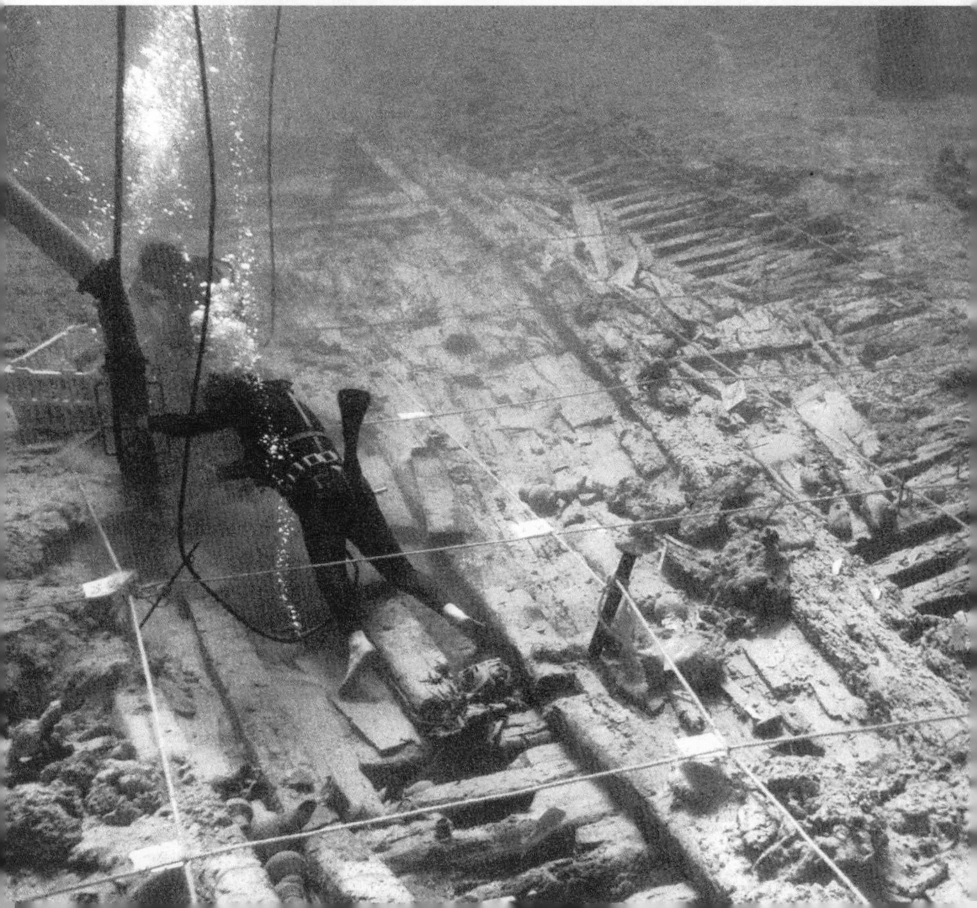

GARRETT

chests of pearls, emeralds and other gemstones, and agricultural products such as sugar, tobacco and dyestuffs. After 1565, when the Manila galleons began making the perilous voyage between the Philippines and Acapulco, on the west coast of Mexico, exotic products from the Far East were added to the shipments destined for Seville. Oriental goods were unloaded at Acapulco and carried by pack animals across the mountains to the port of Veracruz on the Gulf of Mexico where they were put aboard the transatlantic galleons.

During the first half of the sixteenth century Spanish ships made transatlantic voyages alone or in small convoys. A dramatic increase in attacks by pirates and privateers from the nations that had been excluded from the Treaty of Tordesillas in 1495 led to the establishment of a new convoy system. Starting in 1552, three separate fleets sailed each year. The New Spain or Mexican Fleet called first at Veracruz to load treasure and exotic Oriental goods and then headed for Havana. The Tierra Firme Fleet picked up gold and emeralds from the Colombian mines at Cartagena and then went on to Panama. A great mercantile fair was held in Panama, either in Nombre de Dios or Porto Bello. The treasures from Peru, Chile and Ecuador, consisting chiefly of gold and silver specie and bullion, were brought to Panama City on the Pacific side of Panama and then transported across the isthmus by mule to the fair to await the arrival of the third fleet, which was called the Armada of Tierra Firme or the Galleons. After all of the treasures were embarked on the galleons, both fleets sailed together to Havana to join the New Spain Fleet and sail for Spain. The combined homeward-bound fleet, which at times numbered over 250 ships, must have been a stirring sight as it headed up the Straits of Florida.

Throughout the Colonial Period, many ships (known as *registros*) sailed alone or in small groups from Spain to the New World and back again. Lacking the protection of the large fleets, they were preyed on by pirates and privateers. However, they offered

Marx holds gold coins he found with his *Sea Hunter* off Cuba.

An early eighteenth century Spanish galleon under sail.

the advantage of carrying contraband treasure and off-loading it either off the southern coast of Portugal or at small Spanish ports to evade customs officials. Each year some six to ten *avisos* or mail boats also sailed between Spain and the New World. Although officially forbidden to carry any treasure on the return voyage, as a rule, they carried large amounts of unregistered treasure.

Early in the sixteenth century the Spanish established pearl fisheries on the islands of Cubagua and Margarita off the northern coast of Venezuela. The supply of indigenous Carib divers was soon exhausted. Many died from European diseases. Others died from overwork at the hands of their greedy employers, who forced them to dive as many as sixteen hours a day. The next source of divers were enslaved Lucayan Indians from the Bahamas. The Spanish historian Oviedo, writing in 1535, gave an account of a visit to the pearl fisheries of Margarita where he observed the divers, who were considered the best divers in the New World.

Bronze cannons from a late sixteenth-century Spanish galleon recovered by Marx in 1962 and currently on display in an Azores Islands museum.

He marveled at their ability, noting that they were able to descend to depths of 100 feet (30 meters) and remain submerged as long as five minutes. They had more stamina than the Caribs and could dive from sunrise to sunset, seven days a week, without appearing to tire. As Old World divers had done for millennia, they descended by grasping stone weights in their arms. They dove naked except for a net bag around their necks in which they deposited oysters they found on the bottom. So great was the demand for the Lucayan divers in the pearl fisheries that in only a few decades the Bahamas were bereft of their former inhabitants, the first natives seen by Columbus on his epic voyage of discovery. Negroes from Africa replaced them as divers.

The Spaniards also used divers in salvage work. Every year from 1503 onward, ships from Spain carried supplies across the Atlantic to sustain its new settlements in the New World. On the return voyages these ships carried the treasures and products of the colonies back to the mother country. Because of frequent storms and careless navigation, many ships were lost at sea. In major colonial ports like Havana, Veracruz, Cartagena and Panama, teams of native divers, and subsequently African slaves, were kept aboard salvage vessels that were ready to depart on short notice to attempt recovery of sunken treasure. Contrary to popular belief, contemporary divers were able to recover over 90 percent of the treasures lost on the Spanish ships in the New World. From the sixteenth century to the end of the eighteenth century, divers recovered more than 100 million pesos ($1,250,000,000 in modern currency) from Spanish wrecks. On more than one occasion, they saved the Spanish Crown from bankruptcy.

CHAPTER 2

CANADA'S RICHEST SHIPWRECKS

Canada, the second largest country in the world, has the world's longest coastline. Canada's maritime history is fascinating. A thousand years ago Viking ships plied the waters and Basque whalers began fishing off Labrador in the 1420s. In 1497 John Cabot claimed Canada for King Henry VII, and by 1502 England received the first shipment of Canadian fish. For centuries the rich Grand Banks fisheries off Newfoundland attracted ships from France, Portugal, Spain and England, and countless of them sank. However, very few ships with treasure were lost in Canadian waters because almost all the ships plying these waters were merchantmen, warships, immigrant ships and fishing vessels. I have found records of over 1,000 ship losses off Canada during the Age of Sail but only the six below meet the criteria for inclusion in this book.

Harsh weather, rough seas and ice cold water throughout most of the year make Canada one of most challenging areas in the Western Hemisphere for shipwreck exploration and salvage. In fact, most Canadian divers interested in finding shipwrecks head for Bermuda, the Bahamas and the Caribbean. However, there have been some very interesting shipwreck finds in Canadian waters.

Canada's major treasure salvage operation took place during the summers of 1965 and 1966 when three amateur divers located the eighteenth-century French warship *Le Chameau* off Cape Breton Island, Nova Scotia. They found the site by dragging a grappling hook where the ship was known to have sunk, and when

These Spanish silver coins were discovered on an unidentified shipwreck near the entrance to Halifax Harbor.

it snagged something, a diver went down to investigate. The wreck was first located in 1914, when a helmet diver surveying a modern shipwreck spotted gold and silver coins on the sea-floor. He planned to recover the treasure as soon as he finished the shipwreck survey, but he drowned a few days later without having revealed the location. The 1960s salvors worked with a 2 to 3-knot current ripping across the wreck site in water that never rose above 45°F (7°C)—conditions I encountered when diving there in 1979. The divers recovered over 2,000 louis d'or coins and 11,000 silver livre coins, as well as a silver pocket watch and other interesting objects.

In 1978 a team of underwater archaeologists from Parks Canada discovered the oldest known wreck in Canadian waters. She was the Basque whaling ship *San Juan*, lost in 1565 in the harbor of Red Bay, Labrador. To survive in the icy waters, divers had hot water from the surface continuously circulated through their rubber suits. Though frigid, the waters were crystal clear, which greatly facilitated the collection of archaeological data. It was a particularly significant find because it furnished scholars with

The port of Halifax, Nova Scotia, in 1766.

tens of thousands of fascinating sixteenth-century artifacts, many of them rare, including a bronze navigator's astrolabe, the ship's compass, intact wooden barrels for storing whale oil, and even the ship's whaleboat, the only one of its kind in existence. After seven summers of intense work, the archaeologists discovered two other Basque whaling ships of the same vintage, also in an excellent state of preservation due to the cold water. Lack of funds has prevented further excavation.

1725: French frigate of war *Le Chameau* carrying a valuable cargo of gold and silver coins was lost off the southeast corner of Cape Breton Island, Nova Scotia. It was discovered in 1965 and worked on by various treasure hunters, including myself, but the bulk of her treasure still lies undiscovered.

1758: British warship HMS *Tilbury* was lost off the south side of Cape Breton Island. She was the pay ship of Admiral Edward Boscawen's fleet and carried over £500,000 sterling in gold and silver specie. In 1979 I discovered this wreck about 8 miles (13 kilo-

(Left) French silver coin recovered from the *Chameau* off Louisburg, Cape Breton. *(Below)* Two Spanish coins, known as "bust dollars," recovered from an unidentified wreck off Scatarie Island near Louisburg, Cape Breton.

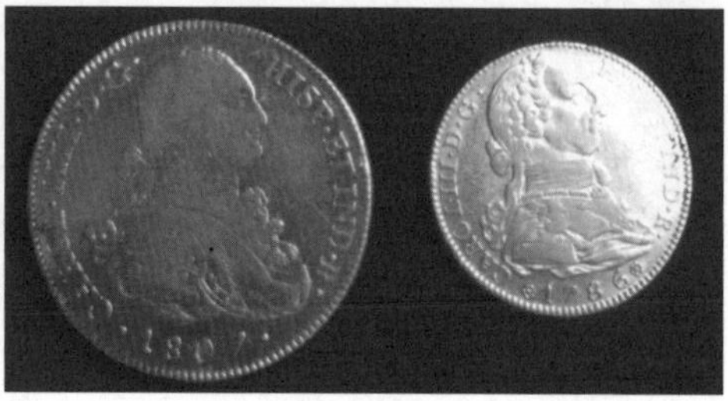

meters) east of Louisbourg on a shoal of rocks named Tilbury Reef. However, the Canadian government has not granted an excavation permit.

1796: The British warship HMS *Active*, commanded by Captain Edward Leverson Gower, was lost near the entrance of the St. Lawrence River carrying over £300,000 sterling in silver specie.

1798: During a gale in Halifax Harbor, many ships were sunk, including the HMS *Lynx*, a British warship carrying £75,000 sterling in gold and silver specie.

1812: The British warship HMS *Barbados* was lost on Sable Island off the coast of Nova Scotia, carrying over £500,000 sterling in gold and silver bullion and specie.

1822: The French ship *L'Americaine*, carrying over $1 million in gold and silver specie and bullion, was lost on Sable Island, off the coast of Nova Scotia.

Over 30,000 of these British copper pennies, all dated 1801, were recovered off a merchantman off Scatarie Island, near Louisburg.

Marx's major salvage vessel *Rio Grande*—a 110 foot long, all aluminum vessel with twin blasters.

Chapter 3

Florida's Richest Shipwrecks

Spain lost over 1,000 treasure-laden ships during the Colonial Period (1492–1830). It is not surprising that the waters surrounding Florida have been the focus of the most intense shipwreck exploration in the world. No area in the Western Hemisphere boasts more sunken treasure. The seas off the Florida Keys and Cape Canaveral claimed hundreds of Spain's treasure-laden ships. In many cases original documents furnish only the vaguest wreck location, such as "lost on the coast of Florida." In 1591, for instance, 27 ships of the combined fleets of Tierra Firme and New Spain were lost after leaving Havana. Manuscript documents simply state "lost between the Florida Keys and Cape Canaveral," so they can be anywhere along 200 miles (322 kilometers) of coast. This book covers only those few with relatively precise locations.

From the time of Columbus until the introduction of the steamship, all vessels returning from Spain's New World colonies to Europe sailed up the dangerous Bahama Channel, the passage between Cuba and the Florida Keys, also known as the Straits of Florida. Hurricanes and faulty navigation took a heavy toll on these ships.

Each year, after leaving Veracruz and heading for Havana, the New Spain Fleets sailed across the Gulf of Mexico and made first landfall around the Dry Tortugas, the small group of islands at

Author Marx with two tin ingots recovered from a British wreck carrying over 100 tons of tin, lost off of Lousbourg Nova Scotia, Canada.

Primitive charts, such as this one dated 1545, were used in the sixteenth century to navigate the ships, and were no doubt responsible for the loss of many ships.

the end of the Florida Keys archipelago, or at the Florida Keys. This served as a checkpoint in navigation before the ships sailed towards Havana, which lies only 90 miles (145 kilometers) from Key West. During moonless nights and in bad weather, the flat cays and islands were invisible and many ships struck coral reefs. This treacherous area claimed so many lives that it appeared on Spanish charts as "The Martyrs." This is where the famed Spanish galleon *Atocha*, found by Mel Fisher, was lost in 1622.

After setting sail from Havana, both the New Spain and Tierra Firme fleets first headed about 50 miles (80 kilometers) east before starting up the Bahama Channel to steer clear of the Florida Keys. However, prevailing easterly winds and hurricanes drove many ships upon the Keys' myriad reefs. Once ships entered the Straits of Florida, they sailed north. To minimize danger, they tried to clear the Keys, but after one day's sail they headed closer to the coast, following standard sailing directions to the navigational checkpoint of Cape Canaveral. The sighting of this jut of land, which bears the oldest place name in North America, indicated a ship was far enough north to avoid the shallows of the perilous Little Bahama Bank. Ships then set a course northeast for Bermuda, another navigational checkpoint. Unfortunately, even on days with optimal visibility, many ships foundered on submerged shoals and reefs off Cape Canaveral.

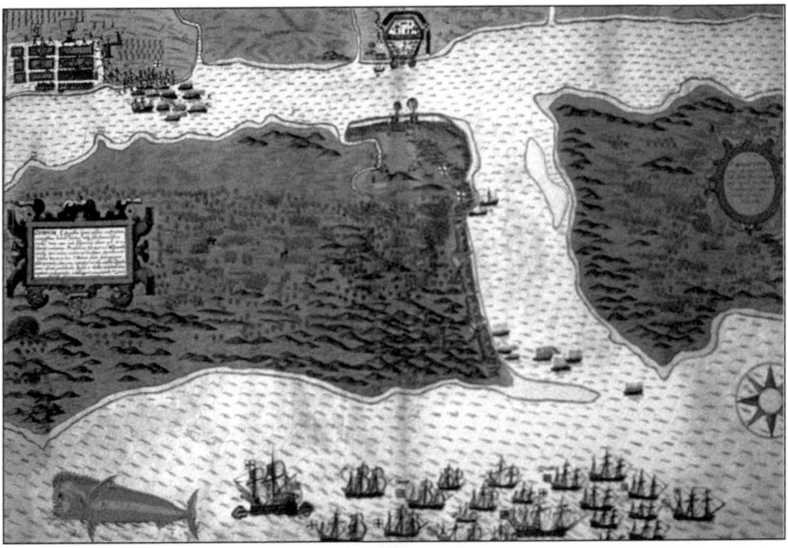

Sir Francis Drake attacking St. Augustine, Florida, in 1586.

Only a small number of Florida wrecks were salvaged, either because their locations were too imprecise or because by the time salvors arrived the remains were invisible under shifting sands or widely scattered. Actually, Florida's coastal Indians were sometimes more successful at recovering treasure than the Spaniards. In 1556 when a galleon wrecked off Cape Canaveral, Ais Indians recovered over 1 million pesos in treasure, which they buried ashore. Soldiers sent down from St. Augustine used torture to force the Indians to give up the treasure.

1549: Three unidentified Spanish merchantmen, sailing from Veracruz to Havana with a total of 980,000 pesos in gold and silver, wrecked in a hurricane near the south end of Key Largo. Most of the people made it ashore and lived there for several years in great hardship before a passing ship rescued them.

1563: The Spanish galleon *La Madalena,* (250 tons/254 tonnes), commanded by Captain Critical Rodriguez, was returning to Spain from Veracruz when she wrecked during a storm off Cape Canaveral. Sixteen out of the 300 souls aboard survived, reaching shore in a small boat. At the time she sank, she was carrying over 50 tons (50 tonnes) of

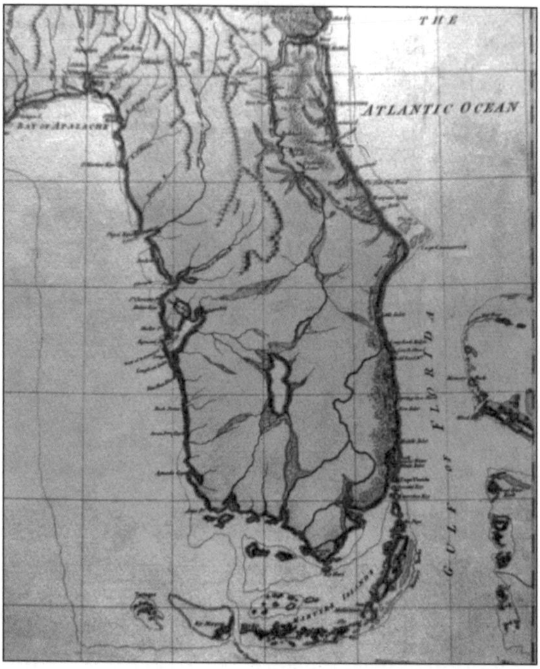

By 1763 when this chart was made, there was much improvement in the accuracy of the chart. Here the Bahama Channel, or Straits of Florida, is called the Gulf of Florida.

silver in specie and bullion, 170 boxes of worked silver (candlesticks, plates, etc.), 1,100 pounds (500 kilograms) of gold, plus jewelry and pearls. Repeated Spanish attempts to locate *La Madalena* were fruitless. In 1970, nearly 400 years later, a shrimper's net snagged a large bronze cannon dated 1560, which is believed to be from this wreck.

1571: Two galleons, the *San Ignacio,* (300 tons/304 tonnes, 22 cannons), under command of Captain Juan de Canova and the *Santa María de la Limpia Concepción* (340 tons/345 tonnes), sailed in the New Spain Fleet from Veracruz with over 1.5 million pesos in treasure. A hurricane struck the fleet in the Gulf of Mexico, separating the two galleons from the others. After making necessary repairs they reached Havana, only to find that the New Spain Fleet had already sailed for Spain. Sailing together, they made their way up the Straits of Florida, and when they were several hours' sail south of Cape Canaveral, the galleons were further damaged in a storm. The captains decided to run their ships aground at the cape to save lives and treasure, but while trying to get close to shore, they both wrecked on a shoal about 1.5 leagues offshore. There were no survivors, but Spanish soldiers on the shore where a small wooden fort had been erected to aid shipwreck survivors witnessed the disaster.

1578: An unidentified Spanish ship was lost "3 or 4 leagues" south of Matanzas Inlet, where the Spaniards had a small fort. (A league is a unit of distance equal to 3.0 statute miles or 4.8 kilometers.) Indians reported the disaster and soldiers from the fort found many bodies on the beach and a small box with dozens of gold rings and other jewelry. Two years later the governor of Havana wrote to the king, stating that he was sending a salvage vessel to find "the very rich ship lost south of Matanzas Inlet," but there is no record that it was found.

1588: This year only one ship, *Santa María Del Camino* (280 tons/284 tonnes), commanded by Captain Alonzo Martín Morejón, was dispatched to Nombre de Dios in Panama to pick up all of that year's treasures from South America. She took on 1.8 million pesos in gold and silver in Panama and then an unspecified amount of gold, emeralds and pearls in Cartagena, Colombia. A hurricane drove the ship ashore and it was dashed to pieces near St. Lucie Inlet on the east Florida coast. Indians massacred most of the survivors, but kept some of them prisoners until they were rescued several years later by Spaniards from Havana who were searching for ambergris.

1589: In 1588 Spain's sadly misnamed "Invincible Armada" attempted to attack England. It was soundly defeated and over 100 ships were wrecked along the coasts of Ireland and Scotland. A year later Spain suffered another major loss of ships. On September 9, 1589, three Spanish treasure fleets joined together and set sail from Havana for Spain. Fewer than a dozen of the more than 100 ships ever reached the motherland. As the massive convoy entered the mouth of the Bahama Channel, a hurricane struck. One of the richest of the galleons, the *Magdalena* (650 tons/660 tonnes), commanded by Captain Antonio Jorge, laden with over 1.25 million pesos in treasure plus a probable equal amount in contraband treasure, began firing her cannon for assistance. The other ships, struggling to free themselves from the Florida reefs, couldn't respond. The galleon went down north of present-day Miami and all but three of the 700 people aboard drowned. Many of the other ships were also lost along the east coast. Fifteen of the remaining vessels sank in a second hurricane near the Azores.

1600: An unidentified galleon of 400 tons (406 tonnes), commanded by Captain Diego Rodríquez Garrucho, stayed behind in Veracruz after this year's New Spain Fleet departed for Havana and Spain. The ship was waiting to carry treasures, which was being brought from the Philippines and points east. When the galleon finally set sail, she carried over 700,000 pesos in gold and silver, plus 245 chests and boxes of Oriental goods of unspecified value, which would have included Chinese porcelain and objects made of gold, silver, jade, ivory and sandalwood, and possibly precious gemstones. The ship bypassed the usual stop at Havana and started up the Straits of Florida after leaving the Gulf of Mexico. During a moonless night she wrecked on a shoal several leagues offshore near Cape Canaveral. Only seven men and a boy managed to reach shore. They walked up the beach to the Spanish town of St. Augustine. The governor there sent a salvage vessel to find the treasure wreck. Sand can move amazingly quickly, as the Spanish salvors discovered. By the time they reached the site, the wreck was almost entirely buried under the sand and they recovered only three bronze cannons. A salvage attempt the following year proved fruitless.

1611: After the New Spain Fleet of Captain-General the Marquis de Cadereyta sailed from Veracruz, they encountered a bad storm and the galleon *Santa Ana María del Juncal* (650 tons/660 tonnes), commanded by Captain Bernardo de Torres and carrying over 2 million pesos in treasure, separated from the convoy and was wrecked near Cape Apalache. Salvors sent by the viceroy of Mexico found timbers and flotsam from the wreck on the beach, but were unable to find any of her treasure.

1622: A hurricane off the Florida Keys struck a Spanish treasure fleet, sinking nine ships in the Florida Keys and three more south of the Dry Tortugas. The *Atocha* and the *Margarita,* which sank south of the Tortugas, were discovered by the late Mel Fisher and have produced vast amounts of treasure. The third Tortuga wreck, the *Nuestra Señora del Rosario,* sank in shallow water and was thoroughly salvaged by the Spaniards. About twenty years ago, it was relocated. The National Park Service worked on it, finding only a few artifacts. The other undiscovered shallow water wreck sites have tremendous amounts of treasure. A fisherman accidentally located one of the three unidentified deep wrecks in 1,400 feet (427 meters) of water. Seahawk Deep Water Technology partially salvaged it in 1990 and 1992.

1624: The Spanish galleon *El Espíritu Santo El Major* (600 tons/609 tonnes), commanded by Captain Juan de Olozabal, was lost near Key Largo, Florida. She was one of more than forty ships of the Tierra Firme treasure fleet under the command of Don Antonio de Oquendo. The fleet sailed from Havana and as it entered the Bahama Channel, a sudden squall struck near Cape Canaveral. When the fierce storm was over, the *El Espíritu Santo El Major* and her cargo of 2.2 million pesos had disappeared without a trace in deep water.

1641: As the New Spain Fleet of Captain General Juan de Campos was sailing up the Straits of Florida, they were struck by a hurricane. Running before the storm, they passed Cape Canaveral and five of the ships, carrying a combined total of 2.35 million pesos in treasure, were wrecked on the coast between 5 and 10 miles (8 and 16 kilometers) north of St. Augustine and there were no survivors. Seven others sank on the high seas in this same area. Another ship in the fleet picked up fourteen survivors. Another, the *Nuestra Señora de la Concepción*, which served as the *Almiranta* of the fleet, lost all her masts and drifted for weeks before wrecking on Silver Shoals north of Hispaniola. This was the wreck described in Chapter 7 that was salvaged forty years later by Sir William Phips, who recovered most of the 2 million pesos in silver she carried.

1683: The Spanish galleon *Santissima Concepción* (700 tons/711 tonnes), commanded by Admiral Manuel Ortiz Arosemena, sailed late in 1682 from Spain for Peru and Mexico with a cargo of mercury. At Cartagena she took 77 chests of pearls and 49 chests of emeralds on board. In Porto Bello and Veracruz she took on over 1.8 million pesos in treasure and 217 chests of goods from the Orient. As she approached Cape Canaveral, she was struck by a hurricane and driven upon a shoal about 3 or 4 leagues off the cape. Of the 500 souls on board, only five reached the shore by clinging to pieces of rigging. Repeated attempts failed to locate the wreck. A chest of clothing containing personal gold jewelry, valued at 1,500 pesos, was found on the beach a month after the disaster.

1715: On July 31 a powerful hurricane struck a treasure fleet of twelve ships, sinking eleven of them between St. Lucie Inlet and St. Augustine. Modern-day salvors have found only six of these wrecks. The flagship of the fleet, the galleon *Nuestra Señora de la Regla* (471 tons/478 tonnes), commanded by Captain-General Esteban de Ubilla, with fifty bronze and iron cannons, wrecked 2 miles (3 kilometers) south of Sebastian Inlet (there was no inlet at the time). She went down with over 3 million pesos in registered treasure, dozens of chests of jewelry made to order for the queen of Spain, as well as unknown amounts of contraband treasure. Contemporary Spanish salvors established a salvage camp on the shore and spent several years recovering about 25 percent of her silver. Some of the salvaged

Replica of the flagship of the 1715 treasure fleet. Originally it was an English ship named *Hampton Court.*

treasure was robbed when pirates from the Bahamas attacked the camp. The *Almiranta* lies about 8 miles (13 kilometers) south of the *Nuestra Señora de la Regla* off Vero Beach. During the hurricane she struck bottom about 3.5 miles (5.5 kilometers) offshore. The bulk of her 3 million pesos in treasure have never been discovered. Three of the 1715 fleet sank in deep water. Two sank off Cape Canaveral and have not been located, and one unidentified galleon sank in 1,000 feet (305 meters) of water, 60 miles (96 kilometers) east of St. Augustine. In 1965 a shrimp boat accidentally discovered this wreck when she pulled up copper cooking cauldrons in her nets. In 1990 and again in 1991, I spent seven weeks on this site with Seahawk Deep Water Technology, using the *Johnson Sea-Link,* a manned submersible, and we found many artifacts and coins.

1733: A fleet of 22 Spanish galleons in the New Spain Fleet of Admiral Rodrigo de Torres was lost in the Florida Keys. Salvage efforts began immediately. Owing to the huge amounts of contraband, salvors recovered over twice the amount of treasure listed in the cargo manifests. However, a great deal of treasure still remains on these wrecks. In modern times some of the wrecks have been located and worked on with varying results.

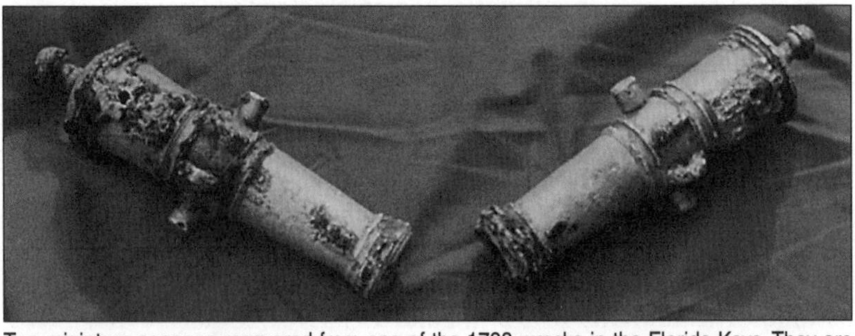

Two miniature cannons recovered from one of the 1733 wrecks in the Florida Keys. They are made of platinum. The Spaniards also used this metal, which was valueless in those days, to counterfeit silver coins.

Two Spanish pieces of eight—one as found and the other after cleaning—from the *San José.*

(Left) These three gold rings also came from the Spanish galleon *San Jose*, lost in 1733 in the Florida Keys.

(Below) Gold coins and other objects recovered from one of the 1715 shipwrecks off Florida's Atlantic coast.

(*Right*) Twelve-foot-long gold chain holding a gold religious reliquary from the flagship of the 1715 fleet, lost off of Sebastian Florida.

(*Below*) Marx entering the *Sea-Link I* submersible prior to making a dive on one of the 1715 fleet galleons lost in 1,200 feet (366 meters) of water off St. Augustine, Florida.

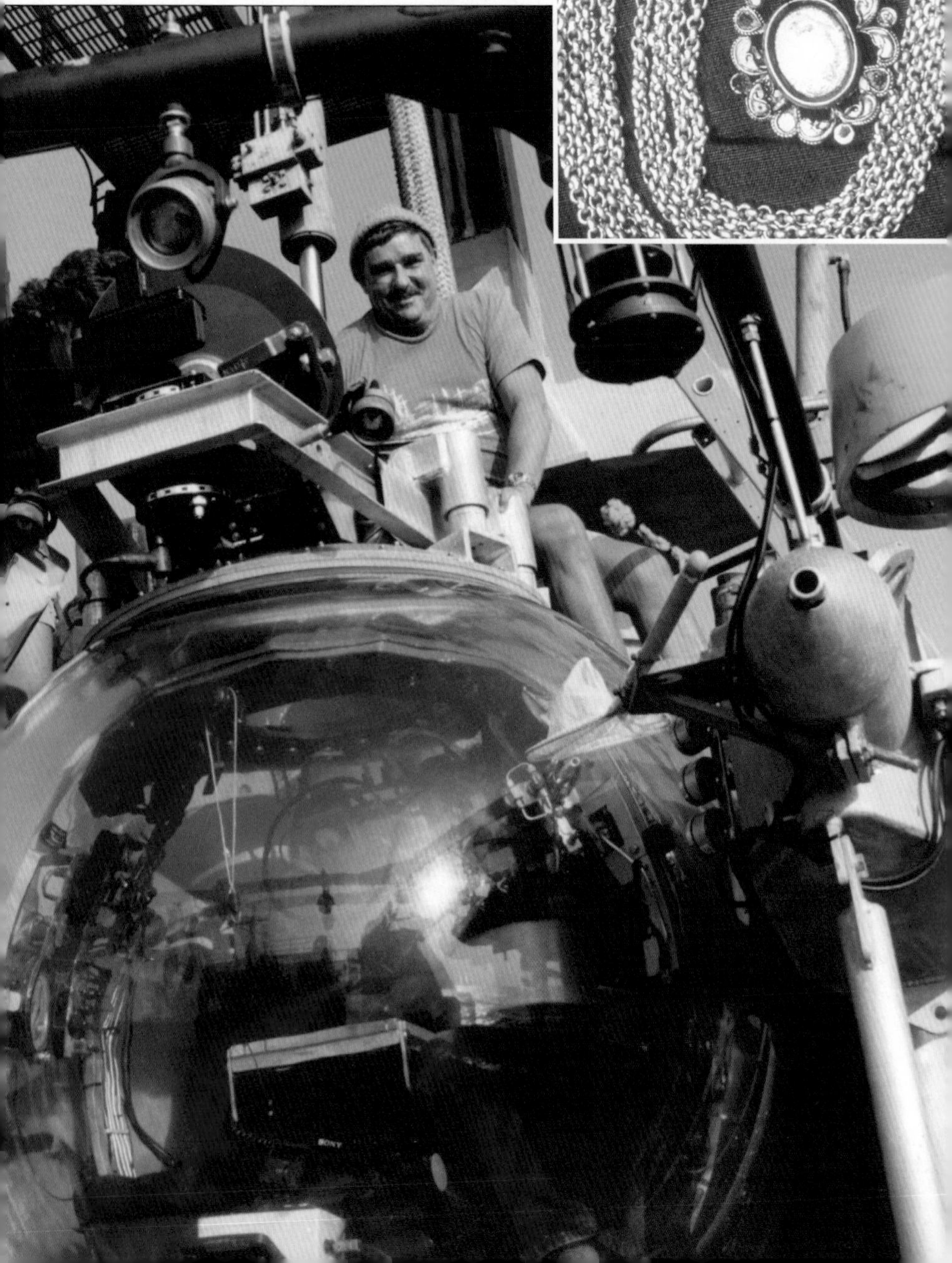

CHAPTER 4

U.S. EAST COAST'S RICHEST SHIPWRECKS

In 1565, fifty-two years after Ponce de Leon sailed along the coast of Florida, Pedro Menéndez de Áviles founded St. Augustine, which is the oldest permanent existing European settlement in the United States. It was never terribly important. A shallow sandbar blocking the port's entrance limited its use to small vessels. Annually a small *patache* was sent from Havana with about 100,000 pesos in treasure to pay royal officials, the military, and missionaries residing there. St. Augustine was totally dependent on this subsidy for its existence because it had no trade products.

In 1624 the Dutch founded New Amsterdam (New York), which soon became a flourishing trade center. The English, eager to cash in on the wealth of the New World, followed with settlements in New England, Virginia, and along the Delaware River. Shipping between these areas and Europe doubled each year. By the end of the seventeenth century, over 500 vessels a year engaged in transatlantic sailings.

I have documented 2,167 ship losses off the East Coast, excluding those in Florida waters, during the Colonial Period. However, very few meet the criterion of $10 million worth of cargo for inclusion in this book. During the American Revolutionary War, over 500 ships were lost. Six hundred were lost in the American Civil War, but by that time engines of various sorts propelled most ships and only a small number of the lost vessels were sailing ships.

Rum bottle, brass musket trigger guard, clay smoking pipe, and brass ladle found on a late seventeenth-century merchantman off Wilmington, North Carolina.

1520: The Spanish caravel *Buen Jesús,* commanded by Captain. Lucas Vásquez de Ayllón and sailing between Santo Domingo and Spain, was lost in a hurricane near Cape Romain, South Carolina. She carried six chests of gold nuggets and dust valued at over 150,000 pesos, as well as three chests of pearls from the Margarita Island pearl fisheries. Seven years later, a Spanish vessel exploring the coast found two survivors from this wreck who told them that all the other survivors died from starvation and Indian attacks.

1553: The New Spain Fleet left Veracruz for Havana and Spain and was struck by a hurricane. Eighteen ships went to the bottom. Several were wrecked on Padre Island, Texas. They were the galleon *San Estevan* (220 tons/223 tonnes), commanded by Captain Francisco del Mecerno and carrying 440,000 pesos in treasure; the galleon *Sancta María de Yciar* (220 tons/223 tonnes), commanded by Captain Alonso Ozosi, with 367,000 pesos in treasure; and another unidentified merchantman with an unknown amount of treasure. Two of these ships have been partially salvaged in modern times, but the bulk of the treasure the fleet carried, valued between 3 and 4 million pesos, lies at the bottom of the Gulf of Mexico.

1738: The German ship *Princess Augusta,* commanded by Captain Brook and carrying 350 German immigrants from Amsterdam to New York, was wrecked on the northern tip of Sandy Point, Block Island, at the eastern entrance to Long Island Sound. Prior to the disaster, 250 of the passengers and some of the crew had died from drinking contaminated water. In addition to a considerable amount of personal valuables belonging to the immigrants, the ship also carried more than £2 million sterling in gold and silver coinage for a New York bank.

1750: A hurricane on August 18 wrecked four galleons on the North Carolina coast. They were part of the New Spain Fleet commanded by Captain-General Juan Manuel de Bonilla. The *Nuestra Señora de la Soledad* wrecked 10 leagues north of Ocracoke Inlet; the *El Salvador* 5 leagues farther north; the *San Vicente* near Topsail Inlet; and the *San Pedro* at Drum Inlet. Spanish and English salvors recovered a great deal of the treasure, but another 2 million pesos in treasure still lies buried under the sands that hindered the eighteenth-century salvors.

1750: Five other ships of this same fleet were driven north to Virginia by the hurricane. Two—the *Capitana, Nuestra Señora de Guadeloupe* and the *Zumaca*—reached Norfolk and temporary safety. Three others were lost: the *Nuestra Señora de los Godos* sank near Cape Charles; the *La Galga* 15 leagues north of Cape Charles; and an unidentified brigantine disappeared about halfway between the other two. Very little of their precious cargoes was ever recovered. Six weeks later, the *Guadeloupe* and the *Zumaca* started for Spain. Only a few hours into the voyage another hurricane struck, and both ships sank within sight of the coast, taking over 4 million pesos to the bottom. Twelve English ships were lost in the vicinity of Norfolk in this hurricane, but nothing is known about their cargoes.

1761: During a hurricane on May 4, five ships were lost off Charleston, South Carolina. One of them, the British merchantman *Success,* en route from Jamaica to London, went down with over £1 million pounds sterling in gold and silver. The gold and silver aboard the *Success* had been recovered from a Spanish shipwreck somewhere in the Caribbean.

1779: The British warship HMS *Hussar,* with 28 cannons, and commanded by Captain Charles Maurice Pole, was lost at Hell's Gate on the East River off New York City. She was the pay ship of the British fleet and carried over £300,000 sterling in silver specie. In 1985 the *New York Times* reported that the wreck had been discovered, but to date no treasure has ever been recovered.

1779: The worst maritime disaster suffered by the Americans during the Revolutionary War occurred in May when British Navy warships under the command of Admiral George Collier burned and destroyed 148 American naval and merchant vessels at Norfolk, Virginia, and the surrounding area. Ironically, many of these ships were actually insured by Lloyds of London, which reported the overall loss of cargoes and ships at over £4 million sterling, £1 million of it in gold and silver specie.

1785: The Spanish merchantman *Nuestra Señora del Rosario* (550 tons/559 tonnes), commanded by Captain Celestino Prado de Miranda, sailed alone from Veracruz with 1.5 million pesos in treasure on board and made the customary stop in Havana where she picked up mail and some passengers before starting for Spain. Near Cape Canaveral she encountered a hurricane and was driven far north off the regular route back to Spain. She was badly damaged and the captain decided that Boston was the nearest safe port to make repairs.

While heading there she wrecked off the east end of Long Island near Montauk Point with only 79 people of the 254 people aboard saved. Coins from this wreck were reportedly found for many years on the beach after strong storms.

1785: The Scottish immigrant ship *Faithful Stewart*, en route to Philadelphia, sank near Cape Henlopen, Delaware. More than 200 people perished and over $1 million in personal and ship's treasures were lost.

1798: The British warship HMS *De Braak* (sixteen cannons), commanded by Captain James Drew, carried £220,000 pounds sterling in gold and silver specie, plus 70 tons (71 tonnes) of copper ingots. It capsized and sank near Lewes, Delaware. Several years after the sinking, a fisherman snagged a large iron chest in his nets. He opened it to find it crammed with silver coins. The chest is displayed in the Lewes Historical Museum. Over the years many divers tried to locate this wreck, which was finally discovered in 1983. While the ship's lower hull was raised in a salvage attempt, many artifacts and some of the treasure fell off and sank into the soft mud on the bottom. Most of the treasure is still there to be found.

1802: The Spanish warship *Juno* (34 cannons), sailed from Mexico for Spain carrying 300,000 pesos in treasure and 425 people. It sank off Cape May, Virginia, with a total loss of lives and treasure. Several years ago a salvor claimed to have found this wreck, but he failed to prove it was the *Juno*. Despite confirmation of the identity of the wreck, the Spanish government went to court and was awarded its ownership.

1804: The Spanish merchantman *Santa Rosa* (670 tons/681 tonnes), sailing alone between Havana and Spain, was blown far off course during a hurricane. She was lost on Cape Fear Shoals near Wilmington, North Carolina, carrying over 1 million pesos in gold and silver specie. There were only 19 survivors.

1813: The French merchantman *Tamerlane*, sailing between Martinique and Guadeloupe Islands and France with over 340,000 livres in Spanish gold and silver specie, was captured by an American privateer. While sailing to New York, both ships were wrecked on Cape Henry, Virginia, and only a small part of the treasure was saved.

1817: The American packet boat *Canton*, with over $300,000 in Spanish specie and other valuable cargo, was preparing for a voyage between Boston, Massachusetts, and England when for some unknown reason she suddenly blew up with a total loss of lives and cargo in Boston Harbour.

Salvor inside a large clam shell bucket, which was used to recover over 6 tons (6.09628 tonnes) of silver coins, recovered from the Spanish ship *Cazador*, lost in the Gulf of Mexico in 300 feet (91.5 meters) of water, in 1798.

UNITED STATES OF AMERICA
TEN D.

CHAPTER 5

U.S. WEST COAST'S RICHEST SHIPWRECKS

Long before the Christian era, ships were lost along the west coast of the United States. Early settlers in California, Oregon, and Washington found the remains of hulks along beaches. Some contained Oriental objects dating back 2,000 years. It is likely they were the remains of Asian trading and fishing vessels that lost their masts in storms or a rudder on a rocky bottom. At the mercy of prevailing winds and the Japanese current, these vessels would have drifted helplessly until wrecking on the American coast. There are dozens of reports in nineteenth-century ships' logbooks recording the sighting of vessels from the Orient drifting along the west coast, some with people still aboard. In California archaeological excavations at several Indian occupation sites have revealed Japanese pottery and other artifacts dating back to 1500 B.C.

There was very little shipping activity along the west coast of the United States until after the discovery of gold in California. During the Colonial Period, only six to eight Manila galleons and a few exploratory vessels passed through this area. Ships with substantial treasures came after the Gold Rush era, but most were not sail-driven, so are not included in this book.

(Facing, top) Gold coins, dated 1857 and minted in San Francisco during the California Gold Rush, were recovered from an unidentified wreck off Monterey, California.

(Facing, bottom) This diver recovers a piece of gold using his Infinium LS metal detector.

Bronze bell recovered from the Manila galleon *San Agustin*, lost in 1595 in Drake's Bay, California.

1582: The Manila galleon *Santa Martha* (1,200 tons/1219 tonnes), commanded by Captain Sebastián de Miranda, sailed from Manila for Acapulco with a cargo of Oriental treasures valued at 4,385,000 pesos. She was lost off San Nicolas Island, one of the Channel Islands off southern California. Commercial abalone divers have found jewelry and other objects from this wreck, but her main hull has not been found.

1595: The Manila galleon *San Agustín,* commanded by Captain Sebastian Cermeño and sailing between the Philippines and Acapulco, was lost in Drakes Bay, about 25 miles (40 kilometers) west of San Francisco. She carried a large cargo of Oriental luxury items and porcelain. I located her in 1950 and relocated her in 1989, but was unable to get permission to excavate. Documents state there were more than 2 million pesos' worth of Oriental treasures on board when she was lost and very little has been discovered.

Manila galleons brought back tons of gold objects, such as this gold chain and manicure set.

ca. 1650: Cannon Beach, Oregon, is so called because of a dozen iron cannons exposed when beach sand washes away during storms. The cannons appear to be of mid-seventeenth-century Spanish manufacture. From their size it appears they may have come off a Manila galleon. Keep in mind that many Manila galleons, like other classes of ships, disappeared without a trace and we have no documentation on their whereabouts.

1707: The Manila galleon *San Francisco Xavier* (1,900 tons/1,930 tonnes, 44 cannons), commanded by Captain Francisco Obregon y Ávila and sailing between Manila and Acapulco with over 3 million pesos in Oriental treasures, wrecked near the mouth of Oregon's Nehalem River. Over 600 souls perished. Artifacts such as Chinese porcelain shards have been found on the beach, but the wreck has not been located.

1854: The American ship *Yankee Blade* sank off San Francisco, California, carrying $153,000 in gold specie, plus unknown amounts of gold from miners heading home. Current numismatic value for these coins would be at least $50 million dollars.

1860: On the southwest coast of Oregon there is a place called Gold Beach because of gold coins that wash ashore during storms. The coins were minted in San Francisco in the 1860s, but no records exist indicating the name of the wreck that must lie offshore.

CHAPTER 6

BERMUDA'S RICHEST SHIPWRECKS

During the past five centuries, more than 1,000 ships have been lost off Bermuda. In fact, this beautiful group of islands was first settled in 1609 by shipwrecked English colonists headed for Virginia. A nineteenth-century historian aptly dubbed the island a "graveyard of ships." The waters around Bermuda conceal more shipwrecks than any other area in the Western Hemisphere, with the possible exception of the Florida Keys. In several areas the Bermuda sea floor has two and, in one case, three ships from different periods lying on top of each other.

On modern maps Bermuda appears as a small dot in the Atlantic some 569 miles (916 kilometers) off Cape Hatteras, North Carolina. However, it played a key role in early navigation and is shown disproportionately large on old maritime charts. Bermuda Island is one of the largest of 300 coral isles, islets and rocks that make up the British colony of Bermuda. It was known to early mariners as the Isle of Devils because of its perilous waters.

From earliest times Bermudans engaged in shipwreck salvage. When seventeenth-century treasure hunter William Phips first reached *Nuestra Señora de la Concepción* on Silver Shoals, north of Hispaniola, he discovered that Bermudan wreckers had beaten him to the galleon and recovered a substantial amount of treasure.

1533: The Spanish merchantman *Santa María de Portugalete* (110 tons/112 tonnes), commanded by Captain Juan de León, was personally owned by the king of Spain and was returning to Spain with over 2 million ducats in Aztec golden plunder captured by Cortez and his conquistadors. She was one of the richest ships ever lost at Bermuda. Three years later a passing ship saw signal fires on the beach and rescued the survivors.

1543: A Portuguese slave ship coming from Santo Domingo with over 500,000 pesos in treasure, was wrecked on a reef 4 leagues from the nearest land off the north end of the island. The thirty survivors built a small vessel from wreck timbers and managed to return to Santo Domingo, where they reported seeing signs of two other recent shipwrecks. These are believed to be two Spanish *naos* carrying a combined total of 1.3 million pesos in treasure, which disappeared in 1541 when the New Spain Fleet was struck by a hurricane within sight of these islands.

1550: The Spanish galleon *Santa María de la Bella* (120 tons/122 tonnes), commanded by Captain Francísco Pérez and carrying 1 million pesos in gold and silver, was en route to Spain when she wrecked on the western reefs off the main island. Some survivors got ashore and were rescued four years later by a passing ship.

1551: The *Capitana* (flagship) of the Tierra Firme Fleet of Captain-General Sancho de Viedra (350 tons/356 tonnes), commanded by Captain Juan Quintero, carried 2.5 million pesos in treasure. She sprang a serious leak and was deliberately run up on one of the western reefs of the islands during a hurricane. She broke up before any of her people and treasure could be saved. Another ship of this fleet, the *Santa Barbola* (400 tons/406 tonnes), commanded by Captain Juan Alvarez de los Ríos, wrecked on a nearby reef, but most of her people and all of her treasure was saved.

1560: During a hurricane, the galleon *Nuestra Señora de los Milagros* (400 tons/406 tonnes), commanded by Captain Matías de Rodas, in the Tierra Firme Fleet of Captain-General Pedro de la Roelas, went down in deep water off the south side and within sight of these islands. She was carrying over 2 million pesos in treasure, as well as other objects of unknown value from the Orient.

1563: Still another hurricane caused the loss of the *Capitana* of the New Spain Fleet of Captain-General Juan Menéndez de Áviles and four other galleons. They were carrying over 3 million pesos (most of

Teddy Tucker, Bermuda's most successful treasure hunter, has been working on shipwrecks around the island for over fifty years.

the treasure was on the *Capitana*) and were lost on the western reefs near these islands. Due to bad weather, the fleet was unable to stop for survivors and over 1,250 souls perished.

1584: When the fleet of 51 ships in the New Spain Fleet of Captain-General Antonio Manrique was close to Bermuda, a hurricane struck, sinking three galleons with 3.5 million pesos on them and three merchantmen with unknown amounts of treasure on them on the western reefs.

1595: The Spanish galleon *San Pedro* (340 tons/345 tonnes), commanded by Captain Simon Garcia de la Vega and carrying over 500,000 pesos in treasure, wrecked on a reef due to faulty navigation. Teddy Tucker discovered a section of this wreck in 1955 and recovered several million dollars in jewelry and gold ingots, but the main treasure site has yet to be located.

1622: During a storm that struck the New Spain Fleet of Captain-General Fernando de Sousa, two ships wrecked on reefs off the western side of Bermuda. One was the *nao San Ignácio* (150 tons/152 tonnes), commanded by Captain Domingo Hernández and carrying 270,000 pesos in treasure; the other was the *nao Nuestra Señora de la Limpia Concepción* (116 tons/118 tonnes), commanded by Captain Juan Calzado and carrying 320,000 pesos in treasure. English inhabitants then living on the island recovered some treasure from the *San Ignacio,* but sand quickly covered the other *nao.*

1644: An English chart dated 1740 bears the following information: "Amongst these rocks which extend above 3 leagues to the northwest of the island are a great number of wrecks and amongst others that of a rich Spanish ship lost about the year 1644. It was once discovered,

The General Archives of the Indies building, which houses tens of millions of pages or original documentation dealing with the New World, and especially shipwrecks.

but it is now fished for in vain. Off the southwest and west sections of the island are great number of rocks at 3 to 4 leagues distance from land, whereby an abundance of ships have been lost."

1684: The Spanish galleon *San Salvador* (567 tons/576 tonnes), commanded by Captain Pedro de Arvíde and carrying over 2 million pesos in treasure, sprang a bad leak while attempting to get close to the islands wrecked upon the western reefs. The Spaniards set the ship on fire and then fled for the shore to prevent English inhabitants from salvaging any of the treasure on the wreck. Local divers retrieved a small part of her treasure before shifting sands covered the wreck.

1792: The French merchantman *Le Grand Aanictl* (350 tons/356 tonnes), commanded by Captain Caiserques, sailed from Hispaniola for Marseilles with a valuable cargo that included 785,000 pesos in Spanish gold and silver specie. It struck on a reef off the western side of these islands and then slid off into deep water. Most of the people aboard survived. The ship lay in such deep water that salvors couldn't recover any of the treasure.

Marx displays Spanish gold bars he recovered from a 1622 shipwreck off the Dry Tortugas.

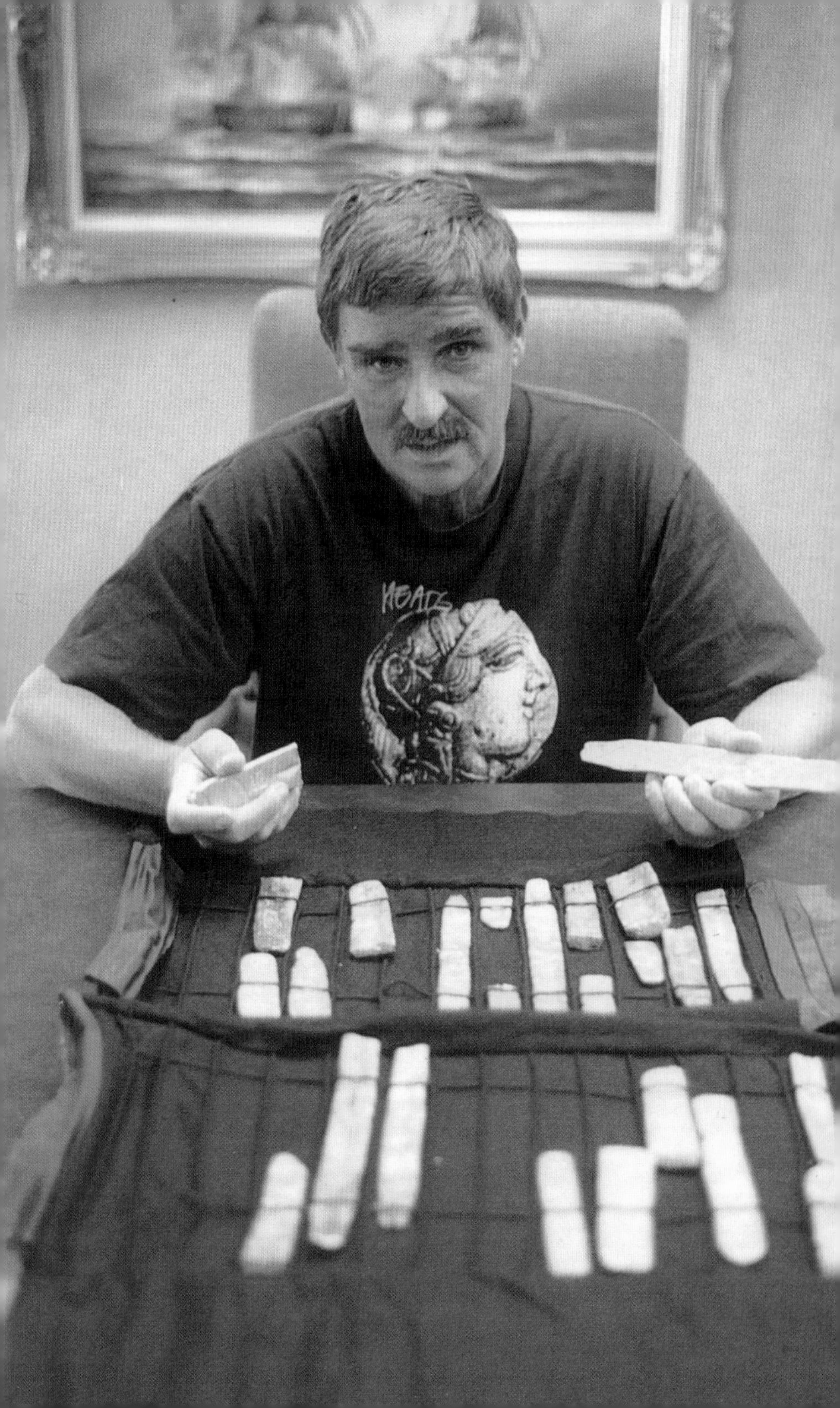

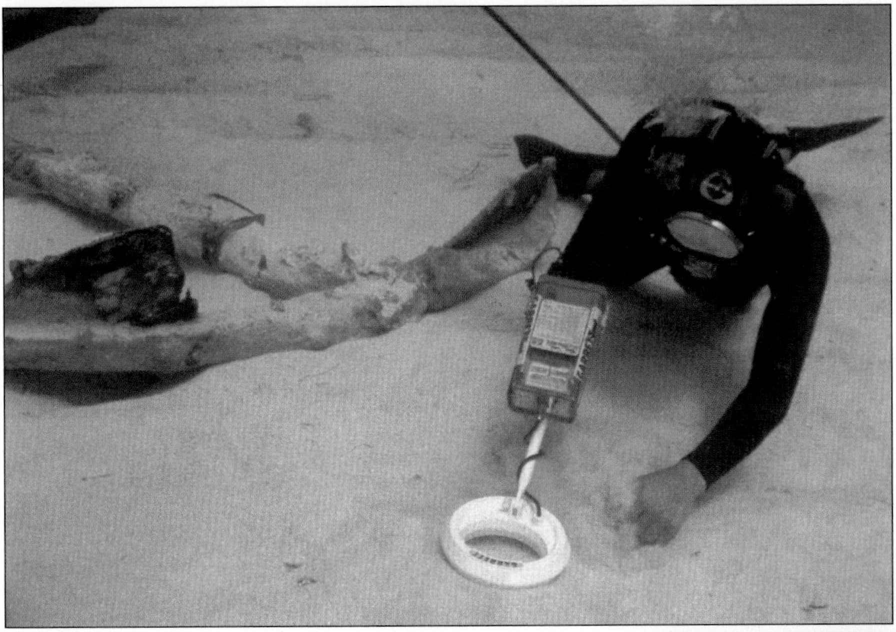

(Above) A diver swims by the anchor of a Spanish galleon in the Bahamas while scanning with his detector.

(Right) A gold and emerald cross found by Teddy Tucker in the 1595 *San Pedro* shipwreck off Bermuda.

(Below) From mid-15th century through the 18th century, the astrolabe was the main navigational instrument used to establish latitude at sea.

(Facing page) Bob Marx on deck with silver bars and stacks of coins brought up from the galleon *Nuestra Señora de las Maravilla.*

Bob Marx (second from right) kneels with other members of his team in 1956 before thousands of artifacts recovered from the Spanish merchant ship *Matanceros* off Mexico's Yucatan Peninsula.

Ten of millions of silver pieces of eight were minted at both the Potosí and Lima mints in Peru and circulated throughout the entire world during the Colonial Period.

CHAPTER 7

THE BAHAMAS' RICHEST SHIPWRECKS

The 700 islands, islets and cays of the Bahamian archipelago offer one of the most interesting and lucrative areas for shipwreck exploration in the Western Hemisphere. An island country in the Atlantic Ocean east of Florida and Cuba, the Bahamas offers gin-clear water, near ideal weather conditions and a staggering number of shipwrecks. Between 1492 when Columbus dropped anchor off San Salvador Island and the end of the American Civil War in 1865 more than 3,000 ships were lost in the Bahamas. The island nation's proximity to the United States and its familiar culture make it relatively easy to work in. Shipwreck projects in the Bahamas are less expensive than those in far-flung waters because they can generally be mounted and supplied from a Florida base.

No sooner had the conquistadors discovered that the fastest way home was to sail up the treacherous Bahama Channel than they began losing ships. While taking advantage of the fast northerly-flowing Gulf Stream, they wrecked on the myriad reefs and shoals that border the deep waters of the channel also known as the Florida Strait, which separates the Bahamas from Florida. These disasters often occurred out of sight of any coastline, cay or rock, making it impossible to record a wreck's location. Contemporary salvors dispatched from Havana and Santo Domingo were generally thwarted in their attempts. Most sites were too vaguely described to locate, and those they found were typically already covered over by shifting sands.

The Spaniards weren't the only ones searching for sunken cargoes. Within a few years of Bermuda's settlement by the English, "wracking" or salvaging shipwrecks had become the islanders' major occupation and the Bahamas was their prime hunting grounds. In the early 1600s, a century before Nassau was founded, Bermudan "wrackers" established numerous bases in the Bahamas. Merchants from all over the Caribbean and coastal North America flocked to these makeshift camps to purchase salvaged goods from Spanish shipwrecks and those of other nations. After Nassau was settled, "wracking" was an important occupation in the Bahamas until the end of the Civil War. Many of today's wealthy Bahamian families made their fortunes through the "wracking" business.

In 1933 some fishermen made a well-publicized find in the Abacos. They discovered a large safe on a reef on the north side of Green Turtle Cay. In it they found over $100,000 in glittering American gold coins from the Civil War period. Three years later, a fisherman working in the Exumas Islands recovered hundreds of big silver bars and several Spanish gold bars. He took them to Miami and sold them for metal value, not realizing how much more they would bring on the antique market. In 1947 fishermen digging in the sand for turtle eggs on Gorda Cay, east of Grand Bahama Island, uncovered Spanish coins and five silver bars. News of the find spread and the following year the late Art McKee, a treasure hunter from the Florida Keys, appeared on the scene. The fishermen, who had no idea their treasure trove came from a wreck, told Art that just offshore there were two mounds of "river pebbles," the term fishermen use for ballast piles. Limestone, the only rock available in the Bahamas, isn't suitable for ballasting a sailboat, so fishermen traditionally picked up shipwreck ballast stones elsewhere. Even today fishermen on some of the outer islands use ballast from old shipwrecks for their boats.

More treasure has been found in Bahamian waters by serendipitous accident than by professional treasure hunters. Hundreds of Bahamians dive commercially for lobsters, and almost every year one of them makes a noteworthy find. Most lobstermen's treasure finds occur on the reefs stretching northward from the western tip of Grand Bahama Island up to Mantanilla Shoals and then eastward toward Walkers Cay. Unfortunately, these lobster divers create a major problem for shipwreck searchers. They usually pick up all the cannon and anchors they stumble across so that visual clues are missing. Also, by removing all traces of ferrous metal, they make it impossible for a magnetometer to pinpoint the site. Several years ago the Bahamian government greatly added to this problem when, in an effort to curtail illegal salvage activity on the Little Bahama Bank, they offered to pay $50 for every cannon and anchor delivered in Nassau.

In January 1965 four very lucky diving instructors working out of Freeport, Grand Bahama Island, struck pay dirt. Two of them were leading a dive on what is now called "Treasure Reef," just outside the entrance to the port, when they spotted a cannon in only 6 feet (2 meters) of water. They said nothing to the tourists, but as soon as they could, they returned to explore the site. Hand fanning sand pockets in the shallow reef, they picked up Spanish silver coins as fast as they could grab them. Although the find was valued in the press at over $20 million, the actual value of the trove of some 20,000 silver coins was more like $2 million to $3 million—not bad for a chance discovery! Many hopeful divers followed in their wake, but traces of the actual shipwreck where the coins and cannons came from were never discovered. This is because the galleon first struck on the reef where chests of coins spilled out of a hole ripped in the ship's bottom, and because the cannons fell overboard as the ship listed and the storm forced the ship further to the east along the coast where it and another ship were wrecked. These were two Spanish galleons lost in 1628 (further described below).

For obvious reasons, not all shipwreck finds are publicized; major discoveries in the Bahamas have generally been kept quiet. One such find occurred in 1969 when a French sailboat, on an around-the-world cruise, stopped in the Berry Islands after crossing the Atlantic. While spear-fishing, the crew found a mound of

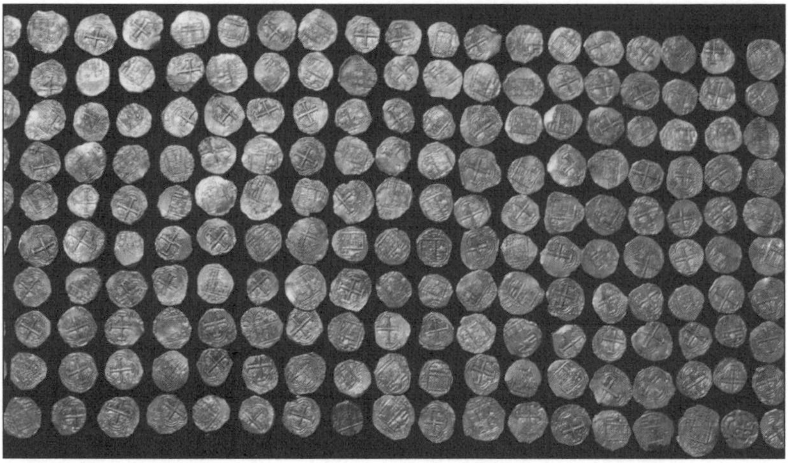

Some of the thousands of Spanish gold doubloons recovered from the *Maravillas.*

almost 2,000 large Spanish silver bars paving an area the size of a tennis court. They picked up a few samples and later returned and salvaged over 60 tons (61 tonnes) of silver, cancelled the remainder of their voyage, and returned to France enriched beyond their wildest dreams.

My discovery in 1972 of the Spanish galleon *Nuestra Señora de las Maravillas,* lost in 1656 on the Little Bahama Bank north of Grand Bahama Island with over 5.5 million pesos in treasure, remains the most significant discovery made in the Bahamas. The bulk of the treasure she carried, including a life-size statue of the Madonna and Christ Child, has not been found. From the spot where she initially wrecked (the area I worked on in 1972), the *Maravillas* broke up in two pieces. The main section of the ship traveled over 8 miles (13 kilometers), scattering treasure all along the trail.

The Bahamas is littered with wrecks. Just about anywhere one jumps in the water, there are traces of a shipwreck to be found. In Nassau Harbor, for example, over the centuries more than 300 ships met their doom. In 1816 about 100 hundred ships sank in a single hurricane. Thousands of ships anchored there over the years, and bottles, clay smoking pipes, crockery and countless other items were thrown overboard. Trash yesterday, they are

Commemorative medal struck in London with the silver salvaged by Phips from the *Concepción*. It shows King William and Queen Mary.

treasures today. Patient, keen-eyed divers can often locate wreck sites visually. The government has no objections to a tourist diver picking up a souvenir or two; however, if you chance upon a chest of doubloons, that is another matter.

1528: Spanish *nao Santa María de la Concepción* (110 tons/112 tonnes, 14 iron cannons), commanded by Captain Blas de Navarra Oleo, was sailing directly from Mexico to Spain with what was described as a "vast amount of Aztec treasures" that Cortez had robbed from Montezuma and his people. It must have been a phenomenal amount since the crew had to jettison all the ship's ballast in Mexico before setting sail to make room for it. A storm wrecked the ship. Only two men survived, subsisting on a small cay until rescued eight years later. Bimini was not named at this time, but the latitude given for the disaster places the wreck off either North or South Bimini.

1552: The Portuguese slave ship *San Anton do Brasil*, also known as *El Dorado* (120 tons/122 tonnes), sailed from the west coast of Africa to Nombre de Dios, Panama, with a cargo of slaves. While in port, she was seized by the Spanish port captain and placed in the service of the Spanish Crown. An immense Inca treasure had been discovered in a cave near Cuzco, Peru. Rather than wait for the arrival of the annual treasure fleet to carry it to Spain, authorities used this Portuguese ship for the passage. Most of the treasure consisted of gold figurines, ingots and jewelry valued at over 780,000 pesos. The ship made a brief stop at Cartagena, Colombia, where she picked up quantities of lustrous pearls from Margarita Island and an undisclosed amount of gold and emeralds from Bogotá. She sailed on and 8 miles (13 kilometers) north of Bimini, encountered a fierce storm and sank. A shoal in this area is named El Dorado Shoal after this disaster. In 1981 with the aid of a magnetometer, an instrument that detects ferrous metal, I located three of the *El Dorado*'s iron anchors. A few days later I was attacked by a mako shark that ripped open my upper arm and shoulder. By the time I returned to the wreck six weeks later, the anchors had disappeared and the location was lost again. All of the galleon's cannons are bronze, so frustrating months of magnetometer work failed to find her because the only ferrous materials on the wreck were the anchors, which had been removed. Since then a number of groups have unsuccessfully sought the wreck.

1559: The Spanish galleon *Santa María de Llos Remedios* (300 tons/305 tonnes, 32 iron cannons), was sailing from Veracruz to Spain without making the customary stop at Havana to avoid pirates reported in that area. She was carrying 768,440 pesos in gold and silver, plus an unspecified cargo of exotic goods from the Orient such as porcelain, jewelry, jade, silks and spices. A sudden storm struck as the *Remedios* worked her way up the Bahama Channel and she was separated from the other 87 vessels in the convoy. The vessel's rudder and one of her masts were destroyed, and she was helpless before winds and currents that drove her on a reef 3 to 4 leagues east of Great Isaac's Cay near the northwestern edge of the Great Bahama Bank. A few survivors reached Cuba in a ship's longboat, but repeated attempts to locate the wreck failed.

1564: The Spanish galleon *Santa Clara* (300 tons/305 tonnes), commanded by Captain Juan Diaz Bozino and carrying 1,217,000 pesos in treasure, was driven off course during a storm and wrecked several miles north of Memory Rock on the Little Bahama Bank, most likely on the reef called the Dry Bar. Salvors reported they had found the *Santa Clara* and were recovering the treasure, but when it was taken to Havana, royal officials were surprised to find the salvaged treasure was from another Spanish wreck, which had disappeared without a trace four years earlier. Salvors returned to the area the following season, but failed to find the galleon.

1628: Dutch privateers, commanded by Admiral Piet Heyn, captured the entire Spanish treasure fleet in Matanzas Bay, Cuba, where the Spaniards had run the ships aground. The Dutch, unable to cram all the plunder on their own ships, managed to refloat five of the largest galleons. A storm struck the victorious fleet as it was about to pass Grand Bahama Island and two of the richly-laden Spanish galleons, the *Santa Gertrudes* and the *Santa Ana,* both 600 tons (610 tonnes), were separated from the convoy and driven eastward. One first struck on a shallow reef off present-day Lucaya (Freeport) and then wrecked about 3 miles (5 kilometers) to the east. The other was reported to have wrecked "within a cannon- shot distance" to the east of the first galleon. They would be in the vicinity of Pinder Point Village. A place there is called Golden Rock because, according to local lore, fishermen about 150 years ago found a large amount of gold and silver on the sea-floor.

1641: The Spanish galleon *Nuestra Señora de la Concepción,* returning to Spain in a treasure fleet convoy, encountered a hurricane while passing through the Bahamas, losing masts and rudder. Drifting at the mercy of wind and currents, she eventually wrecked on the north side of Silver Shoals (so named because of this disaster) All 450 souls aboard perished and her treasure of over 1.5 million pesos sank with the ship. In 1687 American-born William Phips salvaged about 90 percent of her treasures. Most of the profit went to his investors and he kept 16 percent. The king of England, who received 10 percent, knighted Phips and appointed him the first governor of Massachusetts. The wreck was found again in recent years and more treasure was recovered. However, a great deal more remains buried under coral reefs.

1656: The second richest Spanish galleon ever lost in the Western Hemisphere was the *Nuestra Señora de las Maravillas,* commanded by Admiral Mathias de Orellanas, lost on the Little Bahama Bank. She went down with over 5 million pesos in treasure, and for twenty years contemporary divers worked on her, bringing up about 1.5 million pesos before she was completely covered over by shifting sands. William Phips found the wreck in 1681 and salvaged a small amount of treasure. After a search of many years, I rediscovered the wreck in 1972 and recovered a considerable amount of her treasures, but the majority of what she carried, including a solid gold life-size statue of the Virgin and Child, awaits discovery.

1669: The Spanish galleon *Nuestra Señora de Esperanza,* also known by the nickname *Genovesa,* commanded by Captain Domingo Ypenar-

The smiling author examines numerous silver coins and large bars from the *Maravilla*.

(Below) Each of the *Maravilla* silver bars contained unique markings which identified the bar. This one weighed 72 pounds.

reita (650 tons/660 tonnes, 32 cannons) and carrying 3,250,000 pesos in treasure, wrecked during a fierce norther on the Little Bahama Bank near the edge of the Gulf Stream. She lies in less than "five fathoms of water." One fathom equals 6 feet (1.8288 meters). The location is 10 miles (16 kilometers) north of Memory Rock. Another ship in the fleet rescued 63 of the 478 people aboard. When salvors from Havana found the wreck site in April 1670, it was already almost covered over by sand and they found nothing but two anchors. A salvage effort in 1671 failed to find any trace of the treasure galleon.

1678: A Dutch ship carrying salt (essential for treating the herring, which was a staple of the Dutch diet), from St. Martin's Island to Holland was passing close to Ambergris Cay, south of Grand Turk Island. The Dutch spotted wreckage on this small deserted cay and on shore they found the bones of over 200 Spaniards. Apparently they had been on a richly laden ship that wrecked and had been able to get a lot treasure ashore because the Dutch found 3 tons (3.048 tonnes) of gold ingots, 43 tons (44 tonnes) of silver bars and 340,000 pesos in silver specie. They also found a starving dog that they took back to Holland. A salvage expedition, sent from Amsterdam to locate the wreck and determine if there was any more treasure on it, couldn't find the site.

1741: The Spanish galleon *Nuestra Señora del Buen Viaje* (640 tons/650 tonnes), 38 cannons), commanded by Captain Jaime Solas de Casanova, was sailing alone as a "register ship" from Porto Bello and Havana for Spain, carrying 375,000 pesos in gold and silver specie and bullion, plus other "products of the land." About a half day's sail from Cape Canaveral, she encountered a fierce storm and was forced to run before it for two days. The ship lost all three masts and the rudder and was at the mercy of wind and currents. She drifted for six weeks until wrecking on Ambergris Cay, one of the Turks and Caicos Islands in the eastern Bahamas. Luckily, 240 of the 330 souls on board managed to get ashore on the cay with a few barrels of water and a bit of food. The captain and five men set off in the ship's long boat to find assistance. They reached Porto Plata, Hispaniola, four days later and were then taken overland to the city of Santo Domingo, where they notified the governor of the plight of those left on the desolate waterless cay. Instead of sending a vessel to immediately rescue the stranded survivors, the governor had a ship detour to Margarita Island to pick up pearl divers to be sent to Santo Domingo. By the time the rescue/salvage boat was sent to the cay, over two months had passed and the rescuers found the cay littered with the skeletons of those left behind. Most of the wreckage had been covered over by shifting sands and divers found only seven iron cannons, two anchors, and the ship's bell.

1765: The Spanish galleon *El Santiago El Grande,* sailing between Havana and Spain with over 2 million pesos in treasure aboard, wrecked and sank in 17 feet (5 meters) of water on the Great Bahama Bank 35 miles (56 kilometers) southeast of Bimini and 7 miles (11 kilometers) southeast of Beak Cay in the Riding Rock Chain. Huge seas caused the ship to be driven far onto the shallow bank before it finally broke up and was covered by shifting sands. Within a few years of the disaster, the exact location of this wreck appeared on printed navigation charts. Despite this pinpoint location, recurring attempts by contemporary and modern salvors have failed to locate this tantalizing wreck.

1800: The English warship HMS *Lowestoffe* and eight merchant ships were smashed against the reefs on the southeast corner of Great Inagua Island and totally lost. The Lowestoffe was carrying over £400,000 in Spanish coinage, valued then at 400,000 pounds sterling. There are no reports that any of it was ever recovered.

1801: In July over 120 ships anchored in Nassau Harbor were destroyed in one of the most destructive hurricanes to ever strike the Bahamas. They sank with treasure and cargoes valued then at over £4 million pounds sterling. In 1961, during construction of the bridge linking the city of Nassau and Paradise Island, one unidentified ship of this date was accidentally discovered and over $200,000 in Spanish gold and silver specie was found on her.

1811: The British packetboat *Prince of Wales,* commanded by Captain Proctor, sailed from Port Royal, Jamaica, for Nassau and England with the mail, passengers, and £228,000 pounds sterling in Spanish gold and silver specie. It was wrecked on Saltpond Reef on the southwest side of Great Inagua Island. A vessel sailing with her saved all of the people aboard. Within a day, over a dozen Bahamian vessels appeared and "wrackers" began diving on the site. What they brought up is unknown.

1812: The British warship HMS *Southampton* (32 cannons), commanded by Captain Sir James Lucas Leo, was sailing between Jamaica and England and carrying "sixty-eight chests of Spanish specie" when she wrecked on a reef that still bears her name, about 9 miles (14.5 kilometers) north of Conception Island. The exact position the ship's navigator gave for the wreck is 24 degrees and 3 minutes north latitude and 69 degrees and 57 minutes west longitude. Six years after the disaster, admiralty documents indicate that "only about half of the specie was ever recovered." Several years ago, while leading sports divers from a cruise ship, well-known underwater photographers Ron and Valerie Taylor briefly visited this reef and came upon a number of cannons. From photographs they sent me, it appears that they chanced upon *Southampton* without realizing she still contained a great deal of silver coinage.

1815: Two Spanish merchantmen en route from Havana to Spain were reported lost, one at the beginning of the year and one at the end, 2 to 3 miles (3 to 5 kilometers) north of West End, Grand Bahama Island, close to the edge of the Little Bahama Bank. On January 6 the *Barcelones* had part of her cargo salvaged, but over 100,000 pesos in gold and silver coins were never found. The *Juncta,* commanded by Captain Capillo, was lost on December 26 and a passing ship rescued the crew. A fraction of the more than 175,000 pesos in coinage that went down with her was reportedly recovered by Bahamian salvors.

(Upper left) Ping-pong-ball-size emerald with two gold lockets recovered from the *Maravilla.*

(Upper right) Fragment of marble statue of Roman goddess, accidentally located off of Vera Cruz, Mexico. How did it get there?

(Lower) Marx (wearing cap) and another diver with part of the 80,000 brass crucifixes recovered from the *Matanceros* (*Matanzeros*), a Spanish merchantman lost in 1739 off the coast of Yucatan. To this day, more crucifixes from this wreck still wash ashore after storms.

CHAPTER 8

MEXICO'S RICHEST SHIPWRECKS

Acapulco, on Mexico's Pacific coast, boasts one of the finest natural anchorages in the world. It is breathtakingly beautiful: a deep, semicircular bay, nearly landlocked and accessible by land. Acapulco was founded in 1565 on the narrow ribbon of land between the bay and steep, encircling mountains. In the Colonial Period, Acapulco never amounted to much as a town. A conglomeration of a few shacks, a little chapel, and a small fort, it was not a popular place to live. Most of the year the only inhabitants were a few slaves and a small contingent of soldiers manning the fort. Located in an earthquake zone, the town was hot, humid and mosquito-infested except from December to April when the weather was tolerable. With its location in the Pacific Ocean, Acapulco was not a link in the chain of seaports that conveyed silver from either Mexico or Peru to Spain, and at first glance it seems mystifying that a town should have been built in such a place at all. Acapulco existed for only one reason: to handle the most fascinating Spanish commerce of the sixteenth century: the Manila galleon trade between the Philippines and Mexico.

When the Manila galleons arrived in Acapulco crammed with treasure and luxury goods from the Orient, a fair like the one at Nombre de Dios was held. The buying and selling went on until the cargoes were disposed of. Goods consigned to Peru were

(Facing) Diver inspecting large ballast pile with two iron cannons at wreck site in the Bahamas. This shows how objects can be heavily camouflaged by marine growth.

Port of Acapulco around 1600. The Manila galleons sailed from this port to the Philippines and returned here with the fabulous treasures of the Orient.

shipped to Panama to await lading onto the Armada of the South Seas. Goods consigned to Mexican destinations were transported by mule train, as were those for Spain, which went all the way to Veracruz to await the next New Spain Fleet. After the fair, Acapulco, like Nombre de Dios, went to sleep for the rest of the year.

It was during the sleepy season in 1579 that Francis Drake, soon after his attack on Callao, sailed north along the Pacific coast of Mexico toward Acapulco. On the way he captured a merchant ship from Acapulco, obtaining victuals and water but very little in the way of plunder except for a handsome gold falcon with an emerald set in its breast. He sailed the *Golden Hind* into the Bay of Acapulco. However, he didn't attack the town, possibly because he concluded from interrogating the Spaniards on the merchant ship that there wasn't much to get in Acapulco. In the bay he refitted his ship for the long voyage home.

In 1519 Hernán Cortez set out from Cuba with eleven vessels to conquer Mexico. Soon after his arrival, he founded a town on the coast, La Villa Rica de la Veracruz, or Rich Town of the True Cross, so named because gold was found there. As a seaport, Veracruz left much to be desired. The harbor was open and unprotected. Ships at anchor there were exposed to the ravages of hurricanes in summer and northers in fall and winter. Over the years more than 200 large ships were lost in and around the port. At the entrance was a shallow bar that only small ships could cross; large ships had to anchor at San Juan de Ulúa, a small island 15 miles (24 kilometers) down the coast. A fort was erected there to protect anchored ships. Large ships unloaded cargo onto small boats, which carried it up to Veracruz. However, the position of Veracruz made it suitable for handling commerce between Mexico and the mother country, and soon it became Mexico's leading seaport.

Veracruz was the first port of call for the majority of the ships in the New Spain Fleet. Besides being the clearinghouse for the precious Mexican metals and for Manila goods destined for Spain, Veracruz had an item of its own to contribute to trade: cochineal, highly prized as a source of purple and scarlet dye. Each year prior to the arrival of the New Spain Fleet, Veracruz underwent the transformation usual in treasure fleet ports. Merchants, customs and treasury officials, tavern keepers, and slaves flocked there, and mule trains laden with the year's output from the Mexican silver mines began to arrive. In Veracruz, as in Nombre de Dios and Acapulco, there was a fair of several weeks' duration, after which the New Spain Fleet sailed for Havana and Veracruz became, once again, a drowsy tropical town.

1574: Four unidentified Spanish galleons in the New Spain fleet of Captain-General Antonio Manríquez, sailing between Veracruz and Havana and then to Spain with over 2 million pesos in treasures, were wrecked near Coatzacoalcos and totally lost, with over 1,000 fatalities. Contemporary salvors recovered none of the treasures, which had been covered by shifting sands.

1590: As the New Spain Fleet of Captain-General Antonio Navarro de Prado was only a few miles off Veracruz, coming from Spain with over 600 tons (610 tonnes) of urgently needed mercury used in the amalgamation process of refining gold and silver, a violent storm totally destroyed sixteen ships. Among them were seven galleons carrying all of the mercury. This was a major disaster and caused great financial problems in Spain.

1600: Six ships of the sixty-ship convoy of the New Spain Fleet of Captain-General Pedro d'Escobar Melgarejo were wrecked when a hurricane hit the fleet about 60 miles (96.5 kilometers) east of Veracruz in the Gulf of Mexico. Coming from Spain, they carried no listed gold or silver, but rather a vast amount of mercury that is today worth over $200 million.

1610: The Spanish galleon *Nuestra Señora de la Piedad* (250 tons/254 tonnes, 2 cannons), commanded by Captain Martín Ruiz, set sail from Callao, Peru, for Acapulco. She carried over 1 million pesos in gold and silver treasure, which was to be placed aboard one of the Manila galleons sailing for the Philippines the following year. When the ship was about a league off the port of Zacatula, Mexico, a sudden squall caused her to capsize and sink with all her treasure. Three hundred-fifty people persons drowned and 32 were saved. Many pieces of wreckage drifted ashore the same day, but because she is in deep water, divers recovered only a small amount of treasure.

1611: Just as the New Spain Fleet was ready to sail for Havana and Spain, a bad storm struck the port of Veracruz and four large galleons carrying over 3 million pesos in treasure were sunk. They were the *San Lorenzo*, the *La Concepción*, the *Nuestra Señora del Rosario y Santo Tomás*, and the *Nuestra Señora de la Antigua*. The ships all broke up and their cargoes were so widely scattered that divers recovered very little treasure.

1614: The New Spain Fleet, consisting of 41 ships, set sail from Cádiz, Spain, under the command of Captain-General Juan de la Cueva y Mendoza . After the customary stop for refreshments at the island of Guadeloupe, the fleet headed for Veracruz. Due to misjudgment by the flagship's senior pilot, the fleet found itself in treacherous shallow waters off the coast of Yucatán between Cape Catoche and Isla Mujeres, where seven of the largest ships of the fleet wrecked and sank. Over 1.5 million pesos in merchandise was aboard these merchantmen as well as 680 tons (691 tonnes) of mercury, which is very valuable today. The ships broke up quickly, and shifting sands soon covered their cargoes. Salvage boats from Havana recovered only a few cannons and anchors.

1623: As the Portuguese slave ship *Nossa Senhora de la Piedade*, coming from Angola with 282 slaves, was approaching the coast of Yucatán, she was chased by pirates and wrecked on the east side of Isla Mujeres. Her crew and the slaves made it ashore after the Portuguese set the ship on fire. An investigation revealed that she was carrying seven large chests of gold nuggets and dust, plus several tons of ivory (elephant tusks).

1623: The Spanish galleon *La Candelaria* (250 tons/254 tonnes), commanded by Captain Juan de Paternina and sailing in the Tierra Firme Fleet with 765,000 pesos in treasure, was separated from the fleet in a storm near Jamaica. She went to Santo Domingo for repairs and then headed for Havana to join any other ships sailing for Spain. En route she wrecked in a storm on the northeast coast of Cozumel Island with only a few survivors. In recent years fishermen found several thousand Spanish silver coins, which appear to be from this wreck, on the beach near the Mayan ruin called El Castilla.

1631: The New Spain treasure fleet, sailing from Veracruz to Havana and Spain, was struck by a hurricane in the Gulf of Mexico and several ships were lost. Among them was *Capitana, Nuestra Señora del Juncal,* which sank about 20 miles (32 kilometers) north of Campeche, carrying an enormous treasure. Only 35 of the 335 people on board reached the shore in a small boat.

1668: The Manila galleon *Santa María de los Valles* (1,500 tons/1,524 tonnes, 68 bronze cannons), commanded by Admiral Nicolas Curi de Leyba, set sail from Manila with 778 people aboard and a cargo valued at over 3 million pesos. After passing through the Straits of San Bernardino and turning north toward Japan, she was struck by a fierce typhoon and huge waves carried away seven of her crew and many boxes and chests of cargo stored on the main deck. After weathering the storm, she had an uneventful voyage, making landfall at Cape Mendocino on the coast of California and then cruising along the coast until reaching Acapulco two days before Christmas of that year. Two hours after dropping anchor and while waiting for officials to arrive, fire broke out and the ship was totally consumed and sank within the hour, taking over 330 of those aboard to the bottom, along with her fabulous treasure.

1702: As the New Spain Fleet of Captain-General Fernando Chacón was leaving Veracruz for Havana and Spain, the galleon *Almiranta, Santa María de Teasanos*, commanded by Captain Martín Gonzalez de Vergara and carrying 1.75 million pesos in treasure and "many chests and boxes from the Orient of unknown value," struck a submerged object—possibly an old wreck—about 2 miles (3 kilometers) off the port and quickly sank. Only 47 of the 390 people aboard were saved.

1711: The Spanish galleon *Santa María y San Josef,* carrying a vast amount of jewelry valued at over 2 million pesos, especially made in the Orient for the queen of Spain, as well as over 1 million pesos in gold and silver specie and bullion, went down in the Gulf of Mexico near Alacranes Reef during a hurricane. There was a total loss of life and treasure.

1715: Shortly before the New Spain Fleet of Captain-General Juan Estevan de Ubilla was to sail from Veracruz to Havana, a violent storm struck, sinking twelve of his ships, which carried 4.85 million pesos in treasure, plus precious Oriental merchandise. Very little was ever recovered from them. The storm was so strong that many buildings in the port were blown down and many small vessels were lost.

1719: A squadron of three galleons—the *Capitana,* the *Almiranta,* and the *Santo Cristo de Maracaibo*—commanded by Admiral Francisco de Cornejo and carrying 287 tons (292 tonnes) of mercury and other cargo was totally lost on the coast about 3 to 4 leagues west of Campeche. There were very few survivors.

1725: The *Capitana, Nuestra Señora de Belém,* commanded by Admiral Antonio Serrano and carrying over 2 million pesos in gold and silver, caught fire and sank about 10 miles (16 kilometers) northeast of Campeche in the Gulf of Mexico. Over 400 lives were lost.

1752: Five unidentified galleons in the New Spain Fleet of Captain-General Cristóbal de Eraso, carrying 2.8 million pesos in treasure, were wrecked in a storm on the coast of Tabasco between Coatzacoalcos and Paraiso. Salvors recovered about a quarter of the treasure on the wrecks.

1798: The Spanish frigate *Nuestra Señora de Guadalupe,* sailing between Honduras and Spain with 2.5 million pesos in silver bullion and specie, was totally lost on Chinchorro Reef off the Yucatán Peninsula near the border with Belize. She was only partially salvaged.

1801: The British warship *Meleager* (32 cannons), commanded by Captain Thomas Bladen Capell, sailed from Veracruz for London with 88 chests of Spanish silver specie. She was wrecked on coral reefs surrounding Triangle Bank. Most of the crew made it to safety on a nearby deserted cay. Two weeks later, a passing ship rescued them.

Chapter 9

Central America's Richest Shipwrecks

In 1513 the explorer Vasco Nuñez de Balboa crossed the Isthmus of Panama, then called Darien, mounted a hill, and became the first European from the Western Hemisphere to set eyes on the Pacific Ocean. Six years later, Spain established a town at the site of a native fishing village on the Pacific coast at the narrowest part of the isthmus. Named Panama, the town served as a base for the expeditions that marched across the isthmus to embark on the exploration and conquest of Peru, and soon acquired such importance that by 1521, it was constituted a city. The harbor was shallow, exposed to the sea, and subject to great tides that limited it to small vessels. Large ships went to Perico, 6 miles (10 kilometers) to the west, where several small islands formed a protective anchorage. The cargoes from these ships were ferried by lighters to the port.

Yet so strategic was the location of Panama City that its growth kept pace with the expanding Peruvian trade for which it served as an emporium. A visitor in 1575 described the city as having several very handsome buildings used by the president and other royal officials, a huge cathedral, three monasteries, and 400 wooden houses. The majority of residents were engaged in the flourishing mercantile trade as merchants or transportation agents. Virtually all the items exchanged between the Pacific coast of South America and the mother country had to pass through Panama City. Shipping merchandise from Panama to Callao took two to three times

Panama City in 1697 where all of the treasures were brought up from South America before being transferred by mule across the Isthmus to Porto Bello.

longer than the route ferrying treasure to Panama because of contrary winds and currents.

Transporting goods across the isthmus was far more challenging. The river route took from three to twelve days, depending on how high the river was. Frequently, because of floods or droughts, the river route could not be used and the journey had to be made entirely over land, which was always difficult. Mules are notorious for their recalcitrant nature and the Panama mule trains, often 100 or more mules, had good reason to balk. They traveled with extremely heavy loads (as much as 300 pounds/136 kilograms of silver was loaded on a single mule), so that during any journey across the entire isthmus, several perished on the trail.

Like Panama City, Nombre de Dios was founded to handle traffic with Peru and it had nothing but its position at the narrowest point of the isthmus to recommend it as a seaport. The location was open to the sea, offering little protection from the elements or enemy attack. In 1565, during a norther, an entire fleet was lost at anchorage in Nombre de Dios.

Nombre de Dios was the site of a great mercantile fair that began with the arrival of the annual Tierra Firme Fleet from Spain. No sooner were the ships anchored in the harbor than seamen came ashore to erect an enormous tent made from sails in the town's square. Into this tent went the cargoes of wine, olive oil and manufactured goods unloaded from the ships. Meanwhile, the mules began to arrive. They were relieved of their burdens, and silver bars were piled high in the streets like bricks. The buying and selling took place amid a tumult that suggested a carnival. Once the fair was over and the fleets left, the port, all but abandoned because of its unhealthy climate, sank back into tropical torpor.

Francis Drake knew just how drowsy and ill-defended Nombre de Dios was from two reconnaissance missions to American waters in 1570 and 1571. He convinced Queen Elizabeth that attacking Nombre de Dios was a practical venture. On May 24, 1572, he left Plymouth with two small ships. Spanish spies in England told him he would find the port almost deserted. But Nombre de Dios was not deserted, for the Tierra Firme Fleet was due to arrive and preparations were well underway for the fair. Drake launched his attack at three o'clock in the morning, landing and marching into town before the alarm was sounded. Surprised Spaniards put up a fight and there was a brief skirmish, during which a musket ball wounded Drake in the thigh, but the English prevailed. Several prisoners led Drake to the cellar of the governor's house, where he beheld a sight beyond his wildest imagination. On the earthen floor lay a stack of silver bars 70 feet (21 meters) long, 10 feet (3 meters) wide, and 12 feet (4 meters) high. Each bar weighed between 35 and 70 pounds (16 and 32 kilograms). In all there were 60 tons (61 tonnes) of silver, worth at least 1 million pounds sterling.

Nombre de Dios's climate was pestilential and hundreds of people died each year from tropical diseases. In 1584 Philip II ordered the town to be moved to a more salubrious site several miles to the northeast. Porto Bello, as it was named, boasted a far better harbor, and in 1596 it became the Caribbean terminus on the isthmus and the port for the Tierra Firme Fleet. When both the Tierra Firme Fleet and Armada were in Porto Bello, more than 150 ships lay at anchor.

Each year throughout most of the Spanish Colonial Period, two large galleons, called the *Naos de Honduras*, were sent from Honduras to Havana carrying large amounts of gold and silver from the

An Anglo-Dutch fleet attacking Spanish galleons in the port of Porto Belo, Panama.

mines of Guatemala, Honduras and Nicaragua, as well as products such as dye woods, mahogany and indigo. At Havana they joined other Spanish ships for the voyage to Spain.

The countries of Costa Rica, Nicaragua and El Salvador had small Spanish agricultural settlements, and none of the ships visiting their ports brought or exported treasure.

One area rich in shipwrecks lies east of Central America in the western Caribbean where numerous reefs and shoals, such as Serrana and Serranilla, have accounted for the loss of many ships over the centuries. The first known ship lost off Serrana was a small unidentified merchantman lost in 1526 between Santo Domingo and Margarita Island off the coast of Venezuela. It sank in a storm off Southwest Key on Serrana Bank.

1545: Honduras: The Spanish merchantman *Nuestra Señora de la Limpia Concepción* (380 tons/386 tonnes), commanded by Captain José de la Camera and carrying over 7 tons (7.11233 tonnes) of gold, plus an unknown amount of silver, set sail from Puerto

Caballos for Spain, but was wrecked in a storm at Cabo de Honduras. Most of the people and all of the treasure were lost.

1552: Panama: The Spanish galleon *La Limpia Concepción* (375 tons/381 tonnes), in the Tierra Firme Fleet of Captain-General Francísco de Mendoza, carried over 700,000 pesos of treasure and was lost shortly after leaving the Caribbean port of Nombre de Dios, then the terminus for trans-shipping all treasure from South America to Spain after it was brought across the Isthmus of Panama from Old Panama City. Nombre de Dios served as the Caribbean terminus for treasure fleets until 1596 when Sir Francis Drake destroyed it. The Spaniards then transferred the terminus to Porto Bello, and over the years more than fifty treasure galleons were lost there, many in attacks by pirates and privateers.

1552: Serranilla Bank: Over the years countless Spanish galleons sailing between Panama and Colombia to Havana and Spain were lost off this western Caribbean island and the small cays around it. The Spanish merchantman *Santa Catalina* (200 tons/203 tonnes), commanded by Captain Alonzo Galdemez, was sailing from Cartagena to Havana with 330,000 pesos in treasure on board, and wrecked on reefs on the eastern end of Serranilla Bank. Only nine of the 237 people on board reached a small cay, where they sustained themselves with great hardship for four years, maintaining a signal fire fueled with driftwood. Finally, a passing ship saw the fire and rescued the survivors. After reaching Havana, they told of having seen another ship strike the reef in 1554, but all aboard were lost so the ship could not be identified.

1605: Honduras: The two Honduras galleons sailed from Spain with merchandise for the colonies and were just entering the port of Trujillo when one, the *Almiranta*, was struck by lightning. She caught fire and sank quickly with over 100 men and her cargo. In consequence, 1605's accumulated Honduran treasures were crammed aboard the remaining galleon, the *Capitana*. Twelve hours after setting sail, the Capitana ran into a hurricane. Attempting to return to port, she was driven on the coast just 2 leagues north of Trujillo and went to pieces. Fragments of the wreck, including bodies and a few bars of gold and silver, were found on the beach, but the wreck was never located.

1605: Serranilla Bank: The worst disaster occurred in 1605 when four large and rich galleons—the *Capitana* named *San Roque* (600 tons/610 tonnes), commanded by Captain Ruy Lopez; the *Almiranta* named *Santo Domingo* (747 tons/759 tonnes), commanded by Captain Diego Ramírez; the *Nuestra Señora de Begonia* (500 tons/508 tonnes), commanded by Captain Pedro Muñoz de Salto; and the *San Ambrosio* (450 tons/457 tonnes), commanded by Captain Martín de Ormachea—in the Tierra Firme fleet of Captain-General Luis de Córdova were lost with over 8 million pesos in treasure. This was one of the greatest treasure losses the Spaniards sustained in the seventeenth century. Although there were no survivors from these four wrecks, the Spaniards sent out salvage teams all over the western Caribbean, trying unsuccessfully to locate them. Then in 1667, fishermen from Cuba accidentally discovered two of them on Serranilla Bank and recovered an undisclosed number of silver coins. During the following six years, Spanish authorities sent many expeditions to salvage the wrecks, but none was able to relocate them. Several modern expeditions, including one of my own in 1963, have attempted to locate these rich wrecks, but prevailing bad weather and incessant large seas that break over the reef where the wreckage lies have foiled us all.

1607: Honduras: A Dutch squadron of warships attempted to capture two Spanish galleons, which were loading treasures for Spain in the port of Trujillo. During the battle, one of the Dutch ships laden with half a million guilders in treasure, captured from a Spanish galleon off Colombia, exploded and sank. Both galleons survived and later reached Havana and then Spain. In 1979 an American yachtsman, spear fishing near the entrance of Trujillo, accidentally found two small Dutch bronze cannons, which he took back home as souvenirs.

1631: Panama: The Spanish galleon *San José* (600 tons/610 tonnes) sailed from Callao, Peru, for Panama with a large amount of treasure on board, and wrecked on a reef, which now bears her name, between the islands of La Galera and Garachine in the Bay of Panama, about 120 miles (193 kilometers) south of Panama City. Divers were quickly sent to the wreck and recovered 25 of the ship's 28 bronze cannons and over 1 million pesos in treasure. A year later, the president of Panama reported that more than 400,000 pesos in silver specie and 44 large silver bars remained but couldn't be recovered because sand had covered the wreck.

1633: Serrana Bank: Two galleons—the *San Juan* (400 tons/406 tonnes), commanded by Captain Gaspar de Caranza, and the *Santa*

Margarita (450 tons/451 tonnes), commanded by Captain Lorenzo de Oliva, with 3 million pesos aboard—met their fate. Other ships in this Tierra Firme Fleet of Captain-General Antonio de Oquendo rescued a total of 47 men from both galleons. Salvors sent by the governor of Havana a few months later were unable to find either wreck, and several subsequent attempts were also unsuccessful.

1641: Old Providence Island: This small island east of Nicaragua in the western Caribbean Sea was a pirate haunt for many years. Henry Morgan and others of his ilk used it as a base to attack shipping plying between Cartagena and Havana. In 1641 the Portuguese ship *Santa María de la Ayuda,* en route from Brazil to Lisbon, was blown into the Caribbean by a hurricane. She sought safety in Cartagena, only to learn that Portugal had gone to war with Spain the previous year. The Portuguese concealed the treasure beneath the ballast of their ship and hoped to retrieve it after the ship reached Spain, but she sank off Old Providence.

1659: Belize: The *Ayuda* (230 tons/234 tonnes), with a large treasure of diamonds and other precious stones from Brazil, was lost. The Spanish galleon *Santiago,* sailing between Cartagena and Havana and Spain in the Tierra Firme Fleet of Captain-General the Marquis de Villarubia with over 2 million pesos in treasure, was totally lost during a storm on the coast where today the northern border of Belize faces the southern boundary of the Mexican state of Quintana Roo. About 300 survivors were rescued after two months on a small cay. In the Archives of the Indies in Seville, I located two charts showing the exact location of this wreck. Both gave the name of the ship but one had the date as 1659 and the other as 1669. One document gave a location on the east side of Cozumel but this ship was most likely one of the other three ships of this fleet also lost in the storm.

1660: Honduras: The Spanish galleon *Santiago* (450 tons/457 tonnes), commanded by Captain Rodrigo de Torres and sailing in the Tierra Firme Fleet of Captain-General Juan de Echeverria from Cartagena to Havana with 675,000 pesos in treasure on board, separated from the convoy during a hurricane and was badly damaged. While seeking a safe haven for repairs, the ship was wrecked on a deserted island east of Cape Gracia de Dios. Most people survived and reached the island, where they spent 53 days building a vessel from wreck timbers. They sailed it to Trujillo, claiming all treasure had been left behind, but royal officials found about 50,000 pesos in gold ingots hidden in their clothing and personal effects. By the time a salvage attempt was organized six months later, the wreck site was largely covered by sand.

1675: Costa Rica: Two Spanish galleons—the *Nuestra Señora de Begoña* and the *Nuestra Señora de Buen Viaje*—sailing between Peru and Acapulco, wrecked while passing along Costa Rica's Pacific coast near Cabo Blanco on the Nicoya Peninsula. They were carrying over 1 million pesos in silver bullion and specie, as well as several tons of mercury.

1681: Panama: The Tierra Firme Armada, commanded by the Marqués de Bienes, took on treasure and set sail from Porto Bello for Spain. A sudden storm scattered the fleet along the coast of Panama. The galleon *Espiritú Santo* (650 tons/660 tonnes), commanded by Captain Antonio de Lima, struck a reef off Punta de Brujas and quickly broke up and sank, carrying 280 souls and over 1.5 million pesos to the bottom. In the same storm, the merchantman *Chaperon* sank near the mouth of the Chagres River and another ship, *La Boticaria*, wrecked on a reef near Isla de Naranjas, from which a small amount of treasure was recovered.

1690: Honduras: A severe shortage of mercury in Mexico, which hindered the refining of gold and silver, prompted the viceroy of Mexico to send a small ship, the *San Juan* (130 tons/132 tonnes), with over 1 million pesos in silver specie to buy mercury in Peru. While sailing down the Pacific coast of Honduras, the ship encountered a bad storm and was wrecked southwest of the Gulf of Fonseca on a point of land, which today bears the name of the ship. Sand had covered the wreck and salvors recovered only a small part of the silver specie.

1799: Honduras: A British squadron attacked the port of Omoa, Honduras, where over 1 million pesos in gold and silver had been accumulated for shipment to Spain. The booty was loaded aboard the British warship HMS *Leviathan* and just as she left the harbor, a storm struck and she sank about a quarter mile (.40 kilometer) offshore.

Diver surfacing with a wine bottle recovered from a wreck in Porto Bello Bay.

(*Left*) The ruins of the original Panama City, which was destroyed by Henry Morgan in 1670. A new city was built 6 miles (10 kilometers) to the west.

(*Below*) Close to shore off the Custom's House in Porto Bello, Marx found these objects, which include gold tooth picks, earrings, a crucifix and buttons; silver sewing thimbles, holy medallions and a cross; and two large diamonds.

(*Below*) Treasure chart showing the location of the galleon *San Diego*, which was lost in Darien province in 1599 while sailing from Peru to Panama with a large cargo of treasure.

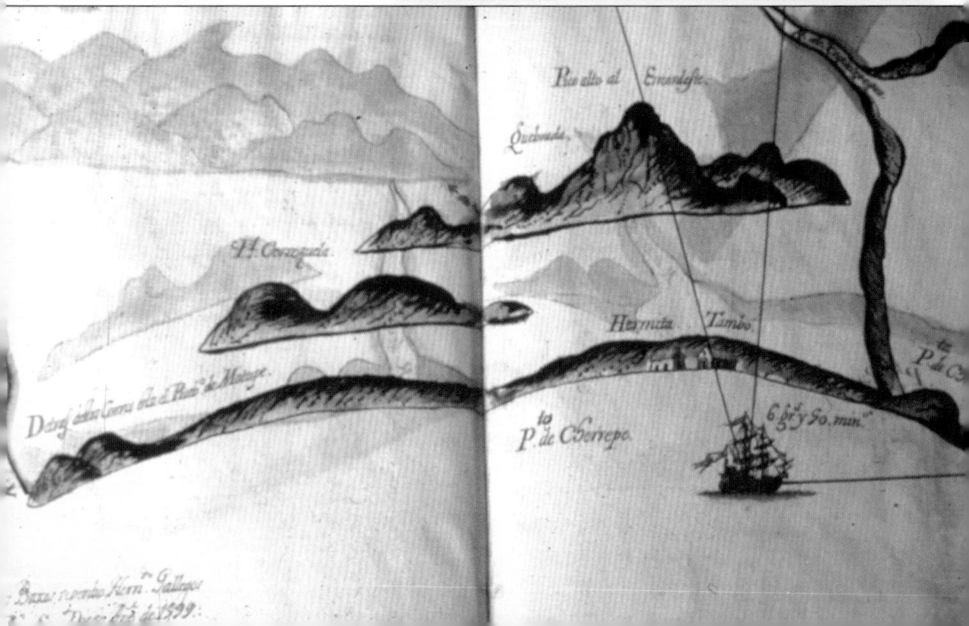

CHAPTER 10

GREATER ANTILLES' RICHEST SHIPWRECKS

The Greater Antilles includes the Caribbean islands of Hispaniola (Dominican Republic and Haiti), Cuba, Jamaica and Puerto Rico. In 1492 Columbus founded the first Spanish colony in the New World on Hispaniola, the second largest island in the West Indies. Although there are many shipwrecks of historical importance, few (if any) carried treasure. Columbus obtained a small amount of gold there and more was discovered when settlers panned streams and rivers. However, the supply was soon exhausted and ships sailing to Spain from Hispaniola carried hides and sugar instead of treasure.

Cuba, in contrast, was the assembly point for the treasure fleets sailing to Spain and the only port in the New World consistently visited by the Tierra Firme Fleet, the Armada of Tierra Firme and the New Spain Fleet. Unlike the majority of scruffy seaports in the Spanish colonies, Havana, established in 1519 on the west side of Havana Bay, was truly an imposing city, boasting handsome buildings and a large population. Its deep-water harbor, the finest in the West Indies, accommodated 1,000 ships, and the entrance to the harbor, a narrow channel, could be easily defended. Havana began to boom when commerce between Spain and her American colonies hit its stride. Most ships returning to Spain called there. The city offered water, victuals from the surrounding farmland and replacements for crewmen who had died on the voyage or deserted. Havana became the leading shipbuilding port of the

Two views of the port of Havana, ca. 1600, where all of the treasure ships stopped prior to sailing back to Spain.

Western Hemisphere as well as a stopping-off place for ships to make repairs before beginning the long transatlantic voyage.

Spain regarded Jamaica, which had little precious metal, as the least important of the their colonies in the Western Hemisphere. In 1655 the poorly defended island fell to Oliver Cromwell's forces. It was the first time Spain permanently lost one of its New World colonies. An English fortification was constructed at the end of a sandspit separating Kingston Harbor from the Caribbean. The town of Port Royal grew up around it, attracting merchants, craftsmen, tavern-owners, prostitutes, privateers and pirates. Ideally situated in the middle of the Caribbean, the city became the hub of contraband trade and the main pirate center in the Western Hemisphere until an earthquake and tidal wave toppled it into the sea in 1692. It was the richest city in the hemisphere, notorious as the "wickedest city in the world."After Port Royal was rebuilt, the British Crown was determined to suppress piracy and it became the most important British naval base outside of England. During the Colonial Period, over 900 ships of many nations wrecked in Jamaican waters, but very few of them carried substantial amounts of treasure. In the Port Royal area alone, over 100 ships were lost and some are mixed in with the remains of the sunken city.

San Juan, Puerto Rico, founded in 1509, is one of the best and safest ports in the West Indies, but large ships rarely used it during the Age of Sail. Like Jamaica, the island had little of value to Spain. It was used primarily as a port of call for ships needing repairs.

Co-author Jenifer Marx recovering gold and silver coins from Spanish galleon located off of Jamaica.

The three Cayman Islands, part of the Lesser Antilles, are a mecca for sport divers who enjoy their crystalline waters, abundant marine life and friendly people, but there is little for the treasure seeker. None of the more than 350 documented shipwrecks in the Caymans appear to have been carrying treasure. However, the Caymans lie almost on the direct route for galleons sailing between the Spanish Main and Cuba, so logic dictates that some sank in these waters.

1502: While Columbus was in the port of Santo Domingo, Governor Bobadilla prepared a fleet of thirty ships to sail back to Spain with a tremendous amount of gold seized from the natives. Sensing an approaching hurricane, Columbus tried in vain to prevent the fleet's departure. Under the command of Admiral Antonio de Torres, the fleet set sail around the beginning of July and little more than a day later the hurricane struck, destroying all but four ships and killing more than 500 people. Most wrecked 20 to 30 miles (32 to 48 kilometers) east of the port of Santo Domingo. The flagship, the *Santa Monica*, with the largest amount of gold, including a gold nugget described in documents as "the size of a plate," sank close to Mona Island, located between Santo Domingo and Puerto Rico. None of the precious cargo was ever recovered.

1515: An unidentified Spanish caravel of 80 tons (81 tonnes, six cannons), commanded by Captain Alonso Donato, set sail from Santo Domingo en route to Spain laden with 235,000 pesos in gold nuggets and gold dust. Shortly after leaving port, a hurricane struck. The leaking ship ran before it for several days before sinking in the port of Cumanacan, at the mouth of the Bani River in Cuba. Indians killed everyone aboard except for two young boys, who were ransomed some ten years later.

1525: Conquistador Don Pedro de Alvarado ordered a *nao* of 150 tons (152 tonnes) and 12 bronze cannons, under the command of Captain Martín de Narváez, dispatched for Spain "with an immense cargo of gold" the Spaniards had amassed in the conquest of Guatemala. During a wild storm, the ship was dashed to pieces on the shore about a league north of Cape San Antonio on Cuba. The only three survivors were rescued two years later, along with survivors from another ship lost to the north of them.

1531: The Portuguese East Indiaman *Santa María da Conceição,* commanded by Captain Nuño da Acunha and returning to Lisbon from the Orient with a cargo valued at over 2 million crusadoes, was severely damaged in a storm off the Cape of Good Hope. Unable to reach Portugal, she put in at Salvador, Brazil, for repairs. Sailing alone from there she encountered a hurricane and was blown to "one of the larger Leeward Islands." The ship was repaired and set sail for Portugal, but was soon struck by yet another hurricane and driven toward the western Caribbean. The vessel was becalmed for a week or so and many of those on board suffered from a "fever." When the winds picked up, she sailed north. On the night of November 24, due to faulty navigation, and "not bad weather," she struck upon the southeast coast of Cuba 2 to 3 leagues to the east of Santiago de Cuba and only "a few souls of the more than 400 aboard were saved." Fishermen from Santiago who were sent to salvage her valuable cargo found only floating bales of silk and six of her bronze cannons. The cargo would have consisted of silks, spices, porcelain and exotic objects made of gold, silver, ivory, jade, etc. Most Portuguese East Indiamen at that time carried precious stones and pearls as well.

1534: An unidentified Spanish *nao,* commanded by Captain Sancho Pardo, was sailing from Villarica (near Veracruz), Mexico, to

Spain with gold treasure valued at 330,000 pesos. During a January norther she struck upon a shoal well off the coast of western Cuba in the vicinity of Cape San Antonio. The shoal was named after her captain, Sancho Pardo, and appears on both old and modern charts. Only three aboard the ship survived by clinging to the vessel's mast and drifting ashore.

1544: An unidentified Spanish *nao*, carrying "over 700,000 pesos in gold," set sail from Nombre de Dios in Panama for Havana and Spain. Her treasure was most likely plunder amassed by Pizzaro, who was then conquering Peru and stripping the Incas of their accumulated riches. En route to Havana, the ship was attacked and captured by a French pirate vessel from the port of St. Malo, France. All of the *nao*'s crew were "put to the knife," the ship was set on fire, and the pirate vessel took off with an immense amount of plunder. She was struck by a storm in mid-October and wrecked at Cabo Frances, between Cape San Anton and the Isle of Pines.

1544: The Spanish *nao Santa María de la Isla* (180 tons/183 tonnes, 32 iron cannons), commanded by Captain Vicente Martín and sailing between Nombre de Dios and Havana and then Spain, wrecked due to faulty navigation on the coast "3 leagues more or less to the west of the entrance to Havana port." Huge waves quickly broke the ship up and many people drowned. She was carrying 1,347,400 pesos in gold and silver, plus pearls and precious stones of unknown value. Shifting sands quickly covered the wreck and nothing was found but some timbers thrown on the shore several weeks after the disaster. Contemporary salvors who spent three summers in the area recovered only a few cannons.

1550: The Spanish merchantman *Santa María de Jesús* (330 tons/335 tonnes), commanded by Captain Diego Bernal and carrying over 2 million pesos in gold and silver, was too severely damaged by a hurricane in the Bahama Channel to reach Spain, so she went around the northern Bahama Islands and headed to Puerto Rico for repairs. She wrecked in a storm 3 to 4 miles (5 to 6.5 kilometers) west of the entrance to the port of San Juan with an almost total loss of lives. Repeated salvage attempts failed to recover anything significant.

1551: After the Tierra Firme Fleet sailed from Nombre de Dios with that year's South American treasures, a galleon (presumed to have sunk sailing between Peru and Panama City) arrived with over 2 million pesos in treasure. The late arrival's precious cargo was transferred overland to Nombre de Dios to await the Spain-bound fleets the following year. However, when pirate vessels were sighted in the area, the governor feared an attack on the port and ordered the *Santa María de Finisterra,* the only large vessel available, to carry the treasure to Havana to await an escort back to Spain. On January 7, 1552, while at anchor in Havana harbor, the ship sank suddenly in 120 feet (36.5 meters) of water. Repeated salvage attempts failed to recover any of her ill-fated treasure.

1553: The Spanish *nao La Santa María y Espiritú Sancto* (120 tons/122 tonnes, 24 cannons), commanded by Captain Alonzo Perez Maldonado and sailing between Veracruz and Havana, was lost at Cape San Antonio directly beneath the lookout station of La Vigia. During a norther, the ship opened and began taking on more water than the pumps could handle. Realizing that he must run the ship aground to save as many lives as possible, Captain Maldonado sel-ected Cape San Antonio since there would be people at La Vigia to assist them in getting ashore. Only 27 of the 256, plus slaves, reached safety because of the rocky coast and big waves. The ship was carrying 980,000 pesos in gold and silver, plus "gifts for the king." According to various accounts, La Vigia was the highest part of Cape San Antonio where there was a small garrison of soldiers.

1557: The Spanish galleon *Nuestra Señora del Candelaria* (425 tons/432 tonnes), was sailing in the New Spain Fleet when a hurricane struck in the Gulf of Mexico. After the winds and seas subsided, treasure from two sinking galleons was transferred to the *Candelaria,* increasing the value of treasure she carried to 1,695,000 pesos. A storm prevented the galleon from entering Havana harbor, so she headed to the port of Matanzas. En route a violent storm arose, and she wrecked on a reef about midway between Havana and Matanzas. Salvors recovered 664,200 pesos in treasure before the ship slipped off the reef and sank in water too deep for the divers.

1557: The Portuguese slave ship *Rainha de Portugal,* commanded by Captain Ferrão de Castello Branca, was wrecked on the south side of Cayo Grande, in the Archipelago de los Jardines de la Reina, off Cuba's south coast. After the Tierra Firme Fleet sailed from Nombre de Dios, one of the galleons sprang a critical leak and returned to port. Authorities deemed her unfit to sail and transferred all 800,000 pesos of her treasure onto this Portuguese slaver, which they seized with the pretext that she was trading in contraband goods. The *Rainha* was attempting to catch up with the fleet in Havana when she was lost in a storm.

1570: An unidentified Portuguese slave ship entered the Cuban port of Matanzas on the pretext of desperately needing fresh water and victuals. After a drunken seaman boasted about treasure hidden under the ship's ballast, customs officials searched the ship and found over 250,000 pesos in Spanish silver specie, three chests of gold dust and 112 ivory elephant tusks. The Portuguese were all imprisoned and a Spanish crew was put aboard to sail the prize to Havana. En route she was attacked by two French pirate vessels and, while attempting to return to Matanzas, she wrecked in a sudden storm on the coast 3 to 4 leagues west of Matanzas. The Spaniards set her on fire to keep the booty out of the hands of the pirates. Salvors recovered only three chests of silver specie and seven ivory tusks.

1581: An unidentified Spanish *patache* was sent from Cartagena as an advice boat carrying despatches to Spain. English pirates appeared near the entrance to Havana, so she headed for Matanzas with the pirates close behind. When capture seemed inevitable, the crew set fire to the ship about a half mile (.80 kilometer) off the port of Matanzas and rowed to shore in two small boats. The pirates captured one boat and killed everyone in revenge for frustrating their capture of the *patache*. A subsequent inquiry revealed that the advice boat was carrying over 4 tons (4.064 tonnes) in contraband gold ingots and three chests of emeralds.

1593: The Spanish galleon *El San Crucifixo de Burgos* (600 tons/610 tonnes), carrying over 1 million pesos in treasure, was heading back to Spain in a convoy when it was damaged in a hurricane and sought refuge in the port of Santo Domingo on Hispaniola Island. The ship was still there when word came that Sir Francis Drake was heading there to attack the port. In order to thwart Drake, the galleon was hastily dispatched for Havana, but on the way there it wrecked on the coast during a nocturnal storm 2 leagues east of Cape Cruz, near the southeast point of Cuba.

1593: Two treasure-laden Spanish galleons were sailing between Veracruz and Havana and Spain in the New Spain Fleet of Captain-General Martín Pérez Olezabal—the *Santa María de San Vicente* (180 tons/183 tonnes), commanded by Captain Miguel de Alcata, and the

Nuestra Señora del Rosario (220 tons/223.5 tonnes), commanded by Captain Cristóbal Castellanos. Both went down during a storm, sinking in deep water less than half a league northwest of the entrance to Havana Harbor. When I wrote *Shipwrecks of the Western Hemisphere,* the sixteenth-century document I used stated that all treasure was removed from both ships before they sank. I subsequently found other documents that state only a small part of the gold and silver could be off-loaded to other ships in the convoy before they sank.

1606: After leaving Cartagena for Havana, the Tierra Firme Fleet of Captain-General Alvarez de Áviles encountered a hurricane and the ships all were separated. Áviles took his *Capitana* and eight other ships, with a total of over 2.5 million pesos in treasure, into the port of Santiago, Cuba, for badly needed repairs. Three weeks later they all set sail for Havana, but several hours after leaving port they encountered still another hurricane and all the ships wrecked on reefs 4 leagues from the eastern end of Los Jardines de la Reina. Áviles and many other men were rescued from several of the wrecks. Áviles outfitted a vessel and returned to the wreck of his *Capitana,* hoping to salvage some treasure. He recovered eight of the 44 bronze cannons and some rigging, but the treasure was already buried under the sand in 4 fathoms of water. Nothing was recovered from any of the other wrecks.

1607: The Spanish galleon *San Roque* (650 tons/660 tonnes), sailing between Porto Bello and Havana with 1.1 million pesos in treasure on board, wrecked on a coral reef during a storm 6 leagues east of Cayo Grande in the Archipelago de Los Jardines de la Reina, off the south coast of Cuba. Most of the ship was still intact and sticking above the water when a salvage ship from Santiago arrived five days later. However, a storm came up and the wreck slid off into deep water. The salvors recovered only 620,000 pesos of treasure.

1627: The Portuguese East Indiaman *Santa María da Conceição,* carrying over 2 million crusadoes from the Orient to Lisbon, was severely damaged in a hurricane and unable to reach Portugal, so she went to the Caribbean to seek a port where repairs could be made and wrecked about 10 miles (16 kilometers) east of Santiago, Cuba.

1628: Spain's greatest marine disaster was not the Spanish Armada in 1588 but the loss in 1628 of the entire New Spain Fleet in Matanzas Bay, Cuba. Over the centuries hundreds of galleons and other Spanish ships were lost to pirates and privateers, but this was the only time that an entire fleet was captured. The treasure convoy of 24 ships was approaching Havana from Veracruz when a formidable fleet of Dutch warships, commanded by Admiral Piet Heyn, was sighted. The Spanish galleons changed course, heading for Matanzas Bay where they hoped to offload the treasure before the Dutch could plunder them. Unfortunately, upon entering the bay, all 24 ships ran aground. Instead of trying to save the treasure, the Spaniards fled for shore. Without firing a shot, the Dutch grabbed over 25 million pesos in treasure.

There was so much treasure that they had to refloat the four largest Spanish galleons to carry the bulk of it. Two of these Spanish ships were separated from the Dutch convoy by a storm and wrecked near present-day Freeport, Grand Bahama Island. A section of one with some silver coinage was discovered in 1965. I visited the site in 1968 and recovered 450 silver coins and some artifacts. We can assume that three of the four galleons that escaped from Matanzas made it to Havana. However, one was wrecked 4 leagues east of Havana. There is no mention of what it carried or if it was salvaged. Although this was the greatest treasure ever captured at sea, had the Dutch only known that at the first sight of the enemy, the Spaniards had concealed huge amounts of gold and precious stones under the ballast in their ships, they could have seized twice the booty. Before setting sail for Holland, Heyn ordered his men to burn the remaining twenty Spanish galleons and their hidden treasure sank into the soft mud of the bay where most of it still remains today. In 1957 local fishermen recovered 27 80-pound (36-kilogram) silver bars from one of these wrecks.

1641: The Spanish galleon *Nuestra Señora de la Pena de Francia* left Havana for Spain in the fleet of Captain-General Juan de Campos, which was struck by a hurricane in the Straits of Florida. The ships were scattered and the *Francia,* carrying over 1 million pesos in treasure, was badly damaged. With only one mast intact, the captain decided to try to return to Havana. This was a challenge because the fast-flowing Gulf Stream prevents sailing ships from heading south. The galleon had to circle around the Bahamas, enter the Old Bahama Channel and then head west to Havana. While attempting to do this, she wrecked 6 leagues east of Havana. A young boy was the only survivor.

1666: The Spanish galleon *Nuestra Señora de la Guia* (700 tons/711 tonnes, 48 cannons), picked up 925,000 pesos in treasure, plus the per-

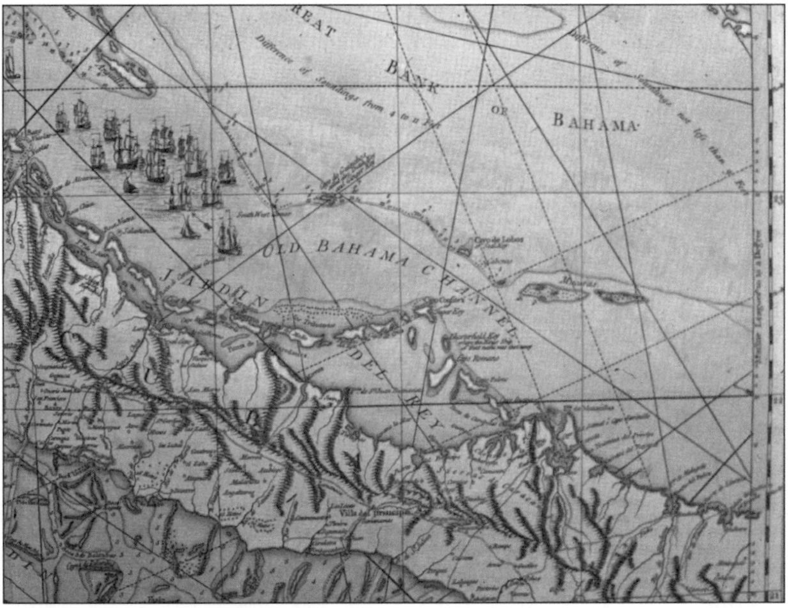

English chart of the north coast of Cuba and southern Bahamas showing Chesterfield Key, where the HMS *Chesterfield* was lost in 1762.

sonal property of the archbishop of Lima, Peru, in Porto Bello and then embarked "many chests of pearls and emeralds" in Cartagena before sailing for Havana. En route to Havana, a hurricane struck and the galleon wrecked on the third cay at the eastern end of Los Jardines de la Reina, east of Cape Cruz, on Cuba's south coast. Only seven lucky souls reached the cay where they subsisted on turtle blood and turtle meat for over a month before being rescued by fishermen. Numerous expeditions failed to find the wreck.

1691: Four Spanish galleons of the Tierra Firme Fleet of Captain-General Marques de Vado were wrecked on Pedro Shoals, about 125 miles (201 kilometers) south of Jamaica, carrying over 6 million pesos in treasure. Fishermen from Port Royal rescued 776 people from the wrecks, but twice that number were lost. Despite intensive salvage operations by salvors from nearby Jamaica and by Spaniards soon afterward, more than half of the treasure still remains on these ships.

1711: As the New Spain Fleet approached Havana from Veracruz, a "norther" struck and five of the ships were wrecked "about 5 leagues" west of the port. Salvors almost immediately recovered

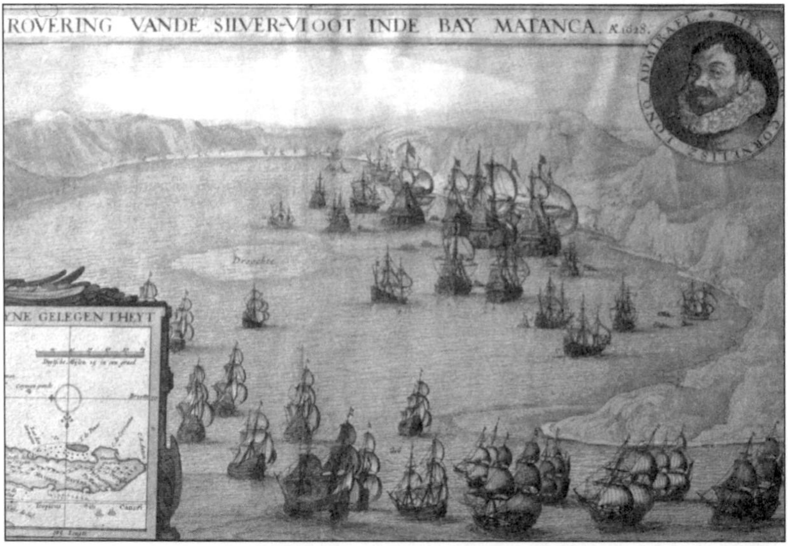

The Dutch fleet, under the command of Admiral Piet Heyn, entering Matanzas Bay to capture the New Spain treasure fleet in 1628.

over 1.7 million pesos from four of the ships, which had wrecked on the beach. But repeated efforts over several decades failed to find the fifth ship, the *Santissima Trinidad* (64 bronze cannons), commanded by Captain Diego de Alarcón y Ocaño, which was the *Almiranta* of the fleet, with 1.2 million pesos in treasure on board. She struck a reef within sight of the other four ships and disappeared. Most likely she slipped off into deep water.

1727: The governor of Cuba wrote the king that during a recent storm, hundreds of gold coins, dated 1716 and 1717, had been found on a beach near Playa Honda, and he surmised they came from a wreck, but since no one knew of a ship having been lost in that area, it was a bit of a mystery. Salvors spent two months searching, but failed to find any traces of a wreck. In 1732 a royal official in Havana wrote to the president of the House of Trade in Seville, stating that in the same area after a hurricane, 127 small bars of gold, over 900 gold coins, several large gold chains, and a small box of emeralds were found on the beach. Another salvage attempt failed to find any traces of the wreck, which most likely is in deep water farther offshore than they searched.

1730: The richest galleon ever lost on Pedro Shoals was the *Genovesa*, commanded by Captain Francisco Guiral. In 1730, due to a

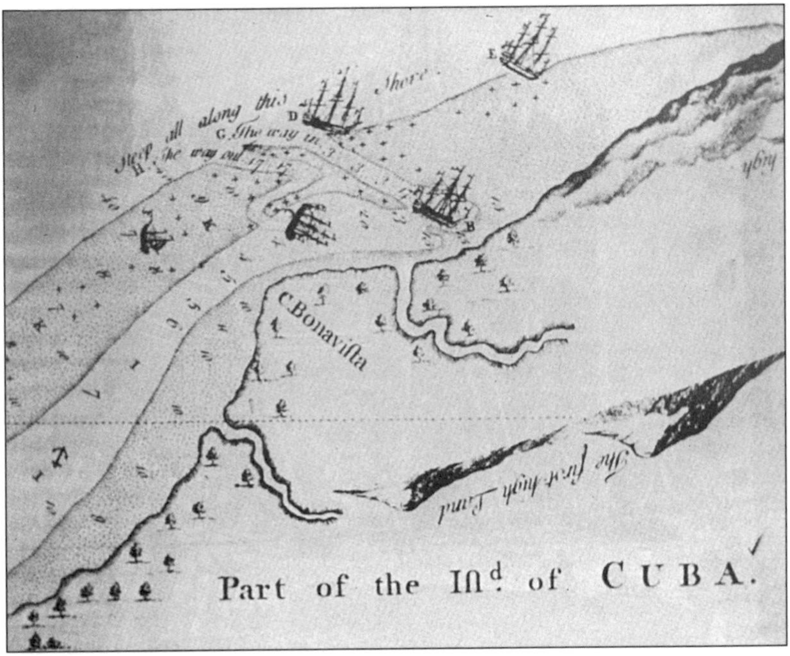

Early chart of the northwest area of Cuba showing the locations of five British merchantmen lost in 1699.

scarcity of ships, no fleets were sent to the New World and all of the treasures from South America were loaded aboard this one galleon armed with 54 cannons. Accounts differ, but she carried between 3 and 5 million pesos in treasure. After leaving Cartagena and heading for Havana, she struck on a reef due to faulty navigation and was totally lost. Survivors from the *Genovesa* reached Kingston, Jamaica, prompting the British to send a salvage vessel to the site. When English salvors reached Pedro Shoals, they located a wreck and started bringing up considerable amounts of treasure. They assumed they had found the *Genovesa*. In fact they were about 10 miles (16 kilometers) away on the site where, several days after the *Genovesa* sank, another Spanish ship, the *Santa Isabela*, had sunk with about 1 million pesos in treasure.

1730: The three Cayman Islands were pirate strongholds throughout the Colonial Period, even after the British settled there in 1655. The only recorded shipwreck, which could be considered a "treasure site," is on Little Cayman. She was the Spanish galleon *San Miguel*, lost carrying over 50 tons (51 tonnes) of mercury, which on today's market would be worth over $13 million.

1740: The richest single ship ever lost in Cuban waters was the Spanish warship *Invencible* (70 bronze cannons), commanded by Admiral Rodrigo de Torres and carrying over 4 million pesos in gold and silver. Arriving from Veracruz, she anchored in Havana Harbor. Shortly after the admiral went ashore to pay his respects to the governor, lightning struck the ship, which blew up, taking all 470 men aboard to a watery grave. Thousands of coins from the wreck showered the waterfront, but the rest of her treasure is buried somewhere under the harbor mud. Over the centuries hundreds of Spanish ships sank in New World ports such as Veracruz, Cartagena, Porto Bello and Nombre de Dios. However, the largest concentration of Spanish colonial shipwrecks is in Havana Harbor. In the other ports shallow water made it possible for salvors, both colonial and modern, to recover precious cargoes. Today, dredging operations have obliterated most of the shipwrecks. Fortunately, very little dredging has been done in Havana Harbor, and the water, while too deep for earlier salvors, is well within reach today. In October 1768 a hurricane struck Cuba, destroying 5,000 buildings in Havana and laying waste to the surrounding countryside. Sixty-nine ships sank in the harbor, among which were 17 galleons and merchantmen carrying over 7 million pesos in treasure.

1794: The British West Indiaman *Covert*, commanded by Captain John Lawford and sailing between Jamaica and England with 43 chests of Spanish silver specie on board, wrecked due to faulty navigation on Baja Nuevo Reef, located between Grand Cayman Island and Pedro Shoals off Jamaica. A few of her people were saved by another ship in the same convoy.

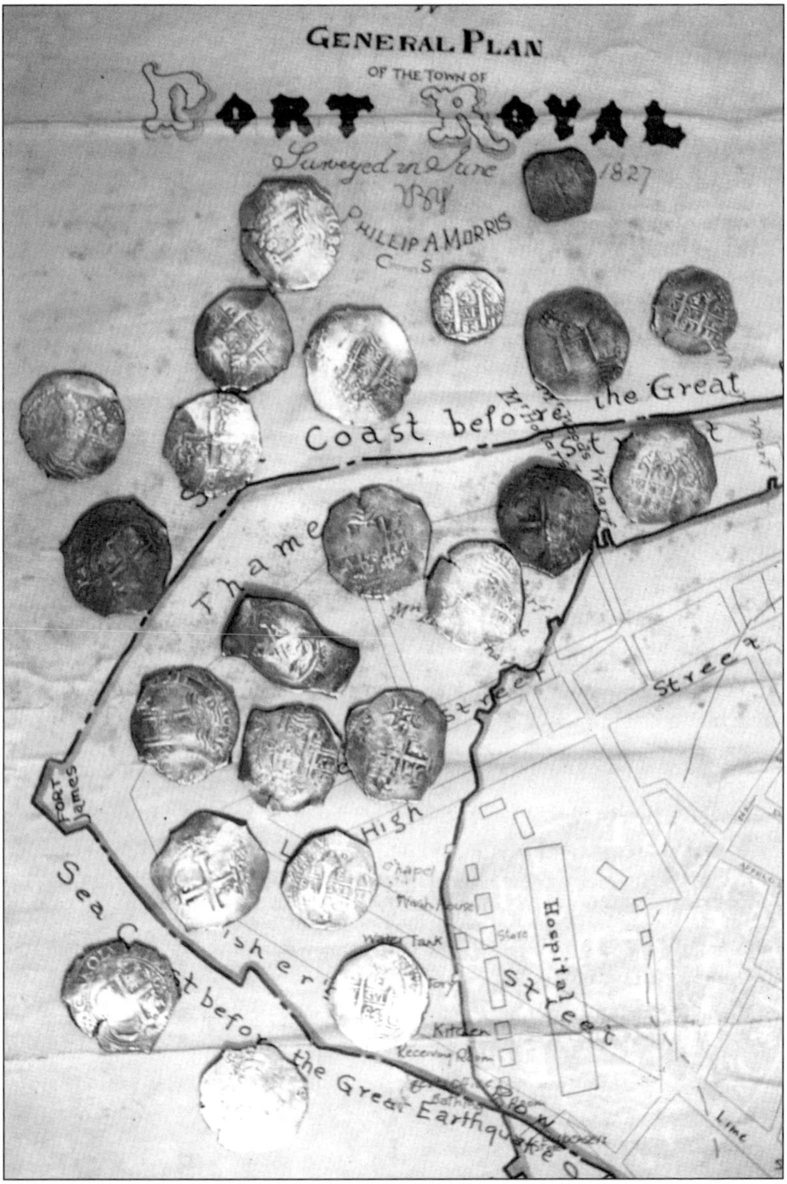

(Above) These Spanish silver coins were among the many treasures, relics and artifacts recovered by the authors from the sunken city of Port Royal.

(Facing, top) Spanish silver pieces of eight with the brass keyhole plate and part of the key from a treasure chest found at Port Royal. *(Facing, lower)* Jenifer Marx surfaces with a human skull during their three-year excavation of the sunken city.

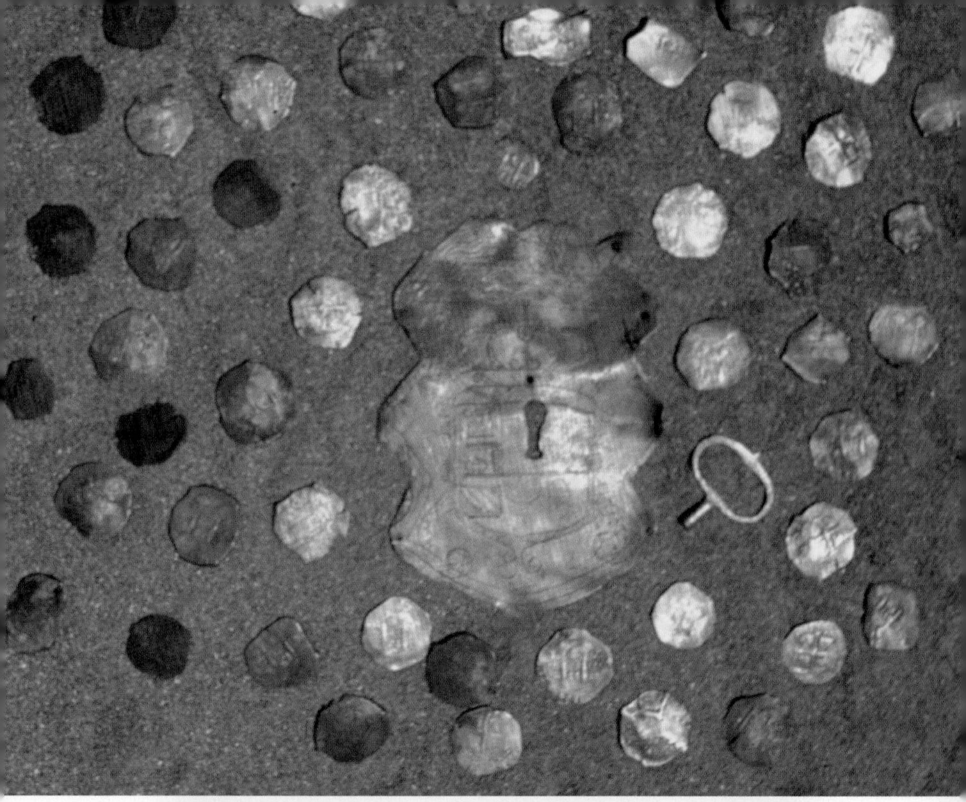

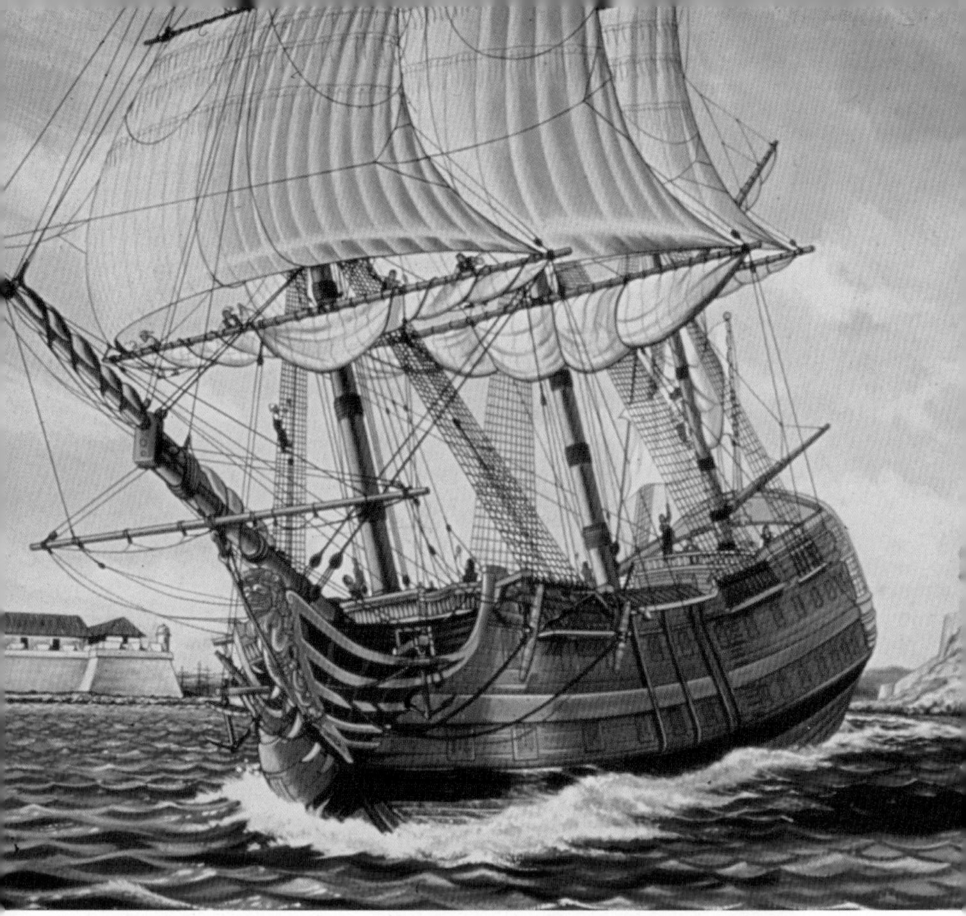

French warship leaving the island of Guadeloupe en route to France.

Three pistols and lead musket balls recovered by Marx from Jamaica's sunken Port Royal city.

CHAPTER 11

LESSER ANTILLES' RICHEST SHIPWRECKS

There are very few treasure ships in the Lesser Antilles, an island group in the eastern part of the West Indies, which extends in an arc from Curaçao to the Virgin Islands. Ships returning with treasure from the New World didn't pass this way except when blown off course by hurricanes. Ships coming from Spain and elsewhere in Europe sailed by these islands on their way to ports such as Cartagena, Nombre de Dios, Porto Bello and Veracruz, but they were carrying general merchandises for colonists. Some carried mercury, but few of these were lost, mainly because the voyages from Spain to the New World took place during the spring months, long before the hurricane season started.

1567: As the New Spain Fleet under Captain-General Juan Velasco de Barrio was about to set sail from Veracruz for Spain, word came that two English fleets were waiting to intercept them, one off Havana and the other at the entrance to the Bahama Channel. To protect the treasure the king so desperately needed, de Barrio decided to take an unusual route back to Spain. Hugging the coast of Yucatán, the fleet turned southward and passed to the south of Jamaica. He planned to sail to the Virgin Islands and then head for Spain. However, when nearing Puerto Rico, the ships were forced to run eastward before a storm and six of the major galleons, carrying over 3 million pesos in treasure, wrecked near the northwest tip of Dominica Island. Several of them slipped into deep water. The lost ships were the galleon *Capitana, San Juan* (150 tons/152 tonnes), commanded by Captain Beneto de Santana; the galleon *Almiranta, Santa Barbola* (150 tons/152 tonnes),

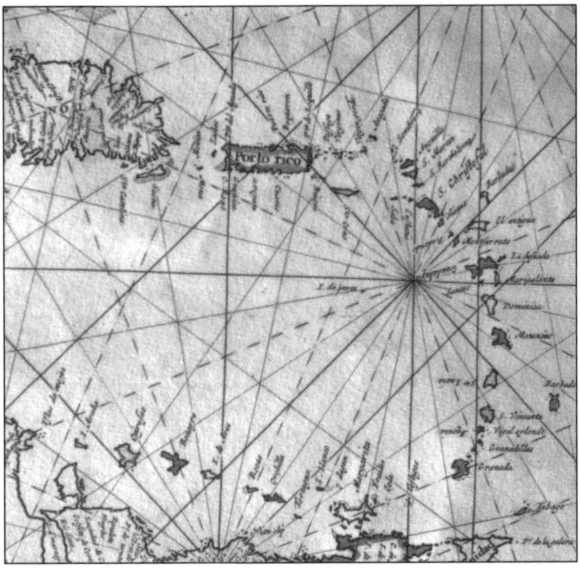

On this old chart, the chain of islands on the right-hand side are the Lesser Antilles.

commanded by Captain Vincencio Garullo; the galleon *San Felípe* (120 tons/122 tonnes), commanded by Captain Juan Lopez de Sosa; the *nao El Espíritu Santo* (120 tons/122 tonnes), commanded by Captain Juan de Rosales; and two unidentified *naos* of 120 tons (122 tonnes) each. The storm prevented the other ships in the fleet from picking up any of the treasure or survivors, most of whom reached shore, where they were massacred by Caribe Indians.

1603: The island of Guadeloupe lies just north of Dominica and each year the treasure-laden fleets stopped there for refreshment. In 1603, when the New Spain Fleet of Captain-General Fulgencio de Meneses made the customary stop, a sudden squall caused three galleons to wreck near a river mouth at the southwest end of the island. One of the lost vessels was the *Capitana, San Juan Bautista* (700 tons/711 tonnes, 45 bronze cannons). She also carried over 275 tons (279 tonnes) of mercury, today worth a king's ransom. Several Spanish attempts to recover the flasks of liquid metal and the artillery were thwarted by hostile Carib Indians.

1630: An unidentified Spanish galleon of the New Spain Fleet of Captain-General Miguel de Echazarreta was en route to Veracruz when it wrecked on the east side of St. Kitts island in a nocturnal squall. Over 300 souls were lost, and 55 tons (56 tonnes) of mercury.

The Dutch island of St. Eustatius, also known as Statia, was used as both a major contraband port by all nations during the seventeenth and eighteenth centuries and as a pirate base.

1687: The Dutch town of Orangestad on St. Eustatius Island was struck by an earthquake and cast into the sea. Orangestad was then a pirate and privateering hangout, and it is estimated that over £1 million pounds sterling in treasure was lost. Some of the buildings are visible today, protruding through the sandy bottom.

1687: The same earthquake that destroyed St. Eustatius also destroyed Charleston on Nevis Island where losses were estimated at over £250,000 pounds sterling. I explored this site in 1960 and found many artifacts but no treasure. I had no excavation equipment at that time and was limited to picking up visible objects on the sea floor.

1689: Tiny deserted Bird Island, located 130 miles (209 kilometers) southwest of Guadeloupe Island in the eastern Caribbean, was the site where the Spanish galleon *Santa Ana Maria* went down carrying 78 tons (79 tonnes) of mercury and other merchandise. Most of those aboard survived, but were marooned on the island for five months before being rescued.

1731: An unidentified Spanish galleon, sailing between Spain and Veracruz with a cargo of 80 tons (81 tonnes) of mercury destined for the mines of Mexico, was wrecked on the reefs on the north side of Anegada Island in the British Virgin Islands. Nothing was ever salvaged, most likely because the heavy mercury quickly sank under the sand.

1758: The Italian merchantman *Due Compagni,* carrying over 200,000 Spanish pieces of eight, left the port of St. Eustatius and was rounding the island's northern tip when a squall caused her to capsize. Contemporary salvors recovered a small portion of the coins.

1775: An eighteenth-century chart of the British Virgin Island notes: "On Anegada is Ye Treasure Point, so called by the freebooters [pirates] from the gold and silver supposed to have been buried there abouts after the wreck of a Spanish galleon." This may be so because often treasure fleets were struck by hurricanes after they left Havana and entered the Bahama Channel. When they were unable to reach Spain, they were ordered to go around the northern part of the Bahamas and make their way back to Havana, Puerto Rico or Santo Domingo and in some cases were wrecked in the Virgin Islands.

1780: The greatest Caribbean hurricane ever recorded occurred on October 12, 1780, destroying an estimated 1,000 ships throughout the Lesser and Greater Antilles. The biggest losses were on Martinique Island, where 150 large ships sank, some with treasure.

1781: The Portuguese merchantman *Santissimo Trinidade*, commanded by Captain Dos Santo and sailing from Brazil to Lisbon, with over 3 million cruzadoes in Oriental treasures, was driven by a hurricane and wrecked on the eastern side of St. Martin Island. More than 500 souls perished and only a small amount of her treasure was recovered at the time.

1788: The Portuguese merchantman *Armida*, commanded by Captain da Silva, sailed from Brazil for Lisbon, with over 1 million crusadoes in treasure. Due to faulty navigation, she wrecked off Point Saline on the southern tip of Grenada Island. Most of the people were saved, but none of the treasure.

1804: The Portuguese East Indiaman *Francizhena*, sailing from the Orient to Lisbon with over 3 million crusadoes in Oriental treasures, stopped in Brazil where she took on an unknown amount of gold, diamonds and other precious stones. En route to Lisbon, she was wrecked in a hurricane on the east side of Barbados Island. Over 450 souls perished and none of her treasure was ever recovered.

1804: The British warship *Magnificent* (74 cannons), commanded by Captain William Henry Ricketts Jervis, was carrying over £200,000 pounds sterling in gold and silver specie, which it had captured from several French ships. She set sail for England and soon afterwards struck upon the Black Rocks, a shoal off the Isle de Saints, south of Guadeloupe Island, and then sank in deep water. Other warships in the fleet saved most of the crew.

Chapter 12

Spanish Main's Richest Shipwrecks

In 1533 Spaniards founded Cartagena de las Indias at one of the most spacious bays on the coast of Colombia, then known as New Granada. A mere two years later, Cartagena superseded Santa Marta as the principal port on the Spanish Main (the northern coast of South America, touching the Caribbean Sea). Santa Marta was closer to the mouth of the Magdalena River, the river on which gold and emeralds were transported down from Bogotá, but Cartagena boasted a fine harbor, more than 10 miles (16 kilometers) long and spacious enough to offer safe anchorage to hundreds of large ships. Narrow Boca Chica, or Small Mouth, was the only navigable entrance, so Cartagena could have been one of the most secure settlements in America, with forts on both sides of the entrance and a chain boom across the opening.

However, the wheels of Spanish colonial administration turned very slowly and Cartagena's first fort hadn't been completed ten years later, when the town was besieged and sacked by French privateer Robert Baal. That incident stimulated completion of construction and soon the town had, along with the completed fort, thick surrounding walls and batteries at points along the shore all the way to Boca Chica and on both sides of Boca Chica itself. These fortifications were necessary because Cartagena was very attractive to Caribbean pirates and privateers. It was the first port of call for the majority of the ships in the Tierra Firme Fleet and the Armada and, even more important, it was the rendezvous for all

During the seventeenth and eighteenth centuries, the Dutch island of Curaçao was a center of contraband trade with the Spanish New World colonies.

the ships after they had collected their treasures from the separate ports of the Spanish Main. Despite ever increasing defense measures, Cartagena was successfully attacked again in 1586 by Drake, who took the city, obtaining 110,000 pesos in ransom.

1542: Three unidentified Spanish merchantmen sailed from Nombre de Dios for Cartagena with over half a million pesos in gold and silver. One also carried 39 chests of gold Inca objects. They struck a reef while entering Boca Chica, then used as the entrance to Cartagena Harbor, and all three sank soon afterwards. Divers reported that the wrecks were too deep to be salvaged and, at the governor's orders, the chief pilot was hung for causing the disaster. He was accused of being drunk in his bunk when he should have been on deck supervising navigation into the harbor.

1559: An unidentified galleon, sailing from Nombre de Dios with 900,000 pesos in gold and silver aboard, separated in a storm from the other ships in the Tierra Firme Fleet and attempted at night to enter Cartagena Harbor, but the pilot was off the mark and missed the entrance by 2 miles (3 kilometers). The ship ran aground quickly and broke up in heavy seas. Only a small part of her treasure was recovered.

1564: The Spanish galleon *Nuestra Señora de Tarragona* (500 tons/508 tonnes), commanded by Captain Felipe Mascaras and coming from Nombre de Dios with 690,000 pesos in treasure aboard, struck upon a reef several leagues before reaching Cartagena, then slid off and went down in deep water before any of her treasure could be taken off by other ships. Only 16 people were lost, but disgruntled merchants who

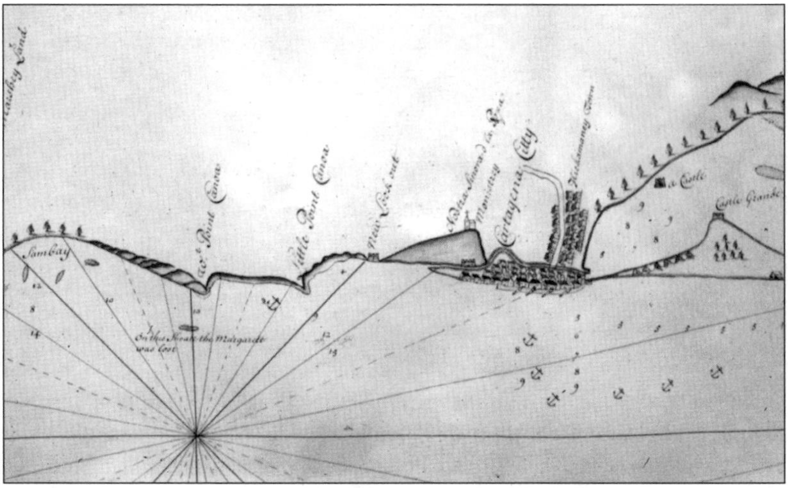

English chart showing the location of the wreck of the Spanish galleon *Nuestra Señora de Margarita* (called the "Margarett" here), lost in 1706 with treasure on board.

lost their fortunes and blamed the captain for the loss later allegedly murdered the captain in the port.

1570: The Portuguese East Indiaman *Nossa Senhora de Belém* (11,400 tons/1,422 tonnes, forty cannons), commanded by Captain João Mendes de Vieria and coming from the Orient with over 8 million crusadoes in cargo, first made a stop in Salvador, Brazil, for fresh water and to put some sick men ashore, then continued for Lisbon. A week later it ran into a hurricane and was severely damaged, losing two of its four masts, then headed for a safe haven in the Caribbean. While attempting to enter the port of Puerto Cabello, Venezuela, it struck upon a reef and quickly broke up in strong seas. Only 44 people were saved. Pearl divers from Margarita Island were sent to salvage the wreck, but recovered only 68 bales of silks, 134 chests of spices, and six bronze cannons.

1572: The Spanish galleon *San Felipe* (550 tons/559 tonnes, 36 cannons), commanded by Captain Galdomez and sailing between Nombre de Dios and Cartagena with 840,000 pesos in treasure, caught on fire when the ship was only a few hours from the port. Her captain ran her aground on Tesoro Island, but she blew up before any of her treasure could be saved. All but 16 aboard her perished.

1594: A late seventeenth-century English book on sailing directions, which had been copied from a Spanish book, stated that

Sir Francis Drake attacked Cartagena in 1543 and obtained a large ransom in return for not destroying the city.

between the St. Jago River and port of San Matheo on the Pacific coast of Colombia, "there comes out seaward a league and a half some rocks on which was cast away Juan Philipo Castro, a great pilot of these seas, in the ship *Clarius* in the year 1594 and in said ship was a vast treasure and many other ships have also been cast away on the same rocks." The ship was most likely a galleon in the Armada of the South Seas making a voyage from Peru up to Panama when lost. All Spanish ships generally used religious names, but many also had nicknames such as this ship. She would have been carrying between 1 and 2 million pesos in treasure.

1610: During the voyage of the Tierra Firme Fleet from Spain to Cartagena, the *Capitana, San Felipe* (850 tons/864 tonnes, 42 bronze cannons), commanded by Captain Gaspar de Vargas, as well as an unidentified *patache,* were wrecked at night on the east side of Bonaire Island. Over a period of five years pearl divers from Margarita Island salvaged all of the bronze cannons, but only 42 tons (43 tonnes) of the 110 tons (112 tonnes) of mercury the *Capitana* had on board, which would be worth a fortune today.

1634: The Spanish galleon *Los Tres Reyes* (560 tons/569 tonnes), carrying 1,545,000 pesos in treasure, had just arrived in Cartagena from Porto Bello and was waiting for the other ships in her fleet to arrived when it caught fire and blew up, killing all 324 men aboard. Salvors using grappling hooks were able to recover only some of her rigging and nothing more.

1640: As the Tierra Firme Fleet was approaching the Caribbean on a voyage from Spain to Cartagena, they intercepted a Portuguese fleet commanded by Admiral Rodrigo Lobad da Silva, sailing from Brazil

A 1708 view of Cartagena from the sea. It is shown as a very active port.

to Lisbon with over five crusadoes in gold, diamonds, precious stones, plus other types of treasures from the Orient. War had broken out between Spain and Portugal, and although the Portuguese admiral was unaware of this fact, he suspected foul play. As the combined fleets entered Cartagena Harbor, the Portuguese deliberately wrecked the three largest ships, which were carrying the bulk of the treasure. Very little was ever recovered from them.

1669: At the entrance of Lake Maracaibo, Venezuela, the pirate Henry Morgan used a fire ship to destroyed two unidentified Spanish galleons, commanded by Admiral Alonso de Espinosa, which the pirates believed had no treasure on board. Unknown to the pirates, the local inhabitants of several towns on Lake Maracaibo had transferred their treasures to these ships when word arrived that Morgan was coming. The ships were to depart for Cartagena, but Morgan arrived just as they were departing.

1708: The richest Spanish galleon ever lost in the Western Hemisphere was the *San Jose,* which carried over 11 million pesos in treasure. Due to the War of Spanish Succession, no treasure had been sent from South America to Spain for six years. In 1708 half of the 22 million pesos picked up by the fleet in Porto Bello, Panama, was loaded on the *San Jose,* which was the *Capitana* of the fleet. As the fleet approached Cartagena, Colombia, an English squadron, commanded by Commodore Wager, appeared on the scene and a furious battle ensued. The *San Jose* received the brunt of the attack. Her powder magazine caught fire and she blew up and sank in a matter of minutes with only five of her crew of 600 surviving. The English captured one of the other ships; another was run aground by the Spaniards and later salvaged. The *San Jose* sank in about 2,000 feet (610 meters) of water.

1815: The Spanish galleon *Almiranta, San Pedro Alcántara* (1,000 tons/1,016 tonnes, 64 cannons), commanded by Captain Javier de Salazar, was part of a fleet sent to suppress the revolution in Venezuela. It blew up while anchored near Coche Island off the coast of Venezuela. The more than 800,000 pesos in silver specie and large cargo of munitions and arms were scattered over a wide area due to the tremendous explosion. Contemporary divers from Margarita Island recovered only about half of the silver specie.

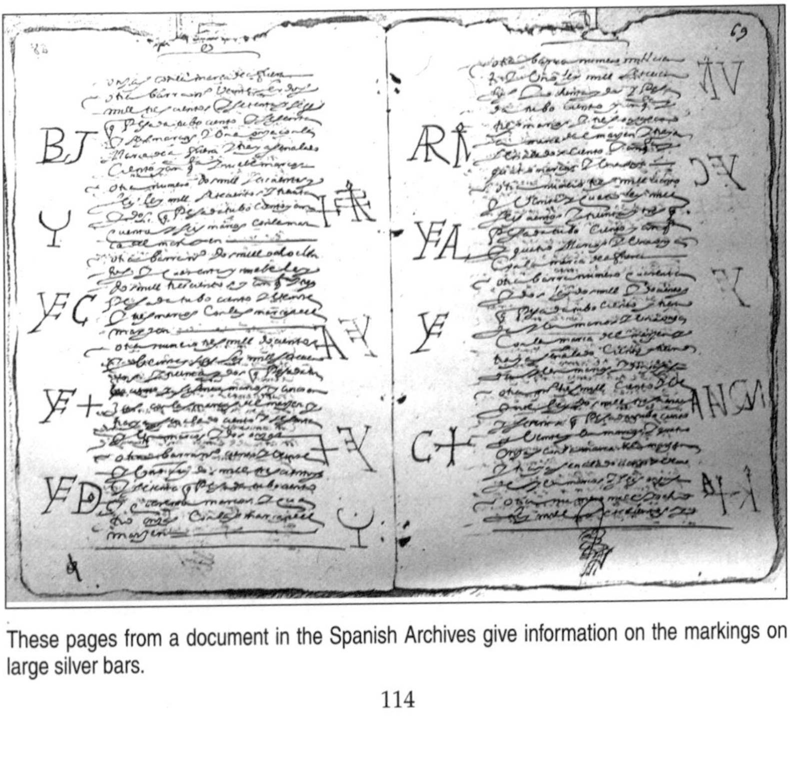

These pages from a document in the Spanish Archives give information on the markings on large silver bars.

CHAPTER 13

SOUTH AMERICA: EAST COAST'S RICHEST WRECKS

For centuries the most important Portuguese seaport in the New World was Brazil's São Salvador de Bahia de Todos os Santos, better known as Bahia or Salvador. Bahia, roughly 1,000 miles (1,609 kilometers) northeast of Rio de Janeiro, was founded in 1549 and served as the capital until 1763. It became a major entrepôt for the lucrative trade in sugar and African slaves, as well as a port of call for the returning Portuguese East Indiamen. Rio de Janeiro served as a transfer point for gold and diamonds from the Minas Gerais area, which were carried to Bahia on ships that joined the Brazil Fleet. This annual fleet usually consisted of 100 to 150 ships, which sailed to Lisbon via the Azores Islands. Salvador was also notorious as the largest contraband center in South America. Huge amounts of gold and silver were smuggled down the Plate River from Peru to Buenos Aires and then sent up to Bahia, where the precious metals were used to purchase European manufactured goods, as well as exotic objects brought over from the Orient on the Portuguese East Indiaman. By 1650 colonists in Peru were obtaining more goods via the Plate River than through legitimate transactions for goods brought over by the treasures fleets to Panama and then carried on the Armada of the South Seas to Callao.

Not surprisingly, such great wealth attracted pirates and privateers. The most notable attacks occurred in 1624 and 1627 under the brilliant leadership of Admiral Piet Heyn, Holland's most famous naval hero. In 1624 a powerful fleet of 34 ships carrying 6,500 men

The port of Salvador, also called Bahia, around 1580.

was sent to capture Salvador. When this formidable fleet appeared off the heavily fortified city, the unprepared inhabitants panicked. The Dutch captured the city, plundering waterfront warehouses and taking fifteen treasure-laden Portuguese ships that lay at anchor, ready to sail for Lisbon. Heyn left a garrison to hold the city and sailed for the Caribbean in hopes of intercepting a treasure fleet. The following year, a combined Spanish-Portuguese armada arrived and retook the city. Undaunted, Heyn returned again in 1627 and captured 22 of 26 rich merchantmen at anchor there, taking over 2 million guilders in treasure and other cargo. Heyn's most notable accomplishment—the capture of the New Spain Fleet off Matanzas, Cuba, in 1628—lives on in a well-known Dutch song.

Buenos Aires, now capital of Argentina, was founded in 1536 but not permanently settled until 1580. It is strategically located at the mouth of the Rio de la Plata, the River of Silver or Plate River. Contraband trade with Peru via the Plate River was the city's chief activity. After the 1770s the treasures from Peru, Chile and Ecuador were no longer sent to Panama for trans-shipment to Spain. Instead, Spanish ships braved the terror of rounding Cape Horn and made their first stop at Buenos Aires for refreshments. In 1717 the Portuguese established a fortified town at Montevideo on the other side of the mouth of the Plate River. Montevideo became a center of contraband activity with Peru. Spain attacked the town in 1726 and expelled the Portuguese, making Montevideo the port station for the Spanish fleet in the South Atlantic.

The port of Buenos Aires, Argentina, around 1610.

1561: The Portuguese East Indiaman *Drago* (1,200 tons/1,219 tonnes, thirty cannons), commanded by Captain Lourenço de Carvalho and coming from India to Lisbon with a "valuable cargo, including twenty chests of precious stones and diamonds," was forced to head for Brazil as contrary winds and calms prevented her from reaching Lisbon. She was low on water and provisions and headed for Salvador and wrecked on Itaparica Island, facing Salvador.

1573: The Portuguese East Indiaman *Santa Clara* (1,500 tons/1,524 tonnes), was the flagship in a fleet of 33 ships commanded by Don Francisco de Sousa. She left Goa with over 8 million crusadoes in treasure aboard. While rounding the Cape of Good Hope, two ships of the fleet began leaking badly. They eventually sank, but their treasures, totaling over 6 million crusadoes, had already been transferred to the *Santa Clara*. No ship had ever returned to Portugal with such an extraordinarily valuable cargo. After a stop of a few days at Salvador, Brazil, the fleet set sail for Lisbon. About six hours after leaving Salvador, a storm struck and the *Santa Clara* was wrecked on a reef and the slid off into deeper water. Only six of the 667 people aboard managed to reach shore. None of her treasures was ever recovered.

1593: The Portuguese East Indiaman *São Pedro* (1,600 tons/1,626 tonnes, 44 cannons), commanded by Captain Pedro Gonçalves and sailing from India to Lisbon with a cargo of Oriental goods valued at over 1 million crusadoes, was badly damaged in a storm off the Cape of Good Hope. She sailed for St. Helena Island for repairs, but was unable to find this island, so she headed for Salvador, Brazil. She sank in a storm while in Salvador for repairs and found new crew to replace more than 130 who died from scurvy during the voyage. Some people survived and many bales of silk, which had been on the main deck, floated to shore.

1596: The Portuguese East Indiaman *São Francisco Xavier* (1,400 tons/1,422 tonnes, 44 cannons), commanded by Captain Manoel de Almeida and returning to Lisbon from Malacca and Mozambique, encountered severe storms off South Africa and was badly damaged. She headed to Salvador for repairs. An epidemic swept through the vessel when she reached Salvador, and only a dozen of the 770 people on board were healthy enough to man the ship. After the ship was repaired and a new crew found, she sailed for Lisbon with a cargo valued at 1.2 million crusadoes, but off Cape San Augustine, Brazil, she capsized in a storm and sank with very few survivors.

1609: The Portuguese East Indiaman *Nosso Senhor de Jesus* (1,800 tons/1,829 tonnes), 56 cannons), commanded by Captain Antonio Barroso, in the armada of Captain Manuel de Meneses, was returning from India with a cargo valued at 450,000 crusadoes. She was badly damaged in storms off South Africa and went to Salvador for repairs where she sank at anchor with no loss of life. Many boxes of cinnamon on deck floated to shore, but none of her Chinese porcelain or other treasures was recovered.

1614: The Portuguese East Indiaman *Nossa Senhora da Conceição,* also known as the *Nossa Senhora da Esperança* (1,250 tons/1,270 tonnes, 32 cannons), commanded by Captain Francisco de Sousa Pereira and sailing from Lisbon to Malacca with gold and silver valued at 375,000 crusadoes, suffered badly in a storm off Senegal on the coast of West Africa. Her captain decided to head to Brazil for repairs. She wrecked 4 leagues south of Maceió, Brazil, and only some of her people were saved. Another unidentified ship sailing with her also wrecked off Paraiba.

1625: The Dutch West Indiaman *Delft* (34 cannons), commanded by Captain Cornelis van der Bols, was sailing between Salvador and Holland with over 1 million guilders in gold and silver specie and bullion, seized from two Portuguese ships near Rio de Janeiro. She capsized during a storm off Cape San Augustine, Brazil, and sank about a league from shore. Several men reached land, but were beheaded by Portuguese soldiers from a fort on the cape.

1637: The Portuguese East Indiaman *Nossa Senhora da Caridade* (880 tons/894 tonnes, thirty cannons), commanded by Captain Manuel de Morais Sarmento and sailing from Lisbon to India with gold and silver specie valued at 280,000 crusadoes, was separated from her armada during a storm off the west coast of Africa. The captain decided to head for Brazil, where she wrecked off Ilhéus in a storm. Only 18 men survived.

1637: The Portuguese East Indiaman *Nossa Senhora da Conceição* (1,400 tons/1,422 tonnes, 44 bronze cannons), commanded by Captain João da Costa and sailing from India with a cargo worth more than 1 million crusadoes, was attacked by four Dutch warships and forced to enter the Bay of Macas, Brazil. The Portuguese burned their ship to prevent it from being captured. Some of the crew made it safely to shore, but the Dutch caught and beheaded many men.

1637: An unidentified Portuguese East Indiaman, sailing from India to Lisbon with a cargo valued at 890,000 crusadoes, was trying to reach Salvador for badly needed repairs when she was attacked by a Dutch warship under the command of Admiral Lichthart. Her crew set her on fire in the port of Villa dos Ilhéus, Brazil, to keep the Dutch from getting the cargo. Most of the crew made it to shore, but many of them were captured and killed.

1647: The Portuguese East Indiaman *Nossa Senhora do Rosario* (1,850 tons/1,880 tonnes, 46 cannons), commanded by Captain Pedro Carneiro and returning from Macau and Goa with a cargo valued at 640,000 crusadoes, stopped in Salvador, Brazil. While there she was attacked by two Dutch ships and blew up with a total loss of life and cargo.

1648: The Dutch warship *Utrecht* (48 cannons), commanded by Admiral Witte de Witt and carrying over 400,000 guilders in Oriental treasures, made a stop at Recife, then in Dutch hands. From there she was sent to blockade Portuguese-controlled Salvador. When they saw the *Utrecht* approaching, the Portuguese sent out two large warships. In the ensuing action the *Utrecht* grappled one of the Portuguese ships and as Dutch mariners swarmed aboard his ship, the captain set fire to his powder magazine and both ships exploded and sank, taking 550 men to watery graves.

1669: The Portuguese warship *Sacramento*, coming from Lisbon with 478,000 pesos in Spanish gold and silver specie, sank with a great loss of life off Salvador during a storm. In recent years local divers have recovered forty bronze cannons and many valuable artifacts, but none of her treasure.

Silverware—including a large platter, plates, and cutlery—recovered from the *Utrecht.*

1698: An unidentified Portuguese East Indiaman, sailing between India and Lisbon, with a cargo valued at 570,000 crusadoes, including an unknown amount of diamonds and gold bullion, stopped at Salvador to repair damage inflicted by storms off the Cape of Good Hope. Leaving Salvador, she wrecked on the coast of French Guiana and only three of the 400 or so people on board made it ashore.

1698: The Portuguese East Indiaman *Nossa Senhora de Belém* (1,500 tons/1,575 tonnes), commanded by Captain Matias de Gouveia and returning to Lisbon from the Far East with over 1.5 million crusadoes in cargo, was totally lost near present-day Georgetown, British Guiana. Only nine men survived out of 700.

1700: The Dutch East Indiaman *Voetboog* (626 tons/636 tonnes, 46 cannons), commanded by Captain Jakob Landsheer and sailing between Batavia and Holland with 233,000 guilders in Oriental treasures, plus spices and porcelain, was wrecked in a bad storm on the coast just south of Recife, Brazil. Only seven men survived.

1722: The Portuguese East Indiaman *Rainho dos Anjos* (1,450 tons/1,473 tonnes, 38 cannons), sailing from Macau to Lisbon with a cargo valued at 470,000 crusadoes, plus a present valued at 300,000 crusadoes for Portugal's king from the emperor of China, made a stop in Brazil because of bad weather. In the harbor of Rio de Janeiro, lightning ignited a fire and the ship exploded and sank with a total loss of life and treasure.

1726: The largest amount of gold ever lost in the Western Hemisphere was aboard the Portuguese flagship *Santa Rosa,* which sank off the coast of Brazil. Powerfully armed with 66 bronze cannons and a crew of over 700 men, she had picked up over 26 tons (26.41 tonnes) of registered gold bullion and coins in Salvador, Brazil, and then set sail for Recife further up the coast, before crossing to Lisbon. A fire broke out when the ship was only a few hours south of Recife in the vicinity of Cape San Augustine, and she blew up and sank as an anguished crowd ashore watched helplessly. Several of the other 49 ships in the fleet rescued six survivors.

1737: The Portuguese merchantman *Nossa Senhora da Assunção* (1,400 tons/1,422 tonnes), commanded by Captain Alvaro Sanchez de Brito, was in a fleet of 62 ships preparing to sail back to Lisbon from Salvador. Part of her cargo consisted of three chests of diamonds and 44 boxes of gold bullion and specie. For no apparent reason, the ship sank, most likely because she was overloaded. Later it was learned that several tons of contraband gold bullion and specie had been concealed under bales of cocoa and dyewood.

1750: The Spanish merchantman *La Purísima Concepción y San Francisco de Asís* was lost at the mouth of the Plate River between Argentina and Uruguay. She carried over 500,000 pesos in treasure, as well as several chests of diamonds and other precious stones.

1752: The Spanish galleon *Nuestra Señora de Luz* (1,200 tons/1,219 tonnes), sailing between Peru and Spain via Cape Horn, was lost near Rio de Janeiro, and everyone but the captain perished. She sank with over 600,000 pesos in treasure aboard, plus an unknown amount of treasure the archbishop of Lima was shipping to Spain. Salvors recovered some of her rigging and three bronze cannons.

1752: The French East Indiaman *Prince,* commanded by Captain Morin and returning from the Far East with a cargo of treasures valued at over 5 million livres, was coasting along Brazil when she caught fire near the port of Natal. To save lives, the captain ran her aground near a beach, but before people could abandon ship, the *Prince* exploded, killing all but nine of the 400 people aboard. Contemporary salvage attempts failed.

1753: The Spanish galleon *Nuestra Señora del Rosario* (900 tons/914 tonnes), carrying over 800,000 pesos in gold and silver from Peru to Spain via Cape Horn, sank at the mouth of the Plate River between Argentina and Uruguay after anchoring there to repair damage sustained in a storm off Cape Horn.

1757: The Portuguese merchantman *San Francisco Xavier* (1,500 tons/1,524 tonnes, fifty cannons), part of a fleet of 44 ships ready to sail for Lisbon from Salvador, Brazil, was found to be too leaky and rotten for the voyage. Only after it was unloaded, stripped and burned did officials discover that merchants had hidden seven boxes of diamonds and 43 boxes of gold coins under the ballast to avoid custom duties. These treasures sank with the ship.

1765: The Spanish warship *San Leandro* (320 tons/325 tonnes, 32 cannons), commanded by Captain José Quiroga and serving as a packet mail boat between Peru, Chile, Buenos Aires and Spain, was badly damaged in a storm off Cape Horn on the voyage between Chile and Buenos Aires. She headed to the Falkland Islands to make repairs. She was struck by another storm and wrecked on the westernmost island in this group of deserted islands. Four survivors who were picked up two years later told the authorities there had been half a million pesos in contraband gold and silver on the wreck.

1777: In a battle between a fleet of Portuguese merchantmen and Spanish warships off the island of Santa Catalina, Brazil, three unidentified Portuguese merchantmen were sunk with cargoes valued at 790,000 crusadoes in gold bullion and specie.

1783: The Spanish frigate *Diamante* (650 tons/660 tonnes, sixty cannons), commanded by Captain Martín de Arcinagas and sailing between Callao, Peru, and Spain with over 2 million pesos in gold and silver, never arrived in Buenos Aires where she was supposed to pick up mail and passengers for Spain. The ship, with 450 people on board, was presumed lost in a storm. Six years later, a fishing boat from Gallegos, Argentina, was blown to the uninhabited Falkland Islands in a storm. There, among makeshift huts, the fishermen found traces of the wrecked *Diamante*, including two chests of 6,000 silver pieces of

Late sixteenth-century Spanish pieces of eight and one piece of four, recovered off a wreck near Buenos Aires, Argentina.

eight and a box of mail, which proved the identity of the wreck. The following year a salvage vessel dispatched from Buenos Aires to find the wreck and treasure recovered only a gold chalice and two silver candelabra on the beach.

1787: The Portuguese merchantman *Santissimo Sacramento e Santa Arrábida* (900 tons/914 tonnes), sailing from Lisbon to Rio de Janeiro with 280,000 crusadoes in Spanish silver specie on board, caught on fire while anchored off Rio de Janeiro and sank, but only six men were lost.

1805: The British merchantman *Britannia,* carrying silver bullion valued at £1.74 million pounds sterling, sank in deep water after striking coral reefs off the south side of Rocas Islands, located about 250 miles (402 kilometers) east of the Brazilian mainland.

1809: The Portuguese merchantman *Nossa Senhora da Graça* (670 tons/681 tonnes), was sailing from Rio de Janeiro to Recife with gold specie, diamonds and precious stones valued at over 560,000 crusadoes, and then back to Lisbon. Hours before her departure from Recife, she caught on fire and was destroyed.

Lead merchant packing seals from an unidentified mid-sixteenth-century Portuguese merchantman lost off Salvador.

Chinese porcelain objects, one a jar with pepper cloves in it, off the Portuguese East Indiaman *Nossa Señhora de Rosario*, lost off Salvador in 1737.

Clump of sulphated Dutch ducatoon coins off the *Hollandia*, Admiral Piet Heyn's flagship, which was lost in 1625 during his attack on Salvador.

(Above) Hundreds of thousands of silver bars such of these were cast from silver from the Potosí Mine in Peru over the centuries. The bars had markings indicating their weight, the fineness of the silver, the mine the silver came from, markings proving that taxes were paid to the king and church, and the owner's initials of the bar. *(Below)* Most of the ships used off the west coast of South America were built in Guayaquil, Ecuador.

CHAPTER 14

SOUTH AMERICA: WEST COAST'S RICHEST WRECKS

In 1537 Francisco Pizarro, the Spanish conquistador who subjugated the Incas of Peru, founded Callao to serve as a seaport for the capital city of Lima 8 miles (13 kilometers) inland. It boasted a fine natural harbor protected by a large offshore island where one fort stood, and a long promontory on the mainland pointing to the island, where a second fort was constructed. The port served as the main base for the Armada of the South Seas, a fleet averaging about six heavily armed large galleons used to transport Inca gold and silver to Panama. After the discovery of Potosí in 1545, Callao achieved prominence, for all the silver from that incredible mine came there for shipment to Spain. Two forts defended the town.

The inhabitants considered Callao unassailable. Francis Drake, scourge of Spanish America, did not agree. In 1579, while making the historic voyage with the *Golden Hind* that was to carry him around the world, the English privateer attacked Callao and plundered thirty vessels in the harbor. Learning that a galleon had recently departed for Panama laden with some of the annual Peruvian treasure, Drake sailed in pursuit and caught up with her off Ecuador. The *Nuestra Señora de la Concepción*, more commonly called *Cacafuego*, was easily taken, and the booty obtained was staggering: 26 tons (26.41 tonnes) of bar silver, 80 pounds (36 kilograms) of gold in bars, 13 chests of coins, and a small chest of precious stones; the total was valued at between £150,000 and £200,000 sterling.

The Spanish galleon *Cacafuego*, carrying a large amount of treasure while sailing between Peru and Panama, was captured by Francis Drake. She carried so much treasure that Drake could take only about half of it.

The port of Guayaquil, Ecuador, was the main ship building port on the west coast of South America, providing all the galleons for the Armada of the South Seas and the majority of merchantmen plying those waters. Unlike the oak and pine ships used in the treasure fleets, which lasted an average of six years, those made in Guayaquil of local hardwood had an average life span of forty years.

Each year a large galleon, called the Gold Ship, sailed from Guayaquil to Panama, carrying large amounts of gold mined around Quito, as well as emeralds. Over a dozen of these rich ships were lost over the years, but no documentation survives giving their locations. Unfortunately, this is also true of other ships that sank carrying treasure from Valparaiso, Concepción, and Valdivia in Chile.

1545: An unidentified Spanish *nao* set sail from Callao for Panama, carrying "a vast amount of Inca golden treasures" plundered by the conquistadors under Pizarro's command. As she left the port, she struck a submerged rock near a small island, which became known as Golden Rock because of the great treasure lost there when she sank. The soft mud in this area quickly swallowed up the wreck and nothing was ever salvaged from her.

(Right) Chart of San Matheo, Ecuador in which the rich galleon *Clarius* was lost in 1594.

(Below) Blowup of text regarding the *Clarius*.

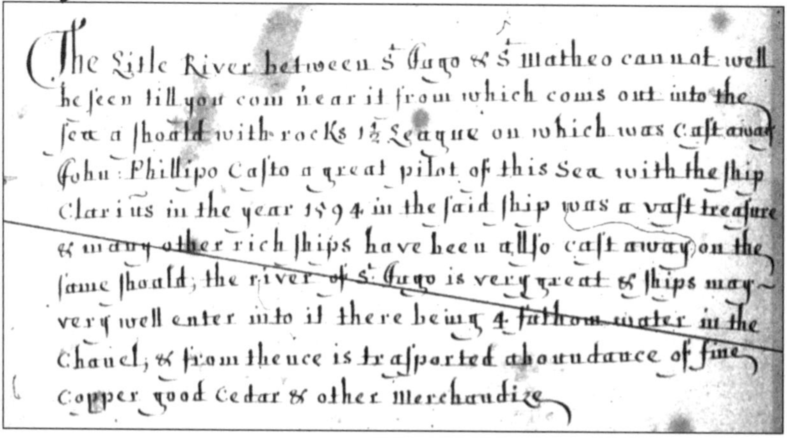
The Litle River between S. Jago & S. Matheo cannot well
be seen till you com near it from which coms out into the
sea a shoald with rocks 1½ League on which was cast away
John Phillipo Casto a great pilot of this Sea with the ship
Clarius in the year 1594 in the said ship was a vast treasure
& many other rich ships have been allso cast away on the
same shoald; the river of S. Jago is very great & ships may
very well enter into it there being 4 fathom water in the
Chanel, & from thence is trasported aboundance of fine
copper good Cedar & other Merchandize

1571: An unidentified Spanish galleon sailing between Peru and Panama was lost due to faulty navigation off the Rock of Colache near Punta Santa Elena, Ecuador. Primary documents, without being specific, state that she carried "a vast treasure."

1577: In the port of Callao, the Spanish merchantman *Nuestra Señora de Lorento* (400 tons/406 tonnes, 24 cannons), commanded by Captain Hernán Mendoza de Áviles, had loaded most of her cargo of 2.2 million pesos in gold and silver in preparation for sailing when a suspected pirate vessel appeared, bearing down on the port. In a frenzy to keep her out of hostile hands, the captain gave orders to set fire to his ship. While she was still burning, the other vessel came into the port and anchored. To everyone's consternation, she proved to be a Spanish merchantman coming up from Valparaíso, not a pirate ship.

1586: At least 150 ships were lost in the port of Callao during the Colonial Period. In a 1586 earthquake, three heavily laden unidentified Spanish galleons in the Armada of the South Seas, carrying 6.7 million pesos of treasure, were capsized by huge waves resulting from the earthquake. Over 1,200 people went down with the ships. More than thirty other vessels also sank.

1594: Four Spanish galleons sailing between Callao and Panama in the Armada of the South Seas were lost near the mouth of the Santiago River near the town of St. Matheo and Galera Point, Ecuador. Only one, the *Clarius*, was identified. Her master, Felipe Castro, wrote that they carried "a prodigious treasure."

1599: An unidentified Spanish galleon of Captain Melchor de Sechura was lost with over 2 million pesos in gold and silver on the Shoal of Zana located about 15 miles (24 kilometers) northwest of Punta Pacasmayo, Peru. Salvors were unable to locate the wreck despite the presence of ship's timbers on the shore and decided that she must have slipped off into deeper water.

1599: Four large Spanish galleons in the Armada of the South Seas sailed from Callao to Panama with 11.89 million pesos in treasure, 320,000 pesos of which divers had recovered from a ship lost in Callao the previous year. After passing Cape Santa Elena, Ecuador, a fierce storm struck and only two of the vessels reached Panama. One of the missing galleons wrecked between the port of Esmeraldas and Punta Galera, which takes its name from a rich galley carrying Inca plunder lost there in 1538. Bodies and timbers from the sunken galleon washed up on the beach, but none of her treasure was ever recovered.

1605: A large unidentified Spanish merchantman sailing between Panama and Callao with over 100 tons (102 tonnes) of mercury for the gold and silver mines of Peru, worth a large fortune today, was totally lost on a reef still known as Las Hormigas, northwest of the port of Callao. Many ships have been lost there.

1610: An unidentified Spanish galleon (850 tons/864 tonnes, 38 cannons), sailing between Callao and Panama with over 1 million pesos in gold and silver, was lost about 10 miles (16 kilometers) south of Chiclayo, which is north of Trujillo, Peru. Contemporary divers recovered only 150,000 pesos of the treasure.

1610: The Spanish merchantman *Santa María* (450 tons/457 tonnes, 34 cannons), commanded by Captain José Rodríquez de la Costa and carrying 880,000 pesos in treasure, was not ready when the Armada of the South Seas sailed for Panama. A month later, against the advice of many people, she set sail alone. Several leagues south of Chiclayo, Peru, a pirate vessel chased her. The captain had her run aground and set on fire. All but six of her people made it to safety. When some of the pirates boarded the ship to extinguish the fire, it suddenly blew up. Salvors recovered only 150,000 pesos of her treasure. The captain and the owner of the ship were later hanged for sailing alone and for losing treasure belonging to the king, the church and merchants.

1612: An unidentified Spanish galleon, commanded by Captain Domingo Annoto and owned by Gonzalo Beltrán, was sailing between Callao and Panama when she was wrecked on a shoal off the Fama River, north of Cape Santa Helena, Ecuador. According to a 1669 English chart, "in her was an abundance of plata (silver) and other treasure."

1623: During an attack by the Dutch in the port of Callao, eleven large Spanish galleons, five of which were loaded with 6.44 million pesos in treasures and made up the Armada of the South Seas, were ready to leave for Panama. The five galleons with all of the treasure were set on fire to keep the treasure from the enemy. All were sunk. There is no documentation on cargoes of the other six ships.

1647: The Spanish galleon *San Nicolás* (640 tons/650 tonnes, 38 cannons), carrying 2 million pesos in gold and silver, caught on fire while anchored a half league off the port of Arica, Chile, and blew up with a total loss of life. Using grappling hooks, salvors recovered four of her bronze cannons, two anchors and 16 chests of silver specie. Arica was the port where all the gold and silver from Potosí and the other mines were collected for shipment to Callao.

1650: The Spanish warship *San José* (44 cannons), with over 125,000 pesos in treasure aboard, was totally lost at Punta Datalonguen near Valdivia, Chile.

1654: Four galleons comprising the Armada of the South Seas set sail from Callao for Panama with several years' accumulation of treasure from the mines of South America. During a moonless rainy night, the *Capitana, Nuestra Señora de la Concepción,* commanded by Admiral Francisco de Sosa, wrecked on Chanduy Reef, near the mouth of Ecuador's Guayaquil River. She went to pieces quickly and almost everyone drowned. Contemporary salvors recovered about half of the more than 3 million pesos in treasure aboard. Within days of the disaster, shifting sands had covered the site.

1665: The Spanish galleon *Santa Ana* (750 tons/762 tonnes, 32 cannons), commanded by Captain Casimiro de Tarifa, suffered in a bad storm for three days, losing two masts and her rudder before wrecking near Punta Humos (now Punta La Vieja), Chile. She carried over 500,000 pesos in gold ingots, but contemporary salvors recovered only six bronze cannons.

1673: Two galleons, the *Nuestra Señora de Carmona* (44 cannons), commanded by Captain Jorge de la Manca, and an unidentified galleon of 38 cannons, commanded by Captain Francisco de Acevedo, carrying over 3 million pesos in gold and silver, were preparing to sail from Arica, Chile, for Callao when an earthquake struck, causing enormous waves that inundated both ships and sent them to the bottom, killing all aboard.

1681: The Spanish galleon *Santa María de la Consolación,* commanded by Captain Juan de Lerma, was fleeing from the infamous pirate Bartholomew Sharpe when she was forced to run aground on Santa Clara Island in the Gulf of Guayaquil, Ecuador, and the crew set her on fire before fleeing for the safety of the nearby island. Spanish records do not indicate how much treasure she carried, but the pirates claimed she had 100,000 pieces of eight on board. This is too small an amount for a galleon sailing between Peru and Panama at that time. My guess is she had 1 to 2 million pesos in treasure on board. Seven years ago salvors located a section of this wreck and recovered about 80,000 silver coins. They are searching for the main section of the wreck, where they expect to find a huge amount of treasure.

1684: The Spanish merchantman *San Juan de Dios,* carrying over 350,000 pesos in gold and silver, was lost near Punta Panquecito, Chile. Only a few iron cannons were ever recovered.

1685: The Spanish galleon *San José,* chased by pirates, sought refuge in the port of Paita, Peru, and was wrecked near the entrance of

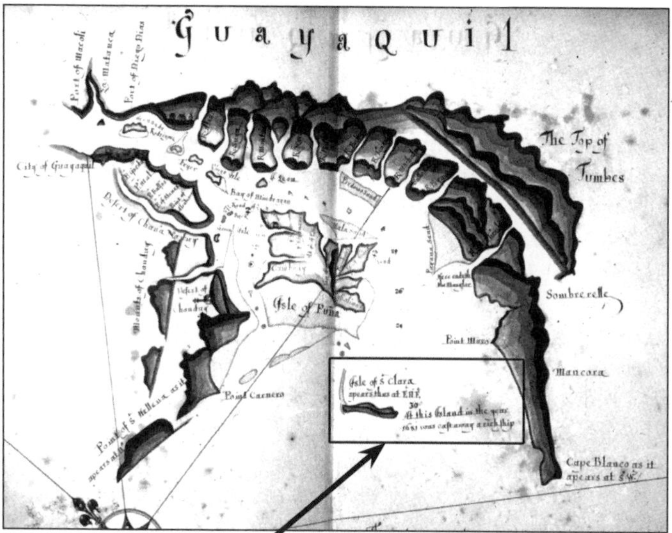

(Above) Chart of the Bay of Guayaquil, showing in the center Santa Clara Island. *(Left)* Blowup of Santa Clara Island. States, "At this Island in the year 1681 was cast away a rich ship".

this port. The crew set her on fire and she blew up with over 3 million pesos of treasure just as the pirates were boarding her.

1746: On October 28, Peru suffered the worst earthquake since the Spanish Conquest. When the three treasure-laden ships of that year's Armada of the South Seas sank at anchor, it created the greatest financial disaster in Peru's history to that time. The ships were fully laden and ready to sail when the disaster occurred. The *Capitana* of this fleet, the *San Fermín* (thirty cannons), went down with over 3 million pesos in gold and silver. Her sister ships sank with a total of 4.5 million pesos. Twenty merchant ships in port also sank. Very little of the lost treasures was ever salvaged.

1767: During the Colonial Period earthquakes, fires, storms and enemy attacks sank at least fifty large ships in and around the port of Valparaíso, Chile. The Spanish galleon *Nuestra Señora del Buen Viaje* (800 tons/813 tonnes), with over 400,000 pesos in gold bullion and specie, was lost a half league north of the port in a storm and 89 of the 367 people on board were saved, but none of the gold.

1770: When this great loss occurred the Spaniards had begun sending their South American treasures directly from Peru to Spain around the southern tip of South America, rather than up to Panama and then by galleon through the Caribbean as in the past. The *Orriflamme,* originally a French warship, was the largest vessel to undertake the long hazardous Cape Horn route up to that time. Her cargo, valued at over 4 million pesos, consisted chiefly of gold and silver specie and bullion. During a storm she sank on the coast near Valparaíso, Chile. Only a few of some 700 crew and passengers survived. Repeated salvage attempts met with scant success.

1800: The Spanish galleon *Santa Leocadia* (34 cannons), commanded by Captain Antonio Barreda, was lost at Punta Santa Elena, Ecuador, northwest of the modern port of Guayaquil. About 140 people perished in the disaster. Contemporary salvors recovered about 90 percent of the more than 2 million pesos in treasures she carried, but there is still a lot left. Gold and silver coins come ashore during storms on nearby beaches, so her approximate location is easy to determine.

1857: The British ship *Valdivia* wrecked on a reef due to faulty navigation off Llico, Chile, while sailing between Valparaíiso and Puerto Montt with over £200,000 pounds sterling in gold and silver bullion. Some was salvaged by contemporary salvors.

Old World

Chapter 15

Introduction To Old World Shipwrecks

At no time in history was precious metal more of a critical factor in shaping the destinies of men and nations than in the period following the Spanish Conquest when gold and silver in unprecedented amounts poured into Europe through Spain. In 1492 the prevail-ing mood in Europe was one of disillusionment and pessimism. Most of the continent lay exhausted from years of internecine strife, and Spain was impoverished from the long struggle against the Moors. The specter of Islam haunted a disunited Christendom. The Turks pressed ever closer to the European heartland. They blocked the logical routes of expansion east and south to the spices of the Indies and the fabled gold of Cathay and Japan, which Marco Polo had brought to the attention of men and nations always hungry for precious metal. Gold was the object of virtually every voyage of discovery and every exploratory effort.

European nations had insufficient precious metal to meet the needs of expanding commerce. Barter worked when transactions were small scale and local but was largely supplanted by the exchange of coinage for goods or services. Silver and gold were needed for all but the simplest transactions, but the low production of gold and silver in Europe's few mines limited the amount of coins in circulation and economies stagnated. All this changed after Christopher Columbus returned to Spain with news of a New World.

With Spain's conquest of the two great civilizations of America—the Aztec and the Inca—the floodgates opened. A deluge of gold and silver flowed into Europe. For the next 250 years the New World was the major source of gold. By 1550 the stocks of European gold and silver had increased by half as much again as had existed when Columbus set sail in 1492. Post-conquest Europe erupted in a sunburst of splendor. Much of the American treasure found its way into the hands of merchant bankers who gradually gained control of the vast gold supplies once in royal hands. American treasure financed currencies in almost every nation. A new wave of commercial expansion and prosperity followed the Conquest, and precious metal figured more dazzlingly than ever in the pomp and ceremony of courts and churches. The rivers of newly mined gold and silver infused into the European economy aided the rise to power of manufacturing states, such as England, Germany and the Low Countries. Ironically, the treasures of the New World ultimately sapped Spain's strength.

In the early years Spanish adventurers made colossal fortunes, and the Spanish Crown was gratifyingly enriched. But after the great silver mines of Potosí opened in 1545, little of the gold and silver that sailed up the Guadalquivir River to Seville remained in non-industrial Spain. It went immediately to pay for imported manufactured goods to pay on the crushing debts owed to the great banking houses, notably the Fuggers and the Welsers of Augsburg. The lure of treasure emptied Iberia of much of her able-bodied male population. Spain never developed a manufacturing base, and what gold and silver the Crown managed to hang on to was used to finance perennial and costly Catholic-Protestant wars as well as fostering extravagance and decadence.

It was the Portuguese who pioneered the maritime expansion that marked the beginning of the modern world. With Venetians, Genovese, Catalans and Arabs dominating trade in the Mediterranean, the Portuguese ventured into the Atlantic and were the first Europeans to reach India and the Far East. By 1480 the Portuguese had reached down the coast of Africa, and braved uncharted Atlantic waters to colonize the Azores. Intrepid Portuguese fished the rich waters off Newfoundland with the Basques and Bretons.

A sixteenth-century cannon foundry where good bronze artillery pieces were cast.

Portugal has always lived by harvesting the seas. Her rocky coast, hammered by the Atlantic, was the gateway to a wider world. They invented the caravel, a swift, light ship used for exploration of the African coast, and later developed the larger carrack for the long voyages to the Orient.

The Portuguese saw no conflict between passion for God and lust for riches. Prince Henry the Navigator, Crusader, scientist and founder of the first commercial exploration companies, vowed that spreading the Christian faith was more important than developing trade. A Crusader, he wanted to spread Catholicism beyond Islamic Africa to areas where medieval Europeans believed a great Christian king ruled (the legend of Prester John). But he also regarded wealth gained from the exploitation of foreign lands, looting and slave trading as God's blessing. The combination of greed and godliness was the driving force for Spanish exploration as well and, to a lesser extent, for British, French and Dutch expansion.

Portugal's piratical expeditions to the Orient were incredibly barbarous and profitable. The Portuguese bombarded rich and prosperous ports, set fire to the houses, plundered the warehouses

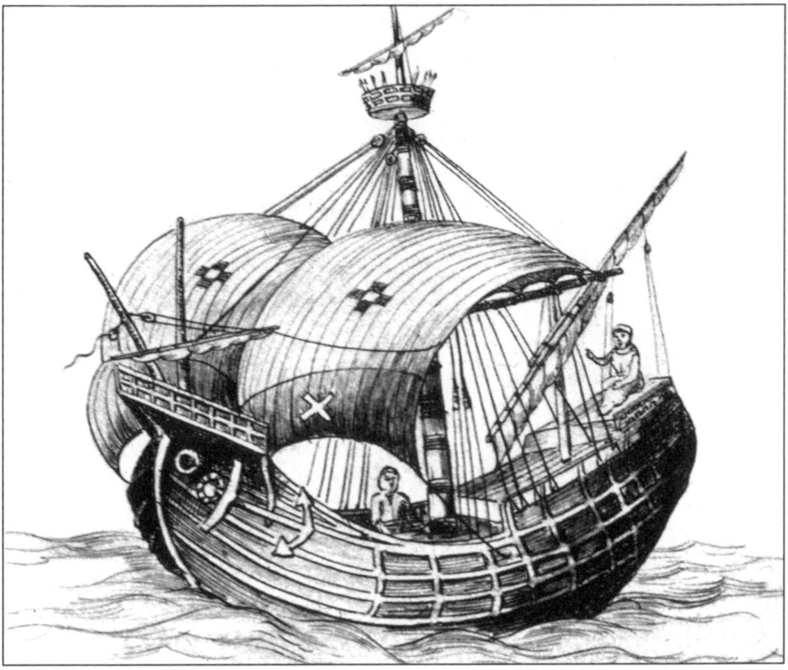

Portugese merchant ship circa 1600.

and slaughtered the inhabitants, whom they regarded as soulless heathens. In the early days they stole almost as often as they traded. In the process they destroyed the long established routes that had bound the Far East and Muslim world in a web of mutually profitable and largely peaceful commerce.

In the early fifteenth century, the Portuguese were heirs to Arab and Jewish advances of the late Middle Ages: the astrolabe for establishing latitude, cartographic skills, and shipbuilding design that produced sailing vessels, which if cumbersome by seventeenth-century standards, were marvels of maneuverability that made short work of the junks and dhows of the Orient and Indian Ocean. Prince Henry established a base for exploration on the southwest coast where he gathered men gifted in navigation, cartography, astronomy and shipbuilding. The center included a school for the study of geography and navigation, a naval arsenal (Portuguese ships had the best artillery from Dutch and German founders) and an observatory. The school emphasized log keeping and mapping. With successive voyages knowledge grew about Atlantic currents, wind systems and navigation. Most of the navigators on Spanish ships were Portuguese. The nearby port of Lagos became a center for shipbuilding.

By the middle of the sixteenth century, the Portuguese empire spanned half the world, enriching a small percentage of its people while the vast majority remained subsistence fishermen and farmers. By the end of the sixteenth century, the Portuguese had become very conservative, reluctant to adjust to a changing world. While Spain and other nations developed far better ships, the Portuguese clung to their ancient, clumsy carracks, making them even larger and more cumbersome, which led to greater losses. First the Dutch, then the British and the rest of western Europe's maritime states surpassed them in navigation and shipbuilding.

By the middle of the sixteenth century, the Dutch were Europe's maritime leaders. Some 3,000 fishing vessels and over 75,000 seamen were fishing the North Sea for herring and other fish. At least one-quarter of the male population of the Netherlands was involved with maritime trade, fishing or other sea-related activities. Through clever exploitation of the sea, they eventually became a great nation. The plentiful supply of fish made the Dutch less vulnerable to famine than other people. What they did not consume, they shipped to other nations, especially the Catholic countries, e.g., Spain, Portugal, France and Italy, where religion gave an impetus to fish consumption.

Dutch merchant ships carrying salted fish also carried a variety of trade goods, including about 80 percent of the goods that Spain and Portugal transshipped to their global colonies. Communications with their far-flung colonies required large fleets. They depended on Dutch shipping for bringing them most of the materials needed in ship construction and maintenance. The Dutch obtained timber, masts, spars, cordage, canvas and pitch from countries bordering the Baltic Sea. The Spaniards paid in the silver and gold that were essential to the Netherlands' commerce.

From the Portuguese the Dutch obtained porcelain, spices, sugar, drugs, cork and salt. The latter two products were indispensable to the fisheries: cork for fishnet and salt for preserving the catch. This trade was so important that it flourished even when the Dutch were at war with Spain and Portugal.

At the beginning of the seventeenth century, the Dutch decided to wrest control of the East Indies spice trade from Portugal. In 1602 the States General of the Netherlands incorporated the Dutch East India Company (*Vereenigde Oostindische Compagnie*, or VOC) and granted it a commercial monopoly extending from the Cape of Good Hope eastward to the Strait of Magellan, with sovereign rights in whatever territory it might acquire. The VOC is considered the first company to issue stock shares. From Batavia (today Jakarta), which was founded in 1619, Dutch influence and trade spread throughout the Malay Archipelago, to China, Japan, India, Iran and the Cape of Good Hope. It supplanted the Portuguese in most of present-day Indonesia and in the Malay Peninsula, Ceylon (now Sri Lanka), the Malabar Coast of India and Japan. In 1652 the company established the first European settlement in South Africa on the Cape of Good Hope.

The Dutch were brilliant businessmen and mariners. They had more ships, better ships and better artillery and crews than other nations. Dutch vessels were much faster and could make headway in light breezes. In contrast, it took half a gale to get lumbering Portuguese carracks and *naus* moving. Portuguese ships resembled massive castles and were built more for the comfort of a large number of passengers and the capacity to carry large cargoes than for speed or warfare. The Portuguese and Spaniards lost around 5 percent of their ships on long voyages, while the Dutch lost less than 1 percent.

Throughout the sixteenth and seventeenth centuries, the Dutch and Germans were the best cannon founders in Europe. Most of the bronze cannons used by European nations during this period were of Dutch and German manufacture. Dutch bronze cannons were so highly prized in the Far East that the king of Java once sold

With each new discovery, the Portuguese erected stone monuments to claim that area.

the beautiful Princess Taruroga for three pieces of artillery. From 1590 onwards most large ships carried only bronze pieces. Iron guns were less reliable. They often overheated and exploded after a few firings.

Officers on French, Spanish and Portuguese ships, many of whom bought their positions or took them because of political connections, generally had little seagoing experience. In contrast, Dutch officers generally worked their way up from the lower deck and had many years of experience. Seamen on Dutch ships spent their early careers on fishing boats in the rough North Sea and signed on voluntarily, whereas the British and French depended on press gangs to provide seamen, most of whom had never been to sea. The soldiers and artillerymen on Spanish ships were usually Spanish, but the actual sailors were from many nations, particularly Ireland.

Britain, France and Sweden also formed East India companies in the seventeenth and eighteenth centuries to establish trade in the Far East. These companies, which had varying degrees of governmental support, grew out of the associations of merchant adventurers who organized voyages to the East Indies in the wake of the Dutch. They received charters from their respective governments, authorizing them to conduct trade, negotiate treaties and acquire territory wherever they could.

These companies operated on a smaller scale than the Portuguese and Dutch East India companies with the exception of the British East India Company (1600 to 1874), chartered by Elizabeth I, which became one of the most powerful commercial enterprises of its time and took on military and governmental functions in India, the "jewel in the crown."

The company received a monopoly on trade for any areas that had no prior concessions from any Christian ruler, but sometimes ignored this restriction. An immensely profitable voyage to Japan whetted the company's appetite, and in 1610 they set up the first trading factories or trading posts in the provinces of Bombay and Madras, India. Under a new charter granted by King James I, they competed with the Dutch trading monopolies in Indonesia and the Malay Peninsula.

British East India Company merchantmen were well armed and were used at times to attack Portuguese, Dutch and French possessions and shipping. Some years more profit came from plunder than trading. In 1655 the company absorbed several rival companies incorporated under the Commonwealth of Lord Oliver Cromwell. In 1657 Cromwell ordered it reorganized as the sole joint-stock company with rights to the Indian trade. During the reign of Charles II, the company acquired sovereign rights in addition to its trading privileges. The charter was renewed several times in the eighteenth century, each time with financial concessions to the Crown, and the company soon became the dominant power in India, but by 1813 their monopoly of the Indian trade was abolished. Twenty years later, the British East India Company lost its China trade monopoly, and in 1874 the company was dissolved.

In 1664 King Louis XIV's finance minister organized the French East India Company (*Compagnie des Indes Orientales*), which was founded to compete with the Dutch and British in trade in the Eastern Hemisphere. Its first trading post was established at Surat, north of Bombay in 1675. The following year it set up its principal Indian base at Pondicherry on the Coromandel Coast. The company prospered and began trading with China, Vietnam and Persia (Iran). In 1719 the company was reorganized with the American and African French colonial companies as the *Compagnie Perpetuelle des Indes*. A year later the company suffered severely with the collapse of the Mississippi Scheme, an ambitious plan for the colonization and commercial exploitation of the Mississippi Valley and other French colonial areas. Then it lost its slave trade with Africa, its trade with Louisiana in 1731, and in 1736 its coffee trade with the Americas. However, in India the company prospered for a few decades until the British capture of Arcot in 1751, limiting French control to southern India. In 1761 the British captured Pondicherry. Company operations were suspended by royal decree in 1769, and in the following year it turned over its capital of more than 500 million livres to the Crown.

Seventeenth-century aristocrats craved porcelain, jade, silks, carved ivory and other Oriental products, decorating their mansions with them and creating whole galleries to house their collections. In 1731 the Swedish East India Company *Svenska Ostindiska Companiet* (SOIC) was founded, inheriting most of its know-how from the Austrian *Ostende* company, which had been trading in China for over fifty years. During its existence, which lasted until 1813, the company sent only one or two ships to the Orient in most years.

The Danes made unsuccessful, financially disastrous attempts to gain a share of the East India trade in 1616 and 1634, and both times most of their ships were lost at sea. In 1729 King Frederick IV of Denmark chartered and largely financed the Danish East India Company, centered on trade with India. It prospered until the end of the eighteenth century when the British began encroaching in their areas. The final blow occurred in 1801 when British naval forces destroyed the Danish navy in several battles in the

Baltic Sea and the company went bankrupt. Great Britain purchased their two main Indian possessions of Srampore and Tranquebar in 1845.

The voyages made by the European trading ships, called East Indiamen, were long, arduous and very dangerous. It is not surprising that more than 2,000 of these ships were lost during three centuries of this global navigation, sinking in the waters of the Far East, in the Indian Ocean and the Atlantic. On homeward-bound voyages, most East Indiamen stopped at the Azores or passed close to them as a checkpoint in navigation, and more than 150 were lost in the area. More than 300 East Indiamen, many laden with immensely rich cargoes, sank off South Africa, especially around the Cape of Good Hope.

The toll of East Indiamen in 1647 alone illustrates how treacherous this area is. In February sixteen of a fleet of 17 Portuguese carracks rounding the Cape wrecked. The surviving ship reached Madagascar, but sank soon after anchoring. In December 1646 a fleet of eight Portuguese carracks set sail from Goa "very fully laden with the most beautiful goods which had come from the East over many years." In early June 1647, as this fleet rounded the Cape of Good Hope, it too was overcome by a violent storm; six vessels went to the bottom during the first hour and two others were wrecked on the coast.

(Above) The caravel, invented by the Portuguese around 1400, was the main vessel used for explorations by both the Portuguese and Spaniards.

(Center) Small iron 16th century Portuguese cannon. This small type was primarily used as anti-personnel, to prevent pirates from boarding the ship and for repelling mutinies.

(Lower) The Tower of Belem, located several miles south of Lisbon on the Tagus River, was the starting and ending point for all of the Portuguese ships engaged in exploration and trade with the Orient.

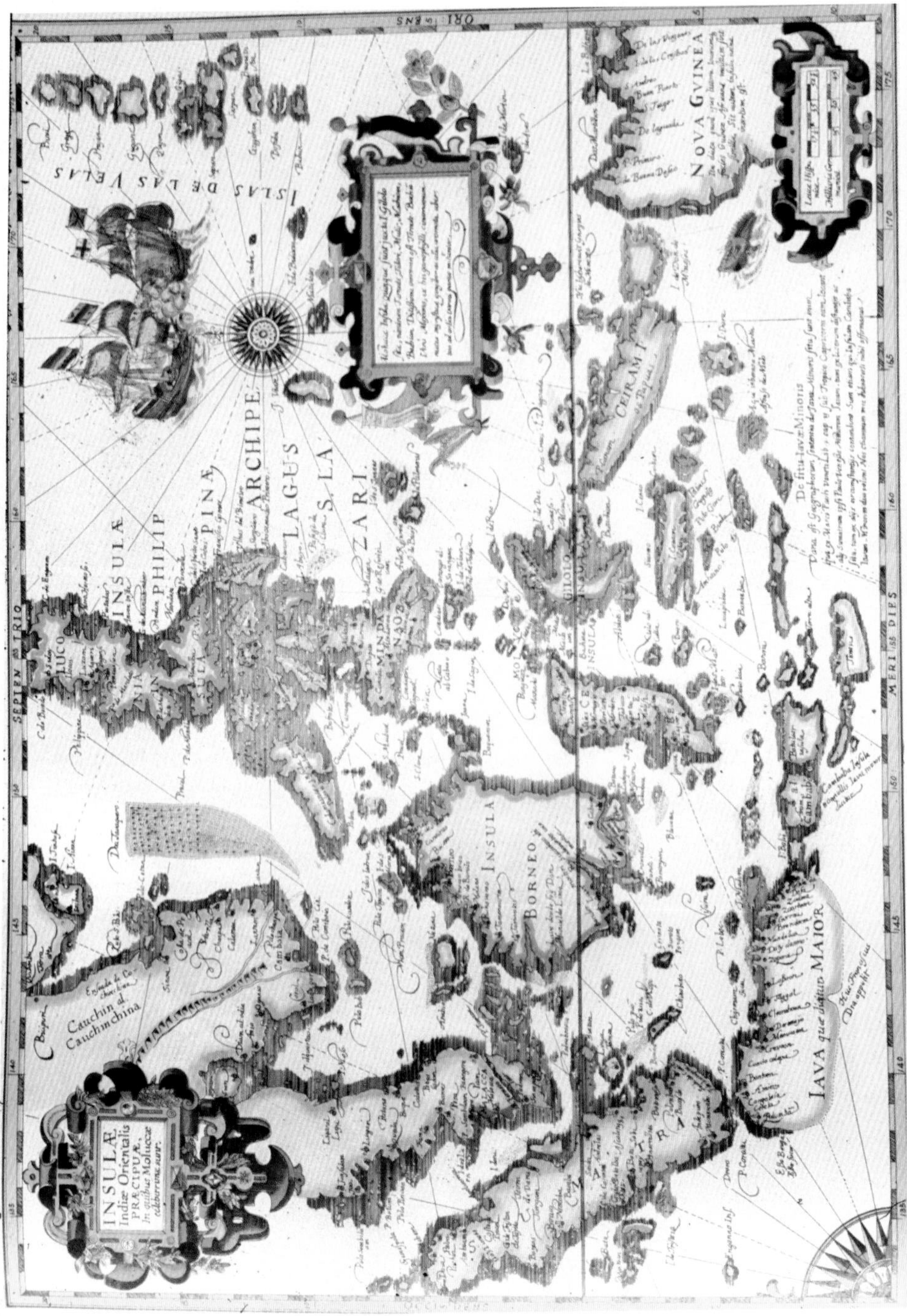

A beautiful chart of the Orient made in 1595 by a Dutch cartographer.

Chapter 16

British Isles' Richest Shipwrecks

At an underwater archaeological conference about twenty years ago, archaeologist Dr. Margaret Rule, known for her work on Henry VIII's flagship the *Mary Rose*, said that more than 20,000 shipwrecks lay in the waters of the British Isles. She went on to state that fewer than 100 are of any significant archaeological value, which upset many of the archaeologists present who believe that every shipwreck has archaeological value. As an example, Dr. Rule mentioned the Goodwin Sands, a stretch of shoals and sandbars about 10 miles (16 kilometers) long, lying between Ramsgate and Deal off England's southeast coast. This dangerous area was created when an island named Lomea submerged during a great storm in the late eleventh century. Over the years more than 1,000 ships were lost on the Goodwin Sands, which has the ability to swallow even the largest ships and cover them so quickly that they are obliterated. Myriad wrecks spanning millennia lie jumbled together in a concentrated area, making archaeological excavation of a particular ship impossible.

Like the Phoenicians long before them, the British depended on sea commerce and trading for their existence, a necessity for a nation with few natural resources and no precious metals. During the Medieval Period, the Hanseatic League, a confederation of free cities in northern Germany and surrounding areas, dominated most of maritime commerce, forcing the British to trade with the Iberian Peninsula and Mediterranean. Once the

A British East India Company trading ship, *ca.* 1650. They were similar in design to the Dutch East India Company ships, but usually larger and slower at sea.

Hanseatic League's monopoly ended in the late sixteenth century, the British and the Dutch took over, dominating maritime trade all over Europe, and later in the West Indies and North America. The defeat of the Spanish Armada in 1588 opened the sea-lanes to British commerce since Spain and Portugal barely had sufficient ships to maintain their far-flung empires and were unable to prevent the British from trading wherever they wished.

Spain and Portugal were totally dependent on the European manufactured goods supplied chiefly by the British and Dutch. In 1623 the papal nuncio wrote to the pope that when the treasure fleets reached Cádiz, over half of the gold and silver aboard was transferred directly to British ships to pay for the goods they had supplied to Spanish New World colonies. British merchants

(Facing) Prince Charles, who worked as a volunteer diver on the excavation of King Henry VIII's flagship *Mary Rose*, lost in 1551 off Portsmouth, admires one of the bronze cannons recovered from this wreck.

(Above) Trade goods recovered from an unidentified British East Indiaman lost off Mauritius Island around 1750, probably en route to India.

(Below) Divers showing hundreds of silver coins and two pewter plates that they recovered from the *HMS Association*, lost in 1707 on Gilstone Reef in the Scilly Isles.

sometimes went bankrupt when British warships captured or sank homeward-bound Spanish ships and the merchants went unpaid.

In the sixteenth and seventeenth centuries British merchants trading with Spain were paid with New World gold and silver. That changed in the eighteenth century when Portugal benefited from the vast amount of gold coming out of the newly discovered mines of Brazil. Gold coins have always held a great fascination for mankind and some of the most beautiful ever minted were the Portuguese *moidore* coins from Brazil. Copious amounts of these "Joes," as the Anglo-Saxons called them, reached Great Britain along with tons of gold ingots, which the British minted into gold coins. Very few documents detailing gold shipments have survived, except for the period 1730 to 1740 when over 500 tons (508 tonnes) of Portuguese gold reached England.

Initially, British traders had to be content acting as middlemen ferrying the goods of one nation to another. Once British colonies were established in the West Indies and North America and the British East India Company started bringing spices and exotic products back from the Orient, these traders became major players in international trade. Their first great profits were derived from the production of sugar and tobacco in the New World, which the rest of Europe hungered to obtain. They also brought back large amounts of contraband gold and silver obtained from Spanish colonies.

By 1700 Great Britain had become the world's leading naval power. European ships were no match for Britain's massive, well-armed frigates, which defeated most of Europe's navies. In the 1798 Battle of the Nile in Egypt's Aboukir Bay, they annihilated Napoleon's French navy. In 1805 they defeated the combined French and Spanish at the Battle of Trafalgar. Britannia ruled not only the waves, but also world trade.

Fourteenth century: A document from the fourteenth century records that an unidentified French ship, carrying 100,000 gold coins, wrecked in a storm off Rye, England, and none of her gold was recovered. This was a payment to indemnify the British for the loss of

One of the many pieces of gold jewelry recovered from the 1588 Spanish Armada ship *Girona*, off Northern Ireland.

one of their ships, carrying an equal amount of gold, which had been lost in a battle with several French privateers during a time of peace between both nations.

1467: The Spanish merchantman *Nuestra Señora de Burgos*, sailing from San Sebastián, Spain, to Germany with 16 chests of gold coins, was lost in a storm on the Skerries, a group of islands in the South Irish Sea not far from Wales.

1537: An unidentified Spanish merchantman, coming from Bilboa with 27,000 gold coins en route to Flanders, was driven westward by a storm and wrecked close to Cork, Ireland, with a total loss of life and treasure.

1588: Spain lost more than 100 galleons of the Invincible Armada off the coasts of Scotland and Ireland. Although these ships were not treasure-laden, they all carried considerable amounts of precious objects. The galleon *Girona*, salvaged by Robert Stenuit in 1967, for example, contained 45 beautiful pieces of jewelry, 405 gold coins and 756 silver coins.

1589: The New Spain Fleet of Captain-General Martín Pérez de Orozabal was approaching the Azores when English warships attacked, capturing eight rich galleons. One unidentified galleon "with a large treasure on board" later sank inside Mounts Bay in Cornwall, England. Contemporary salvors were able to recover several tons of silver bars and 23 chests of silver coins, but the rest was quickly covered by sand.

1592: The British merchantman *Golden Lion*, sailing with a large cargo of silver specie and bullion, from London to Oporto, Portugal, to purchase wine and brandy was lost on the Goodwin Sands with a total loss of life and treasure.

1598: One of the first Dutch fleets to sail to the Orient was commanded by Gerald Le Roy, who sailed on the *Maan* (400 tons/406 tonnes). While firing a salute off Dover, England, the ship capsized and quickly sank with a heavy loss of life. She was carrying an unknown amount of gold and silver bullion and specie to buy Oriental products.

1627: Two Dutch East Indiamen—the *Vliegende Draak* (320 tons/325 tonnes) and the *Kampen* (300 tons/305 tonnes)—sailing to Batavia from Holland with unknown amounts of treasure, were lost on the Needles of Wight, England. The *Kampen* was discovered and partially salvaged in recent times.

1640: Spain suffered a maritime disaster reminiscent of the 1588 Invincible Armada debacle. A Spanish fleet, commanded by Captain-General Antonio de Oquendo, and a Dutch fleet, under Admiral Tromp, engaged in several days of furious battle. The Spaniards lost 43 large warships and some smaller vessels in the English Channel. More than 6,000 men perished. Some of the Spanish ships were carrying large amounts of gold and silver specie.

1645: British East Indiaman *John*, commanded by Captain John Mucknell, sailed from London to the East Indies carrying £220,000 sterling in gold and silver specie. When the ship stopped in the Comorro Islands, some of the crew mutinied. The captain aborted the voyage and returned to England. Upon reaching Bristol, they learned that war between the Royalists and those backing Cromwell was raging all over England. The captain then decided to become a pirate. The crew agreed with him, and they set sail for the Canary Islands where they plundered many ships. Returning to England with the hold full of swag, they were attacked by warships loyal to Cromwell and driven onto the rocks off the Scilly Islands, England.

1656: The Dutch East Indiaman *Rotterdam* (480 tons/488 tonnes), commanded by Captain Wilhem Schoutsz and coming from the Orient with a cargo valued at 340,000 guilders, was wrecked on the Isle of Mull, Scotland. Only some of her people were saved.

1664: The Dutch East Indiaman *Kennermerland* (950 tons/965 tonnes), carrying 120,000 guilders in silver specie from Holland to Batavia, wrecked on Stoura Stack in the Outer Skerries of the Shetland Islands and all hands were lost.

1665: Two returning Dutch East Indiamen—the *Maarsseveen* (1,210 tons/1,229 tonnes), commanded by Captain Jan Hermansz with 371,000 guilders in cargo, and the *Oranje* (1,200 tons/1,219 tonnes), commanded by Captain Reinier Reiniersz and with 340,000 guilders in cargo—were intercepted by English warships and sunk in a battle off Lowestaff, England, in the North Sea.

1665: The Dutch East Indiaman ship *Zeepard* was wrecked on Westray Island in the Orkney Islands while sailing from Holland to Batavia with 365,000 guilders in silver specie on board. Contemporary salvors using a diving bell were unable to recover any of the treasure and two divers were killed in the operation, which was plagued by strong currents and rough seas.

1666: The Danish East Indiaman *St. Michael the Archangel* (1,750 tons/1,778 tonnes), commanded by Captain Christian Hansen and sailing with 430 chests of Spanish pieces of eight to make pur-chases in the Orient, was wrecked in a storm on the west side of Little Minch Island in the Outer Hebrides, off the northern tip of Scotland. Only six men survived.

1667: The Dutch East Indiaman *Walcheren* (840 tons/853 tonnes), was returning from Batavia to Holland with a cargo valued at 364,000 guilders, excluding a large consignment of Chinese porcelain, which

The British were constantly improving the various types of equipment used in diving and salvage of wrecks, such as this diving bell at work on a wreck around 1700.

was used as ballast, a normal practice on Dutch ships returning from the Orient. She wrecked on one of the Faeroe Islands and most of the people aboard died.

1667: The British East Indiaman *Charles Royal* (860 tons/873 tonnes), returning from India and Mauritius Island with a cargo valued at £310,000 sterling, wrecked on the south side of the Isle of Wight, England. Her masts and superstructure protruded from the water, but before salvors could work on the site, a Dutch warship appeared and burned the ship, and salvors recovered very little.

1668: The English merchantman *Peter of Hamburg* (90 tons/91 tonnes), commanded by Captain Peter Mansel Plattle and coming from the West Indies with a general cargo plus 47 chests of Spanish pieces of eight (such chests normally held 3,000 coins), wrecked on rocks about a mile off Llanell on the south coast of Wales. Most of her people were rescued, but none of the coins were recovered.

1670: The Dutch East Indiaman *Wapen Van Vlissingen* (725 tons/737 tonnes), carrying 320,000 guilders in gold and silver bullion and specie to Batavia, was totally lost on the Goodwin Sands on the south coast of England, and only a few souls were saved.

1673: The Dutch East Indiaman *Wapen Van Hoord* (756 tons/768 tonnes), sailing from Holland to Batavia with "a substantial amount of silver specie,"was lost in the Scilly Isles and most of the people aboard drowned.

1680: The British East Indiaman *Phoenix* (880 tons/894 tonnes), commanded by Captain John Penn and returning from the Orient with a cargo valued at £389,000 sterling, which included "many boxes of diamonds and pearls," wrecked near Hugh Town in the Scilly Isles off the southwest tip of England. Not far from there a Dutch merchantman, *Peace of Amsterdam,* coming from the West Indies with a cargo of unknown value, had been totally lost the year before.

1682: The royal pinnace *Gloucester,* commanded by Captain Sir John Berry, was carrying James II, king of England, when it wrecked on the Lemon and Ore Shoal in the North Sea off the east coast of England. The king and some aristocrats traveling with him were rescued, but "a large amount of gold plate belonging to the king" was lost.

1688: The Dutch merchant ship *Tobias Leidsman,* sailing from Holland to Oporto with 120,000 guilders in coinage to purchase wine, was lost on Hanglip Shoals in the Shetland Islands, Scotland.

1689: Four Dutch East Indiamen—the *Pijdwaart* (600 tons/609 tonnes) with 120,000 guilders in Oriental products; the *Kapelle* (647 tons/657 tonnes) with 131,000 guilders; the *Land Van Schouwen* (1,120 tons/1,138 tonnes), commanded by Captain Gerrits Bruijn, with 210,000 guilders; and the *Wapen Van Alkmaar* (892 tons/906 tonnes) with 485,000 guilders—were totally lost off the northern Shetland Islands near Baltasound Yell while sailing between Batavia and Holland. More than 1,000 crew and passengers drowned and three salvage attempts were unfruitful.

1695: The British East Indiaman ship *Henry* was returning from India with a cargo of unknown value, plus a chest of diamonds valued at £75,000 sterling when it was lost in Dingle Bay, Ireland.

1711: The Dutch East Indiaman *Liefde* (1,009 tons/1,025 tonnes), commanded by Captain Barend Meikens and sailing between Holland and Batavia, was totally lost on Moux Reef in the Shetland Islands. Salvors were unable to recover any of the 312,000 guilders in gold and silver bullion and specie.

1711: The Dutch East Indiaman *Weerestein* (240 tons/244 tonnes, 22 cannons), commanded by Captain Jan Krijnebak, and sailing to Batavia from Holland with 225,000 guilders in gold and silver specie, was wrecked in the Shetland Islands.

1713: The Dutch East Indiaman *Rijnenburg* (618 tons/628 tonnes), commanded by Captain David Brouwer and sailing for Batavia with "a large consignment of silver bullion and specie," was lost on a reef in the Shetland Islands.

1717: The English merchantman *Scanderoon* (440 tons/447 tonnes), commanded by Captain Edward Pulleson, sailed from Lisbon for England with a general cargo, plus £120,000 sterling in Spanish coins. She wrecked near Swansea on the southeast coast of Wales, and only some of her people were rescued.

1719: The Dutch East Indiaman *Loosdrecht* (805 tons/818 tonnes), commanded by Captain Willem Dekker, enroute to Batavia with 340,000 guilders in gold and silver specie, was wrecked on the Isle of Wight, England. About half of her treasure was recovered by contemporary salvors.

1721: The Dutch East Indiaman *Aagtekerke* (800 tons/813 tonnes), commanded by Captain Nikolaas Rabodus, sailed for Batavia with 287,000 guilders in gold and silver specie and was lost near Plymouth, England. About half of her treasure was saved.

1725: The Dutch East Indiaman *Astrea* (800 tons/813 tonnes), commanded by Captain Jakob Thoorn, sailed for Batavia with 290,000 guilders "in treasure" on board and was wrecked 1 league east of Plymouth. None of her treasure was saved.

1728: The Dutch East Indiaman *Adelaar* (810 tons/823 tonnes, 48 cannons), commanded by Captain Willem de Keizer, sailed to for Batavia with 340,000 guilders in "gold and silver" and battled a fierce storm for three days, ending up totally destroyed on the rocks of Barra Island, Scotland.

Set of silverware recovered from an unidentified British East Indiaman lost off Madagascar Island around 1700.

1736: The Dutch East Indiaman *Loosdrecht* (850 tons/864 tonnes), commanded by Captain Willem Vroon, sailed for Batavia with 340,000 guilders in gold and silver bullion and specie. She was totally lost on the Goodwin Sands.

1738: The Dutch East Indiaman *Boot* (650 tons/660 tonnes), commanded by Captain Jakob van Duinen and bearing a cargo valued at 200,000 guilders on returning to Holland from Batavia, was totally lost in a storm near Dartmouth, England. Only a few of the crew was saved.

1740: The Dutch East Indiaman *Rooswijk* (850 tons/864 tonnes), commanded by Captain Daniel Ronzieres, sailed for Batavia with 360,000 guilders in gold and silver specie and was totally lost on the Goodwin Sands.

1742: The Dutch East Indiaman *Amsterdam* (850 tons/864 tonnes), commanded by Captain Pieter Visser and sailing from Batavia with a cargo valued at 265,000 guilders, not including the value of diamonds, precious stones and porcelain on board, was totally lost on Yell Island, the northernmost of the Shetland Islands. Only seven men survived.

1745: The British warship *HMS Fox* was sailing between Lisbon and Portsmouth "with a very large amount of gold and silver" when she sank in the English Channel about 2 leagues south of

Late seventeenth-century pewter ware and a brass barrel tap recovered from an unidentified British merchantman on the Goodwin Sands.

Dover with a great loss of life during a storm. *La Nymphe*, a richly laden pirate vessel, wrecked in the same storm at Weymouth on England's south coast.

1747: The British East Indiaman *Dolphin* (370 tons/376 tonnes), commanded by Captain George Newton and carrying forty chests of silver weighing over 6 tons (6.096 tonnes), was sailing between London and Bombay when she was lost on the Goodwin Sands. All lives were lost and nothing was ever recovered from her.

1748: The Dutch East Indiaman *Amsterdam* (1,150 tons/1,168 tonnes), commanded by Captain Willem Klump, sailed for Batavia with 300,104 guilders in silver coins and bars. She was wrecked between Hastings and Beachy Head, and some of the silver was recovered. Over the centuries the coastline has expanded and the wreck is now under the beach sands. At certain low tides, parts of the ship's hull are exposed. For more than 25 years archaeologist Peter Marsden has excavated this wreck, recovering a great deal of her general cargo. Because the entire lower hull is intact, the Dutch government attempted to build a cofferdam around the site and raise the hull. The effort was unsuccessful, but they did construct a full-scale replica of the ship, which is on display at the Maritime Museum in Amsterdam.

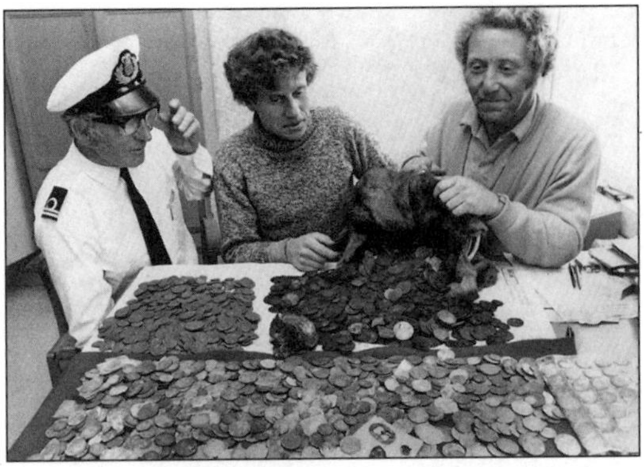

Divers showing the Receiver of Wrecks hundreds of silver coins they recovered from the *HMS Association*, lost in 1707 on Gilstone Reef in the Scilly Isles.

1753: The Danish merchantman *Prince Christan* (140 tons/142 tonnes), commanded by Captain Peter Jargenson, was sailing between Bordeaux, France, and Copenhagen with "a great quantity of gold and silver on board" when it was wrecked at Beachy Head in the English Channel.

1756: The Dutch East Indiaman *Nieuwvijvervreugd* (1,150 tons/1,168 tonnes), commanded by Captain Marinus de Jonge and returning from Batavia with a cargo value at 330,000 guilders, wrecked in St. Magnus Bay, Shetland Islands, and exploded before any of those aboard could get off the ship.

1758: The Spanish merchantman *Nuestra Señora de la Guardia* (360 tons/366 tonnes), commanded by Captain Lorenzo Janones, sailed from Cádiz for Havre de Grace, France, with a cargo that included 35,000 pieces of Chinese porcelain. She wrecked in the English Channel near Beachy Head.

1765: The British East Indiaman *Albion* (1,850 tons/1,880 tonnes), sailed from England for India carrying £650,000 sterling in gold and silver, and wrecked near Ramsgate in southeastern England. Salvors recovered three-fourths of the treasure, but quite a bit still remains.

1778: The Dutch East Indiaman *Wassenaar* sailed from Holland for Batavia with over 300,000 guilders in gold and silver specie and bullion. She wrecked on the south side of the Isle of Wight. Contemporary salvors recovered a small part of the treasure.

1778: The British East Indiaman *London* (1,700 tons/1,727 tonnes), sailing for India with £477,000 sterling in Spanish coinage and other cargo, collided with the warship HMS *Russell* shortly after leaving Portsmouth and sank soon after, taking down most of the people on board.

1780: Two Danish East Indiamen, the *Wilhem* and the *Prins Frederik,* both carrying large amounts of gold and silver, sank in a fierce storm in the English Channel about 2 miles (3 kilometers) southeast of Margate. There were few survivors.

1783: The Dutch ship *Oostereem* (1,150 tons/1,168 tonnes), commanded by Captain Axel Land and chartered by Prussian merchants for a voyage to China, was carrying "a large amount of gold and silver" when she was wrecked on the Goodwin Sands.

1785: The Dutch East Indiaman *Neerlands Vrjheid* (566 tons/575 tonnes), commanded by Captain Frederik Floor, was en route to Batavia with 389,000 guilders "in gold and silver" when she was wrecked near Land's End, Cornwall, England.

1786: The Dutch East Indiaman *Ganges* (1,150 tons/1,168 tonnes), commanded by Captain Jan Frederik Schuts, left Holland with 440,000 guilders in gold and silver specie, bound for China, and was totally lost at Padstow in Cornwall. When she ran aground, the weather was moderate and plans were made to salvage her treasure and other cargo, but a winter storm struck and the ship quickly went to pieces. Most of the 377 people aboard her had been taken off before the storm.

1786: The British East Indiaman *Haleswell* (758 tons/770 tonnes), commanded by Captain Richard Pierce, sailed for India with 77 chests of Spanish pieces of eight (4,000 coins in each chest), plus other cargo, and was wrecked during a storm on the east end of Purbeck Island, off St. Alban's Head on the south coast of England in the English Channel.

1790: The Dutch East Indiaman *Valk* (600 tons/610 tonnes), commanded by Captain George Gottlieb Hebner, sailed for Batavia with 378,000 guilders in treasure and was totally lost on the sand banks off Yarmouth, England. Contemporary salvors recovered about half of her treasure.

1794: The French warship *L'Impetueux* (74 cannons), was one of six prizes captured by Lord Howe's fleet and taken into Portsmouth harbor and anchored there. The British were unaware there were 300,000 pesos of Spanish treasure on board. French prisoners on board set the ship on fire and she sank. Later, about half the treasure was recovered by divers using a bell.

1795: A convoy of over 200 ships, under the command of Rear-Admiral Christian, was struck by a violent storm in the vicinity of Weymouth, England. More than 25 ships sank. One of them, the *Catherine*, carrying 21 chests of gold specie, was totally lost off Langton and about half those on board drowned.

1795: The Dutch East Indiaman *Hougly* (1,150 tons/1,168 tonnes), commanded by Captain Arnold Rogge, sailed from Batavia with a cargo valued at 130,000 guilders and was captured by the British at St. Helena Island where she stopped for fresh water. Weather prevented the British and the prize ship from reaching Portsmouth, and they headed for Cork, Ireland. Just as the ships were entering Cork harbor, the Dutch set their ship on fire, and it exploded and sank.

1795: The English captured another Dutch East Indiaman, the *Zeelelie* (1,150 tons/1,168 tonnes), commanded by Captain Kornelis Adriaansz, sailing from Batavia with 716,000 guilders of cargo. Bad weather prevented the English warship and her prize from sailing directly to Portsmouth, and as they headed for Shannon, Ireland, the Dutch ship wrecked in the Scilly Islands.

1796: The American East Indiaman *Washington* (750 tons/762 tonnes), sailed from India and was lost in a gale at Lizard Point. Salvors recovered silks, muslin and Indian hemp, but none of the chests containing gold jewelry, precious stones and pearls, valued at £265,000 sterling.

1798: The *HMS Colossus,* carrying £125,000 sterling in Spanish coins, was anchored off St. Mary's in the Scilly Isles when a hurricane struck, causing her to wreck on rocks known as the Southern Wells. Many on board had fought alongside Lord Nelson in the Battle of the Nile and were taking back plunder from various French ships they had captured.

1799: The Danish merchantman *Hoefnung,* sailing from Denmark to Malaga, Spain, with "a large amount of gold and silver specie," wrecked on the Goodwin Sands in a gale and quickly went to pieces.

Most of the people on board got ashore on floating timbers from the wreck.

1801: The Swedish East Indiaman *Sophia Magdalena,* sailing from India to Copenhagen, was wrecked near Kingstown on the South Foreland, England. The bulk of her cargo was tea and was salvaged, but none of the "many chests and boxes of precious stones and gold jewelry" were found.

1802: The British East Indiaman *Melville Castle,* sold to the Dutch government and renamed the *Vryheid,* was ferrying soldiers to the Cape of Good Hope and Batavia. She sailed from Amsterdam with over 330,000 guilders in gold and silver specie on board and wrecked in a storm between Dymchurch and Hythe on the south English coast. Only 18 of the 472 people on board survived. Numerous contemporary salvage attempts failed to find any of her treasure.

1803: The East Indiaman *Hindostan* (1,248 tons/1,268 tonnes), sailing from England for China and India with £343,000 sterling in treasure (Spanish gold and silver specie) and other cargo, wrecked in the English Channel off Margate on the shoals known as Wedge Sands. Divers employed by the British East India Company recovered only a small part of her treasure.

1805: In a fleet of British East Indiamen that sailed from Portsmouth was the *Earl of Abergavenny,* commanded by Captain Wordsworth. When struck by a fierce storm she tried to reach safety in Portland Roads and wrecked on the Shambles. She quickly went to pieces, and only about 120 people of the 420 on board were saved. There are various reports about the amount of treasure she had board, but an account two years after the disaster states that only 62 chests of the more than 300 she carried had been salvaged.

1809: The British East Indiaman *Admiral Gardner,* sailing from England to India, was wrecked on the Goodwin Sands, but everyone aboard was saved. She carried over £200,000 sterling in silver and copper specie. In modern times commercial salvors have recovered around 50,000 of her copper coins, but none of the silver.

1811: The British warship *Pomone* (38 cannons), commanded by Captain Robert Barrie, sailed from Constantinople with the retiring British ambassador to Persia, who carried his own personal fortune of unknown value, plus 55,000 pesos in Spanish silver specie. She struck upon a hidden rock and sank very close to Needles Point.

1815: The British West Indiaman *Queen Charlotte*, sailing from Greenock to Jamaica with £230,000 sterling in silver specie, wrecked during a storm on one of the Isles of Scilly and only 14 men were saved. In the 1960s sports divers recovered a small amount of coinage from the wreck.

1845: The Dutch East Indiaman *Delft*, sailing from Batavia with 14 tons (14.22 tonnes) of gold bars from China and other valuable cargo, wrecked in a storm between Dover and Folkestone in the English Channel.

1859: The English merchantman *Royal Charter*, coming from Australia with 40,000 ounces in gold coins and 87,000 ounces in gold bullion, plus gold belonging to passengers who worked in the Australian gold fields, was wrecked in a storm in Wharf Bay, near Bangor, Wales. Salvors worked over four years to recover about half of the gold.

CHAPTER 17

SPAIN'S RICHEST SHIPWRECKS

Throughout history Cádiz has been the most important seaport in the south of Spain. From the dawn of history ships sailed from Cádiz and made their way there. Phoenicians, Greeks, and Romans traded for Iberian silver, tin and gold. Cádiz is the oldest continuously inhabited city in Europe. The Phoenicians established a trading post there in 1,100 B.C. and called the town Gadir (meaning enclosure), a name that later transmuted to Gades under the Romans. Hannibal lived in the city and Julius Caesar first held office here and planned his great empire.

I have spent thousands of hours exploring countless shipwrecks in and around the Bay of Cádiz. Hidden beneath its waters is the largest amount of sunken treasure of any port in Europe, not to mention a vast treasure in archaeological information. Four thousand years of history are hidden in the bay, history that, in the last few decades, is rapidly being destroyed by land reclamation.

Cádiz is one of the most important underwater archaeological sites in the world. Under the auspices of the Archaeological Museum of Cádiz, I conducted a visual survey of the bay over a three-year period from 1960 through 1962, before magnetometers were used to locate shipwrecks. Sub-bottom profiling sonar, which detects objects buried beneath the sea-floor, was not invented yet and side-scan sonar was of no use since everything was buried. I used long metal probes to detect buried objects and then dug test holes using an airlift. Within a 2-mile (3-kilometer) radius of the

Cadíz around 1700 when over 500 large ships of many nations were using it annually. It was the main port for returning New World treasure ships.

modern port, I located 54 Classical Period shipwrecks and 97 of later date, including many New World Spanish galleons.

Modern Cádiz is a major port. Soon after I completed my survey, dredging and landfill operations began to enlarge the port for deeper draft ships. The dredging and filling obliterated huge numbers of shipwrecks. At the request of King Juan Carlos, who is an avid diver and history buff, I conducted a new survey in 1985, this time using a magnetometer and a sub-bottom profiling sonar. Sadly, I found that many of the ships I had discovered in my earlier surveys no longer existed.

UNESCO aided a frustrating campaign I mounted to save the remaining shipwrecks. The Save Cádiz Bay Foundation convinced the government to prevent further dredging and landfill operations in certain areas I had designated, but destruction of shipwrecks has continued in other parts of Cádiz Bay. Despite this, there are still many undiscovered shipwrecks with treasure awaiting discovery.

Tradition says Carthaginians founded Cádiz in 800 B.C., but recent finds of Egyptian amphorae indicate that the port was being used as long ago as 2,000 B.C. The earliest mariners most likely came there to trade for the region's abundant gold. Documented research reveals that the Cádiz area has over 4,000 shipwrecks and the remains of at least five submerged settlements: two Phoenician and three Roman. In addition to Egyptian shipwrecks, many Phoenician, Greek and Roman merchantmen and war galleys were lost at Cádiz. During the Medieval Period it was one of the most important seaports in Europe, and hundreds of trading vessel went to the bottom in storms. Even the Vikings came to grief at Cádiz. In A.D. 957, after months of sacking various ports of the Mediterranean, a fleet of about seventy plunder-heavy Viking ships sank in Cádiz Bay when they sought refuge from a storm.

Once trade with the New World was established, Cádiz became the most important port in the world. Throughout the Colonial Period, thousands of ships sailed from this port bearing goods to New World colonies and returning with prodigious amounts of treasure. Cádiz was not an ideal port. It is poorly protected from storms and ships were subjected to constant attacks from North Africa's Barbary pirates and others who coveted a share of Spain's great wealth. Sir Francis Drake attacked Cádiz in 1587, sending many large galleons to the bottom. In the sixteenth century, over 600 richly laden treasure galleons returning from the New World sank in the bay before their treasures could be off-loaded. Cádiz is second only to the Azores in the amount of treasure waiting to be found.

The majority of ships lost in and around Cádiz Bay lie at an average depth of 50 feet (15 meters). Limited recoveries were made with the use of grappling hooks, but contemporary salvors recovered little because underwater visibility, even for divers operating out of diving bells, was very poor and the bottom is very fine silt, causing objects to quickly sink beneath the sea floor.

The Guadalquivir River, which connects the city of Seville with the Atlantic Ocean, has been navigated at least since the time of the Phoenicians, some of whose ruins, including a smelting works, have been found along the bank. During the sixteenth century, many Spanish ships plying between Spain and the New World used Seville as their home port. Coming and going they had to cross the Bar of Sanlúcar de Barrameda, a treacherous area of shoals at the river's mouth. Around 1550 Cádiz supplanted Seville

Bronze apothecary mortar and pestle recovered from a wreck in Cadíz Bay.

as chief port for New World traffic. However, some ships from the Americas still crossed this bar and anchored off Bonanza, a nearby port on the river where their cargoes were off-loaded to be sent up the river to Seville. Over the centuries hundreds of ships, many of then treasure-laden, were lost on the Bar of Salutary.

Barcelona, Bilbao, Cartagena and Málaga are important Spanish seaports that were widely used by the Phoenicians, Greeks and Romans, but declined during the Colonial Period when all New World shipping was confined to the Andalusian ports of Cádiz, Seville and Sanlúcar. It was strictly forbidden for any other ports to have direct commerce with the New World. Although there are many shipwrecks of great archaeological importance elsewhere, few hold treasure and will not be listed below.

1543: An unidentified Spanish caravel, sailing from Panama and Havana "with a large cargo of Inca gold figurines and other gold," was wrecked near Rota in Cádiz Bay. None of her cargo was recovered because the sea-floor is silt and anything touching bottom is immediately swallowed and concealed.

1555: The Spanish galleon *Santa Cruz,* returning from Cartagena and Havana with 1.34 million pesos in treasure, was wrecked along with three other unidentified galleons on Playa de Zahara, located about midway between Cádiz and Gibraltar. Only a small part of her treasure was salvaged. Periodically silver coins from these wrecks are found on the beach after a severe storm.

1557: The Spanish merchantman *La Trinidad* (220 tons/223.5 tonnes, 26 cannons), commanded by Captain Sebastian de Quesada and sailing from Spain to Panama with 120 tons (122 tonnes) of mercury used in the refining of gold and silver, wrecked on the Bar of Sanlúcar and then slid into deeper water. Most of people were saved, but none of the valuable mercury.

1563: The Spanish galleon *Espiritu Sancto* (600 tons/610 tonnes), commanded by Captain Gaspar Gonzalez and carrying 430,000 pesos in treasure, was wrecked at the mouth of the Rio Tinto near Palos. Only a few of her people were saved.

1566: As the Tierra Firme Fleet, sailing from Havana, approached Cádiz Bay with a large amount of treasure, three of her ships sank. The *San Antón,* commanded by Captain Benito Pérez Carrasco, with 650,000 pesos in treasure, wrecked on the Bar of Sanlúcar; the *Santo Antonio,* commanded by Captain Juan Arze and carrying 330,000 pesos in treasure, wrecked at Arenas Gordas just west of the mouth of the Guadalquiver River; and the *San Gabriel,* commanded by Captain Juan Gonzalez, with 289,000 pesos in treasure, sank in deep water about 3 miles (5 kilometers) off Cádiz Bay.

1573: When the New Spain fleet of Captain-General Francisco Luxan was departing from Spain for Veracruz, the galleon *San Miguel* (300 tons/305 tonnes), commanded by Captain Francisco Ruiz and carrying 67 tons (68 tonnes) of mercury, sank on the Guadalquiver River at Chipiona, just north of Sanlúcar de Barrameda, after hitting the ballast pile of a wreck, causing several bad leaks that could not be contained by pumps. Later that year when this fleet was returning from Mexico, the galleon *La Madalena* (400 tons/406 tonnes), commanded by Captain Cristóbal Sánchez and carrying 460,000 pesos in treasure, wrecked in a storm on Arenas Gordas, just west of the entrance to the Guadalquiver River.

1577: The Spanish galleon *Nuestra Señora de Buen Viaje* (560 tons/569 tonnes, 44 cannons), commanded by Captain Rodrigo Benevides de Carmona and returning from Veracruz and Havana with over 2 million pesos in treasures, was totally lost at Arenas Gordas in a storm. Only five men reached the shore.

1579: An unidentified Spanish merchantman sailing from the New World to Cádiz was forced to run before a bad storm and sank near Tarifa. Salvors recovered 135,000 pesos of the 378,000 pesos she carried in treasure.

1581: As the New Spain Fleet under the command of Captain General Alvaro Manrique de Lara was leaving Sanlúcar, the galleon *San Miguel* (400 tons/406 tonnes), commanded by Captain Martín de Lecoya, carrying 80 tons (81 tonnes) of mercury, was wrecked on the Bar of Sanlúcar. Several hours later, another ship of this fleet, the *Nuestra Señora de Guadalupe,* commanded by Captain Domingo Fernandez, was wrecked near Cádiz. Two months later as the Tierra Firme Fleet of Captain-General Francisco de Luxan was approaching Cádiz, five unidentified galleons with a treasure totaling 1.74 million pesos were lost. Two wrecked at Arenas Gordas, two others inside Cádiz Bay, and one inside the port of Sanlúcar.

1587: The Tierra Firme Fleet, returning from Panama and Havana and commanded by Captain-General Álvaro Flores de Quinones, encountered a bad storm as it approached Cádiz Bay. Six rich galleons were lost with a total of 2.18 million pesos in treasure. The *Santa María de Madalena* (300 tons/305 tonnes), commanded by Captain Francisco Romero, was one of five ships wrecked on the Bar of Sanlúcar. Another, the *San Juan* (150 tons/152 tonnes), commanded by Captain Gonzalo Milanés de Torres, sank about a half league off Portimao, Portugal.

1589: Three galleons in the Tierra Firme Armada of Captain-General Diego de la Rivera—the *San Pablo* (550 tons/559 tonnes), commanded by Captain Francisco Márquez; the *San Pedro* (450 tons/457 tonnes), commanded by Captain Alonso Maldonado; and the *San Miguel* (250 tons/254 tonnes), commanded by Captain Diego Osorio—carrying a total of 1.3 million pesos in treasure, were wrecked on the Bar of Sanlúcar. The vessels broke up and sank quickly in bad weather. There were survivors, but no cargo was saved.

1592: As the Tierra Firme fleet of Captain-General Francisco Martínez de Leyba was sailing from Cádiz, a bad storm arose, sinking the three galleons, which carried a total of 355 tons (3361 tonnes) of mercury. The *San Pedro* (500 tons/508 tonnes), commanded by Captain Blas Milanés, wrecked on a rock known as El Pichaco, and quickly broke up; the *Santa Catalin*a (350 tons/356 tonnes), commanded by Captain Juan Bautista Musdientes, wrecked on a dangerous rock called Diamante; and the *Santo Alberto* (250 tons/254 tonnes), commanded by Captain Pedro Rodriquez, capsized and sank about a league off the port.

1596: A fleet of Spanish galleys attacked and destroyed three towns in Cornwall, England. To avenge this deed, an outraged Queen Elizabeth I sent a fleet of 126 ships, augmented by 25 Dutch ships, under the command of Lord Effington and the earl of Essex, to attack Cádiz. Upon arriving there, they found 63 Spanish ships, the majority of which had just arrived from the New World with their treasures on board. To prevent the more than 25 million pesos in treasures from falling into the hands of the enemy, the Spaniards set fire to most of their ships and the English finished some of them off with cannon fire. The English managed to capture two galleons, but unfortunately they were among the few that had already been unloaded. The Spaniards paid a ransom of 500,000 ducats in gold to prevent the enemy from destroying the city.

1605: Two ships coming from Honduras in the New Spain Fleet—the *Nuestra Señora de Rosario* (450 tons/457 tonnes), commanded by Captain Santiago de Arrita, and the *Santa Monica* (400 tons/406 tonnes), commanded by Captain Diego Granillo—were wrecked on the Bar of Sanlúcar, losing over 1 million pesos in treasure.

1612: As the New Spain Fleet of Captain-General Antonio de Oquendo arrived in Spain, two galleons—the *San Estevan* (400 tons/406 tonnes), commanded by Captain Bernardo Andino, with 760,000 pesos in treasure; and the *Nuestra Señora de Consolación* (350 tons/356 tonnes), commanded by Captain Pedro de Urbina Cervera, with 487,000 pesos in treasure—wrecked on the Bar of Sanlúcar. The

San Estevan was fairly intact and salvors expected to remove the treasure, but the wind drove her seaward and she went down nearby in deep water. Nothing was saved except for most of her people.

1619: The Spanish merchantman *Nuestra Señora del Socorro* (120 tons/122 tonnes), commanded by Captain Antonio de la Pena, was a "register ship,"a vessel that had permission to sail to and from the New World alone to sell merchandise. Such ships were forbidden to carry more than 50,000 pesos in treasure on the return. The *Socorro* actually carried 265,000 pesos in treasure, and her captain decided to make landfall at Vigo, a northern Spanish port where custom officials were more likely to turn a blind eye to this illegal activity. While sailing to Vigo, she sank in a storm on the Pontevedra River.

1616: Five returning Spanish galleons, carrying a total of 2.3 million pesos in gold and silver—unable to enter Cádiz Bay, which was blockaded by Barbary corsairs—fled through the Straits of Gibraltar into the Mediterranean and wrecked in a storm on the beaches of Almería. Silver coins from these wrecks still come ashore in rough weather.

1625: The Portuguese East Indiaman *São Cristoval* (1,800 tons/1,829 tonnes and 68 bronze cannons), en route from Goa to Lisbon, was driven by a storm to the north of Spain. She wrecked about 5 miles (8 kilometers) west of La Corunna and went to the bottom with over 2 million cruzadoes in cargo and all but five of the 378 souls on board drowned.

1626: The Portuguese East Indiaman *São Filipe* (1,400 tons/1,422 tonnes, 28 cannons), commanded by Captain Dias de Andrade and returning from India with a cargo "great value,"was unable to enter Lisbon because enemy Dutch ships were waiting there. She headed north and wrecked during a fierce storm near Cabo Ortegal on the northwest tip of Spain.

1626: The Portuguese East Indiaman *São João* (1,500 tons/1,524 tonnes, 36 cannons), commanded by Captain Sebastiao da Costa Valente and returning from India to Lisbon with a cargo valued at 760,000 crusadoes, was lost on the coast of Viscaya near Gijón and only a few men were saved. Another Portuguese East Indiaman, the *São Jose* (400 tons/406 tonnes and thirty cannons), commanded by Captain Antonio de Meneses and sailing in the same armada as the *São João*, was wrecked 2 leagues east of this ship.

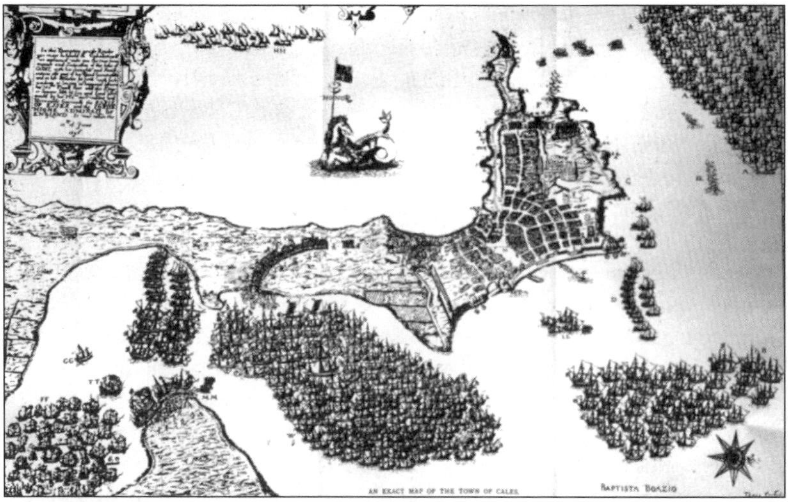

An English fleet of warships attacking a returning New World treasure fleet in 1596 in Cadíz Bay. The letters MM, GG and TT indicate the locations of three rich New World galleons lost in this battle.

1629: The Portuguese East Indiaman *Santo Estevao* (1,400 tons/1,422 tonnes), commanded by Captain Vicente Leitao de Quadros and returning from India with a cargo valued at 673,000 crusadoes, was unable to enter Lisbon because a fleet of Barbary pirates were cruising there. She headed north and wrecked in Vigo Bay. Some people, but no cargo, were saved.

1633: More than forty ships sank during a storm in Cádiz Bay. The loss was valued at over 4.5 million pesos in treasure and other cargo. The only ships identified were the *San Buenaventura* (230 tons/234 tonnes), commanded by Captain Mauricio Salgado, with 73 tons (74 tonnes) of mercury on board; and the *San Diego* (135 tons/137 tonnes), commanded by Captain Nicolás Caballero, with 43 tons (44 tonnes) of mercury. Both ships were part of the New Spain Fleet, preparing to sail for Veracruz.

1639: An armada of ten Spanish warships sailed from Cádiz to Flanders, carrying supplies for the war against the Dutch. The flagship of the fleet, the *Capitana,* was also carrying 1.5 million pesos in gold and silver specie. A fleet of French warships attacked the armada and burned and sank seven ships, including the *Capitana* with the treasure, off Guetaria on the northwest coast of Spain. Two vessels were captured and one escaped.

1656: The same year that the *Nuestra Señora de las Maravillas* was lost in the Bahamas, her sister ship, the galleon *San Francisco Xavier* (700 tons/711 tonnes), sank in the Bay of Cádiz with over 2 million pesos in treasure on board. After an uneventful voyage of 58 days from Havana, she was almost home when an English squadron, commanded by Vice Admiral Goodson, surprised the returning fleet. During a bloody six-hour battle, the English sank two Spanish merchant ships and captured another. The *Xavier* broke away and appeared able to reach the safety of the port, when suddenly she blew up and sank with an almost total loss of life. Because Spain's coffers were nearly empty, every effort was made to recover the ship's cargo. Salvage attempts using weighted nets failed because the ship lay 20 fathoms deep. About ten years ago, a fisherman snagged two chests of seventeenth-century gold coins in his nets, which may be from the sunken galleon.

Not long after the *Xavier* sank, an English squadron, led by Admiral Stayner, blockaded Cádiz Bay. Four galleons of the Tierra Firme Fleet of Captain-General Juan de Hoyos had been separated from the rest of the convoy during a storm off Bermuda and were the first to reach the coast of Spain. The English captured two of the galleons with 2 million pesos in treasure on each and sank two others with a like amount of treasure aboard. One went down in 25 fathoms of water 3 miles (5 kilometers) south of Rota; the other in much deeper water south of Santri Petri, several miles east of Cádiz.

1662: The Spanish merchantman *San Estevan* (400 tons/406 tonnes), commanded by Captain Juan de Hoyos, and carrying over 1 million pesos in treasure from Mexico, was anchored in Cádiz Bay when she caught fire and sank. The king ordered several royal officials to serve life sentences as galley slaves when he learned that the ship had been in port for three days, waiting to be unloaded, but customs officials enjoying a local fiesta didn't turn up for work.

1666: The Spanish merchantman *Nuestra Señora de Begoña* (440 tons/447 tonnes), commanded by Captain Marcos de Aranburu and coming from Panama with 473,000 pesos in treasure, was attacked and sunk by Algerian corsairs about 2 leagues south of Cape Santa María. The pirates captured all survivors and later ransomed them. Two weeks later when the coast appeared clear of marauders, many merchantmen set sail for various destinations. Once offshore, the same Algerian corsairs appeared and sank eight Dutch merchantmen: the *Zale, Wildman, Evangelista, Fortune, Chestnut, Cat, Golden Hare* and

Profhet Elias. Combined they carried over 2 million guilders in treasure and other cargo, most of which had been brought back from the New World by the Spaniards.

1667: The Spanish merchantman *Sancta Clara de Genova* (470 tons/477.5 tonnes), commanded by Captain Melchoir de Lobrano and bringing 230 tons (234 tonnes) of mercury for the mines of the New World, struck upon the dangerous rock known as El Diamante in Cádiz Bay and sank. Contemporary salvors recovered only about 10 tons (10.16 tonnes) of mercury, which is so heavy that the rest disappeared under the bay's deep, soft silt.

1672: The Spanish merchantman *Isabela*, commanded by Captain Juan de Ugarte and carrying over 220,000 pesos in treasure, which had been captured from a Moorish ship off Morocco, wrecked near Cape Santa María.

1682: The Spanish warship *Nuestra Señora de Concepción* (60 cannons), was sailing between Cádiz and Genoa with 390,000 pesos in gold and silver specie, when it encountered a French warship near Alicante. The French captain demanded that the Spaniards fire salvos to salute the French. Instead the Spaniards opened fire with shot. The French shot back and, after a three-hour battle, the *Concepción* sank.

1688: The Spanish merchantman *Nuestra Señora de Buen Viaje* (24 cannons), coming from Genoa with 156 tons (158.5 tonnes) of mercury on board, sank about half a league off the east side of Ibiza, one of the Balearic Islands and only a few of her crew made it ashore.

1695: An English squadron of warships under the command of Sir George Rooke was cruising off Cape St. Vicente near Gibraltar when the Spanish galleon *Nuestra Señora de Rosario* (800 tons/813 tonnes), commanded by Captain Mario de Corcovado and bringing 2.5 million pesos from Buenos Aires, was driven ashore on the treacherous area of Arenas Gordas in the delta of the Guadalquivir. Contemporary divers recovered about half of this treasure. Soon after, the same English ships attacked the Spanish galleon *Santa Teresa de Ávila*, commanded by Captain Diego Asencio de Vicuña and coming from Havana with 1.32 million pesos in treasure, forcing her to seek safety in Lisbon. While entering the Tagus River, she wrecked on a shoal near Setúbal and was a total loss.

Drawing of a 11th century Crusader ship.

1696: The Spanish warship *San Carlos* (84 cannons), coming from Naples with over 2 million pesos in treasure, sank close to Santi Petri in a storm while attempting to reach Cádiz and over 150 men perished.

1702: An Anglo-Dutch fleet intercepted a French-Spanish treasure fleet sailing from the New World to Spain off the Spanish coast. Unable to reach Cádiz Bay, the fleet fled north and entered Vigo Bay where all 29 ships ran aground. Some were set on fire, to prevent their treasures from falling into enemy hands. Only a small portion of treasure was removed before the British and Dutch warships came into the harbor. The British warship HMS *Monmouth* was towing the captured Spanish galleon *Santo Cristo de Maracaibo* to England. She carried more than 2 million pesos in treasure and had been badly damaged. She struck an unmarked rock and sank in 300 to 400 feet (91 to 122 meters) of water. The cost to Spain in treasure, ships, and cannons was estimated at over 30 million pesos, making it one of Spain's greatest losses. Over the years numerous expeditions have failed to recover any of the treasure because the wrecks lie under deep mud. In 1893 a San Francisco syndicate sold $750,000 in stock to finance salvaging these ships, but was thwarted by the mud. During the past three decades at least five groups have failed to find this elusive wreck.

1704: The Spanish merchantman *Nuestra Señora de San Andrés* (675 tons/686 tonnes, 26 cannons), commanded by Captain Marcos de Aramburu and sailing between Cádiz and Genoa with 356,000 pesos in silver specie, was dashed to pieces in a storm off the northwest side of Mallorca, one of the Balearic Islands. Only two men were saved.

1706: The Dutch East Indiaman *Hazelnoot* (630 tons/640 tonnes, 42 cannons), commanded by Captain Jakob de Boer and returning from Batavia with 785,000 guilders in cargo, was chased by Barbary Coast corsairs off northwest Spain. Rather than lose the ship and cargo to the pirates, the captain ran the *Hazelnoot* aground and set it on fire 4 leagues west of La Coruña.

1750: The Dutch East Indiaman *Wapen Van Hoorn* (850 tons/864 tonnes), commanded by Captain Jakob Greef and coming from Ceylon with a cargo valued at 280,000 guilders, sank in deep water during a storm off Cape Finisterre, a rocky promontory in extreme northwest Spain. Only two of the crew survived.

1751–53: During a furious storm more than twenty large ships were lost in Cádiz Bay, including the galleon *Santissima Trinidad* (1,200 tons/1219 tonnes), which carried more than 3 million pesos in treasure. None of the treasure was ever salvaged. The following year a storm caused the total loss of over 100 large ships, including two unidentified French ships with over 750,000 livres in gold and silver. And once again in 1753 a storm sank over forty large ships in the bay, including the warship *Neptune*, which had just arrived from Mexico, carrying 235,000 pesos in treasure.

1772: The Portuguese ship *São Joseph*, returning from Brazil "with a large quantity of gold," was making for Lisbon when a tempest forced her to run way to the north and she was totally lost at Cape Oregal on the northwestern tip of Spain. A concealed bag of diamonds worth over 125,000 crusadoes was found on one of the survivors who struggled ashore.

1772: Two Spanish galleons, the *Belle Limenna* and *San José*, returning from Mexico with a combined treasure valued at 674,000 pesos, struck upon the Bar of Sanlúcar and were total losses.

1801: Two Spanish galleons—the *Nuestra Señora de Barcelona*, and the *Nuestra Señora del Popolo*—carrying a total of over 3 million pesos in treasure from the New World, were close to their final destination in Cádiz when a large English warship attacked and sank them off Cabareta Point, not far from Cádiz.

1821: The Portuguese merchantman *Doña María* (2,000 tons/2032 tonnes, 44 cannons), had just left Cádiz for Lisbon with 288 chests of Spanish silver specie, when a storm arose. The ship first hit some rocks and then sank in deeper water. Most of her people were saved, but none of the silver was recovered.

(Facing, top image) The anaerobic muddy sea floor of Cadíz Bay provides excellent preservation of wooden shipwrecks, as evidenced by this bow of a late fifteenth-century caravel, which was pulled up in a fisherman's net. *(Facing, lower image)* The walled enclosed port city of Dubrovnik (formerly Ragusa), Yugoslavia, as it looks today.

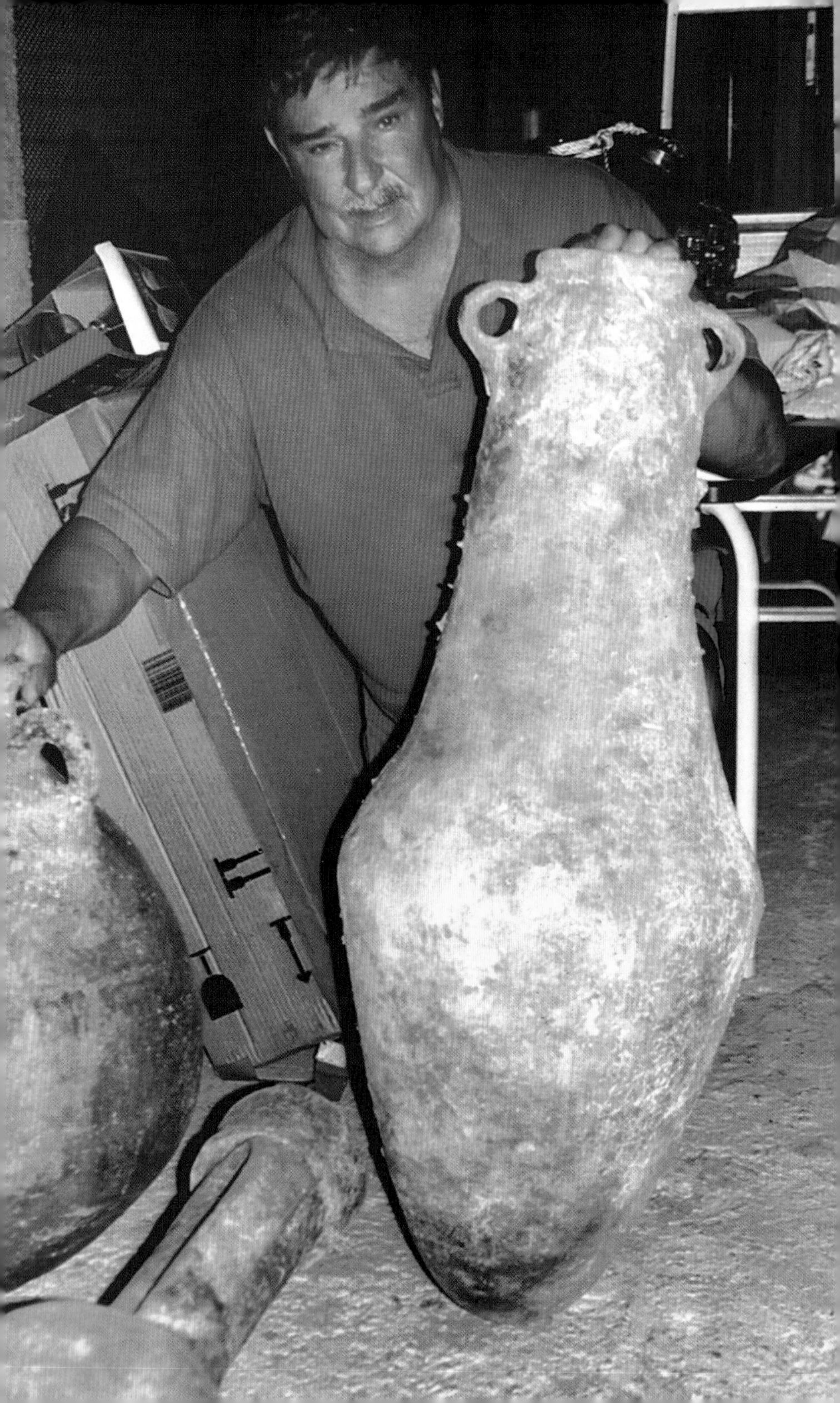

CHAPTER 18

EUROPE'S RICHEST SHIPWRECKS

There is speculation that as long ago as 6000 B.C settlers from Sicily reached the Maltese Islands via raft or other primitive vessels. Throughout the ages these three Mediterranean islands, strategically located midway between Sicily and north Africa, have been at the crossroads of history. The prehistoric Phoenicians, Minoans and Egyptians all used their good harbors to break their north-south and east-west voyages. During the Punic Wars the Romans captured the islands. They were beneficent rulers for 750 years. Trade increased, and the islands prospered. In A.D. 60 St. Paul was shipwrecked on Malta.

The Byzantine Empire governed the islands from 533 until ousted in 870 by Arabs, who found the islands a perfect place from which to launch piratical attacks on Christian shipping. Crusaders, led by Count Roger of Normandy who had established a kingdom in Sicily, took the islands in 1090. In 1283 an important naval battle was fought between Aragonese and Angevins in Malta's main harbor. Two Angevin ships sank with a large amount of gold. In 1530 the Knights of Malta, who began a rule that lasted for 275 years and focused on battling the Ottoman empire and protecting Christian shipping, fought the swarm of Muslim pirates under control of the Sultans in Constantinople.

(Facing) Robert Marx with an eighth-century B.C. Phoenician amphora he found off Majorca Island, Spain.

The Vikings sailed far and wide for centuries, raiding and plundering ports and even inland cities throughout Europe and the Mediterranean.

The greatest seafarers and traders of antiquity were the Phoenicians, an ancient maritime people who sailed farther and traded better than anyone else. Along the way they founded colonies, notably Carthage, and introduced the world's first alphabet based on symbols for sounds. They sailed from ports in present-day Syria and Lebanon to Africa, Arabia, the British Isles and to the far-off Azores Islands. Many believe they even reached Brazil. Around 1,200 B.C. they started making voyages to Cornwall on the southwest coast of England to obtain copper and tin, metals essential for making bronze tools, weapons and other trade goods. They also sought gold, ivory and other products. In return they traded carved furniture and timber made from the legendary cedars of Lebanon, which they also used in shipbuilding. They also traded Tyrian purple (a precious dye made from the murex shell), silk, cloth, glass (which they invented) and other trade items.

The port of Amsterdam in 1657, the home base of the Dutch East Indiamen.

The Scandinavians, who are remembered today for the prowess of the Vikings and the explorations of the Norsemen, were relatively slow to develop shipbuilding and seafaring skills. Until the seventh century they took to the icy northern seas in small skin-covered vessels, but once they were ready to sail far, there was no stopping them. By 874 Norsemen reached Iceland, then Greenland in 985, and Vinland in 1000 or 1001. The Vikings battered the British Isles and Europe from the eighth to the eleventh centuries, and their fleets, using both sail and oars, terrorized the entire Mediterranean. In 986 a fleet of sixty to seventy Viking ships, returning from a six-month spree in the Mediterranean, were hit by a storm. They went into Cádiz Bay on the south coast of Spain where all but three of the ships sank.

Throughout antiquity the Baltic Sea supplied a large percentage of the herring that were a staple of the European diet. In the latter part of the sixteenth century the herring fisheries declined when the herring migrated into the North Sea, probably because the salinity of the water had decreased. However, the nations bordering the Baltic remained Europe's chief source of masts, rigging, flax and tar.

This Dutch silver ducatoon, dated 1624, was minted in Utrecht, Holland.

The Hanseatic League, a confederation of late medieval merchant associations in Germany and the Baltic, was created in the thirteenth century to undertake large-scale maritime trade. It dominated trade and ship building during the Middle Ages, and by the early years of the fourteenth century, Hansa merchants controlled trade in over thirty ports bordering the Baltic and North Seas, as well as seven ports in England and Bergen in Norway. Their monopoly on sea trade was so great that they even furnished northern Europe with goods from the major ports of Italy, Spain and Portugal. Much of their trade was on the barter system. They exchanged dried herring for Portuguese wines in Lisbon, for example, and in Andalusian ports traded fish, grain, honey, furs and other products for Spanish olive oil, wine, and leather goods. In the late fifteenth century English merchants began challenging their monopolies and soon seized a great deal of their trade. By the end of the sixteenth century, with so much wealth coming to Europe from the New World and the Orient, the Hanseatic League declined in importance and soon after creased to exist.

1476: A Portuguese squadron of warships intercepted a convoy sailing from Cádiz, Spain, to Flanders. A battle ensued and four of

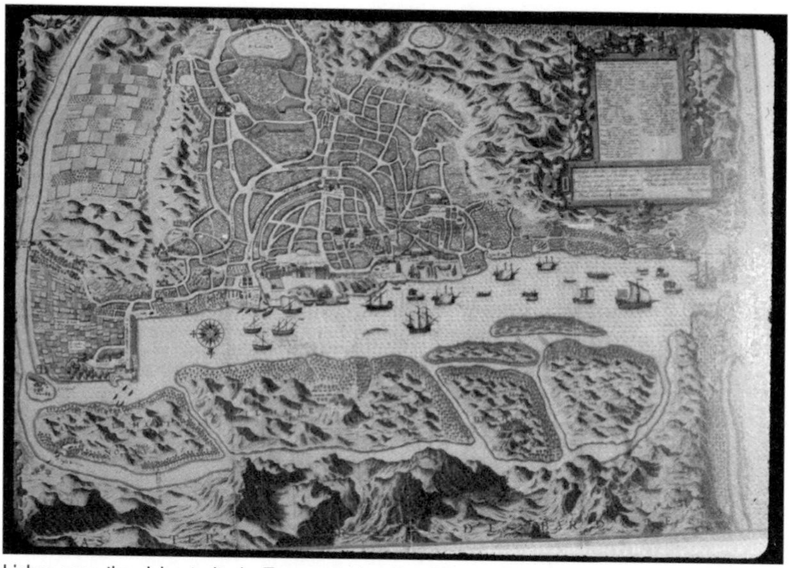

Lisbon was the richest city in Europe during the Colonial Period and the home port of the Portuguese East Indiamen and Brazil fleet ships.

the merchant vessels, including two Genovese ships carrying 180,000 gold coins, were sunk off Cape Santa Maria on the Algarve Coast, Portugal.

1514: A fleet of five Portuguese ships was dispatched by the king of Portugal to Rome to present Pope Leo X with live elephants, black panthers, leopards and some of the most fantastic treasures ever seen. They were part of the colossal amount of treasure that Admiral Afonso de Albuquerque had plundered from many nations in the Orient. The fleet's flagship sank in a storm near Orbetello, on the Tuscan Coast of Italy, with the richest treasure ever lost in the Mediterranean Sea up to that time.

1519: The Portuguese East Indiaman *São Antonio* (1,200 tons/1219 tonnes, 38 cannons), commanded by Captain Manuel de Sousa and preparing to sail to India with 220,000 crusadoes in gold and silver, struck upon the wreckage of a sunken ship at the mouth of the Tagus River, Portugal, and sank soon afterwards. Only a few people were saved.

1522: The Portuguese merchantman *Espera*, sailing from Lisbon and Oporto to Flanders with 230,000 crusadoes in treasure, was wrecked in a storm near Cap Ferrat, France, in the Bay of Biscay.

1524: The Portuguese East Indiaman *São Jorge* (470 tons/477.5 tonnes), returning from Goa with more than 400,000 crusadoes, was lost near Seisembra, not far from Lisbon. Bales of silks and spices came ashore for days afterwards. She was sailing with a vessel of the same name *(see below)* and they were lost in the same area. Just as today, ships often had the same names. In a Spanish fleet there were sometimes a dozen "Rosario"s or "Santa Margarita"s.

1524: The Portuguese East Indiaman *São Jorge* (1,900 tons/ 1,930.5 tonnes, 64 bronze cannons), was returning from India with the last viceroy as a prisoner and with an unknown amount of treasure. Instead of entering the mouth of the Tagus River as was customary, the ship anchored off Seisembra and her treasure and other cargo were illegally unloaded, all of which later proved to be contraband. Her registered cargo was valued at only 250,000 crusadoes, but it was estimated that five times that amount came as contraband. While the unloading was underway, a storm caused the ship to sink.

1525: The Portuguese East Indiaman *Santa Maria do Paraizo* (700 tons/711 tonnes), left for the Far East with 355,000 crusadoes in gold and silver to purchase the exotic products of the Orient. But just three hours after leaving Belém, the port of Lisbon, a storm arose and as the ship tried to re-enter the Tagus River, she struck upon the Shoals of Cachopos and was a total loss.

1525: The Portuguese East Indiaman *São Vicente,* commanded by Captain Francisco d'Anaia and with 250,000 crusadoes in gold and silver on board, was blown on the Shoal of Cachopos while leaving Lisbon's Tagus River. She quickly broke into pieces and only six people and a dog were saved.

1530: The Portuguese East Indiaman *Santa Catarina de Monte Sinai* (890 tons/904 tonnes, 42 cannons), commanded by Captain Pedro Vaz da Cunha and returning from India to Lisbon with a cargo valued at 230,000 crusadoes, was attacked by a French pirate off Cape San Vicente. Ran aground at Lagos in the Algarve, she was a total loss.

1551: The Portuguese merchantman *São Bento,* commanded by Captain Pero Lopes de Sampaio and sailing between Lisbon and Flanders with a cargo of spices and 60,000 crusadoes in silver specie, was wrecked in a storm near St. Nazarre, France, in the Bay of Biscay.

1553: The Portuguese East Indiaman *São Antonio*, commanded by Captain Manuel de Menedez and preparing to sail to India from Lisbon in the armada of Captain Fernão Álvares Cabral with over 400,000 crusadoes in gold and silver already loaded on the ship, caught fire and was totally lost on the Tagus River off Belém, near Lisbon.

1555: Reports reached Madrid that three very rich ships coming from Mexico were wrecked several leagues south of Nazaré, Portugal, and only a few people were saved. Two large chests containing gold jewelry and objects made of silver, jade and ivory were found on the shore among hundreds of bodies.

1556: The Portuguese East Indiaman *São João* (1,500 tons/1,524 tonnes), was returning from India to Lisbon with a cargo valued at over 1 million crusadoes when four Barbary pirate vessels attacked. The captain ran her aground near Faro, Portugal, and set her on fire. The pirates massacred many of the people.

1559: The Portuguese East Indiaman *Nossa Senhora da Barca*, commanded by Captain Jorge de Menendes and returning from India with "a very valuable cargo," was only a few hours' sail from entering the Tagus River when a storm caused her to wreck off Cabo da Roca. Only a few of her people were saved.

1566: The Spanish galleon *Nuestra Señora de la Limpia Concepción* (450 tons/457 tonnes), commanded by Captain Francisco de Áviles, was sailing between Veracruz and Spain with 1.25 million pesos. She stopped in the Azores after being pursued by Barbary corsairs. There she took on an additional 1.9 million pesos in treasure from two galleons, which had been damaged in a hurricane off Bermuda and were unable to sail further. So, with over 3 million pesos in treasure, she headed for Seville when she sank in a fierce storm about 2 miles (3 kilometers) south of Lagos, Portugal. There were very few survivors.

1568: Two Spanish merchantmen returning from the New World—the *Jesus* (220 tons/223.5 tonnes), commanded by Captain Juan Bautista Simon and carrying 235,000 pesos in treasure, and the *San Francisco* (250 tons/254 tonnes), commanded by Captain Benito Martínez and carrying 360,000 pesos in treasure—were attacked by French pirates off Cape St. Vicente, Portugal, and sunk with a total loss of lives and treasure.

1569: The Spanish galley *Nuestra Señora de Atocha*, sailing between Sanlúcar de Barrameda and Naples with 234,000 pesos in treasure on board, wrecked in a storm near the port of Mazzara del Vallo, located on the southwestern tip of Sicily.

1576: Four Spanish galleys, under the command of Captain Domingo de Larrauri and coming from Genoa with 320 tons (325 tonnes) of mercury, wrecked trying to enter Nice, France, and only a few men were saved. Because mercury was essential for the production of gold and silver in the New World, the Spanish mounted a salvage effort, which recovered several tons of mercury; the rest had been covered over by sand.

1587: The Armada of Tierra Firme, returning from Panama and Havana and commanded by Captain General Álvaro Flores de Quinones, was struck by a bad storm as it approached Cádiz Bay. Six rich galleons, carrying a total of 2.18 million pesos in treasure, were lost. The *Santa María de Madalena* (300 tons/304 tonnes), commanded by Captain Francisco Romero, was one of five wrecked on the Bar of Sanlúcar de Barrameda. Another, the *San Juan* (150 tons/152 tonnes), commanded by Captain Gonzalo Milanés de Torres, sank about a half league off Portimáo, Portugal.

1590: The Spanish galley *Buen Jesús*, commanded by Captain José de Miranda and sailing between Cádiz and Flanders with 430,000 pesos in silver specie (the pay for the Spanish army fighting with the Dutch), was totally lost in a storm when she struck on the west side of Isle de Rey, France, in the Bay of Biscay.

1602: A fleet of British warships attacked the port of Coimbra, Portugal, where a number of rich ships were hiding. The *Almiranta, Trinidad* (800 tons/813 tonnes), commanded by Captain Frederico Spinola and with 1.24 million pesos in treasure, was coming from Mexico. The *Trinidad* and four other rich ships were sunk in the fighting. The English captured one unidentified galleon with over 1 million pesos in treasure on board.

1605: The Portuguese East Indiaman *Nossa Senhora da Salvaçao* (1,200 tons/1,219 tonnes, 34 cannons), commanded by Captain João de Castro and returning from India to Lisbon with a cargo valued at 1.8 million crusadoes, plus nine boxes of pearls, diamonds and precious stones, was totally lost on the beach at Cascais, located about 6 miles (10 kilometers) southwest of Lisbon. In 1962 fishermen pulled up three bronze cannons near this beach that may have come from this wreck.

1606: The Portuguese East Indiaman *Nossa Senhora dos Mártires* (1,300 tons/1,321 tonnes, 38 cannons), commanded by Captain Manuel Soares, was returning from India to Lisbon with a cargo valued at 480,000 crusadoes when she wrecked in a bad storm off Torre de São Julião near the Bar of Lisbon. There were some survivors.

1606: An unidentified Spanish galleon returning from the New World "with a large amount of treasure aboard" was unable to enter Cádiz because of a Barbary pirate blockade. She went to Gibraltar and before any of her treasure could be unloaded, six of the pirate vessels appeared. The Spaniards set fire to their galleon and she blew up with a great loss of life and all of the treasure on board.

1607: The Portuguese East Indiaman *Nossa Senhora da Salvaçao* commanded by Captain João de Menezes and sailing from India to Lisbon, was lost just an hour's sail away from Lisbon. She went to pieces off Cascais, loaded with over 1.8 million crusadoes in treasure, including eleven chests of gifts for the Portuguese king from the king of Siam. Several days later another Portuguese East Indiaman, the *Nossa Senhora dos Martyres* (1,600 tons/1,626 tonnes), commanded by Captain Manuel Barreto Rolim and carrying 1.2 million crusadoes in cargo, wrecked at Cabo do Roca, the southwest extremity of Portugal.

1609: The Spanish ship *San Antonio* (100 tons/101 tonnes), commanded by Captain Gonzalo de la Rocha, was sailing between Cádiz and Genoa and carrying 198,000 pesos in silver specie for the purchase of mercury from Austria, was attacked by a Dutch warship and wrecked a league east of Gibraltar. Her crew set her on fire to deprive the Dutch of her coins and she blew up, raining coins all over the beach.

1609: The British East Indiaman *Union*, commanded by Captain Richard Rowles and sailing between the Orient and England with "a very valuable cargo," was wrecked near Audierne on the coast of Brittany, France, and some of her bales of spices washed ashore. Documents state that she carried "fourteen large chests with the golden riches of the East Indies."

The port of Gibraltar showing a rich Genovese merchantman on fire and sinking near the dock, after being attacked by Moorish pirates.

1610: The Portuguese East Indiaman *Nossa Senhora da Oliveira* (1,200 tons/1,219 tonnes, 34 cannons), commanded by Captain Manuel Teles de Meneses and sailing for India with 410,000 crusadoes in treasure on board, was wrecked crossing the Bar of Lisbon and then sank in deep water. Some people were saved. A ship sailing with her, the *Nossa Senhora da Livramento* (960 tons/975 tonnes), commanded by Captain João da Costa Travassos and carrying 673,000 crusadoes in treasure, wrecked on a shoal named El Cabeça Seca near the entrance of the Tagus River.

1612: The Dutch East Indiaman *Bantam* (900 tons/914.5 tonnes; some documents state it was 700 tons), sailing between Bantam, Indonesia and Amsterdam, was totally lost in Amelander Gat in the Friesian Islands in the North Sea. She carried a large cargo of spices, porcelain, and many chests of precious stones, pearls and gold and silver objects.

1612: The Portuguese East Indiaman *Nossa Senhora do Belém* (2,100 tons/2,133 tonnes, 58 cannons), commanded by Captain Manuel Teles de Tavora and sailing from Lisbon to India with "a large amount of gold and silver" on board, wrecked soon after leaving the Tagus River on a reef called el Cabeza Seca.

1615: Although there was a truce between Spain and Holland, the Spanish king sent an armada of warships with 50,000 soldiers to be off-loaded in Flanders, ready to fight when the truce ended. The flagship Capitana, *San Luis* (1,100 tons/1,118 tonnes), commanded by Admiral Diego Brochero and carrying 460,000 pesos in gold and silver specie to pay the soldiers, sank about a half league north of Dunkirk, Belgium, in the English Channel, with a great loss of life.

1616: The Dutch East Indiaman *Gelderland* (500 tons/508 tonnes) had just left the port of Texel with over 240,000 guilders in silver and gold specie when she wrecked during a storm near Flushing, Holland. Three salvage expeditions failed to recover any of her treasure.

1618: The Spanish advice boat *Las Augustias* (50 tons/51 tonnes), commanded by Captain Pedro Diaz Cordero and sailing between Veracruz and Sanlúcar de Barrameda, was sunk in a storm off Cape St. Vincent, Portugal. An investigation into the loss revealed she was carrying 290,000 pesos in contraband treasure and her captain was sentenced to serve in the royal galleys for the rest of his life.

1621: The Portuguese East Indiaman *Nossa Senhora da Conceição* (1,200 tons/1,219 tonnes, 38 cannons), commanded by Captain Luis da Sousa and coming from India to Lisbon with a cargo valued at 430,000 crusadoes, plus 23 chests of diamonds and other precious stones, was attacked by 17 Barbary pirate vessels commanded by Admiral Cara-Mustafa. After a long battle, the captain ran the badly damaged vessel ashore near Ericeira, Portugal, where it was set on fire to keep the cargo out of the pirates' grasp. Salvors soon recovered six of her bronze cannons, but nothing more.

1625: The Portuguese East Indiaman *Santa Helena* (650 tons/660.5 tonnes), commanded by Captain Pedro d'Anaia, was sailing from Goa to Lisbon with a cargo valued at 860,000 crusadoes. Near Lisbon, an advice boat came with orders to head for La Corunna, Spain, to avoid Barbary pirates hovering off the bar of Lisbon. A gale, which kept the ship from entering La Coruña, caused it to sink off Biarritz, France, with a total loss of life. In 1977 a sports diver raised two bronze cannons believed to be from this wreck. They are on display in the Oceanographic Museum in Biarritz.

1625: The Portuguese East Indiaman *São Francisco Xavier* (800 tons/813 tonnes), sailing in the armada of Captain Antonio Telo from

India to Lisbon with 400,000 crusadoes of treasure, plus four boxes of diamonds and precious stones, was lost on the bar of Lisbon. Only 17 men and one box of diamonds and precious stones were saved.

1625: The Spanish galleon *San Juan*, returning from Mexico to Spain with 875,000 pesos in gold and silver, was forced to enter Lisbon because of weather (some documents say to unload contraband treasure, a common occurrence at this time). On entering the mouth of the Tagus River, she struck upon the shoals of Cachopos and was totally lost. Over the years dozens of ships, many of them returning Portuguese East Indiamen, have wrecked on these shoals.

1625: The Dutch East Indiaman *Alkmaar* (650 tons/660.5 tonnes), commanded by Captain Henrik Koster and sailing for Batavia with 380,000 guilders in gold and silver bullion and specie, sank in the roadstead of Texel just hours before sailing.

1625: The Dutch East Indiaman *Schoonhoven* (400 tons/406.5 tonnes, 22 cannons), commanded by Captain Kornelis Hartman, coming from India, was carrying 684,000 guilders in cargo. She was wrecked near Cabo da Roca, Portugal. One hundred ninety-eight people were rescued and imprisoned in Lisbon.

1626: The Portuguese East Indiaman, *Santa Catalina* (1,200 tons/1,219 tonnes), was lost at Cabo da Roca, the southwestern most point of Portugal only a few miles from her destination of Lisbon after an uneventful voyage of over 9,000 miles (1,448 kilometers) from the Far East. She was the flagship of a fleet of seven ships, carrying over 3.5 million crusadoes in treasure, plus 22 chests of diamonds, rubies and other precious stones. She quickly went to pieces in the surf and fewer than a dozen of the 400 people aboard reached shore. A massive salvage effort was initiated, but shifting sands covered the wreck site and contemporary salvors recovered only four of her 56 bronze cannons.

1626: The Dutch East Indiaman *Alkmaar* (600 tons/609 tonnes) was heading for Batavia, carrying over 200,000 guilders in silver specie when lost near Oporto, Portugal. Crew members who got ashore were later ransomed.

1626: The Portuguese East Indiaman *São Bartolomeu*, returning from the Far East with over 1 million crusadoes in Oriental treasures,

Dunkirk and St. Malo, France, were Europe's two main pirate bases from which ships were sent as far as the Orient and the New World.

found the Dutch in wait off Lisbon, and she headed for a port in northern Spain. Four Spanish galleons, also returning from the New World, joined this ship when they learned that the Dutch were also off the coast near Cádiz. The ships were caught in a bad storm in the Bay of Biscay and all five went down with considerable amounts of treasure near Biarritz, France.

1630: One of greatest losses of life in this period occurred with the wreck of the Portuguese East Indiaman *Santo Inácio de Loiola* (1,300 tons/1,321 tonnes, 44 cannons), commanded by Captain Jorge de Almeida. Off the Cape of Good Hope she picked up the crew and passengers of two foundering ships, and off Santa Helena took on more from a storm-damaged ship. With standing-room-only, she headed for Lisbon with over 1,700 people, a cargo valued at 3.78 million crusadoes, and a large amount of Chinese porcelain. She was attempting to pass near the shoals of Cachopos when she wrecked at Oeiras. There were only 118 survivors.

1631: The Dutch East Indiaman *Devente* (550 tons/559 tonnes), commanded by Captain Klaas Jansz Bruin and with over 200,000 guilders in silver and gold specie, sailed for Batavia and sank just outside of the port of Texel, an island in the southwest Friesian Islands off Holland. Contemporary salvors were unable to recover any of her treasure.

1636: The Portuguese East Indiaman *Santa Catalina de Ribamar* (1,900 tons/1,930.5 tonnes), commanded by Captain Luis de Castanheda Vasconcelos and returning from India with a cargo valued at over 1 million crusadoes, was wrecked during a storm on Guincho Beach, Portugal. Only thirty of the 470 people on board survived.

1637: The Portuguese ship *Nossa Senhora da Conceição,* sailing from Lisbon to India and Malacca with 450,000 crusadoes in gold and silver bullion and specie, was attacked by Barbary pirates and caught fire during the battle and sank near Ericeira, Portugal.

1639: The Dutch East Indiaman *Zwolle*, carrying over 250,000 guilders in Oriental treasure and almost home after the long voyage from Batavia, was lost in a storm entering the port of Texel.

1640: The Dutch East Indiaman *Witte Olifant* (1,000 tons/1,016 tonnes, 38 cannons), loaded with a "substantial treasure," was preparing to set sail for Batavia when she sank in a violent storm in the roadstead of Texel. All the people were saved, but none of the treasure.

1643: The Spanish galleon *Santa Ana* (500 tons/508 tonnes), commanded by Captain Felipe Garcia de Salamanca and carrying 690,000 pesos in treasure from Veracruz, Mexico, sank during a storm a league south of Cape St. Vincent, Portugal. King Philip IV was especially upset at the los of this ship because aboard her was a solid gold nugget reportedly weighing about 100 pounds (45 kilograms), a gift to him from the viceroy of Peru.

1649: The Portuguese East Indiaman *Santa Catalina* (1,200 tons/1,219 tonnes), was the flagship of a fleet of seven ships. She carried over 2.5 million crusadoes in treasure, plus 22 chests of diamonds, rubies, and other precious stones. During the night, faulty navigation led the vessel to strike on Cabo da Roca, where she quickly went to pieces. Fewer than a dozen of the 600 people aboard her were able to get ashore.

1649: The Dutch East Indiaman *Rotterdam* (1,100 tons/1,18 tonnes), en route to Batavia with an unknown amount of treasure, put into Goedereede on the west part of the island of Goeree-Overflakkee for repairs. When continuing her voyage, she was totally lost in the Sluise Gat near Wielingen, Holland. There were very few survivors.

1649: The Dutch East Indiaman *Zwolle* (360 tons/366 tonnes, 22 cannons), returning from Batavia with 265,000 guilders in Oriental objects, plus spices and porcelain, was totally lost while trying to enter the port of Texel.

1650: The Portuguese East Indiaman *São Francisco* (1,800 tons/1,829 tonnes), commanded by Captain Luis Dultra Corte-Real, was sailing from Lisbon to India with a first stop in Brazil. She was carrying 1.23 million crusadoes in gold and silver bullion and specie. While passing near the Azores, the ship was badly damaged in a battle with Dutch privateers. She headed back to Lisbon and just north of this port was attacked by English privateers. Her captain ran her aground and set her on fire near Ericeira to keep her treasure from being captured.

1662: The Dutch East Indiaman *Anjelier* (440 tons/447 tonnes), commanded by Captain Barend Barendsz Hans and returning from Batavia with 383,000 guilders in cargo, was wrecked and totally lost at Terschilling Island, one of the West Friesian Islands, belonging to the Netherlands.

1665: A fleet, under the command of Pieter de Bitter and coming from Batavia, was struck by a storm in the North Sea. The Dutch East Indiaman *Amstelland* (700 tons/711 tonnes), commanded by Captain Theunis Gijsbertsz, was forced to seek safety in Bergen, Norway. Leaving there she wrecked on a small island just east of Terschilling Island, Holland. She was partially salvaged at the time, but a report states that most of her 45,000 pieces of Chinese porcelain were not recovered because they were in the bottom of the ship serving as ballast.

1666: The Dutch East Indiaman *Kalf* (320 tons/325 tonnes), commanded by Captain Pieter Korf and sailing between Bengal, India, and Holland with a cargo valued at 206,000 guilders, was lost off Vlieland Island, one of the Netherlands' West Friesian Islands.

1667: An unidentified German merchantman, owned by the Hanseatic merchants of Hamburg, sank close to Belém on the Tagus River with over half a million pesos in Spanish silver specie.

1672: The Portuguese East Indiaman *Nossa Senhora de Ajuda* (1,400 tons/1,422.5 tonnes), sailing in the armada of Captain João Correira de Sa with 480,000 crusadoes of treasure, sailed from Lisbon for Macao. Several hours after leaving the Tagus River, she wrecked at Cabo da Roca.

1674: The Portuguese East Indiaman *Nossa Senhora de Piedade* (1,200 tons/1,219 tonnes), coming from India with a cargo valued at 660,000 crusadoes, first stopped in Brazil where she picked up more cargo, including 16 tons (16.25 tonnes) of gold bars and coins. When approaching Lisbon, she was attacked by Algerian corsairs and wrecked near Cabo da Roca.

1674: The Spanish galleon *San Ignacio* (660 tons/670.5 tonnes, forty-four cannons), commanded by Captain Marcos Velasquez Millian and returning to Spain from Havana with 1.2 million pesos in gold and silver, was lost about 2 miles (3 kilometers) off Cape San Vicente in a storm. There were few survivors.

1675: Six unidentified Spanish merchantmen, in a fleet commanded by Prince Montesarchio and coming from Cádiz, were carrying over 2 million pesos in treasure. They were wrecked in the Straits of Messina, Italy, during a storm.

1677: The Spanish warship *Capitana* and a galleon named *San Gabriel,* in a squadron commanded by Captain-General Juan Roco de Castilla, were both carrying "large amounts of treasure." They sank during a storm near Pianosa Island, located south of Elba Island off the coast of Tuscany, Italy.

1678: An unidentified Venetian merchantman, sailing between Ragusa (now Dubrovnik), Yugoslavia, and Venice and with over 120,000 gold ducats on board, was wrecked and lost near the port of Bari on the southeast coast of Italy. Three salvage attempts failed to recover any treasure.

1683: The Dutch East Indiaman *Tidore* (1,094 tons/1,107.5 tonnes), commanded by Captain Jakob Been, was the flagship of a fleet returning from Batavia under the command of Hendrik van Oudshoorn. She carried 650,000 guilders in Oriental objects and was totally lost on Ameland, one of the Friesian Islands in the North Sea.

1683: The Dutch East Indiaman *Bantam,* was returning from Batavia with 383,000 guilders in cargo aboard, was lost during a storm off Vlissingen on Walcheren Island. English investors who had an interest in her cargo claimed she was really carrying a cargo valued at £2 million sterling.

1693: In December a mighty fleet of 166 merchantmen and forty warships, under command of Admiral Sir Francis Wheeler, gathered off Portsmouth, England, with the eighty-gun HMS *Sussex* as flagship. She carried 9 tons (9.14 tonnes) of gold coins the king ordered to be used to buy the goodwill of the duke of Savoy in England's war with France. The convoy stopped at Gibraltar and soon after set-

The port of Ragusa (now Dubrovnik), Yugoslavia, around 1500, provided a large number of the seamen on Spanish New World ships.

ting sail, the *Sussex* sank in a devastating storm. All hands but two went down with her. Bodies drifted ashore for days on the shores of Gibraltar. Odyssey Marine, of Tampa, Florida, after a three-year search finally located the wreck in 2001 at a depth of over a half-mile (.80 kilometer), and plans are now underway to salvage her. The *New York Times* claimed erroneously that her golden treasure is worth over $4 billion when in fact the figure is most likely between $5 million and $10 million.

1695: A British squadron of warships, under the command of Sir George Rooke, was cruising off Cape St. Vicente when the Spanish galleon *Nuestra Señora de Rosario* (800 tons/813 tonnes), commanded by Captain Mario de Corcovado and bringing 2.5 million pesos from Buenos Aires, was driven ashore on Arenas Gordas, near Sanlúcar de Barrameda, Spain. Soon after, the same British ships attacked the Spanish galleon *Santa Teresa de Ávila,* commanded by Captain Diego Asencio de Vicuña, which was coming from Havana with 1.32 million pesos in treasure, forcing it to seek safety in Lisbon. While entering the Tagus River, she wrecked on a shoal near Setúbal and was a total loss.

1696: The Dutch East Indiaman *Koning William* (1,197 tons/1,216 tonnes), (one of the largest Dutch ships afloat), was commanded by

Captain Jan Hendrik Thim and sailing for Batavia with a large cargo of gold and silver bullion and specie. She was lost on the coast near Zeebrugge, Belgium.

1696: During a storm an unidentified French merchantman, coming from the West Indies with 317,000 livres in gold and silver specie, attempted to enter Oporto and capsized and sank near the entrance to this port. The same storm accounted for the loss of an unidentified Portuguese merchantman coming from London with "a large amount of specie" after it collided with another ship off Viana, Portugal, and sank.

1697: The Dutch East Indiaman *Bantam* (1,138 tons/1,156 tonnes), commanded by Captain Pieter de Rande, was the flagship of a fleet coming from Batavia under the command of Hendrik Pronk, carrying a cargo valued at 385,000 guilders. She was totally lost at Vlissingen in Zealand province. Four other ships in this fleet disappeared and were lost in the Bay of Biscay. Another ship also named *Bantam* sank in the same area in 1683.

1700: An unidentified vessel owned by the Knights of Malta, carrying 55,000 Venetian gold ducats, sank in a storm within sight of Palermo on the island of Sicily and only some of her crew were saved.

1703: The Dutch East Indiaman *Renswoude* (588 tons/597.5 tonnes), commanded by Captain Leendert de Haan and sailing for Batavia with 236,000 guilders in treasure, was lost on Ameland Island, one of the Friesian Islands. Only a few of the crew were saved.

1711: The Spanish royal galley *Capitana*, commanded by Captain Juan Martín de Avila, captured a very rich Barbary pirate vessel with a "prodigious amount of treasure" that it had plundered from numerous vessels over a seven-month period. It was sunk in the Straits of Messina with a total loss of lives and treasure.

1712: The Spanish galleon *Almiranta*, returning from Havana with 1.87 million pesos in treasure, was wrecked in a storm near Faro, Portugal, where only 43 people made it ashore to safety. Three salvage efforts failed to recover any of the treasure.

1713: An unidentified galley, owned by the Pope, was coming from Genoa with 80,000 gold ducats on board when a storm drove it upon some rocks near Ferraio on the Tuscan coast of Italy and all of the gold coins were lost, as well as some of the men on board. Around this time a "very richly laden" Venetian galley, sailing for Ragusa (Dubrovnik), Yugoslavia, was totally lost near Venice.

1718: In a fleet returning from Brazil, the carrack *Nossa Senhora da Boa Viagem* (2,000 tons/2,032 tonnes), carrying over one million gold Brazilian coins, plus 24 tons (24.38 tonnes) of gold ingots, wrecked near Cape Mondego, just north of the port of Figueira da Foz, Portugal. Most of her crew survived, but all the gold was lost. Repeated contemporary salvage efforts have failed to locate it. Three other unidentified ships in the fleet wrecked between Nazarre and Figueira da Foz with unknown amounts of gold.

1720: The Dutch East Indiaman *Ter Nisse* (810 tons/823 tonnes, 48 cannons), commanded by Captain Thieleman Sterling, was two hours out of Texel en route to Batavia when she wrecked on Eijerland Island, Holland, in a tempest. About a third of the 330,000 guilders in treasure aboard her was recovered.

1723: An unidentified "very richly laden" Venetian galley was wrecked in the Gulf of Kvarner off the eastern side of the Istria Peninsula, Yugoslavia. Her loss plunged quite a few merchants in Venice into bankruptcy.

1725: The Dutch East Indiaman *Akerndam* (850 tons/864 tonnes), commanded by Captain Nikolaas de Roy and sailing for Batavia "with a large cargo of gold and silver," was wrecked at Rondoe Island, Norway, and very few men were saved.

1726: The Danish East Indiaman *Queen Anna Sophia* (1,800 tons/1,829 tonnes, 64 cannons), "carrying a vast amount of gold and silver," sank in a storm about half a league north of Lesau Island near the Danish Coast. Some people survived, but all cargo was lost.

1727: The Dutch East Indiaman *Luchtenburg* (850 tons/864 tonnes, 44 cannons), commanded by Captain Adriaan van Leeuwen and sailing for Batavia with 389,000 guilders in gold and silver specie, was lost in a storm near Wieringen Island, which is now connected to the mainland of Holland.

1728: Three Portuguese ships—the *São Joseph, São Vitoria* and the *Nossa Senhora de Graça*—returning from Brazil, first stopped at

Lisbon and then set sail for Oporto in northern Portugal. En route all three wrecked near Póvoa de Varzim, a seaport 18 miles (29 kilometers) north of Oporto. The *São Vitoria* was reportedly carrying "a large amount of Brazilian gold in bars and coins."

1729: The Dutch East Indiaman *Buren* (450 tons/457 tonnes), commanded by Captain Hendrik Huizing, set sail for China with 450,000 guilders in treasure on board, but after only a day out of the port of Texel, she was totally destroyed in a storm at Noorderhaaks, a large sand flat, west of the Marsdiep channel in the Dutch Wadden Sea.

1730: The Portuguese merchantman *Nossa Senhora da Vitoria* (1,800 tons/1,829 tonnes, 36 cannons), caught fire shortly after arriving from Cádiz with "a large amount of Spanish silver specie" and was totally lost in the middle of the Tagus River off Lisbon where she had anchored to unload.

1732: The Dutch East Indiaman *Midloo* (800 tons/813 tonnes), commanded by Captain Pieter Tinnekins and sailing from Batavia with 283,000 guilders in cargo, was totally lost at Terschilling Island, one of the West Friesian Islands in the North Sea. Contemporary salvors were able to recover only spars, rigging and two anchors.

1735: Two Dutch East Indiamen—the *Anna Catharina* (600 tons/610 tonnes), commanded by Captain Jacob de Prinse, and the *Vliegenthart* (850 tons/864 tonnes), commanded by Captain Kornelis van der Horst—sailed from the Dutch port of Rammenkens for the Far East. Both ships carried large amounts of gold and silver specie, as well as other cargo. Within an hour of leaving port, they struck upon the treacherous Schelde sand bank and quickly broke up. All 461 seamen, soldiers and passengers on both vessels drowned. Contemporary divers recovered only a few pieces of artillery. In 1979 two English treasure hunters, John Rose and Rex Cowan, using an archival chart marking the *Vliegenthart's* position, began searching for the ship. They found it the third summer and have recovered a considerable amount of gold and silver coins and other artifacts, but more treasure remains on the site. The *Anna Catherina,* which lies nearby, still has not been located.

1736: The Dutch East Indiaman *Hillegom* (1,150 tons/1,168.5 tonnes), commanded by Captain Jan Almees and en route to Batavia with 480,000 guilders in gold and silver specie, was only a day's sail out of Texel when a bad storm drove it back to port where it was lost.

1741: The Dutch East Indiaman *Oude Zijpe* (650 tons/660.5 tonnes, 42 cannons), commanded by Captain Joost Anker, was returning from Batavia with a cargo valued at 233,000 guilders when a storm caused the ship to be dashed to pieces off the town of Zandvoort in northern Holland.

1741: The Dutch East Indiaman *Bethlehem* (850 tons/864 tonnes), commanded by Captain Ijsbrand Moens, and sailing to Batavia with 450,000 guilders in treasure, was wrecked on a sand bank off Oostende, Belgium.

1742: The Dutch East Indiaman *Watervliet* (650 tons/660.5 tonnes, 34 cannons), commanded by Captain Gerbrand Swaag and sailing for Batavia with 350,000 guilders in gold and silver, wrecked and quickly went to pieces off Calais, France. Only 12 people were saved.

1742: The Dutch East Indiaman *Ananas* (650 tons/660.5 tonnes, 44 cannons), commanded by Captain Jakon Popta, was returning from Batavia with a cargo valued at 246,000 guilders. When she stopped at False Bay in South Africa, she took on 28 chests of silver specie of unknown value from an outward-bound Dutch ship that had sunk in the area two years before. A fierce storm forced the *Ananas* to seek refuge at Calais, and she wrecked entering the port.

1751: The Dutch East Indiaman *Amstelland* (850 tons/864 tonnes), commanded by Captain Hilde Hendriksz Hoek and sailing for Batavia from Texel with 340,000 guilders in treasure, was blown off course by a tempest and totally lost off the North Sea island of Zylt, Germany.

1753: The Dutch merchantman *Constance* (320 tons/325 tonnes), commanded by Captain Kamp and sailing from Texel to Lisbon with 218,000 guilders in silver specie, wrecked during a storm off Belém on the Tagus River, but most of her people were saved.

1758: The Dutch East Indiaman *Delft*, also known as the *Erfprins* (850 tons/864 tonnes), commanded by Captain Pieter Hogendorp and coming from Batavia with 298,000 guilders in cargo, wrecked in a storm near Calais, France. Only a few men were saved.

1759: The Dutch East Indiaman *Buitenzorg* (880 tons/894 tonnes), commanded by Captain Coenraad Dirk Wolk and coming from Batavia with 139,000 guilders in cargo, was totally lost during a storm as she entered Texel. The ship had sailed halfway around the world only to sink at her homeport.

1761: The French warship *Courageux* (74 cannons), commanded by Captain M. Dugue-Lambert, was coming from Santo Domingo with 86 chests of Spanish silver specie when she was captured by a British warship. The prize was taken to Gibraltar, where she sank during a tempest close to a place known as Ape's Hill. The treasure had not been off-loaded, and 470 of the 600 men on board died.

1767: The Dutch East Indiaman *Elizabeth Dorothea*, en route to Texel from Batavia, Indonesia, with a cargo valued at 980,000 guilders, was wrecked off the fishing village of Perten, near Texel. Local inhabitants who plundered some of her cargo were apprehended and punished.

1770: The Dutch East Indiaman *Vrouwe Geertruida* (1,100 tons/1,118 tonnes, 56 cannons), commanded by Captain Willem Vos van Overstraten, and sailing for Batavia with 550,000 guilders in gold and silver, was totally destroyed in a storm near Le Croisic on the coast of Brittany, France. Only a dozen or so men survived the disaster.

1776: The Spanish merchantman *Nuestra Señora de Milagros* (650 tons/660.5 tonnes), commanded by Captain Martín de Carmona Sierra and sailing between Cádiz and Naples with 340,000 pesos in silver and gold specie, wrecked in the Strait of Bonifacio, between the islands of Corsica and Sardinia. Salvors recovered about half of her treasure.

1778: The Dutch East Indiaman *Woestduin* (1,150 tons/1,168.5 tonnes), commanded by Captain Gerrit Berg and coming from Batavia with a cargo valued at 140,000 guilders, was totally lost in Zealand province between Deurloo and Noorderrassen. An inquiry into the cause of the ship's loss established that the captain and several rich merchants were smuggling precious gems worth over 250,000 guilders. This illustrates that the stated value of a cargo fails to reflect the contraband that was on virtually every ship.

1782: Four Spanish galleons in the Armada of Tierra Firme, commanded by Admiral Luis de Cordova, were wrecked at Gibraltar in a

Some of the ceramic cargo recovered from a seventh-century Byzantine wreck which was located off Akko, Israel.

bad storm. One, the *San Miguel* (74 cannons), commanded by Captain Juan Joaquin Moreno, carried 256,000 pesos in gold and silver specie.

1784: The Dutch merchant ship flying the Prussian flag, the *Breslau* (1,150 tons/1168.5 tonnes), commanded by Captain Jan Kornelis Roos and coming from China with a cargo valued at 659,000 guilders, was lost off Boulogne, France. There were very few survivors.

1786: An unidentified French merchantman (570 tons/579 tonnes), sailing between Genoa and Cádiz with 136 tons (138 tonnes) of mercury, was lost while attempting to enter the port of Nice during a storm.

1786: The Spanish galleon *San Pedro Alcántara* (1,483 tons/1,506 tonnes, 68 cannons), commanded by Captain Manuel de Equia, was sailing between Lima, Peru, and Cádiz, Spain, carrying an immense treasure of over 7 million pesos in gold and silver, plus Incan archaeological treasures (including some Incan mummies). She was dashed to pieces off Peniche 45 miles (73 kilometers) north of Lisbon. Intensive salvage operations went on for almost twenty years. Plunderers continue to search for about 1 million pesos in treasure believed to remain on the wreck.

1790: The Dutch East Indiaman *Negotie* (480 tons/488 tonnes), commanded by Captain Herman Driesman and sailing to Ceylon "with a large amount of treasure" aboard, wrecked and quickly went to pieces just an hour after sailing from the port of Texel.

1791: The Dutch East Indiaman *Zaabstroom* (564 tons/573 tonnes), commanded by Captain Jan Josbst Droop and sailing for Batavia with 690,000 guilders in gold and silver bullion and specie, ran aground and quickly broke up off Barfleur, near Le Havre, France. Barfleur was one of the most important ports in medieval Europe and many rich ships were lost there over the centuries.

1793: The French warship *Le Scipion* (74 cannons), commanded by Captain M. de Goy, was captured by Lord Hood at Toulon and taken to Leghorn (Livorno) Harbor, Italy, to be provisioned. After leaving Leghorn she caught fire and exploded 4 miles (6.5 kilometers) from the port, taking all but a few of the 640 souls aboard to the bottom. Silver specie valued at £256,000 sterling also sank with her.

1794: The British warship *Ardent* (64 cannons), commanded by Captain Robert Manners Sutton, was cruising close to the port of Villefranche-sur-Mer, France, with 22 chests of gold and silver specie that had been captured from a French merchantman several days before. She caught on fire and blew up, taking the treasure and all of the more than 500 people on board down with her.

1794: The Dutch East Indiaman *Zorg* (900 tons/914.5 tonnes), commanded by Captain Gerard Olthof and en route to Batavia with "a substantial amount of gold and silver," was first forced into Plymouth, England, because of bad weather. When she was underway again, she ran into another storm and was totally destroyed off Boulogne, France.

1795: After a battle between French and British fleets in the Gulf of Genoa, the damaged British warship *Illustrious* (74 cannons), commanded by Captain Thomas Lenox Frederick, was towed by another British warship and anchored in Valenbe Bay near Avenza, off the coast of Tuscany, Italy. A storm drove her on shore where she caught fire and blew up, taking 125 men and about £220,000 sterling in silver specie to the bottom.

1795: French warship *L'Alcide* (74 cannons), was blown up in a battle by two British warships of Admiral Hotham's fleet and she

A salvage operation underway off Peniche, Portugal, in 1795 on the Spanish galleon *San Pedro Alcantara*. Free divers recovered over 12 million pesos in treasure.

went down near Hyeres Island, France, with 350 men. Some 300 others were rescued, as well as "a large amount of treasure," which was pay for French ships in the port of Toulon.

1796: A French fleet of 44 warships carrying 17,000 men for the invasion of Ireland, under the command of Vice-Admiral Morard de Galles, set sail from Brest for Bantry Bay, Ireland. Due to faulty navigation, the French warship *Seduissant* (74 cannons) struck on a rock near Grand Stevenec in the Passage du Raz, France, and quickly sank, taking 680 of the 1,300 men on board to the bottom, as well as "a considerable amount of treasure." Two salvage attempts failed to find the gold and silver specie.

1800: The British warship *Queen Charlotte* (110 guns), commanded by Captain Todd and cruising between Leghorn and Gorgona Island, caught on fire and blew up, taking over 700 of the 837 men on board to the bottom, along with £185,000 sterling in silver specie.

1804: One of the most sought-after wrecks in modern times is the Spanish galleon *Nuestra Señora de Mercedes* (970 tons/985.5 tonnes), which carried over 5 million pesos in treasure, including 120,000 gold doubloons. During a battle with the British, she blew up and sank in about 1,000 feet (305 meters) of water approximately a mile (1.5 kilometer) off Cape St. Vicente, Portugal.

1810: The Portuguese merchantman *San Juan Principe* commanded by Captain R.F.J. Lobo and carrying 330,000 crusadoes in gold and silver specie, was lost in a storm on the east side of Gibraltar. Only 116 of 315 people on board survived.

1811: The British warship *Minotaur* (74 cannons), commanded by Captain John Barrett, was escorting a convoy of over sixty merchantmen from Sweden to England when she wrecked in a storm, along with several of the merchantmen, on the Haak Sands near the port of Texel. Only 110 of the 590 souls on board were saved. She carried over £330,000 sterling in treasure belonging to Swedish merchants, all of which was lost.

1811: The British East Indiaman *Elizabeth* (650 tons/660.5 tonnes), commanded by Captain Hutton and sailing from England to India with £320,000 sterling in gold and silver specie on board, was wrecked on the Breebauck Shoals near Dunkirk, Belgium, and of the 380 people on board. Only 22 survived. Several attempts failed to recover any of her treasure.

1842: The British East Indiaman *Reliance* (1,500 tons/1,524 tonnes), returning from China with a cargo valued at £250,000 sterling, which included a large number of Chinese gold bars and porcelain, was lost in a storm near Merlimont on France's northwest coast.

Chapter 19

Azores Islands' Richest Shipwrecks

The Azores Island group was the most important maritime crossroads during the Age of Sail. The Azores archipelago accounts for the greatest concentration of sunken treasure in the entire world. It consists of nine volcanic islands in the north Atlantic some 932 miles (1,500 kilometers) west of mainland Portugal. These dramatically beautiful islands, governed by Portugal, were first discovered in 1317 by Portuguese and Genovese mariners, although no settlement was established until 1439. The Azores are generously spread over 350 miles (563 kilometers) of sea, making them difficult to miss for transatlantic voyagers. In the days of dead reckoning navigation, they were a most welcome sight, offering immediate proof of geographic position and the promise of refreshment.

The main port was Angra on the south coast of Terceira Island, despite the unsafe anchorage it offered. During the Colonial Period (1500–1825) Angra was one of the world's most important seaports. At times as many as 200 large ships lay at anchor inside and just outside Angra Bay. A fort with 160 cannons and walls over 3,280 feet (1,000 meters) long guarded the bay, which is exposed to ferocious winds from east to south. In 1832 an English captain stopping there wrote: "Each year five or six ships are lost in this bay." Spanish galleons, Portuguese East Indiamen and ships coming from Brazil put in at Ponta Delgada on San Miguel Island to the south, especially when enemy ships were cruising off Terceira Island or when bad weather mandated finding the nearest port.

The port of Angra on Terceira Island where all the returning New World treasure ships went to join a fleet of warships, which escorted them to Spain through pirate-infested waters.

The majority of the ships wrecked in the Azores were returning home, laden with valuable cargo of some kind rather than outward bound for the Indies, Brazil, or the Americas. Ships that scattered in storms as they crossed the Atlantic or were otherwise separated from their fleet sought the safety of Angra Bay to await a convoy heading home.

Ships flying other European flags also passed through the Azores on their way home. However, only ships of the Catholic nations—Spain, Portugal, France, the Hanseatic League, the papal states and the maritime republics of Genoa and Venice—were permitted to put in at Angra. Protestant ships were forced to seek respite, water and provisions at the two smallest and westernmost islands of Flores and Corvo.

Each year during the Colonial Period it is estimated that between 250 and 300 Spanish and Portuguese ships passed through the Azores. After 1600 other nations began competing with Portugal in the East Indies trade. Many of the East Indiamen returning from the Orient to England, Holland, France and the Scandinavian countries passed through the Azores after wearying months at sea.

(Facing, bottom image) The Dutch East Indiamen used Chinese porcelain for ballast, such as these pieces. Some ships carried over 200,000 pieces of porcelain. *(Following page)* Marx working above a cannon on the wreck of a Spanish armada he discovered.

(Right) The port of Angra as it looks today. Over the years Marx has located and partly excavated seven old wrecks here.

(Below) Enemy and pirate fleets prowled the Azores in search of returning Spanish and Portuguese rich ships. Many were sunk with their treasures.

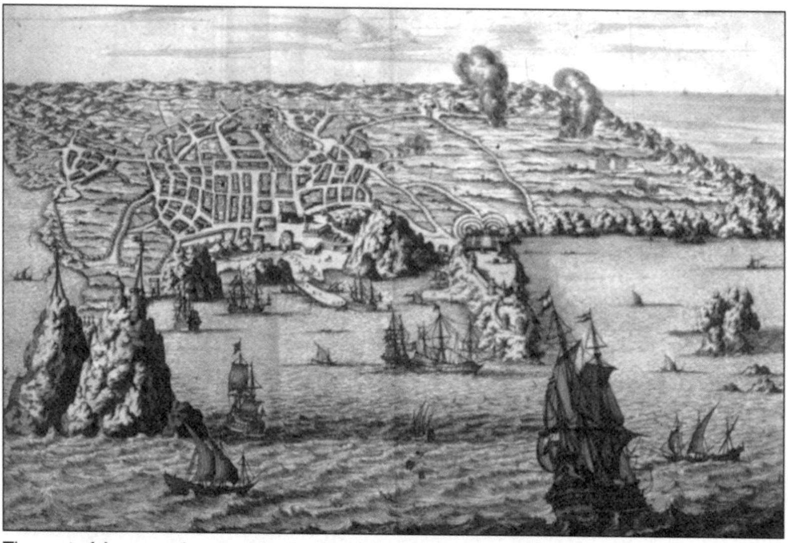

The port of Angra under attack by the Dutch in 1611.

From Brazil, Portugal's New World stronghold, fleets with as many as 125 ships or more sailed each year for the motherland, stopping in the Azores. Although the bulk of their cargoes consisted of sugar, indigo, dyewoods and other agricultural products, many also carried more enduring valuables. By 1680 Brazil was the world's leading producer of diamonds, and by 1700 it was the source of more gold than all of Spain's New World possessions combined.

Fog claimed many ships. Faulty navigation, especially at night, drove many others upon rocky shores. Sea battles accounted for countless other shipwrecks because the Azores was a favored cruising ground for the pirates and privateers of many nations. On various occasions ships were scuttled when there was a chance of their falling into enemy hands.

The Azores is without a doubt the richest area in the world for virgin wreckage of treasure ships. Almost all of them were too deep for contemporary salvors and even for scuba-equipped salvors. Now, however, thanks to the recent development of submersibles and remote-operated-vehicles (ROVs), these priceless capsules of history are within reach.

1504: Although the Portuguese and other Europeans were sailing in the Azores since the first decade of the fifteenth century, the earliest recorded shipwreck occurred in 1504 when a caravel, laden with ivory elephant tusks and 3 tons (3.048 tonnes) of gold from Africa, wrecked on the east end of Terceira island. Her captain was Antonio Nunes da Cunha.

1515: The Portuguese caravel *Trinidade* (140 tons/142 tonnes), coming from Africa with 22 tons (22.35 tonnes) of ivory tusks and 4 tons (4.06 tonnes) of gold, plus 360 slaves, wrecked in a storm near Praia, Terceira island. Six of her crew of 41 survived. All of the slaves drowned.

1517: The Portuguese East Indiaman *Nossa Senhora do Livramento* (850 tons/863.5 tonnes, 44 bronze cannons), described as "the richest ship ever returning from the Orient," was wrecked in a storm near the east end of Terceira Island. Only 16 of the 475 souls aboard her survived.

1522: The most devastating earthquake to ever strike the Azores was felt throughout the islands. Vila Franca do Campo, largest city in the Azores and capital of San Miguel Island, slid into the sea, killing over 3,000 people. The capital was subsequently transferred to Ponta Delgada. Over 150 ships were sunk or wrecked around the islands. Two unidentified Portuguese East Indiamen, coming from India with cargoes valued at over 3 million crusadoes, went down near the sunken city, and a Spanish ship, coming from Mexico with treasures plundered from the Aztecs, was dashed to pieces by a tidal wave 2 leagues west of the sunken city.

1526: The Spanish ship *Santa Maria de la Luz* (150 tons/152 tonnes), commanded by Captain Cristóbal de San Martin, was sent from Mexico by the conquistador Hernán Cortéz with a treasure described as "making the king rich for years." It consisted of tons of gold objects plundered from the Emperor Montezuma and the Aztecs. The ship was trying to enter Angra Bay when a squall caused it to capsize and sink within sight of Monte Brazil, the headland at the entrance to the bay.

1526: An unidentified Portuguese East Indiaman, coming from Malacca and India with a cargo "of great value," was wrecked on the south side of Fayal Island and only a few of the people survived. A week later a small chest full of diamonds was thrown up on the shore and three weeks later a small box full of gold jewelry was also found on the beach near the site.

1528: The Portuguese East Indiaman *Biscainha* (1,100 tons/1,118 tonnes), commanded by Captain João de Freitas, was returning from India with "a valuable cargo" when a deadly epidemic decimated the crew. During a storm she and six others sank in Angra Bay. In the same storm the Portuguese East Indiaman *Nossa Senhora de Belém* (1,200 tons/1,219 tonnes), which sailed from India with a cargo valued at 1.1 million crusadoes, sank 3 leagues south of Angra Bay. The Spanish galleon *Nuestra Señora de los Remedios* (600 tons/610 tonnes), commanded by Captain Juan de Rexual and coming from Mexico with 2,175,000 pesos in treasure, sank about a league west of Angra Bay. A day later in the same storm, three other unidentified galleons, sailing in the same fleet from Mexico with a total of 3.3 million pesos in treasure, also sank within sight of Angra Bay. Four months later nine ships of the Tierra Firme Fleet, coming from Panama and Colombia and heading for Angra Bay, sank in a storm. Only two were identified by name: the *Capitana, Santa Clara* (800 tons/813 tonnes), commanded by Captain Pedro Gonzales with 3.45 million pesos in treasure, and the *Almiranta, Santa Isabel* (750 tons/762 tonnes), commanded by Captain Pedro de Meras, with 2.95 million pesos in treasure. The two flagships sank within sight of Angra Bay; the others wrecked on the rocky coastline. The total loss of treasure in this fleet was over 8 million pesos. Another galleon in this armada, the *La Madelena* (800 tons/813 tonnes), commanded by Captain Domingo de Insaurraga, and carrying 3.3 million pesos in treasure, sank a league south of Ponta Delgada in 40 fathoms of water. Grappling hooks were used to fish up eight bronze cannons.

1529: In a letter to the king of Portugal, a royal official wrote that since 1516 more than twenty very rich ships had been lost around San Miguel Island. Most lay too deep to salvage and, although several lay in shallow water, there were no divers to salvage them. One Portuguese East Indiaman, commanded by Captain Luiz de Lacerda, and carrying a cargo valued at 2.5 million crusadoes, went down about a half league south of Relva in 50 fathoms of water. Using grappling hooks, they were able to recover three of her bronze cannons. Nets were used to pull up nine bales of silk, two boxes of cloves, and three chests of porcelain from another Portuguese East Indiaman lost in 45 fathoms of water between Lagôoa and Aqua de Pau. Further attempts were unsuccessful.

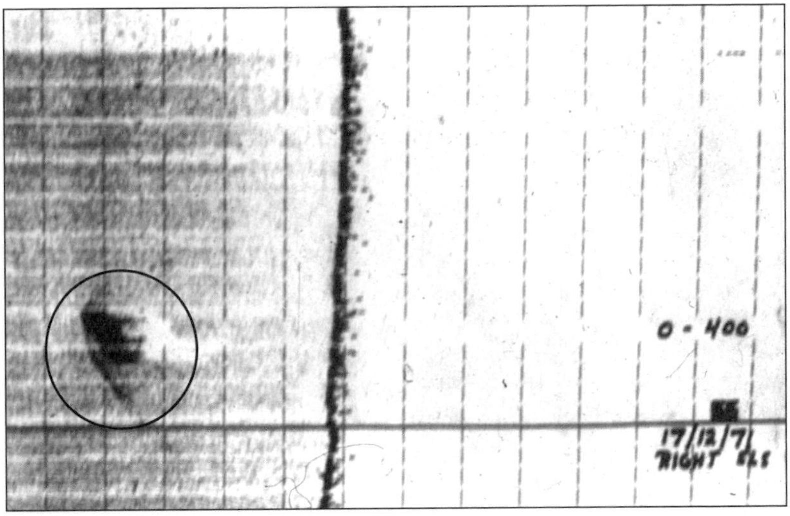

Many of the Azore's deep-water wrecks lie in anaerobic areas, so that ships remain completely intact, as shown in this side-scan sonar graph (see circled area).

1530: The Portuguese East Indiaman *Nossa Senhora da Luz* (1,200 tons/1,219 tonnes, 44 bronze cannons), commanded by Captain Manuel Fialho and coming from India with over 500,000 crusadoes in cargo, sank about a half league off Ponta Delgada in over 50 fathoms of water.

1531: Three Spanish ships, coming from Mexico with over 1 million pesos in golden Aztec objects and other treasure, encountered a storm between Terceira and San Miguel Islands. Two disappeared without a trace. The other, *Nuestra Señora de la Concepción* (110 tons/112 tonnes, ten cannons), commanded by Captain Francisco Bara, was trying to seek shelter at Ponta Delgada, but capsized about a half league distance off Villa de Monestarios, San Miguel Island, and sank.

1533: The Portuguese East Indiaman *Nossa Senhora de Piedade* (1,200 tons/1,219 tonnes), returning from Malacca with 2 million crusadoes in cargo, wrecked several leagues east of Angra. Only 17 of the 500 souls on board survived.

1533: The Spanish caravel San Ildefonso (120 tons/122 tonnes), commanded by Captain Martin Pérez de Gama, was sent from Mexico by Cortéz "with tons of Aztec golden treasure" and was making a stop in the Azores to find some ships to escort it back to Spain. French pirates from Saint-Malo attacked off Fayal Island. While the ship tried to evade capture, a hurricane struck and she sank 3 leagues southwest of the Angra. Only six of her crew survived. All three French pirate vessels sank nearby.

1533: Three Spanish merchantmen, coming from Mexico with gold and silver valued at 1,875,000 pesos, were lost at night in a storm when they struck upon the west side of Fayal Island. Only a few men were saved.

1541: The Spanish ship *San Antonio de Padua* (350 tons/356 tonnes), coming from Veracruz with a cargo valued at 670,000 pesos, was sailing with another ship named *Buen Jesús*, which was wrecked on the reefs of Bermuda. Continuing alone, she made for Angra, but when she was 3 leagues west of the port, she sank in a storm.

1542: An armada of 16 Portuguese East Indiamen, under the command of Admiral Fernao D'Alvares da Cunha and returning from India to Lisbon, went to the Azores to pick up armed escort ships for protection from the Barbary pirates who infested the area. Soon after leaving the port of Angra, the ship *Nossa Senhora de Belém* sank in a squall, with almost 2 million crusadoes in Oriental treasures. Other ships rescued 78 of the 660 people on board.

1542: The Spanish merchantman *San Juan* (150 tons/152.5 tonnes), commanded by Captain Juan Hurtado and coming from Panama and Havana with 450,000 pesos in treasure, was wrecked near Ponta Delgada.

1543: An earthquake struck the island of Terceira, sinking eight ships at anchor in Angra Bay. The only one identified by name was the Spanish ship *San Bernardino* (350 tons/356 tonnes), commanded by Captain José de Villavicencio and coming from Mexico with 635,000 pesos in gold and silver, plus other cargo. Two of the other ships were rich Portuguese East Indiamen coming from India, which sank half a league from shore where they were anchored. Several horrendous tidal waves caused by the earthquake sank the other five: two Spanish ships from Mexico, two Portuguese slave ships coming from Africa, and one wine-laden Portuguese ship from Madeira.

1543: The Portuguese East Indiaman *Nossa Senhora do Bon Viaje*, also known as the *Grifo* (850 tons/864 tonnes), commanded by

Captain Baltazar Jorge de Dias and coming from India with a cargo valued at 900,000 crusadoes, sank while anchored about a half league seaward of Angra Bay.

1548: The Portuguese East Indiaman *Sao João*, coming from Malacca and India with a cargo valued at 540,000 crusadoes, anchored at Ponta Delgada where she soon sank, killing about half of those aboard.

1549: The Spanish galleon *Santa Barbara* (200 tons/203 tonnes), commanded by Captain Pedro Carrasco and returning from Havana to Spain with over 1 million pesos in gold, silver, precious stones and pearls, sank in 20 fathoms off Angra.

1550: A storm caused three returning New World ships to sink in Angra Bay. They were the *Santa Maria* (120 tons/122 tonnes), commanded by Captain Maestre Jorge; the *Santa María de la Piedad* (120 tons/122 tonnes), commanded by Captain Sebastian de Quesada; and the *Santa Maria de Burgoes* (440 tons/447 tonnes), commanded by Captain Juan Basquero. Combined, they lost over 1 million pesos in treasure and other cargo.

1552: Two Spanish galleons heading for Spain from the New World—the *Madalena* (200 tons/203 tonnes), commanded by Captain Miguel de la Borda, and the *Santiago* (220 tons/223.5 tonnes), commanded by Captain Miguel de Oquendo—carrying a total of 1.65 million pesos in gold and silver from Peru, were lost several leagues west of the port of Angra during a storm. There were no survivors.

1554: French pirates attacked a fleet of 14 Spanish ships returning from the New World. The *Capitana*, named *Santa Maria del Camino* (350 tons/356 tonnes), commanded by Captain Miguel de Viso and with over 1 million pesos in gold and silver, sank midway between Pico and Terceira islands. Two of the other ships—the *Almiranta* named *Santa Catalina* (375 tons/381 tonnes), commanded by Captain Tome Nuñez and coming from Panama with 1.35 million pesos in treasure, and the *San Andrés* (320 tons/325 tonnes), commanded by Captain Alonso Cano and coming from Santo Domingo with 400,000 pesos in treasure—sank in a storm off the southwest side of Terceira Island.

1556: Two Portuguese East Indiaman wrecked in a hurricane on the south side of Terceira Island, several leagues east of Angra: the

Nossa Santa Maria da Vitoria (1,800 tons/1,829 tonnes, fifty cannons), commanded by Captain Francisco de Gouveia and bringing a cargo valued at 670,000 crusadoes from Malacca and India, and the *Senhora da Assunção* (1,700 tons/1,727 tonnes), commanded by Captain Jacome de Melo, with a cargo valued at 760,000 crusadoes. There were no survivors.

1558: An unidentified Portuguese East Indiaman commanded by Captain Vasco Lourenzo Figiera de Azevedo and returning from India with 1.8 million crusadoes in cargo, plus 78 boxes of pearls and precious stones, was wrecked during the night on the southeast coast of Terceira island and over 400 lives were lost. Divers recovered only seven of her 66 bronze cannons. For days after the wreck, bales of silk and barrels of spices floated ashore.

1559: The Portuguese East Indiaman *Santa María da Barca*, also called the *Galega* (1,350 tons/1,372 tonnes), commanded by Captain Rui Pereira de Camara and sailing between Goa and Lisbon with over 1 million crusadoes of cargo, was first becalmed for sixty days off Guinea and then went to Brazil to obtain water and victuals. On her way back to Lisbon, she was wrecked in a storm on the south side of Santa Maria Island.

1560: The ships of a large fleet of Spanish treasure galleons, sailing between Havana and Spain, were scattered in a hurricane near Bermuda. Two of these ships—the galleon *La Concepción* (440 tons/447 tonnes), commanded by Captain Gonzalo Monte, with 778,000 pesos in treasure, and the galleon *Trinidad* (300 tons/305 tonnes), commanded by Captain Juan de Heredia, with 645,000 pesos in treasure—were heading for the port of Angra where they expected to rejoin the fleet. During a storm both ships wrecked near the west end of Terceira Island with great loss of life.

1561: Three Spanish merchantmen—the *Santa Catalina, Santa María* and *Santo Antón*—coming from Mexico with a total of 657,000 pesos in treasure, were wrecked on the south side of Fayal Island and only a few people survived.

1562: In November the governor-general of Terceira island wrote to the king of Portugal: "so far this year over forty rich ships from the East Indies, Brazil, and the Spanish New World have been lost from hurricanes, earthquakes, and pirates. The combined value of their cargoes is over 20 million crusadoes. Many bales and boxes have drifted ashore and customs agents have been unable to recover much of these things as the islanders grab them as soon as they come ashore and hide them." He noted that they were able to confiscate one box of cloves and inside it they found two large bags of diamonds and gold jewelry.

1563: A royal official wrote the king of Portugal, stating that during the year the Azores Islands suffered five separate earthquakes, all of which caused enormous tidal waves, washing away entire fishing villages on several islands and causing the loss of over 100 large ships and an equal number of smaller ones. On San Miguel Island one large ship of 400 tons (406 tonnes) was carried over 1,000 paces ashore. Miraculously, most of the people on board survived. The loss of treasure and cargoes far exceeded 50 million crusadoes. The only ship identified was the Spanish galleon *La Madalena* (250 tons/254 tonnes), commanded by Captain Cristóbal Rodriquez Garrucho and coming from Mexico with over 2 million pesos in gold and silver. She went down in Angra Bay, and a large wooden statue of the Virgin Mary that drifted to shore was the only thing salvaged.

1563: A good example of the vast amount of treasures being smuggled back to Spain is the small Spanish merchantman *Nuestra Señora de la Luz*, commanded by Captain Juan Garcia and coming from Santo Domingo with a mundane registered cargo of copper ore, hides and dyewoods. When she wrecked on the beach at Praia on the eastern end of Terceira Island, custom agents rushed to the scene and found she had almost 700,000 pesos in unregistered gold and silver on board. Her captain and owner were later hanged by order of the king to discourage others from smuggling treasure. Sailing with her was the *Espiritu Sancto*, commanded by Captain Bartolomé del Salto, and carrying 275,000 pesos in treasure, whichthat wrecked on St. Jorge Island. Only one person was saved.

1567: The Spanish galleon *La Concepción* (600 tons/610 tonnes), commanded by Captain Luis de Alcalá and coming from Havana with 540,000 pesos in treasure, wrecked about a half league west of Ponta Delgada. Approximately half of her treasure was salvaged. The remainder was concealed under wreck debris and buried under the sandy bottom.

1574: The Spanish advice boat *San Nicolás*, commanded by Captain Juan de Huerto, carried the normal cargo of Spain-bound mail but also

Spanish fascination with pre-Columbian artifacts resulted in vast numbers of objects such as this Mayan jade that can be found on wrecks of Spanish galleons.

large amounts of treasure salvaged from the galleon *La Magdelena*, commanded by Captain Juan Diaz Malamdes, which had wrecked off Tabasco, Mexico, in 1572. Near Corvo Island, Barbary pirates pursued the boat. She headed for safety at Ponta Delgada; however, a storm struck and she sank near La Barria on the west end of San Miguel Island. A week after this disaster, the Spanish galleon *San Ignacio y San Jacinto*, coming from Havana with 445,232 pesos in treasure, sank in a storm near Mostieros on the northwest side of the island.

1579: An unidentified English privateer sank off Gualva, 2 leagues from Angra Bay. It was caught in a bad storm while cruising off this coast and, in a desperate bid to stay afloat, the captain ordered all cannons overboard and then a bit later ordered an "immense amount of treasure" thrown into the sea. Still, the ship went down with over 300 men.

1580: The Spanish galleon *Santa Catalina* (350 tons/355.5 tonnes), commanded by Captain Melchoir and coming from Panama with 500,000 pesos in treasure, was lost off the east end of San Miguel Island in a raging storm.

1584: The Portuguese East Indiaman *Santiago* (1,200 tons/1,219 tonnes), commanded by Captain Afonso Pineiro and coming from India to Lisbon with a cargo valued at 450,000 crusadoes, was wrecked on the west side of Corvo Island and very few men survived.

1585: The Portuguese East Indiaman *Santiago Maior*, also named the *São Filipe e Santiago* (1,800 tons/1,829 tonnes, 42 cannons), commanded by Captain Afonso Pinheiro Teles and returning from Malacca to Lisbon with a cargo valued at 542,000 crusadoes, was lost on the south side of Terceira Island and only a few men survived.

1586: The Spanish galleon *Nuestra Señora de la Concepción* (600 tons/610 tonnes), commanded by Captain Martin de Vitoria and sailing from Veracruz to Spain with treasure valued at 1.8 million pesos, went down in a storm while anchored off Angra.

1586: Another example of smuggling was the case of the small Spanish merchantman *Nuestra Señora de los Remedios* (120 tons/122 tonnes), commanded by Captain Francisco Ximénez. Sailing from Santo Domingo to Spain with hides and ginger, she was forced to run upon the small beach in Angra Bay because she was sinking. While removing her cargo, customs agents found that she was also carrying over 400,000 pesos in unregistered silver bullion and specie.

1586: The Spanish galleon *Capitana, Nuestra Señora de la Concepción* (600 tons/610 tonnes), commanded by Captain Martín de Vittoria and sailing from Mexico to Spain with 1.8 million pesos in treasure, sank in Angra Bay during a storm. She was in only 60 feet (18 meters) of water, so divers recovered most of her cannons, but claimed they couldn't get at the treasure because it was concealed under huge ship's timbers.

1587: An unidentified Portuguese East Indiaman of Captain Cristovao de Figueira de Alvarenga, sailing from India with over 1 million crusadoes in cargo, was attacked by English warships of Count Essex and sunk by cannon fire near Ponta Delgada.

1588: The Portuguese East Indiaman *Santiago* (2,100 tons/2,134 tonnes, 48 cannons), commanded by Captain Francisco de Brito and en route from Lisbon to Malacca with 412,000 crusadoes in treasure, was sailing down the coast of Africa when a storm arose and she was driven all the way to the Azores, over 1,000 miles (1,609 kilometers) to the west. While attempting to enter the port of Angra, the ship wrecked and most of those aboard drowned. Salvage attempts to recover treasure and cannon failed because the water was too deep for divers.

1588: Most of the ships sailing to and from the New World this year were small because the larger galleons were enlisted in the Invincible Armada for the invasion of England. Two of these smaller ships—the *Santiago* (150 tons/152.5 tonnes), commanded by Captain Marcos de Escobar, and the *Nuestra Señora del Rosario* (120 tons/122 tonnes), commanded by Captain Fernández Hernández—combined had over 1 million pesos in gold and silver on board. In the dark of night, they wrecked several leagues west of the port of Angra.

1589: So many ships were lost in the defeat of Spain's Invincible Armada in 1588 that there were few galleons to return from the Americas in 1589 and they had to carry far more treasure than normal. The galleon *Trinidad,* commanded by Captain Miguel de Leturia, was crammed with 4.3 million pesos in gold and silver, making her one of the richest Spanish ships ever lost. She sprang numerous leaks on the crossing and was barely afloat when she limped into Angra Bay, her hold half full of water. While awaiting galleys to tow her into the port, she sank with a heavy loss of life in 100 fathoms of water, making salvage impossible. The following day, a ship that had been sailing with the *Trinidad, Nuestra Señora de Guia* (230 tons/234 tonnes), commanded by Captain Francisco Pérez Granillo and coming from Mexico with 1.235 million pesos in treasure, was fighting against three English warships as she approached Angra Bay. Suddenly she blew up and sank about a league south of the bay with a total loss of life. Three other Spanish ships were sunk off Angra Bay days later by the same English warships—one was the galleon *Nuestra Señora del Rosario* (450 tons/457 tonnes), commanded by Captain Asencio de Vedos and coming from Mexico with 2 million pesos in treasure; the other two were not identified, but each carried over 1 million pesos in treasure. Around the same time an unidentified Portuguese East Indiaman, coming from Malacca with "a very rich cargo," was wrecked at the base of a cliff under the guns of one of the forts in Angra Bay. Divers recovered only a small portion of her cargo.

1590: Two ships sank in the same storm near the port of Angra. One was the Spanish galleon *Nuestra Señora de Begonia* (300 tons/305 tonnes), commanded by Captain Duarte de Quiros and coming from Veracruz and Havana with almost 1 million pesos in gold and silver; the other was a Portuguese East Indiaman, *São Miguel* (1,200 tons/1,219 tonnes), commanded by Captain João Homen de Gouveia and coming from Malacca and Hormuz with a cargo valued at 870,000 crusadoes.

1591: A devastating loss with significant political repercussions occurred when a convoy of two Spanish treasure fleets, coming from both South America and Mexico,` was struck by a hurricane in the Azores. More than 100 of the 150 ships in the convoy, plus four Portuguese East Indiamen returning from the Orient, were lost. Officials estimated the loss of treasure, excluding other types of cargo, at over 40 million pesos on the Spanish ships and over 5 million crusadoes on the Portuguese East Indiamen. This was the greatest treasure loss Spain ever suffered in a single year. The blow sent the near-destitute King Philip II to his quarters, where he shut himself up for a month, praying night and day for a change of fortune.

1592: The Portuguese East Indiaman *Santa Cruz* (1,200 tons/1,219 tonnes), commanded by Captain João Lopes de Azevedo and returning from India, with a very valuable cargo, was attacked by British warships off San Miguel Island. She sustained heavy damage, and the captain ordered her run aground on the south side of the island and burned to keep her out of English hands.

1592: The English had three squadrons cruising around the Azores, waiting to intercept ships returning from the Spanish and Portuguese Indies. While approaching Angra Bay, the Spanish galleon *Santa Cruz* (550 tons/559 tonnes), carrying 810,715 pesos in treasure from Mexico, was forced to run ashore and her crew set her on fire before leaping overboard.

1593: A combined convoy of 121 ships was en route from Havana to Spain heading for Angra, where it expected to pick up protection from the Armada of the Ocean Seas—a fleet of warships that generally met the returning New World treasure fleets in the Bay of Angra and escorted them back to Spain—when a sudden storm struck. The lead ship was less than an hour's sail from Angra. Six of the larger galleons, including the two flagships, the *Capitana* and *Almiranta*, sank with almost a total loss of life. Combined, they carried over 11 million pesos in gold and silver. Some of the other ships that were scattered in the storm wrecked on the north coast of San Miguel Island.

1594: The richest vessel ever lost in the Azores was the ill-fated Portuguese East Indiaman *Las Cinque Chagas*, commanded by Captain Nuño Velho Pereira. When she left Goa, India, she had over 3.5 million crusadoes in gold, silver, precious stones, porcelain, silks and spices aboard. After rounding the Cape of Good Hope, she lay becalmed for several weeks and over half the 1,000 people aboard perished from an epidemic that swept through the ship. In July 1594, when the Azores were finally in view, fewer than seventy men were still fit to work the ship. While tacking through the channel between the islands of Fayal and Pico, they were attacked by four English warships. The massive carrack caught fire, blew up, and sank in deep water with her great treasure.

1595: The Portuguese East Indiaman *São Francisco* (1,600 tons/1626 tonnes, 44 cannons), commanded by Captain Vasco de Fonseca Coutinho and sailing from India for Lisbon with 1.58 million crusadoes in cargo, was chased by British privateers. Her captain had her run aground on the south side of Fayal Island and set on fire. She exploded, but everyone aboard got safely ashore.

1595: The *Earl of Cumberland* was cruising off Terceira Island when an unidentified Portuguese East Indiaman of 2,000 tons (2,032 tonnes) attempted to enter Angra Bay and get under the guns of the forts there. Three of the English warships first raked her with cannon fire and then surrounded her and were attempting to board, when she suddenly blew up and went down with 1,100 souls on board and a cargo estimated valued at over 1 million crusadoes.

1596: Two Spanish galleons in the Tierra Firme Fleet of Captain-General Francisco Martinez de Leyva—one his *Capitana*, the other not identified—were returning from Havana to Spain. Both sank in deep water during a tempest about 2 leagues south of San Miguel Island, with over 3 million pesos in treasure on board.

1597: A French pirate vessel from Saint-Malo captured a Spanish merchantman, *Santa Ana* (150 tons/152 tonnes), commanded by Captain Pedro de Junco, with 113,685 pesos in gold and silver on board. Both ships wrecked on the north coast of Terceira Island while sailing to France.

1597: An unidentified Portuguese East Indiaman, (1,200 tons/1,219 tonnes), coming from Malacca and Macao with a cargo valued at 1.23 million crusadoes, ran into a large fleet of English warships that had been cruising in the Azores for months. Forced to flee to the nearest port, she wrecked on the west side of Fayal Island where her crew set her on fire.

1598: The Portuguese East Indiaman *Santiago* (1,800 tons/1,819 tonnes), returning to Lisbon from the Orient, with cargo valued at 670,000 crusadoes, plus 22 boxes of diamonds and precious stones, was wrecked on the south side of Terceira Island in a storm and only a few people made it ashore.

1599: The Portuguese East Indiaman *Santa Maria de Belém* (2,000 tons/2032 tonnes, eighty bronze cannons), commanded by Captain João Coutinho, was badly damaged by a hurricane and went into the small port of Porto Nova on Terceira Island. While undergoing repairs, a storm blew her out to sea and she sank about half a league offshore. She was also carrying many gifts from the emperor of Japan for the king of Spain (who was also the Kking of Portugal). The first twenty Christian missionaries ever permitted to evangelize in Japan were among the 900 souls who perished.

1600: The Tierra Firme Fleet of Captain-General Sancho Pardo Osorio was scattered during a storm before reaching the Azores and his *Capitana, Santa Ana Maria* (700 tons/711 tonnes, 48 cannons), commanded by Captain Fermín de Iturrica and carrying 2.4 million pesos in treasure, wrecked a league west of Ponta Delgada. Soon after, divers recovered 23 of her bronze cannons, but none of her treasure.

1600: An unidentified galleon in the New Spain Fleet of Captain-General Sancho Pardo Osorio developed a bad leak in a storm on the high seas and was not able to go to Angra Bay with the other ships. Instead she headed for the north west coast of San Miguel Island, where she was deliberately run aground to keep her from sinking. None of the 900,000 pesos of treasure on board could be saved.

1601: The Spanish warship *Santa Teresa* was dispatched from Spain to pick up the treasure and men from the Spanish galleon *Nuestra Señora del Buen Sucesso*, which had run aground on Flores Island the year before. After picking up the treasure and survivors, she set sail for Cádiz. Soon afterwards she was attacked by Barbary pirate ships and sank one of them. Then a storm struck and she wrecked on Fayal Island. Only 17 men were saved.

1604: Three rich unidentified Portuguese East Indiamen were becalmed for three days off Ponta Delgada. No galleys were available to tow them into port, but when it was learned that there were many sick men on all three ships, locals began ferrying them ashore for medical treatment. One boat bringing them ashore was found to be smuggling a large chest containing gold jewelry valued at over 100,000 crusadoes. The water was too deep to anchor and the three ships just drifted about until a tempest came up and they sank with losses of over 2,000 lives and 4.35 million crusadoes in cargo.

1605: The Portuguese East Indiaman *São Jacinto* (1,300 tons/1,321 tonnes), returning to Lisbon from India with a cargo valued at 740,000 crusadoes, plus 19 chests of precious stones and diamonds, was wrecked in a storm near the port of Angra and only her people were saved.

1607: The Portuguese East Indiaman *São Jacinto* (1,800 tons/1,829 tonnes, 46 cannons), commanded by Captain Pedro da Silva, was sailing from Lisbon to India with gold and silver worth 340,000 crusadoes, but off Madagascar she went up on a reef. She got off and went to Mozambique Island for repairs. Instead of continuing for India, she headed back to Lisbon, but was wrecked near Angra. Most of her people survived and a small part of treasure was salvaged.

1608: The Spanish galleon *Capitana* (850 tons/864 tonnes, eighty bronze cannons), carrying over 3 million pesos in gold and silver, collided with another ship while trying to anchor in the port of Angra and soon after sank from a gaping hole. The ship went down in 130 feet (39.5 meters) of water. The Spaniards made an unsuccessful attempt to drag the ship into shallower water with grappling irons.

1608: The Spanish galleon *Capitana, Santa Cruz* (400 tons/406 tonnes), commanded by Captain Constantín Pérez, with 1,788,600 pesos in treasure on board. She was coming from Havana, and sank at anchor shortly after reaching Angra Bay.

1609: The Portuguese East Indiaman *São Salvador* (1,000 tons/1,016 meters, 38 cannons), commanded by Admiral Francisco Ribeiro Rocha and carrying over 2 million crusadoes in cargo, was wrecked near Praia, Terceira Island. Only forty or so of the 950 souls on board were rescued.

1609: Pirates attacked five Portuguese East Indiamen that were under the command of Captain Manuel de Menezes as they approached San Miguel Island. Captain Luis de Bardi was forced to run his ship aground near Ponta Delgada and she suddenly blew up before anyone could get ashore. The archbishop of Goa was aboard with a great personal treasure, which was lost along with her cargo valued at 880,000 crusadoes. The other four ships reached port safely.

1614: The Spanish galleon *Nuestra Señora del Socorro y Buen Viaje* (650 tons/660.5 tonnes), commanded by Captain Juan Quintero and coming from Havana with over 1 million pesos in gold and silver, sank in a storm about a half league off the Bay of Angra.

1614: A dreadful earthquake struck Terceira Island on April 9, destroying over 1,600 homes and taking many lives. At sea around Terceira and all of the other islands, over forty large ships were lost, including several rich Portuguese East Indiamen. Two more earthquakes struck on May 14 and May 24, and another on June 21. Tidal waves created by the earthquakes sank over seventy ships around all the islands. The loss of treasure on the ships exceeded 15 million crusadoes in value.

1614: An armada of five Portuguese East Indiamen was returning from India under command of Captain Manuel Coutinho. One night, while passing through the Azores in good weather, the flagship, *Capitana*, wrecked on Fayal Island. Some people were saved, but the cargo, valued at 1.75 million crusadoes, was lost. Two years later, 34 bronze cannons were recovered from the wreck.

1615: The Portuguese East Indiaman *Nossa Senhora da Luz* (1,800 tons/1,829 tonnes, 46 cannons), commanded by Captain Manuel de Menezes and returning from India to Lisbon carrying 1.85 million crusadoes in cargo, was wrecked near Porto Pim on San Miguel Island.

1616: The Dutch East Indiaman *Surseance* (768 tons/780 tonnes), commanded by Captain Diedrich Wiese and coming from Batavia on Java with a cargo valued at 181,527 guilders, was captured by the English off St. Helena Island. While they were taking her back to England, she wrecked 4 leagues west of Angra Bay.

1616: The Portuguese East Indiaman *Santo Antonio,* commanded by Captain Paulo Rangel de Castelbranco and coming from Malacca with a cargo valued at 780,000 crusadoes, wrecked on the south side of Fayal Island and about half of her people were saved, but none of the cargo.

1619: The Portuguese East Indiaman *Nossa Senhora de Guia* (2,000 tons/2,030 tonnes), commanded by Captain Kuis de Sousa and coming from the Orient with a cargo valued at 1.4 million crusadoes, was attacked by six pirate vessels as she attempted to enter Angra Bay and blew up. Over 1,200 souls went down with her.

1625: The Brazil fleet made a stop in the Azores and the *Almiranta,* with a large amount of gold and silver on board, was wrecked trying to enter the port of Horta on Fayal Island. Some of her people, but none of the cargo, were saved.

1626: Three Portuguese East Indiamen, coming from India, were attacked by three Dutch ships several leagues south of Angra Bay. An unidentified ship, commanded by Captain Lourenço Reixoto Circe and with a cargo valued at over 1 million crusadoes, sank in the battle with all aboard.

1627: The Dutch East Indiaman *Middleburg* (700 tons/711 tonnes), commanded by Captain Willem Jakobsz Koster and returning from Batavia with a cargo valued at 264,764 guilders, wrecked in a storm near the west end of Terceira Island. The few survivors who made it ashore were killed by Portuguese.

1627: A fleet of 24 ships from Brazil heading for Angra Bay was struck by a bad storm, and the *Rainha Santa,* carrying gold and diamonds valued at 11.4 million crusadoes, sank 12 leagues southwest of Terceira Island with a total loss of life.

1628: On June 16 an earthquake struck the Azores. For three hours huge waves battered the archipelago, sinking more than fifty richly laden ships. An island about 5 miles (8 kilometers) long appeared off the south side of San Miguel Island and disappeared several years later.

1630: A Portuguese East Indiaman *Nossa Senhora do Concepção* (1,800 tons/1,829 tonnes), coming from the Orient "with a vast treasure," was anchored about a half league off Vila Franca, San Miguel Island, having lost over half her crew and passengers to disease on board. A violent earthquake struck and she sank with all aboard.

1631: A large unidentified Dutch ship, returning from a voyage in the Caribbean, where it captured seven Spanish trading vessels off Cartagena and Cuba, wrecked in a hurricane on the southwest side of Terceira Island. Two survivors reported the ship carried over 200,000 pesos in gold and silver.

1632: The Tierra Firme Armada, under Captain-General Tomás de la Raspuru, was heading for the port of Angra when a storm arose just north of Fayal Island. The *Almiranta, Nuestra Señora de la Concepción* (600 tons/610 tonnes), commanded by Captain Juan Alonso de Camino, two other richly-laden galleons and ten merchantmen all sank on the high seas within sight of the island. The total loss of gold and silver was in excess of 9 million pesos.

1636: The armada of Captain-General Carlos de Ibarra encountered a hurricane near Bermuda. After the storm, the *Almiranta,* carrying 2 million pesos in treasure, was in a very bad condition, so the captain had the treasure transferred to the *Capitana, San Mateo* (600 tons/610 tonnes), which already had 2.8 million pesos in treasure on board. Off Corvo another storm struck and eleven of his ships sank on the high seas. While anchored about a half league off Angra Bay, the *Capitana* capsized and sank with this enormous amount of treasure. During the same storm the Portuguese East Indiaman *Nossa Senhora de Ajuda* (850 tons/864 tonnes), commanded by Captain Pedro de Menezes and carrying a cargo valued at 1.4 million crusadoes, including 375,000 pieces of Chinese porcelain, sank 2 leagues from the Bay of Angra and only thirty of the 400 people on board were saved.

1647: The Azores suffered from five earthquakes during June and July of that year and not a single building was left standing on Terceira Island. The loss to shipping was catastrophic. At least 120 ships were lost, thirty of which were rich Portuguese East Indiamen and Spanish galleons. Many of the smaller ships were carried far inland by tidal waves. The total loss of treasure was estimated to be in excess of 40 million pesos.

1649: The combined fleets from Tierra Firme and New Spain, under the command of Captain General Juan de Pujadas y Gamboa, were but an hour's sail from reaching the Bay of Angra when a tempest arose, causing four galleons to wreck on the rocky coastline and taking 1,500 lives and 6,590,700 pesos in gold and silver down with them.

1651: The Portuguese East Indiaman *San Pedro de Hamburgo* (700 tons/711 tonnes, thirty cannons), commanded by Captain Francisco de Sa Coutinho and coming from Macao with over 2 million crusadoes in cargo, including 400,000 pieces of Chinese porcelain, was totally lost at Punta de Marenna on the north coast of Terceira Island. She struck the coast, then sank in deep water with no survivors. Sailing with her was another East Indiaman, *Nossa Senhora da Conceição,* with a cargo worth 1.2 million crusadoes, which wrecked off Burarcos on San Miguel Island with a total loss of life.

1651: The Portuguese East Indiaman *São Panteleao* (1,800 tons/1829 tonnes), commanded by Captain João Telles de Menezes and coming from India via Brazil with a cargo valued at 1.3 million crusadoes, wrecked at Villa d'Agua de Pao on Terceira Island in shallow water. Fewer than thirty of the 300 men on board drowned. Two divers drowned in an unsuccessful attempt to recover her bronze cannons.

1660: The Portuguese East Indiaman *Nossa Senhora da Boa Memoria* (2,200 tons/2,235 tonnes), commanded by Captain Garpar Pereira dos Reis and coming from India with a cargo valued at 840,000 crusadoes, wrecked on the east side of Fayal Island and only a small number of people survived.

1663: Three unidentified rich Spanish galleons, carrying over 4 million pesos in treasure from Mexico, sank on the west side of Fayal Island in a bad storm. All aboard perished.

1664: As the combined New Spain and Tierra Firme fleets were approaching the Bay of Angra, a storm arose and four unidentified galleons, carrying a total of 6.58 million pesos in treasure, were wrecked just west of the Bay of Angra. Two other galleons from this convoy wrecked on Pico Island.

1677: The Brazil fleet, totaling 86 ships coming from Rio de Janeiro, Salvador, and Pernambuco, was heading for Angra Bay when a hurricane struck. While it was raging, an earthquake occurred making enormous cross-seas. Forty-two ships were lost on the high seas. More than 6,500 people perished, and the value of lost cargoes, which included vast amounts of gold and diamonds, was over 20 million crusadoes.

1687: A Dutch merchantman, chartered by Spaniards, was coming from Havana with 550,000 pesos in treasure when she wrecked upon a reef formation known as Las Formigas, located about midway between Santa Maria and San Miguel Islands. Some crew and passengers clinging to pieces of the ship were attacked by sharks, and about twenty were rescued by a fishing boat.

1690: During a violent storm lasting over five hours, 14 large, richly laden ships were lost around Terceira Island. Two of these were Portuguese East Indiamen, which sank on the high seas, and other 12 were Spanish galleons coming from Havana with over 8 million pesos on board. They too sank on the high seas close to land. Seven other Spanish galleons wrecked near Angra; they carried over 4 million pesos in treasure. Later that same year, an earthquake struck San Miguel and Terceira islands, and twenty large and small ships were lost with the loss of over 1,500 lives and an unknown amount of treasure. Two months later, two other ships were lost in a bad storm: the Spanish galleons *Nuestra Señora de Santa Maria,* commanded by Captain Pasquez de Iriarte, and the *Nuestra Señora del Mar,* commanded by Captain Ignacio Francisco de Pineda y Salinas. Both were coming from Havana with 2.95 million pesos in treasure on board. They went down on the high seas within sight of land.

1690: The Spanish galleon *Nuestra Señora del Populo,* commanded by Captain Joseph Lopez de Carvajal and carrying 1.32 million pesos in treasure, was hit by a hurricane when passing between Flores and Corvo Island and wrecked on the south side of Fayal Island with a total loss of lives and treasure.

1692: Two Spanish galleons coming from Havana—the *Nuestra Señora de los Remedios y las Animas,* commanded by Captain Martín Blanco del Alamo and with 1.3 million pesos in treasure on board, and the *Nuestra Señora de Cruz de Caravaca,* commanded by Captain Diego de Voja and with an unknown amount of treasure—wrecked off the west end of Terceira Island with a total loss of life and treasures.

1693: The Dutch East Indiaman *Waterland* (1,138 tons/1,156 tonnes, quite large for a Dutch ship at this time), commanded by Admiral Willem Kemp and coming from Batavia with a cargo valued at 234,773 guilders, plus significant personal treasure belonging to the admiral, was attacked by cannon fire from a French warship and sank within sight of the soldiers in the forts of Angra Bay.

1695: The Spanish galleon *Jesús Nazareno* (550 tons/559 tonnes, 44 cannons), with 335 people on board, and commanded by Captain Sebastián Muñoz, came from Havana with over 2 million pesos on board and developed a fatal leak after riding through a hurricane in mid ocean. She sank about an hour's sail from the entrance to the Bay of Angra.

1713: An unidentified French East Indiaman, commanded by Captain Jean Dubois, was sailing between the Orient and France with a cargo valued in excess of 1 million livres when it ran into a hurricane off Terceira Island and sank on the high seas several leagues offshore. There were no survivors. During the same hurricane, the Spanish galleon *Santo Cristo de San Román y Nuestra Señora de Copacabana* (348 tons/353.5 tonnes, sixty cannons), commanded by Captain Martín de Zabala and with over 1 million pesos in treasure, sank on the high seas near Angra with a total loss of life.

1718: During a hurricane, 38 large, richly laden ships were lost around the Azores. Fifteen of 17 lost off Terceira Island were returning Spanish galleons carrying over 11 million pesos in treasure. More than 5,000 people perished.

1720: A devastating earthquake struck Terceira Island on December 8, sinking 18 large, richly laden ships in Angra Bay and drowning over 2,500 men. The value of their treasure and cargoes exceeded 12 million pesos. An unidentified Portuguese East Indiaman, waiting to have her many leaks and rudder repaired, went down in 50 fathoms of water with a cargo from the Orient valued at 2 million crusadoes.

1724: During a hurricane on November 19, seven large ships were wrecked on the north coast of San Miguel. Two of them were very rich Portuguese East Indiamen and one was a ship from Brazil "carrying a vast amount of gold and diamonds."

1726: The Portuguese warship *São Julião* (800 tons/813 tonnes), commanded by Captain Francisco Brandao and carrying 6.5 million crusadoes in gold and diamonds, sank 1.5 to 2 leagues south of Punta de Judeu on Terceira Island, and over 600 people drowned. She was part of a fleet sailing for Lisbon with the most treasure ever to leave from Brazil. Her sister ship, *Santa Rosa,* with over 40 tons (40.64 tonnes) of gold on board, blew up and sank off Cabo de Santo Agostinho 20.5 miles (33 kilometers) south of Recife, Brazil. At this time most of the mines in Peru and Mexico had been worked out and Brazil had become the main source of gold in the New World.

1727: As the Brazil fleet reached the Azores, it encountered a violent storm and the Portuguese warship *Rainha Santa,* with over 7 million crusadoes in gold and diamonds, sank 12 leagues south of San Miguel Island; six other ships also sank in the same general area.

1731: The Spanish galleon *Nuestra Señora del Rosario y San Cristóbal* (732 tons/744 tonnes), commanded by Captain Nicolás de Francia and coming from Havana with gold and silver valued at 675,000 pesos, sank in a storm 2 leagues north of Graciosa Island and 45 of her men were saved.

1734: A fleet of 78 Portuguese ships, en route from Brazil to Lisbon, stopped in the Bay of Angra. While at anchor, a storm came up and two ships collided, causing the *Bom Jesús,* a large merchantman carrying over 3 million crusadoes in gold and diamonds, to sink in 65 fathoms of water, but most of her people were saved.

1739: The Spanish ship *Nuestra Señora de la Candelaria y San Joseph y las Animas* (750 tons/762 tonnes), commanded by Captain Alonso de Yrribar and coming from Veracruz with 2.5 million pesos in treasure aboard, was forced to seek refuge from a storm in the port of Horta on Fayal Island. While trying to enter this port, she wrecked and then slid off into deep water. Only a few people survived.

1741: The Dutch East Indiaman *Hilversbeek* (850 tons/864 tonnes), commanded by Captain Frans de Put and sailing from Batavia for Holland with a cargo valued at 132,000 guilders, excluding about 40,000 pieces of blue-and-white Chinese porcelain, ran aground on the west side of Flores Island and exploded. There were few survivors.

1742: Two Dutch East Indiamen—the *Enkhuizen* (850 tons/864 tonnes), commanded by Captain Dirk Zomerman and coming from China with a cargo valued at 428,000 guilders, wrecked on the south side of Santa Maria island, and the *Abbekerk* (850 tons/864 tonnes), commanded by Captain Dirk van der Poel and coming from Batavia with a cargo valued at 390,000 guilders—were lost on the northeast side of San Miguel Island when an underwater volcanic eruption precipitated several huge tidal waves.

1745: The Dutch East Indiaman *Heuvel* (650 tons/660.5 tonnes), coming from Batavia with a cargo valued at 152,000 guilders, plus a large amount of Chinese porcelain, sunk on Corvo Island's west side.

1755: At the same time that the "Great Lisbon Earthquake" struck, one also occurred in the Azores. San Miguel Island suffered the most. The port of Ponta Delgada was completely inundated by the sea, and most of the homes and thousands of people were carried away into the sea. Seven large ships were lost at this port and two others, one of which was an unidentified Portuguese East Indiaman, sank off Vila Franca. At Terceira Island, five Spanish galleons, coming from the New World and heading for the Bay of Angra, sank about 5 leagues south of the island with a total loss of life and treasure valued at 4.85 million pesos. Two months later, a less catastrophic earthquake struck Terceira Island, causing the Spanish galleon *San Francisco Xavier* (46 cannons), commanded by Captain Domingo Carranza, to sink a half league south of Los Altares on Terceira Island. She was carrying over 1 million pesos of gold and silver salvaged from a wreck off Jamaica.

1758: An unidentified Spanish galleon, coming from Buenos Aires with over 2 million pesos in gold and silver, was wrecked on the west end of Terceira island. Gold and silver coins in large quantities came ashore for months afterwards.

1758: An unidentified Dutch East Indiaman (1,150 tons/1,168.5 tonnes), commanded by Admiral de Graaf and carrying 313,746 guilders of cargo from Batavia to Holland, developed a bad leak and tried to enter Ponta Delgada to make repairs. The local authorities refused her entry and she sank about a half mile (.80 kilometer) off the port.

1761: An unidentified French East Indiaman, coming from China with a very valuable cargo, including 340,000 pieces of Chinese porcelain and 78 boxes of precious stones and pearls, wrecked in a storm near Praia on Terceira Island and over 500 souls perished.

1761: A violent hurricane struck on September 29 and every single ship and boat anchored or sailing around Terceira Island sank, drowning over 8,000 people. Sixteen of the ships were Spanish galleons and merchantmen from the New World with over 14 million pesos in treasure. Fourteen others were Portuguese ships from Brazil with unknown amounts of treasure and cargo. The only locations given were for three large rich Portuguese East Indiamen that were attempting to enter the Bay of Angra when the hurricane struck. They sank within sight of land with a total loss of lives and cargoes.

1772: The Spanish ship *El Buen Cones*, commanded by Captain Albert Cattier and coming from Havana with treasure salvaged from the galleon *El Nuevo Victoria*, commanded by Captain Umaran, which had been lost in the Florida Keys, was wrecked under high cliffs near the west end of Terceira island, but then slipped off in deep water and only her people could be saved.

1774: During a violent hurricane on November 23, four Spanish galleons, coming from Panama and Mexico with over 6 million pesos in gold and silver on board, sank in a bad storm 3 to 4 leagues south of Angra Bay and only 74 men were saved.

1779: A hurricane struck the Azores, sinking seven unidentified ships "with over 1.7 million pesos in treasure" at Horta on Fayal Island. During the storm, the notorious pirate ship *Carmen* (36 cannons), carrying "a large amount of plunder it had amassed over several months," wrecked on Fayal and seven pirates survived and later were tried and hanged.

1781: The Dutch East Indiaman *Concordia* (1,150 tons/1,168.5 tonnes), commanded by Captain Evert Wesseling and sailing from Batavia to Holland, sank during a battle with a British privateer off Flores Island and only a few people were saved.

1789: The worst storm ever recorded in the Azores occurred on October 28 and over 270 ships were sunk or wrecked around all of the islands. The loss of treasure, cargoes, ships and cannons exceeded 45 million crusadoes.

1799: Two earthquakes struck Terceira, Graciosa and Pico Islands in June and December, sinking over thirty large, richly laden ships around the three islands. One of them, a Spanish galleon coming from Mexico with over 1 million pesos in treasure, capsized and stayed afloat for two days upside down before sinking near Praia on Terceira Island.

CHAPTER 20

ATLANTIC ISLANDS' RICHEST SHIPWRECKS

Cape Verde Islands: The Phoenicians were probably the first to visit these islands. Phoenician artifacts have been found on two of the ten volcanic islands in this group, located 320 miles (515 kilometers) off the African coast. The Cape Verdes were rediscovered in 1496 by Venetian navigator Ca Da Mosta, sailing for Prince Henry the Navigator. They were annexed to Portugal in 1596, and the capitol Praia was founded on Santiago Island the same year, replacing Cidade (now in ruins). The scarcity of water, even today, has prevented the islands from attaining importance, except as a haven for ships needing repairs. East Indiamen of all nations passed close to them when heading for the Orient, and numerous ships met their doom on the reefs surrounding these islands. There has been some commercial salvage on several of these wrecks in recent years, but no major finds have been made.

The Canary Islands: Known to the Romans as the "fortunate isles," the volcanic Canaries off the northwestern coast of Africa were rediscovered and claimed by Portugal in 1341. In 1402 the pope arbitrarily awarded the islands to Spain, which continues to govern. During the Colonial Period, they was a major contraband center where European nations sold illegal manufactured goods to ships bound for the New World. Andalusia had a monopoly on selling wine to the New World colonists, but the islands supplied large amounts to American-bound fleets. The Canaries also did a brisk trade in wine for fish with ships from New England.

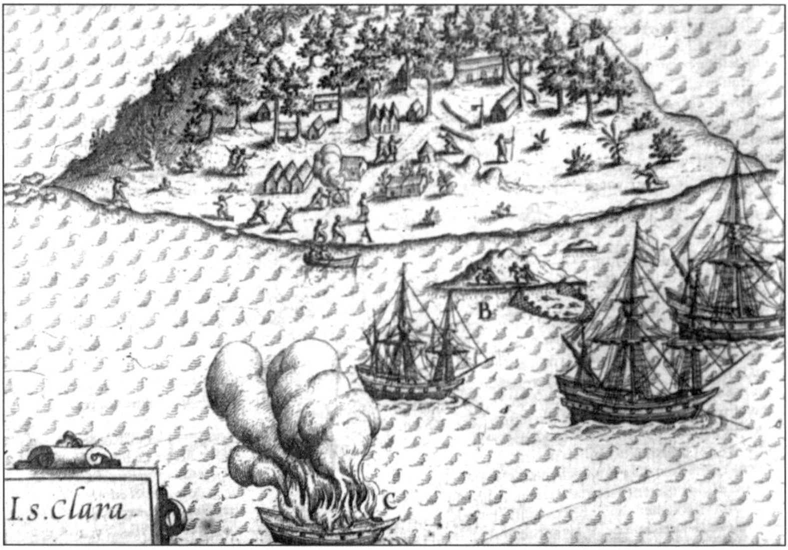

A Portuguese ship on fire during a Dutch attack off Santa Clara Island in the Cape Verde Islands.

Ascension Island: First discovered in 1501 by the Portuguese, this island lies just below the equator, about halfway between Brazil and Africa. Its closest neighbor is St. Helena Island, about 800 miles (1,287 kilometers) to the south. Throughout the era of sail, the island served as a navigational checkpoint for vessels returning from the Orient and the Pacific. Many stopped to obtain water, fish, and turtles to replenish diminished food stores. Others put in to make repairs to their ships, to refresh crews suffering from disease, and sometimes to maroon mutineers and criminals. In addition to two Portuguese East Indiamen lost in 1568 and 1589, other richly laden ships were lost there.

St. Helena: The Portuguese discovered this small volcanic island in the remote South Atlantic Ocean in 1502. For over eighty years, the Portuguese kept their discovery a secret, using the island base to replenish their East India fleet. St. Helena, like Ascension, Island, was a haven for ships returning from the Orient. On numerous occasions rival Dutch and Portuguese East Indiamen put in at the same time, sparking fierce battles. One such encounter occurred in 1613 when two large Portuguese ships fought with four Dutch ships. The Dutch ship *Witte Leew* blew up and sank. In 1976 Robert Stenuit used side-scan sonar to find the wreck. He salvaged it, but never found the large amount of diamonds and other precious stones the ship carried. The island has been in British hands since they seized and fortified it in 1669. Napoleon Bonaparte was exiled on St. Helena from 1815 to 1821.

Madeira Island: Madeira was visited by the Romans from the beginning of the Christian era onwards and then was forgotten for centuries until rediscovered by the Portuguese in 1420. They founded the main port of Funchal in 1421. During the Colonial Period, the island was famous for its wine, known as Madeira, which was in great demand. By the beginning of the nineteenth century, over 100 ships a year from European nations and New England went there to purchase wine. Occasionally Portuguese ships, en route to the Orient and Brazil, made stops for repairs to their ships and to purchase wine.

1508: The Portuguese East Indiaman *São Jorge* commanded by Captain Jorge de Aquiar and sailing between Lisbon and India, wrecked at Tristan da Cunha Island. She had over 300,000 crusadoes in gold and silver specie and most likely is the oldest wreck on this South Atlantic island.

1518: The Portuguese East Indiaman *São Bartolomeu* (1,800 tons/1,829 tonnes), commanded by Captain Lopo Soares and sailing from Lisbon to Goa with 670,000 crusadoes in treasure, sprang a bad leak. Unable to keep the ship afloat, the captain ran her aground on the east side on Tenerife Island, Canaries, where she exploded.

1519: The Portuguese merchantman *São Jeronimo* (1,900 tons/1,930.5 tonnes), sailing from Lisbon to India with "a large amount of treasure," was attacked by pirates off the Moroccan coast. With sails and rigging badly damaged, the vessel put in at Gomera Island, Canaries, for repairs. When they realized the Spaniards there intended to seize the ship, the crew set her on fire and she sank.

1524: The Portuguese ship *Barbosa,* commanded by Captain Francisco de Brito and sailing from Lisbon to Hormuz with 330,000 crusa-

Early sixteenth-century iron cannon recovered from a wreck off Praia Island in the Cape Verde Islands, being prepared for conservation.

does in treasure, was attacked by Barbary pirates. Holed and taking on water, the Barbosa headed for the Canary Islands and sank on the west side of Lanzarote Island.

1568: The Portuguese East Indiaman *Nossa Senhora da Estrella* (1,900 tons/1,930.5 tonnes) commanded by Captain Sebastao Jorge de Faria, was lost on the east side of Ascension Island, carrying over 1 million crusadoes in cargo from the Orient. Only twenty of the 475 souls on her were saved.

1572: As the Tierra Firme Fleet was sailing from Spain to Cartagena, Colombia, the galleon *San Juan* (400 tons/406.5 tonnes), commanded by Captain Andrés d'Escobedo and carrying 180 tons (183 tonnes) of mercury from the mines of Peru, wrecked during a storm on the east side of Lanzarote Island, Canaries.

1586: The Spanish merchantman *San Miguel* (150 tons/152 tonnes), commanded by Captain Francisco de Ribera and carrying 63 tons (64 tonnes) of mercury, wrecked on the east side of Fuerteventura island, Canaries. There were few survivors.

1590: The Portuguese East Indiaman *São Lucas* (1,800 tons/1,829 tonnes), sailing from Lisbon to Malacca with a "large amount of gold and silver" on board, was wrecked in a storm on the east side of Tenerife Island, Canaries. Few people were saved.

1598: The Portuguese East Indiaman *São Tome* (1,400 tons/1,422.5 tonnes), was lost on the north side of Ascension Island with over 2 million crusadoes' worth of Oriental cargo. Only 77 of the 640 souls aboard survived. They were rescued three years later.

1601: The Portuguese East Indiaman *Santiago* (1,300 tons/1,321 tonnes, 38 cannons), returning to Lisbon from India with a cargo worth 350,000 crusadoes, stopped at St. Helena for refreshments. While the *Santiago* was there, she was destroyed by cannon fire from three large Dutch ships that suddenly appeared.

1613: The Dutch East Indiaman *Middleburg* (540 tons/548 tonnes), homeward bound from Batavia (Jakarta) and carrying a cargo valued at over 240,000 guilders, was attacked by two Portuguese ships and sent to the bottom off St. Helena Island. Several modern-day expeditions have failed to locate her.

1615: The armada of Captain Manuel de Meneses, sailing between India and Lisbon, stopped for water at St. Helena Island where it was attacked while at anchor by five Dutch ships. One of the Dutch ships, carrying "a very valuable cargo of Oriental products," was sunk in the battle.

1623: The Dutch East Indiaman *Naarden* (180 tons/183 tonnes), commanded by Captain Aarnoud Koeze and sailing between Holland and India with 210,00 guilders in silver specie, wrecked on the north side of Boa Vista Island, Cape Verde islands.

1624: The Portuguese East Indiaman *Nossa Senhora do Belém* commanded by Captain Francisco de Tavora da Cunha and sailing between India and Lisbon with "a large and valuable cargo," was badly damaged in a storm off the Cape of Good Hope. She went to St. Helena Island for repairs, but sank soon after anchoring there.

1624: The Portuguese East Indiaman *Nossa Senhora do Concecião* (430 tons/436 tonnes), commanded by Captain Antonio Moniz Barreto and carrying 348,000 crusadoes in gold and silver specie, sailed from Lisbon for India, and was wrecked along with five other unidentified ships in the same armada on the Shoals of Santa Ana to the north of Maio Island in the Cape Verde islands group.

1625: The Spanish galleon *Nuestra Señora del Concepción,* on a voyage from Spain to Mexico, detoured to pick up survivors from a Spanish ship wrecked on the Island of Maio in the Cape Verdes and wrecked there herself. She carried 85 tons (86 tonnes) of mercury when lost.

1629: The Dutch East Indiaman *Zoutelande* (100 tons/101.5 tonnes), commanded by Captain Albert Jansz and sailing between Holland and the Moluccas with 220,000 guilders of gold and silver on board, wrecked on the north side of Santo Antão Island in the Cape Verde islands. There were some survivors.

1632: The Portuguese East Indiaman *Nossa Senhora dos Remedios* (1,450 tons/1,473 tonnes), commanded by Captain Francisco Vaz de Almada and returning to Lisbon from India with a cargo valued at 900,000 crusadoes, sank off Funchal, Madeira Island, from a leak incurred while attempting to unload cargo onto another ship.

1635: The Spanish galleon *San Josef,* en route from Cádiz to Mexico with 100 tons (101.5 tonnes) of mercury and other general cargo, was totally lost in a storm off the north side of Madeira Island. She was well off the usual route to the New World having been pursued by Barbary Corsairs. Contemporary salvors recovered only five bronze cannons and two anchors.

1644: The Portuguese East Indiaman *Santo António* (880 tons/894 tonnes, thirty cannons), commanded by Captain Amador Lauzado and sailing from Lisbon to India with 360,000 crusadoes in gold and silver bullion and specie, wrecked during a storm on Fogo Island, Cape Verde islands. There were some survivors.

1645: The Dutch East Indiaman *Sloterdijk* (310 tons/315 tonnes), commanded by Captain Anthonie Koleman and sailing between Holland and Batavia with 210,000 guilders in silver specie, was lost on the east side of São Nicolau Island, Cape Verde islands, and only her crew were saved.

1657: As the New Spain Fleet approached Cádiz, they found that an English squadron under Admiral Robert Blake lay in wait. The fleet headed for the safety of the Canaries and anchored off the town of Santa Cruz on Tenerife Island. They had off-loaded about one-third of 11 million pesos of treasure when the English arrived. The Spaniards scuttled some of their ships to keep them out of the hands of the English. Nothing was ever recovered until the 1980s when several bronze cannons believed to be from one of these ships were brought up.

1664: The French East Indiaman *Taureau* (250 tons/254 tonnes), sailing between France and Madagascar Island and carrying 320,000 livres in gold and silver, anchored off Brava Island, Cape Verde Islands, to obtain fresh water and fire wood. While there she capsized and sank and only some of her people were saved.

1667: The Dutch East Indiaman *Wapen Van Amsterdam* (920 tons/935 tonnes, 58 cannons), commanded by Captain Reinier Brinkmans and returning from Batavia to Holland, was wrecked on the south coast of Iceland; only 14 men were saved. Her cargo, valued at 385,000 guilders, included several chests of precious stones and pearls.

1678: The Dutch East Indiaman *Horstermeer* (310 tons/315 tonnes), sailing from Holland to Batavia with 322,000 guilders in gold and silver, wrecked on Tristan da Cunha Island in the South Atlantic. Six years later, a passing English ship rescued nine survivors from the *Horstermeer*.

1693: The Dutch East Indiaman *Gouden Buis* (660 tons/670.5 tonnes), sailing from Holland to Batavia with 390,000 guilders in treasure, wrecked on the north coast of St. Helena Island. Survivors saved only three chests of coins. In 1728 two of John Lethbridge's divers sent to salvage her were unable to locate the site.

1719: The Dutch East Indiaman *Vansittart* (480 tons/488 tonnes), sailing from Holland to Batavia with 250,000 guilders of silver specie and bullion, was lost on São Nicolau Island in the Cape Verde Island group. In the 1980s several salvage groups worked briefly on this wreck and recovered around 5,000 Dutch silver ducatoon coins and some Spanish pieces of eight.

1729: The Dutch East Indiaman *Graveland* (600 tons/610 tonnes), commanded by Captain Gideon Kuiper and sailing from Batavia to Holland with 362,000 guilders in treasure, stopped at the Cape of Good Hope, then headed for St. Helena Island when she wrecked on Tristan da Cunha Island. A small number of survivors were picked up 14 years later by a British ship.

1732: The Dutch East Indiaman *Slot ter Hoge* (800 tons/813 tonnes), commanded by Captain Willem de Smit, left Holland for Batavia with "a considerable amount of silver and gold" and was wrecked on Maio Island, Cape Verde Islands. Her crew was saved, but the cargo was lost.

1733: The Dutch East Indiaman *Blijdorp* (900 tons/914.5 tonnes), commanded by Captain Haije Blauwhuis and sailing between Holland and Batavia with 350,000 guilders in gold and silver bullion and specie, was lost on Maio Island, Cape Verde Islands, and only the crew was saved.

1742: The Dutch East Indiaman *Westerbeek* (650 tons/660.5 tonnes), commanded by Captain Herman Schutte and coming from Ceylon with a cargo valued at 398,000 guilders, was lost on Hierro, smallest of the Canaries. Most of the crew survived. Soon afterward a Spanish salvage effort recovered little.

1743: The Dutch East Indiaman *Maria Adriana* (650 tons/660.5 tonnes, forty-six46 cannons), commanded by Captain Jan Elswout and coming from Batavia with a cargo valued at 142,000 guilders, wrecked on the south side of Ascension Island. Several months later, an English ship picked up the 97 survivors and took them back to Holland. The English received a generous reward from the Dutch East India Company.

1744: Two Dutch East Indiamen—the *Drechtland* (250 tons/254 tonnes, 28 cannons), commanded by Captain Pieter Krook, had cargo valued at 195,000 guilders, and the *Hofvliet* (1,000 tons/1,016 tonnes), commanded by Captain Pieter Lakeman, with cargo valued at 156,000 guilders—were coming from Batavia when they were lost on a small island located off the coast of Brazil. The *Strjen* (650 tons/660.5 tonnes), with a cargo of unknown value, was sailing with the other two ships when she was lost on nearby St. Paul's Rock. Survivors were rescued by the Portuguese, taken to Salvador, and imprisoned.

1750: The British East Indiaman the *Duke of Cumberland,* sailing from England to India, was lost on the north side of São Nicolau Island, Cape Verde Islands, carrying £320,000 pounds sterling in silver specie. Contemporary salvors recovered about a quarter of this treasure.

1759: The Dutch East Indiaman *Bevalligheid* (850 tons/864 tonnes), commanded by Captain Albert Verzaat and coming from Batavia with a cargo valued at 241,000 guilders, excluding several chests of precious stones and pearls, was fleeing from pirates and ran aground on the east side of Tenerife Island, Canaries. The Dutch blew the ship up as they fled ashore.

1765: The Dutch East Indiaman *Sint Laurens* (220 tons/223.5 tonnes), sailing between Holland and Batavia with 190,000 guilders of gold and silver treasure, was lost in a storm on Boa Vista Island, Cape Verde islands.

1767: The Dutch East Indiaman *Pallas* (1,200 tons/1,219 tonnes, 48 cannons), commanded by Captain Willem van Dalem and carrying over 400,000 guilders in gold and silver bullion and specie, was lost on the east side of Tenerife Island, Canaries. Salvage attempts a year later failed to recover any of the treasure.

1770: The Dutch East Indiaman *Leimuiden* (1,150 tons/1,168.5 tonnes), commanded by Captain Thomas Brunel and sailing between Holland and Batavia, with 230,000 guilders in gold and silver bullion and specie, was lost on the east side of Boa Vista Island, Cape Verde Islands.

1771: The Dutch East Indiaman *Vredejaar* (850 tons/863.5 tonnes, 44 cannons), commanded by Captain Arie Arkebout and sailing between Holland and China with 550,000 guilders of treasure, was wrecked during a storm on the east side of Praia Island, Cape Verde Islands, and only the people were saved.

1773: An unidentified Dutch East Indiaman, the flagship of a fleet sailing from Batavia to Holland, stopped at St. Helena Island for fresh water. Less than half an hour after leaving port, she sank for no apparent reason. Her cargo was valued at over 600,000 guilders.

1777: The Dutch East Indiaman *Duivenburg* (1,150 tons/1,168.5 tonnes), commanded by Captain Gerrit Evertsz Popta and sailing from Batavia to Holland with a cargo of porcelain and exotic Oriental objects of "great value," was lost on the south side of Grand Canary Island.

1779: Two Dutch East Indiamen sailing from China to Holland—the *Abbekerk* (850 tons/863.5 tonnes), commanded by Captain Kasper

Burger, with a cargo valued at 571,242 guilders, and the *Vredenhof* (1,150 tons/1,168.5 tonnes), commanded by Captain Reindert den Uil, with cargo valued at 745,266 guilders—were lost on Ascension Island.

1780: The Dutch East Indiaman *Juno* (850 tons/863.5 tonnes), commanded by Captain Hubert Hendrik Hendriksz and sailing from Holland to Cape Town with 490,000 guilders in gold and silver, was wrecked on the north side of Santo Antão Islands in the Cape Verde islands.

1787: The British East Indiaman *Hartwell*, en route to India with over £400,000 pounds sterling in silver specie and bullion, was lost on a reef now named Hartwell Reef, off the north side of Boa Vista Island, Cape Verde Islands. The ship was lost because of a mutiny on board, which was suppressed by the ship's officers and loyal crew members; however, it is believed that one of the mutineers deliberately ran the ship up on the reef while he was at the wheel.

1795: The British slave ship *Thomas*, commanded by Captain Millar and sailing between Plymouth and the west coast of Africa to purchase slaves destined for the West Indies, was wrecked in a gale on Sal Island, Cape Verde islands. None of the £77,000 pounds sterling in gold specie was saved.

1802: The Portuguese merchantman *Aurora*, commanded by Captain Fabrício João dos Santos and carrying 138,000 crusadoes in treasure, caught fire while anchored off Funchal, Madeira Island, and quickly blew up, shattering windows in many homes near the port. There were only 34 survivors.

1806: The British East Indiaman *Lady Burgess*, sailing from England to India in a convoy of seven ships, wrecked on a reef between Boa Vista and Santiago Islands in the Cape Verde Islands. Thirty-four lives were lost and none of the £180,000 pounds sterling in gold and silver specie was ever recovered.

(Facing, top image) Gold and silver coins recovered from an unidentified Portuguese wreck off Tenerife Island in the Canary Islands. *(Facing, lower image)* Large blue-and-white Chinese porcelain platter recovered from a Dutch wreck off St. Helena Island.

(Above left) Three silver and two copper Portuguese coins recovered from the harbor bottom in Funchal, Madeira. *(Above right)* Mid 16th century bronze Portuguese astrolabe, recovered near Cape Verde Islands. Some of these recovered in recent years have sold for more than half a million dollars because of their rarity. Less than 70 are known to exist in the world.

(Below) Vestiges of many wrecks on the Baixo de India lie in a few feet of water, as evidenced by these two iron cannons and anchor.

CHAPTER 21

AFRICA'S RICHEST SHIPWRECKS

As early as 3000 B.C. the Egyptians were trading along the northern and eastern shores of Africa. The Minoans, Phoenicians, Greeks and Romans followed. The first known mariner to circumnavigate Africa was the Carthaginian Hanno. In 450 B.C. he set out from Carthage, in present-day Tunisia, with sixty ships. The fleet passed through the Straits of Gibraltar, which marked the end of the world, as the ancients knew it, and sailed down the Moroccan coast, establishing a colony at Thymiaterium (modern Mehedia, 70 miles/113 kilometers north of Casablanca). Further down the coast Hanno founded Agadir and Essaouira and four other settlements. The base they made at Arguin Island off Mauritania became West Africa's most important trading colony for 400 years until 146 B.C. when the Romans leveled Carthage.

The Greek historian Herodotus described the silent barter system Hanno pioneered. "They land on the coast, unload their cargo such as blocks of salt that is most esteemed by the natives, then light a fire and return to their ships. The timid people of the country see the smoke, come to the beach, lay down their gold and ivory to pay for the goods, then withdraw inland. Then the Carthaginians come ashore and examine the gold and ivory. If they are satisfied, they pick it up and sail away. If not, they return to their ships and wait for the natives to bring more gold and ivory until the visitors are satisfied."

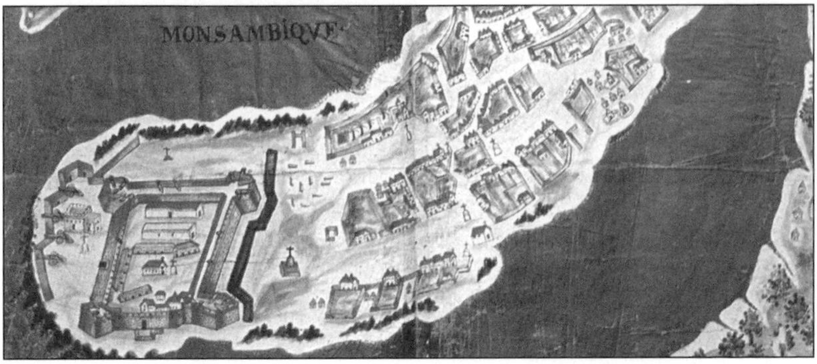

The island of Mozambique, off the coast of Mozambique, was one of the main bases used by the Portuguese East Indiamen. Over the centuries more than 100 rich ships were lost.

After the fall of Carthage the stretch of Saharan West African coast settled by Hanno sank into oblivion for over 1,000 years. In the late Middle Ages, Portuguese expeditions spent half a century rediscovering the places the Carthaginians had discovered and colonized in just a few months.

The Portuguese initiated the Age of Exploration and opened up Africa for the rest of the modern world. In 1143 this tiny nation emerged from centuries of Moorish domination. Soon after, the fledgling Portuguese navy defeated a large Moorish fleet. By 1300 their ships were making trading voyages to France, Flanders and England and along the north coast of Africa. In 1341 they made the first recorded visit to the Canary Islands since Roman times. Overcoming superstition and fear of the unknown, the Portuguese ventured farther into the Atlantic and down the west coast of Africa, discovering the Azores Islands in 1427.

Prince Henry the Navigator founded the school of navigation at Sagres on the southern coast of Portugal with the aim of finding a sea route to the African zone where Moroccans traded salt for gold, pound for pound, with the natives. Like the Phoenicians before them, the Portuguese were very secretive about their ocean voyages. Prince Henry began his systematic explorations mistakenly believing it would take no more than a few years to cover the entire west coast of Africa and reach the East Indies.

The Atlantic desert coast of Africa juts out at Cape Bojador about 150 miles (241 kilometers) south of the Canary Islands. The Cape was considered the edge of the known world and the area below it was the "Green Sea of Darkness," a terrifying zone where even the bravest mariners believed that the sea boiled and relentless tides prevented ships from ever sailing home. Tales abounded of giant sea monsters that rose from the inky depths, swallowing ships whole. Prince Henry ignored these perceptions and in 1419 dispatched an expedition to sail around Cape Bojador and investigate the waters to the south. The closer the ships got to the Cape, the more frightened the mariners became. They finally turned north and sailed home. Undeterred, Henry sent out 13 more expeditions, but each time that the ships ventured within sight of Cape Bojador, fear overcame them and they turned back to Lisbon. Prince Henry's patience and money were running out when, in 1433, he sent Gil Eannes, one of his squires, in a single small vessel. He, too, lost heart and turned about after reaching the Canaries. Henry was obsessed. He sent Eannes out once more, threatening to hang him if he failed and offering rich rewards for success.

Thus motivated, Eannes became the first mariner to double Cape Bojador. After that, expeditions ventured a little farther south each year along the forbidding coast. In 1437 two ships returned with the first cargo of commercial value. They had discovered the area known as Rio de Oro today, where they traded for large quantities of gold. In the 1440s the Portuguese made a settlement at Arguin (Arguim) Island off Mauritania near the present-day boundary with Western Sahara, where the Phoenicians once had their trading base. There they traded wheat and cloth for gold and African slaves, purchased from local chieftains. Almost yearly they pressed further down the coast, about 100 miles (161 kilometers) at a time. By the time Prince Henry died in 1460, his mariners reached about halfway down the west coast of Africa. It wasn't until 1487 that Bartolomeu Dias reached the Cape of Good Hope. Later that year, Vasco da Gama, following in his wake, rounded the Cape and explored a large part of the east coast of Africa.

Throughout these explorations the Portuguese set up fortified trading posts where items of little intrinsic value—such as glass beads, brass utensils, cowry shells, grain and cloth—were exchanged for gold, ivory and, most valuable of all, African slaves. The fruits of the Gold Coast trade greatly enriched Portugal. In 1457 so much gold reached Lisbon that the mint, which had not struck gold coins in over 200 years, began turning out large numbers of gold cruzado coins. The Gold Coast trade was difficult and dangerous, and tropical diseases deterred competitors until the end of the sixteenth century, but Portugal's monopoly inevitably attracted increasing numbers of European adventurers and traders from the Netherlands, Spain, Britain, Denmark, Sweden and Germany.

1441: An unidentified Portuguese caravel, laden with 28 tons (28.44 tonnes) of ivory tusks, gold dust, and 3 tons (3.048 tonnes) of gold nuggets, capsized in a storm and sank less than an hour after setting sail from Arguin Island. All 78 men drowned and the cargo was lost.

1502: The Portuguese ship *São Paulo*, commanded by Captain Antonio Fernandes, was totally lost on a reef off Sofala, Mozambique, from whence it had just embarked after taking on a valuable cargo of gold and elephant ivory tusks.

1504: A squadron of Portuguese warships was sent to dislodge Barbary pirates based at Larache, Morocco, who had been attacking shipping in the Mediterranean and off of Portugal. When the pirates sighted the approaching warships, they transferred loot from warehouses to seven vessels in which they tried to escape. In the ensuing battle off the port entrance, six pirate ships were sunk with their treasures.

1508: The Portuguese merchantman *Santa Cruz* (1,200 tons/1,219 tonnes, 46 cannons), commanded by Captain Duarte de Lemos and sailing between Lisbon and Hormuz with 900,000 crusadoes in treasure, was lost off Mozambique at a place called Baixos de Padua.

1509: The Portuguese merchantman *Santiago Galega* (800 tons/813 tonnes), commanded by Captain Rui de Cunha and sailing from

Lisbon to the island of Mozambique (the major Portuguese port between Lisbon and India used for repairs and obtaining water and provisions) with "a large amount of treasure on board," capsized after reaching the port of Mozambique.

1510: The Portuguese warship *Galega* (1,450 tons/1,473 tonnes), commanded by Captain Pedro Afonso de Aguiar and coming from Goa on its way to Lisbon, carrying a cargo worth 870,000 crusadoes, put into Mozambique Island for repairs and was wrecked there in a storm. Most of her people and about half of the cargo were saved.

1512: The Portuguese East Indiaman *Santo Antonio,* commanded by Captain Francisco Noqueira and sailing from Lisbon to Malacca, Malaysia, with a "large amount of treasure" on board, was totally lost on a reef off Angoche, Mozambique.

1512: The Portuguese warship *Santo Espirito* (1,600 tons/1,626 tonnes), commanded by Captain Francisco Nogueria, in an armada commanded by Captain Jorge de Melo and sailing between Lisbon and Goa, India, with "a large amount of treasure" on board, was lost 3 leagues south of a river mouth on the coast of Angola. Other ships in the fleet rescued some of her people.

1513: The Portuguese merchantman *Santo Antonio,* known as the "Little Antonio," commanded by Captain Afonso Rodriquez and sailing from Lisbon to Goa with 187 chests of gold and silver, was wrecked on the "Baixos de São Lazaro" north of Mozambique.

1516: The Portuguese East Indiaman *São Joãao* (560 tons/569 tonnes), commanded by Captain Joãao de Meneses and sailing from Goa to Lisbon with treasure valued at 470,000 crusadoes, wrecked near Cape Fria in present-day Namibia. Forty-four survivors lived on the shore in great hardship for three years before a passing Portuguese ship rescued them.

1517: The Portuguese East Indiaman *Santa Maria da Luz* (1,200 tons/1,219 tonnes), commanded by Captain Francisco de Sousa and sailing between India and Lisbon with a cargo valued at 670,000 crusadoes, was wrecked between Mafia Island and Dar es Salaam, Tanzania.

1523: The Portuguese East Indiaman *São Miguel* (560 tons/569 tonnes), commanded by Captain Aires de Cunha and coming from

A Portuguese East Indiaman entering the port of Mozambique Island, which was perennially blockaded by ships of rival nations.

India with a cargo worth over half a million crusadoes, was lost on a reef near Mozambique Island.

1531: The Portuguese East Indiaman *Trinidade,* commanded by Captain Diogo Botelho Pereira and returning from India and Malacca with a cargo valued at 330,000 crusadoes, wrecked at Ponta da Padrao near the mouth of the Congo River, Zaire, where the Portuguese had a slave trading post.

1535: The Portuguese East Indiaman *São Miguel* (550 tons/559 tonnes, 22 cannons), commanded by Captain Duarte Tristao and sailing from Malacca to Lisbon with a cargo valued at 660,000 crusadoes, was totally lost on the coast of Somalia in 4 degrees south latitude. Only 17 men survived and eventually reached Mombasa, Kenya.

1537: The Portuguese East Indiaman *Galega* (550 tons/559 tonnes), commanded by Captain Bernardim da Silveira and sailing from India for Lisbon with a cargo valued at 780,000 crusadoes, plus seven chests of diamonds and other precious stones, was wrecked on the east side of Pemba Island, Tanzania.

1541: The Portuguese East Indiaman *Espirito Santo,* commanded by Captain Alvaro Barradas and sailing from India to Lisbon with a cargo valued at 200,000 crusadoes, was lost on the coast of Mozambique at Tintangone and only a few people were saved.

1547: The Portuguese East Indiaman *São Tomé de Borgaleses* (1,870 tons/1,900 tonnes), commanded by Captain Pedro da Silva and sailing from Lisbon to India with 730,000 crusadoes in treasure on board, was totally lost near Angoche, south of Mozambique Island. There were no survivors.

1549: The Portuguese East Indiaman *São Salvador* (1,500 tons/1,524 tonnes), commanded by Captain Joãao Figueira de Barros and sailing from Lisbon to India, was carrying 734,000 crusadoes in gold and silver. She sank in a storm within sight of Mozambique Island and all aboard were lost.

1552: The Portuguese East Indiaman *São Jeronimo*, also known as the *Trinidade* (780 tons/792.5 tonnes), commanded by Captain Lopo de Sousa and sailing from India for Lisbon with a cargo valued at 440,000 crusadoes, plus six chests of precious stones, was wrecked in 8.5 degrees south latitude off the coast of Angola. Another ship in the convoy rescued about fifty survivors.

1557: The Portuguese East Indiaman *Nossa Senhora das Reliquias*, commanded by Captain Antonio Mendes de Castro and sailing from Malacca to Lisbon with a cargo valued at 670,000 crusadoes, wrecked near Dakar, Senegal.

1559: The Portuguese East Indiaman *Garça* was returning to Lisbon from Goa, India, with a valuable cargo of precious stones, objects of gold, jade, ivory and silver and a large consignment of porcelain. She was lost off Vila de João Belo, Mozambique.

1559: The Portuguese East Indiaman *Nossa Senhora das Reliquias* (1,400 tons/1,422 tonnes, 38 cannons), returning from Malacca and Hormuz with a cargo valued at 965,000 crusadoes, developed a bad leak and was run aground on São Tomé Island. Most of her people and about half of her cargo were saved.

1560: The Portuguese East Indiaman *Águia*, having survived a storm lasting 18 days off the Cape of Good Hope, headed for Mozambique for repairs, but was driven off course by another storm and sank in Ungama Bay, north of Mombasa, Kenya. She was coming from Lisbon with over 400,000 crusadoes in treasure and 1,137 people on board, most of whom perished.

1564: The Portuguese East Indiaman *São Martinho* (1,600 tons/1,626 tonnes), commanded by Captain Jorge Fernandes and returning to Lisbon from India with a cargo valued at 400,000 crusadoes, was wrecked in 4 degrees and 30 minutes north latitude on the coast of Liberia.

1564: The Portuguese East Indiaman *Flor de la Mar* (1,900 tons/1,930.5 tonnes, 64 cannons), commanded by Captain Damiao de Sousa and sailing between India and Lisbon with a cargo valued at 620,000 crusadoes, was lost at her anchorage off Mozambique Island during a bad storm and only a few people were saved.

1566: The Portuguese East Indiaman *Tigre* (1,200 tons/1,219 tonnes), commanded by Captain Bartolomé de Vasconcelos and sailing from Macao and Goa to Lisbon with a cargo valued at 680,000 crusadoes, was attempting to make port at Mozambique when she wrecked 4 leagues north of this port.

1568: The Portuguese East Indiaman *Chaga* sailed from Mozambique Island for Lisbon with a cargo worth 320,000 crusadoes. A day later she wrecked at São Jorge Island, Mozambique.

1573: The Portuguese East Indiaman *Nossa Senhora dos Remedios* (1,700 tons/1,727 tonnes), commanded by Captain Pedro de Oliviera and sailing from Lisbon to India with 430,000 crusadoes in gold and silver, was separated from the armada she was with and was totally lost off Cape Verde (not to be confused with the Cape Verde Islands), the western extremity of Senegal.

1576: The Portuguese East Indiaman *São Jorge* (1,900 tons/1,930.5 tonnes, sixty cannons), commanded by Captain Baltazar Pessanha and sailing from Lisbon to Malacca with 700,000 crusadoes of treasure, made a stop at Mozambique Island and, while entering port, struck upon a reef and went to pieces in rough weather, with almost a total loss of life. A salvage attempt soon afterwards recovered nothing but several bronze cannons.

1582: The Portuguese East Indiaman *São Pedro* (1,600 tons/1,626 tonnes, 48 bronze cannons) was lost off the port of Sofala, Mozambique, on a voyage between Lisbon and Goa while carrying over 1 million crusadoes in gold and silver specie.

1582: The Portuguese East Indiaman *São Pedro* (1,400 tons/1,422.5 tonnes, 34 cannons), commanded by Captain Lionel de Lima and sailing from Malacca and Goa for Lisbon with a cargo valued at 430,000 crusadoes, was lost on a reef near the mouth of the Quelimane River, Mozambique.

1590: The Portuguese East Indiaman *São Lucas* (760 tons/772 tonnes), commanded by Captain Rui Gomes da Gracia and sailing from Lisbon to Malacca with "a large amount of gold and silver on board," wrecked between Casablanca and Sale, Morocco. Pirates from Sale rescued 112 people from the wreck and later ransomed them.

1591: The Portuguese East Indiaman *São Luis* (760 tons/772 tonnes, 28 cannons), commanded by Captain Diogo Nunes Gramaxo and sailing from Macao to Lisbon with a cargo valued at over 400,000 crusadoes, including 73,000 pieces of Chinese porcelain, wrecked on the coast of Angola. A ship sailing with her, the *Santo Alberto,* wrecked a day before to the south during a storm.

1592: The Portuguese East Indiaman *Madre de Deus* (2,100 tons/2,133 tonnes, 56 cannons), commanded by Captain Antonio Teixeira de Macedo and sailing from India for Lisbon with 560,000 crusadoes in treasure, was wrecked on the coast of Somalia south of Mogadishu. Another ship rescued some of her crew.

1592: The Portuguese East Indiaman *Bom Jesus* (900 tons/914.5 tonnes), commanded by Captain Correia de Sampaio and sailing from India to Lisbon with a cargo valued at 1.2 million crusadoes, plus personal treasures of the ex-viceroy of India, was wrecked on the coast near Cabo São Braz, Angola, and only a few of her people were saved.

1595: The Portuguese East Indiaman *St. Jago,* also called Santiago, was lost on a reef known as Bassas da India (also named Bassas da Judio on some old charts) with a cargo of over 3 million crusadoes of treasures from the Orient. Only about twenty of the 700 souls aboard survived. In modern times numerous expeditions have gone to this shallow reef, which is about a half mile (.80 kilometer) long, a quarter mile (.40 kilometer) wide, and buffeted by rough seas.

1595: The Portuguese East Indiaman *São Paulo*, commanded by Captain Gonçalvo d'Alvelos, sailed in an armada from Cochin for Lisbon with a cargo valued at 476,000 crusadoes. After passing the Cape of Good Hope, she rescued most of the people from another armada ship that was sinking. Then she wrecked on Cape St. Ann, Sierra Leone, and all but six people drowned.

1595: The Portuguese East Indiaman *São Bartolomeu* (1,800 tons/1,829 tonnes, 46 cannons), commanded by Captain Lopo de Pina de Azevedo and returning from India with a cargo valued at 1.25 million crusadoes, was wrecked in a storm near Lagune Nkomi, Gabon. Some of her cargo and all of her people were saved.

1596: The Portuguese East Indiaman *Nossa Senhora da Vitoria* (1,600 tons/1,626 tonnes), commanded by Captain Joãao Ruiz Carreiro and sailing between Malacca and Lisbon with a cargo valued at 950,000 crusadoes, in addition to a shipment of priceless gifts the Chinese emperor gave to the king of Portugal, wrecked in a storm on Pate Island, Kenya. Most of her crew reached safety in Mombasa. Three salvage attempts yielded nothing of value.

1597: The Portuguese East Indiaman *Santa Maria da Luz* (1,800 tons/1,829 tonnes), returning from India to Lisbon with a cargo valued at 413,000 crusadoes, was lost a few leagues north of Agadir, Morocco, while being chased by Barbary pirates, who rescued 47 survivors and later ransomed them.

1599: The Portuguese East Indiaman *Madre de Deus* was lost on the southeast coast of Somalia while sailing between Lisbon and India, carrying 1.8 million crusadoes in treasure. Natives massacred all survivors.

1599: The Portuguese East Indiaman *Nossa Senhora do Castelo* (1,600 tons/1,626 tonnes, 56 cannons), commanded by Captain Simao de Mendoça and going from Lisbon to India with 646,000 crusadoes in treasure, was lost on the Sofala Shoal, Mozambique.

1603: The Portuguese East Indiaman *São Filipe* (1,900 tons/1,930.5 tonnes, 56 cannons), commanded by Captain Antonio de Mendonça and sailing between Lisbon and Mombasa with 450,000 crusadoes in silver bullion and specie, wrecked near Malindi, Kenya. Most of her people reached Mombasa, but her treasure was a total loss.

An unidentified seventeenth-century Dutch East Indiaman, lost off Angola, yielded over 500 intact Dutch Bellarmine jugs such as these.

1604: The Portuguese East Indiaman *San Filipe* (1,500 tons/1,524 tonnes, forty40 cannons), commanded by Captain Antonio de Mendonça and sailing from Lisbon to Macao with 320,000 crusadoes in gold and silver, was wrecked 30 leagues north of the port of Mombasa, Kenya. Other ships in the armada rescued most of her people.

1605: The Portuguese East Indiaman *Nossa Senhora da Salvaçao* (46 cannons), commanded by Captain Luis de Sousa, sailed in a convoy of three ships from Lisbon to India with a stop in Persia (Iraq) to pick up an ambassador the Persian king was sending to Portugal to negotiate a trade agreement. En route to Persia, the ship ran out of victuals. The captain, officers and merchants had brought their own provisions and had plenty of food, but the crew began to starve. After sailing from Mozambique, the crew mutinied, murdering the captain and six officers. The carrack wrecked on the coast a few hours' sail south of Mombasa, Kenya. Most of the mutineers were eventually apprehended and hanged. None of the treasure was recovered.

1606: Dutch East Indiaman *Zierikee* (760 tons/772 tonnes), commanded by Captain Adriaan Kornelisz, sailed from Holland with two other ships to attack Portuguese shipping in the Indian Ocean and then proceeded to the Moluccas (in Indonesia) for spices. She was carrying 320,000 guilders in gold and silver specie. During an attack on Portuguese ships in the port on Mozambique Island, she ran aground. The crew set her on fire to prevent the treasure from falling into enemy hands and she blew up. Two other Dutch ships rescued the crew.

1607: The Dutch East Indiaman *Mauritius* (700 tons/711 tonnes, 34 cannons), commanded by Captain Jakob Huntum and carrying 240,00 guilders in Oriental cargo, plus cargo taken from a captured Portuguese prize, wrecked on Ilha Caravela 3 miles (5 kilometers) north of the Konkure River mouth in Guinea with only a small number of survivors who were later ransomed.

1607: The Portuguese East Indiaman *Nossa Senhora da Consolaçao* (1,800 tons/1,829 tonnes, 48 cannons), commanded by Captain Diogo de Sousa and sailing from Lisbon to Japan, carrying "a large amount of gold and silver," caught fire while at anchor at Mozambique and was totally consumed. Most of the men survived.

1608: The Portuguese East Indiaman *Nossa Senhora da Palma* (1,600 tons/1,625.5 tonnes, 42 cannons), commanded by Captain João Gonçalves, in the armada of Captain Cristovao Sequeira de Alvarenga, and sailing to India from Lisbon with 146 chests of gold and silver specie, was wrecked on the coast near Angoche, Mozambique. All her people survived, but all treasure was lost.

1608: The Portuguese East Indiaman *Santo Espiritu* (1,800 tons/1,829 tonnes, 38 cannons), commanded by Captain Constantino de Meneses and sailing between Lisbon and India with a great amount of gold and silver, was wrecked near Sofala, Mozambique, and most of her people were saved.

1609: The Portuguese slave ship *Nossa Senhora de Ajuda*, commanded by Captain Miguel Correa Barém, and returning to Lisbon with a cargo of gold and ivory, was lost near the slave port of La Mina, Senegal. Only a few of the crew survived.

1614: The Dutch East Indiaman *Zeelandia* (550 tons/559 tonnes), commanded by Captain Maarten Engels and sailing between Holland and Batavia, carrying over 350,000 guilders in silver specie, was lost near Pointe-Noire, Congo. None of the coins were recovered, but the crew was rescued by another ship in the convoy.

1614: The Portuguese East Indiaman *Nossa Senhora da Conceiçao* (1,450 tons/1,473 tonnes, 46 cannons), commanded by Captain Pedro Mascarenhas and sailing between Lisbon and India with 372,000 crusadoes in treasure, stopped with the rest of the armada at Mozambique Island. In a gale the ship was lost with only a few survivors. A salvage attempt was unsuccessful.

1616: The Portuguese East Indiaman *Nossa Senhora dos Remedios*, commanded by Captain Paulo Rangel and sailing from Goa to Lisbon with a cargo valued at 478,000 crusadoes, was wrecked near Ponta da Marca, Angola, and most of her people were saved by another ship in the armada.

1618: The Portuguese East Indiaman *São Bento* (1,600 tons/1,626 tonnes), commanded by Captain Fernao Soares Cabral, was lost during a battle with the Dutch in the port of Mozambique Island. She was sailing between Lisbon and Goa, India, with 350,000 crusadoes in gold and silver specie and bullion.

1619: The Portuguese East Indiaman *Nossa Senhora da Boa Nova* (1,200 tons/1,219 tonnes, 32 cannons), commanded by Captain João Caetano Melo and sailing from Lisbon to Japan with 470,000 crusadoes in gold and silver specie, separated from the armada and wrecked south of Cap Blanc, Mauritania. Only a few people were saved.

1620: The Portuguese East Indiaman *São Amaro* (1,800 tons/1,829 tonnes, seventy cannons), commanded by Captain Pedro de Moraes Sarmento and sailing from Lisbon to Goa, couldn't enter Mozambique because of a Dutch blockade, so she continued toward Goa, but was totally lost on the coast south of Mombasa, Kenya. Most of her people got ashore and reached Mombasa after a trek of two days.

1621: The Portuguese East Indiaman *São Antonio* (1,100 tons/1,118 tonnes), was lost during a battle with the Dutch in the port of Mozambique Island. She was sailing between Lisbon and Cochin with a large amount of gold and silver specie and bullion. The Dutch pulled a number of survivors out of the water and beheaded them.

1622: The Dutch East Indiaman *Hert* (280 tons/284.5 tonnes), commanded by Captain Quinten Pietersz, sailed from Holland for Batavia wrecked just south of Cap Blanc, Mauritania. Survivors recovered only a small portion of the 230,000 guilders in silver specie she carried.

1622: The Portuguese East Indiaman *Santa Teresa* (1,600 tons/1,626 tonnes), sailing between Lisbon and Goa with 1.3 million crusadoes in gold and silver, was attacked by the Dutch off the port of Mozambique Island and destroyed. Another ship, the São Carlos, carrying 1.2 million crusadoes in treasure, was badly damaged in battle, run aground and blown up by her crew on São Jorge Island off the port of Mozambique.

1622: The Portuguese East Indiaman *São Jose* (1,200 tons/1,219 tonnes, 34 cannons), in the armada commanded by the new viceroy of India, Captain Francisco Henriques, sailed from Lisbon for India with treasure valued at 270,000 crusadoes. She was attacked by Dutch ships in the Mozambique Channel and damaged. She headed for Mozambique Island, but along the way she wrecked on Baixo Mangicale. Another Portuguese East Indiaman, the *Santa Teresa* (1,650 tons/1,676.5 tonnes, forty cannons), carrying over 400,000 crusadoes in treasure, was lost on the same reef.

1623: The Portuguese East Indiaman *São Braz* (1,200 tons/1,219 tonnes), commanded by Captain Cosme Cassão de Brito and sailing between Lisbon and India with a "rich cargo of treasure," sustained severe damage during two storms off the Cape of Good Hope. She sought refuge in Mozambique's port and sank shortly after dropping anchor. In 1987 local fishermen pulled up a bronze bell bearing the name of the ship.

1624: The Portuguese East Indiaman *São Simão* (2,200 tons/2,235 tonnes), commanded by Captain Bento de Freitas Mascarenhas and carrying 850,000 crusadoes in gold and silver specie from Lisbon to Goa, India, was lost in the port of Mozambique Island. About a quarter of the treasure was recovered at the time of loss. During a storm two days later the *Santa Isabel* (1,400 tons/1,422.5 tonnes), commanded by Captain Diogo de Castelo Branco, also sank in this port. Only a small part of the 780,000 crusadoes in treasure she carried and 14 bronze cannons were recovered.

1628: The Dutch East Indiaman *Wapen Van Enkhuizen* (400 tons/406 tonnes, 34 cannons), commanded by Captain Lauens Valerins and sailing between Holland and Batavia with 340,000 guilders in silver specie, stopped off the coast of Sierra Leone in 9 degrees and 30 minutes south latitude to make repairs after a bad storm and blew up for some unmentioned reason.

1629: The Portuguese East Indiaman *Santo Estevao* (1,400 tons/1,422.5 tonnes), commanded by Captain Vicente Leitao de Quadros and sailing between Lisbon and India with "a valuable cargo of treasure," parted from her armada because of a bad leak and headed for Angola, where she wrecked in the Bay of Luciras.

1639: The Dutch East Indiaman *Hof Van Holland* (500 tons/508 tonnes), commanded by Captain Jan Bouwensz van Delft and sailing between Holland and Goree, Senegal, was lost off the port of Goree. Her crew and about half of her 230,000 guilders in silver specie were saved. A Dutch vessel sent to salvage the wreck in 1641 was unable to find her.

1647: The Portuguese East Indiaman *São Pedro de Hamburgo* also called the *Pato* (38 cannons), sailing from India to Lisbon with a cargo valued at 320,000 crusadoes, was wrecked 6 leagues north of Mozambique Island. A salvage attempt proved unsuccessful.

1647: The Portuguese East Indiaman *Bom Jesus,* commanded by Captain Matias Figueira, sailed from Lisbon for Malacca with 670,000 crusadoes in gold and silver, and made a stop at Mozambique Island. A day later she wrecked on that coast further to the north. Most of the people made it back to Mozambique Island, but no treasure was recovered.

1649: The Portuguese East Indiaman *São Lourenço* (800 tons/813 tonnes, 28 cannons), sailing from Lisbon to India with 480,000 crusadoes in treasure on board, wrecked on Baixo de Mongicale, Mozambique. Only 68 out of 678 people on board survived, along with two dogs.

1653: The Portuguese East Indiaman *Nossa Senhora de Belém* (1,800 tons/1,829 tonnes, 56 cannons), commanded by Captain Marcos de Arambreu and coming from Lisbon to India with 764,000 crusadoes in treasure, wrecked on Baixos da India in the Mozambique Channel. There were few survivors.

1670: The Portuguese East Indiaman *Nossa Senhora dos Remedios* (1,600 tons/1,626 tonnes), commanded by Captain Simao de Sousa de Tavora and sailing from Lisbon to Malacca with 470,000 crusadoes in treasures, stopped at Mozambique Island and after leaving, wrecked 4 leagues south of Mombasa, Kenya.

1672: The Dutch East Indiaman *Kranestein* (676 tons/687 tonnes, forty cannons), commanded by Captain Adam van Breen, sailed from Holland for Batavia. Stopping at the Cape of Good Hope, she was rerouted to carry a cargo back to Holland valued at over 400,000 guilders, which had been salvaged from another Dutch East Indiaman.

The *Kranestein* wrecked during a storm on the south side of São Tomé Island.

1711: The Dutch East Indiaman *Baarzande* (768 tons/780 tonnes), commanded by Captain Gijsbert Steen and sailing between Holland and Japan with 440,000 guilders in gold and silver, stopped at Mozambique Island to attack Portuguese ships. She blew up and sank in a battle with two Portuguese warships off this port. There were no survivors.

1717: The Dutch East Indiaman *Schonenberg* (600 tons/610 tonnes), commanded by Captain Jan de Vis and returning to Holland from the Far East with a cargo in excess of 235,000 guilders, was lost near the mouth of the Cunene River, Angola. Two unidentified Portuguese ships sent there in 1672 to purchase slaves were also lost.

1719: The Portuguese East Indiaman *Nossa Senhora da Guia* was lost on Angoche Island about 90 miles (145 kilometers) east of Mozambique Island when sailing between Lisbon and Goa, India. Her cargo of 1.2 million crusadoes in silver and gold specie was never salvaged.

1731: The Dutch East Indiaman *Borsselle* (800 tons/813 tonnes, 48 cannons), commanded by Captain Jacob Jongerheld, left Holland with 523,000 guilders in treasure and headed for a port in Saudi Arabia on the Red Sea. There she picked up a large cargo of pearls and sailed for Batavia, but wrecked in a tempest near Point Ras Hafun on the northeast coast of Somalia.

1738: The British East Indiaman *Sussex* was lost on the Baixos da India in the middle of the Mozambique Channel. Her main cargo was 235,000 pieces of Chinese porcelain. The wreck was recently discovered, but rough seas have prevented excavation of the site.

1742: Two large Dutch East Indiamen—the *Abbekerk* (600 tons/610 tonnes) and the *Maarsseveen* (750 tons/762 tonnes, 44 cannons)— returning from Batavia to Holland, were lost in 11.5 degrees south latitude on the coast of Angola, with valuable cargoes totaling over 500,000 guilders. Survivors lived off the land, resorting at times to cannibalism, for eight years before being rescued. Only 75 of the 467 men survived.

1743: The Dutch East Indiaman *Maria Adriana* (26 cannons), commanded by Captain Jan Elswout and with a crew of 220, returned to Holland from the Far East with a cargo valued at over 500,000 guilders. She was wrecked on the coast about 10 leagues west of Cape Palmas, Liberia.

1747: The Dutch East Indiaman *Eendracht* (1,150 tons/1,168.5 tonnes), commanded by Captain Jan Christoffel Tiede and carrying over 400,000 guilders in Oriental treasures, wrecked on the coast about 30 miles (48 kilometers) south of Dakar, Senegal. Only 27 men were saved. They joined 12 survivors of an unidentified Dutch East Indiaman that had wrecked nearby.

1747: The Dutch East Indiaman *Diemermeer* (850 tons/864 tonnes, 42 cannons), was sailing between Ceylon and Holland, carrying "a very valuable cargo, including many precious stones and pearls," when it wrecked near Walvis, Namibia. Most of the crew survived. A salvage vessel sent out the following year failed to locate the wreck.

1750: The British East Indiaman *Duke of Cumberland* (500 tons/508 tonnes), returning from India with a cargo valued at £438,000 pounds sterling, was wrecked on Goree, the slave-market island off Dakkar, Senegal. Only the people were saved. Two major salvage attempts recovered some of the cargo, a large part of which consisted of gold, jewels and porcelain.

1753: The Dutch East Indiaman *Bredenhof* (800 tons/813 tonnes), commanded by Captain Jan Neilson and sailing between Holland and Batavia, was lost near the port of Beira, Mozambique. Portuguese captured the survivors and later shipped them to Lisbon. She was carrying ten chests of gold ingots, plus 315,000 guilders in cash. The Portuguese failed to recover any of her treasure.

1756: The Dutch East Indiaman *Dieman* (850 tons/864 tonnes, 48 cannons), commanded by Captain Tobias Siekens and sailing between Holland and Batavia with 286,000 guilders in gold and silver bullion, plus 103,542 guilders in cash, was wrecked on Mafia Island off Tanzania.

1790: The Spanish galleon *San Telmo* (1,100 tons/1,117.5 tonnes), commanded by Captain Juan Martín de Ávila and sailing from Lima, Peru, to Spain with over 3 million pesos in treasure, was wrecked at

Essaouira (formerly Mogadore), located 70 miles (112.5 kilometers) southwest of Safi, Morocco. Most of the people on board got ashore, only to be captured. Many were later ransomed.

1798: France's greatest treasure loss occurred in Aboukir Bay, Egypt, while the army of Napoleon Bonaparte was sacking the country. A large fleet of French warships was at anchor there under the command of Admiral de Brueys. On his flagship the *L'Orient,* there was over 25 tons (25.5 tonnes) of gold bullion and specie, plus other treasures looted from several nations. On August 1, a British fleet commanded by Admiral Horatio Lord Nelson suddenly appeared and during a fierce battle thirteen of the French ships, including the *L'Orient,* were sunk. In order to lessen the importance of Nelson's victory, the French never admitted to this great loss of treasure, but historical documents have confirmed it. Over the years the French government has sent numerous secret expeditions to recover the treasure, but none has succeeded. In 1936 a Greek sponge diver was reported to have found several hundred pounds of gold ingots in the area where the ship sank. In 1983 French underwater explorer Jacques Dumas discovered the wreck. He didn't realize he had found *L'Orient* because during his survey he found a bronze nameplate of a ship named *Royal Dauphin,* the name of the *L'Orient* before the French Revolution. French treasure hunter Franck Goddio located the wreck in 1996 and since his main objective was making a documentary film, his divers recovered very little treasure before he moved off to another project. Thus, the bulk of the treasure is still there.

1816: One of the most famous shipwreck disasters off Africa's west coast was that of the French frigate *La Méduse,* lost on the Arguin Bank over 30 miles (48 kilometers) off the coast of Senegal. The ship had 25 barrels with over 120,000 gold coins on board when lost. About 150 of the crew and passengers drifted on a raft for 13 days without food or water. Soldiers killed civilians, some ate the dead, and only 15 survivors made it ashore. A large painting of this raft and the poor souls aboard her is one of the most famous in the Louvre Museum in Paris.

CHAPTER 22

SOUTH AFRICA'S RICHEST SHIPWRECKS

The rough seas around South Africa's vast coastline have claimed the largest number of ships in African waters. The Cape of Good Hope has been a mariner's nightmare since the Phoenicians were the first of record to round it *ca.* 600 B.C. As early as 10 A.D., Muslim trading vessels also visited the shores of South Africa, rounding the cape they called "The Cape of Devils." There is no way to know how many early ships were lost off this coast.

In 1498 Portuguese explorer Vasco da Gama discovered the sea route to the East. The first recorded European ship loss off South Africa occurred seven years later. An unidentified Portuguese trading ship loaded with pepper, which was worth its weight in gold, wrecked in Mossel Bay, 10 miles (16 kilometers) east of the cape. Everyone aboard perished. She was the first of hundreds of Portuguese trading vessels, later known as Portuguese East Indiamen, that went down in the seas off South Africa.

Damage to the majority of their ships rounding the Cape of Good Hope led the Portuguese to establish coastal settlements on the island of Mozambique where repairs could be made and fresh water and provisions obtained. They also founded settlements at Mombassa, Kenya and Goa, on the Malabar Coast of India, which soon became the Indian Ocean's principal spice port. By the second decade of the sixteenth century, an average of 25 Portuguese East Indiamen sailed each year between Lisbon and the East, and

The main wharf in Table Bay, the port for Cape Town, where hundreds of ships stopped each year for supplies and to make repairs.

by the end of the century as many as sixty of these ships plied this lucrative route annually.

The Portuguese monopoly of trade with the East lasted little more than 100 years. At the beginning of the seventeenth century, the Dutch and British formed their own East India companies. The ensuing struggle for supremacy among the Portuguese, British and Dutch lasted for over two centuries. In 1652 the Dutch, who were losing an alarming number of ships, founded Cape Town as a supply station in the extreme southwest part of South Africa. Cape Town became the main port of call for hundreds of ships of the Protestant European nations, which put in for repairs and supplies on voyages to and from Europe. The British captured Cape Town in 1795 but extended port privileges to the Dutch.

The majority of ship losses off South Africa occurred in relatively shallow waters. Since most ships wrecked on the coasts or sank in ports, salvaging should have been relatively simple. However, early divers faced exceedingly hazardous conditions. Rough seas, strong currents and icy-cold water made the work extremely difficult and only a fraction of lost cargoes were recov-

Another view of Table Bay with Cape Town.

ered. Even today, with rubber diving suits to protect divers from the chilly water and sophisticated diving equipment, shipwreck salvage in South African waters is quite difficult and only a small number of ventures have been successful.

1533: The Portuguese East Indiaman *Bom Jesus* (2,000 tons/2.032 tonnes, 68 bronze cannons), commanded by Captain Francisco de Noronha and sailing between Lisbon, Goa and Malacca with 880,000 crusadoes in treasure on board, sank off the Cape of Good Hope about 2 leagues from shore. Only 73 of the 1,089 souls aboard were saved by another ship in the fleet.

1551: The Portuguese East Indiaman *São João Bescoinho* (750 tons/762 tonnes, 26 cannons), commanded by Captain Lopo de Souda and coming from Goa to Lisbon with a cargo valued at 230,000 crusadoes, (a large part of it in Chinese porcelain), wrecked at Ponta do Ouro, so named because a Portuguese ship, loaded with several tons gold, was reportedly lost there some years earlier. There were no survivors from the *Bescoinho*, but some of her wreckage was spotted on a beach by a ship sent in search of her.

1552: The Portuguese East Indiaman *São João* (1,200 tons/1,219 tonnes), commanded by Captain Manuel de Sousa Sepulvida and sailing from Cochin, India, to Lisbon with a cargo valued at 390,000 crusadoes, plus several chests of precious stones belonging to the captain, was lost near the Mtamvuna River on the Natal South Coast. Some survivors made it to Lorenzo Marques (today Maputo) while others waited for a rescue vessel that never came.

1552: The Portuguese East Indiaman *São Jeronymo* (740 tons/752 tonnes, thirty cannons), sailing from Cochin, India, to Lisbon with a cargo worth 463,000 crusadoes, excluding four chests of diamonds and precious stones, which would be appraised in Lisbon, was wrecked a little northeast of the Mtamvuna River. Only two survivors made it up to Maputo.

1554: The Portuguese East Indiaman *São Bento* (450 tons/457 tonnes, 22 cannons), commanded by Captain João D'alvares Cabral and coming from Cochin to Lisbon with a cargo valued at 300,000 crusadoes, was wrecked on the seaward side of the island at the mouth of the Msikaba River on the Pondoland Coast. More than 100 slaves and 44 Portuguese drowned. The survivors numbered 98 Portuguese and 224 slaves, most of whom eventually reached Maputo. Along the way they found survivors from the Portuguese East Indiaman *São João,* which had been lost in 1552.

1565: The Portuguese East Indiaman *Nossa Senhora da Graça,* also called the *Algarvia,* commanded by Captain Vicente Fernandes Pimentel and coming from India to Lisbon with a cargo valued at 640,000 crusadoes, sank in a storm off the Cape of Good Hope with no survivors. Two other ships in the armada disappeared at the same time.

1583: The Portuguese East Indiaman *São Luis* (900 tons/914.5 tonnes), commanded by Captain Luis Caldeira and sailing from Lisbon to India with 630,000 crusadoes in treasure on board, was wrecked in a storm 10 leagues east of the Quelimane River. Few lives were saved.

1585: The Portuguese East Indiaman *São Lourenço* (1,450 tons/1,473 tonnes, 44 cannons), commanded by Captain Fernão Cota Falcão, in the armada of Captain Fernão de Mendonça, sailed from Macau for Lisbon with a cargo valued at 389,000 crusadoes, plus five boxes of diamonds and precious stones. She sprung a leak and sank off the coast of Natal.

1585: The Portuguese East Indiaman *Santiago* (1,800 tons/1,829 tonnes), was sailing between Lisbon and India with 320,000 crusadoes

A British East Indiaman after capsizing while rounding the Cape of Good Hope.

of treasure. Five German merchants, carrying an unknown amount of treasure to purchase spices and drugs in India, were on board as well. The ship survived a bad storm off the Cape of Good Hope, but was separated from the rest of the armada ships. The navigator thought the *Santiago* was off the east side of Madagascar when she was actually in the middle of the Mozambique Channel, and she wrecked on the Bassas da India. Fifty-seven survivors reached the coast in a small boat and walked north for six days to Angoche, where the Portuguese maintained a trading base for buying gold and ivory from the natives.

1588: The Portuguese East Indiaman *São Tomé* (1,500 tons/1,524 tonnes, forty cannons), commanded by Captain Estevão da Veiga and sailing from Malacca to Lisbon with a cargo valued at 430,000 crusadoes, separated from her armada and was wrecked in a storm at Terra dos Fumos on the southeast coast of South Africa. After numerous attacks by the natives, 34 Portuguese and 17 slaves managed to reach Maputo.

1593: The Portuguese East Indiaman *São Alberto* (1,500 tons/1,524 tonnes, 48 cannons), commanded by Captain Juliao de Faria Cerveira and sailing between India and Lisbon with a cargo valued at 670,000 crusadoes, suffered through a bad storm while rounding the southern tip of Madagascar and soon after wrecked at Penado das Fontes on the coast of Natal. About 285 people managed to reach shore, but only 165 survived the 1,000-mile (1,609-kilometer) trek up to Maputo.

1602: The Portuguese East Indiaman *Nossa Senhora da Conceição* (1,800 tons/1,829 tonnes, 44 cannons), commanded by Captain Vicente de Sousa, and sailing from Lisbon to Malacca with "a large amount of gold and silver," was badly damaged in a battle with two Dutch ships and then run aground near the Cape of Good Hope. Most of the people got ashore.

1608: The Portuguese East Indiaman *Santo Espíritu* (1,100 tons/1,118 tonnes, 44 cannons), commanded by Captain Marcos de Abreau and sailing from Japan and India to Lisbon with "a very valuable cargo," including chests of diamonds and precious stones, was wrecked between the Cefane River and East London. Some survived the disaster and reached Maputo in boats fashioned from wreckage.

1619: A fleet of Danish warships, sailing from Copenhagen to Goa, captured two French pirate vessels along the way. They renamed one, laden with plunder from several Muslim ships, the *Jaeger*. The fleet anchored off Robben Island and during a gale, this ship was wrecked.

1620: The Portuguese East Indiaman *São João Evangelista*, commanded by Captain Jose Pinto Pereira and sailing from Lisbon to Malacca with 473,000 crusadoes in treasure, was wrecked at the mouth of the Luabo River on the coast of Natal.

1622: The Portuguese East Indiaman *São João Batista* (2,000 tons/2,032 tonnes), commanded by Captain Luis Maria Rolim and sailing from Lisbon to Malacca with a large amount of gold and silver specie, was attacked by two Dutch ships near the Cape of Good Hope and went down on the high seas with a total loss of life and treasure.

1622: The Portuguese East Indiaman *São Thomé Baptista*, also named the *São João Baptista*, was wrecked near the mouth of the Keiskamma River in 33 degrees south latitude (longitude was not in use). She was sailing from Goa, India, to Lisbon when attacked by the Dutch and sunk. The Dutch recovered six chests of precious stones and pearls, but the remainder of her 2.3 million crusadoes in treasure is still waiting to be found.

1626: The Portuguese East Indiaman *São Gocnçalo* (1,200 tons/1,219 tonnes, thirty cannons), commanded by Captain Martin Teixeira de

Azevedo and sailing from Japan to Lisbon with "a very valuable cargo," was wrecked a few leagues east of the Cape of Good Hope. Most of her people and some of her cargo was saved.

1630: The Portuguese East Indiaman *São Gonçalo* (1,750 tons/1,778 tonnes), commanded by Captain Fernão Lobo de Meneses and sailing between Goa and Lisbon with a cargo valued at 730,000 crusadoes, which included over 45,000 pieces of Chinese porcelain, put into Plettenberg Bay to repair a leak, but a gale caused her to wreck and 133 people drowned. From the wreckage survivors built two small pinnaces. One went to Saldanha Bay and the other to Angola. Those who made it to Angola were rescued by another Portuguese East Indiaman, the *Santo Ignacio Loyola,* which later wrecked on the Bar of Lisbon, and most of those on board drowned.

1635: The Portuguese East Indiaman *Nossa Senhora de Belém,* commanded by Captain Joseph de Cabreya, the admiral in charge of the armada this ship was in, was a very notable disaster when she wrecked at the mouth of the Umizimvubu River, about 125 miles (201 kilometers) south of Durban. Survivors took over a year crossing Africa to reach Angola. Her cargo was valued at over 2 million crusadoes in Oriental treasures.

1644: The Dutch East Indiaman *Eiland Mauritius* (600 tons/610 tonnes, thirty cannons), commanded by Captain Pieter Theunisz and carrying 290,000 guilders in silver specie, sailed from Holland for Batavia. She was lost on a reef shortly after leaving the Cape of Good Hope. All aboard were saved, but none of the coinage.

1647: The Dutch East Indiaman *Haarlem* (850 tons/864 tonnes, forty cannons), commanded by Captain Antonie Biermans, was lost in Table Bay between Robben Island and the mainland while sailing from Batavia to Holland. She carried 183,000 guilders in Oriental treasures, plus Chinese porcelain of unknown value.

1647: The Dutch East Indiaman *Nieuw Haarlem* (500 tons/508 tonnes), commanded by Captain Pieter Pietersz and sailing from Batavia to Holland with a cargo valued at 332,000 guilders, wrecked in a gale near Table Bay. Some of the survivors built a small fort on shore and lived there for a year before being rescued. This prompted the Dutch East India Company to establish a permanent station there where arriving ships could obtain water and food and survivors from shipwrecks would find safety.

1647: The Portuguese East Indiaman *Nossa Senhora de Atalaia do Pinheiro* (2,100 tons/2,133 tonnes), commanded by Captain Antonio de Camara de Noronha, was sailing from Goa to Lisbon with a cargo valued at 1.3 million crusadoes, which included many chests of diamonds and other precious stones, plus 65 bronze cannons made by the Boccaro Foundry in Macau. She was wrecked near the Cefane River, 20 miles (32 kilometers) northeast of East London. Most people aboard drowned, but some survivors walked for five weeks to reach Maputo. Most ships sailing in both the New and Old World were not sheathed until after 1760, but this ship was built in India of teak and completely sheathed with lead.

1665: The Dutch East Indiaman *Maskaatboom*, also called the *Notenboom* (600 tons/610 tonnes), sailing between Batavia and Holland with 330,000 guilders in Oriental treasures and spices, was lost near the Cape of Good Hope.

1668: The Dutch East Indiaman *Schollevaar*, commanded by Captain Romboutz Hackert and sailing from Holland to Batavia, carried 198 chests of silver specie, plus a large number of anchors for use by Dutch ships in Batavia. She wrecked north of Bokpunt near Table Bay.

1669: The Dutch East Indiaman *Zoetendaal* (448 tons/455 tonnes, 28 cannons), commanded by Captain Jan Block and sailing between Sri Lanka and Holland with "a rich amount of cargo," was wrecked in Struis Bay. Only four men drowned.

1672: The Dutch East Indiaman *Zoetendaal* (600 tons/610 tonnes), was commanded by Captain Simon Kerseboom, who died en route to the Cape of Good Hope and was replaced by Willem van der Hop. After leaving the Cape for Batavia, the ship wrecked in a storm 50 miles (80.5 kilometers) east of the Cape. Most of her crew was rescued by another ship, but none of the 330,000 guilders in silver specie was recovered.

1682: The British East Indiaman *Johanna* (550 tons/559 tonnes, 44 iron cannons), commanded by Captain Robert Brown, was lost off the Cape of Good Hope. In 1982 salvors recovered 23,000 Spanish pieces of eight and 27 silver disks. Some treasure was auctioned at Christie's in London. At the time of her loss, she had £125,000 sterling in silver specie, consisting of seventy chests of Spanish pieces of eight. A great deal more treasure is believed to be on her.

1682: The Dutch East Indiaman *Goede Hoop* (1,177 ton/1,196 tonnes), commanded by Captain Anthonie Pronk, sailed from Ceylon for Holland, carrying over 400,000 guilders in cargo. She wrecked in a storm at Table Bay.

1685: The Dutch East Indiaman *Orange* (544 tons/553 tonnes), commanded by Captain Willem Kuif, sailed from Bengal, India, for Holland, with a cargo valued at over 250,000 guilders. She wrecked near Cape St. Lucia, on the coast of Natal. Only about half the crew survived.

1686: The Portuguese East Indiaman *Nossa Senhora dos Milagros* (2,200 tons/2,235 tonnes), commanded by Captain Emmanuel de Silva, was sailing from Goa to Lisbon with "a large amount of valuable goods," three ambassadors from the king of Siam who had presents for the king of Portugal, and a large contingent of Jesuit priests. She wrecked near Cape Agualhas and most of those aboard drowned. Shortly after she sank, a local fisherman served three years in prison for salvaging a great deal of valuable jewelry from the wreck.

1692: The Dutch East Indiaman *Waterland* (1,138 tons/1,156 tonnes), commanded by Captain Willem Kemp, was sailing between Batavia and Holland with a cargo valued at 244,000 guilders. She went into Table Bay because of bad weather and was attacked by a French warship. She sank with a total loss of life.

1692: The Dutch East Indiaman *Hogergeest* (222 tons/225.5 tonnes), commanded by Captain Jakob ter Huisen and sailing between Batavia and Holland with a cargo of valued at 167,000 guilders, was lost in a gale near the Salt River in Table Bay. Only a few of her people drowned, thanks to the heroic actions of a crewman who swam a line ashore which most of the men used to scramble to safety.

1692: The British East Indiaman *Orange* (880 tons/894 tonnes), sailing from England to China with "a large amount of gold and silver on board,"was wrecked in Table Bay and quickly went to pieces. About half of the people aboard drowned.

1693: The Dutch East Indiaman *Gouden Buis* (880 tons/894 tonnes, 44 cannons), commanded by Captain Teunis Kornelisz Baanman, was totally lost in St. Helena Bay on the coast of Natal. None of the 440,000 guilders in gold and silver bullion and specie was saved.

1697: The Dutch East Indiaman *Oosterland* (1,123 tons/1,141 tonnes, and 48 cannons), commanded by Captain Pieter van Ede and sailing between Sri Lanka and Holland with 385,000 guilders of cargo, plus six chests of uncut diamonds, was totally lost in a storm while anchored near the Salt River in Table Bay. A woman, who was the only survivor, gave birth to a boy after reaching shore.

1697: The Dutch East Indiaman *Huis Te Kraaiestein* (1,154 tons/1172.5 tonnes, and fifty cannons), commanded by Captain Jan van der Vijver and sailing between Holland and Batavia with 440,000 guilders in gold and silver bullion and specie, struck a reef near Oudekraal Bay on the Cape Peninsula and then slid off into deeper water. All of her silver specie was in Spanish pieces of eight. Three chests of these coins were removed from the ship, but mysteriously disappeared.

1697: The Dutch East Indiaman *Waddinxveen* (751 tons/763 tonnes), commanded by Captain Thomas van Willigen and sailing between Batavia and Holland with a cargo valued at 330,000 guilders, was wrecked near the Cape of Good Hope. Only four men were saved.

1697: The Dutch warship *Noordgouw*, commanded by Captain Kornelis van de Voet, was sent to the Cape of Good Hope to pick up the cargoes of two ships, valued at 390,000 guilders, which·had been lost in that area. Shortly after loading the cargoes and getting under sail, she capsized and sank in a freak wind.

1702: The Dutch East Indiaman *Merestein* (826 tons/839 tonnes, 34 cannons), commanded by Captain Jan Subbing, was sailing between Holland and Batavia with 340,000 guilders in gold and silver specie when it wrecked at Jutteneiland in Saldanha Bay with only 99 survivors. In 1728 the Dutch East India Company hired the famed pioneer British diver John Lethbridge to salvage the ship and also the *De Hoop*, lost in this same area. There is no record of what he salvaged on either site.

1709: The Dutch East Indiaman *Nagel* (1,130 tons/1,148 tonnes), commanded by Captain Pieter Berkman and sailing between Holland and Ceylon, stopped at Saldanha Bay in bad weather. The ship caught fire and was a total loss. Several chests of silver coins, out of the 330,000 guilders' value of the silver bullion and specie on board, was all that could be saved.

1714: The Dutch East Indiaman *Voorzichtigheid* (850 tons/863.5 tonnes), commanded by Captain van Duren, was sailing between Holland and Batavia with 345,000 guilders in silver bullion and specie, plus four chests of gold church plate. A strong wind drove her onto a reef as she attempted to anchor in Table Bay. She sank in 25 fathoms of water, but most of the people aboard were saved.

1717: A Dutch warship of the type called a *Galjoot* (150 tons/152 tonnes) captured a vast amount of treasure from several Portuguese ships off Mozambique and was preparing to return to Holland when the ship caught fire in Table Bay and was a total loss.

1721: During a storm, two Dutch East Indiamen were totally lost in Table Bay. They were the *Lakenman* (600 tons/610 tonnes), commanded by Captain Herman Branus, and the *Zoetigheid* (600 tons/610 tonnes), commanded by Captain Abraham van der Ceel. None of the 450,000 guilders in silver specie they carried was recovered, except for some 30,000 coins in ten chests from the Lakenman.

1722: The Dutch East Indiaman *Gouda* (220 tons/223.5 tonnes), commanded by Captain Marten Klienkens and with 130,000 guilders in silver specie, sailed from Holland for the Cape of Good Hope (Capetown). She was wrecked and totally lost in Table Bay, although all of the people aboard her were saved.

1722: The British East Indiaman *Chandois* (440 tons/447 tonnes), sailing from Bengal to London with a "cargo of great value," was wrecked near the castle in Table Bay.

1722: The British East Indiaman *Nightingale* (480 tons/488 tonnes), sailing between England and India with 374 chests of silver specie, was wrecked in a gale in Table Bay, but only one man was lost and some of her silver was recovered.

1722: Three Dutch East Indiamen were totally lost while at anchor in Table Bay: the *Schotse Lorrendraaier* (850 tons/864 tonnes), commanded by Captain Adiaan Hijpe; the *Rotterdam* (800 tons/813 tonnes), commanded by Captain Gerrit Fiers; and the *Standvastigheid* (888 tons/902 tonnes), commanded by Captain Jan Kole. They were coming from Holland with a total of 980,000 guilders in gold and silver bullion and specie. Fewer than a dozen souls survived from the ships. In 1727 British diver John Lethbridge recovered 200 silver bars and seven cannons off the Rotterdam. After he left, a local diver recovered 330 gold ducats, 12 cannons and 14 grindstones.

1728: Three Dutch East Indiamen—the *Stabroek* (900 tons/914.5 tonnes), commanded by Captain Barend van der Zalm; the *Haarlem* (850 tons/863.5 tonnes), commanded by Captain Anthonie Biermans; and the *Middenrak* (600 tons/610 tonnes), commanded by Captain Hendrik Juriaan van Beck—sailed from Holland for Batavia and stopped at the Cape of Good Hope, which was the usual practice for all Dutch vessels going to and coming from Holland. A terrifying storm arose, sinking the ships at anchor in Table Bay and taking the lives of all aboard. Together they carried over 1 million guilders in gold and silver bullion and specie. In 1729 two of John Lethbridge's diver working on the *Middenrak* recovered two of her anchors, but nothing else.

1730: The Dutch East Indiaman *Batavia* (610 tons/620 tonnes, 44 cannons), commanded by Captain Jan de Haan and sailing from Holland for Batavia with 430,000 guilders in gold and silver specie and bullion, wrecked near Cape Aqulhas and blew up with a total loss of treasure. Only seven people were saved.

1734: The Dutch East Indiaman *Sterreschans* (850 tons/863.5 tonnes), commanded by Captain Klaas Keuken and sailing from Holland for Batavia with 330,000 guilders in silver specie, ran aground on a reef as it entered Table Bay. While efforts were being made to rescue the crew and treasure, a violent storm sprang up and the ship went to pieces.

1737: The Dutch East Indiaman Petronellla *Alida* (550 tons/559 tonnes), commanded by Captain Pieter Lup and sailing from Holland to Batavia with 463,000 guilders in treasure and cargo, stopped for fresh water in Saldanha Bay where it caught on fire and blew up. Only two men reached the beach, but they died afterward from their burns.

1737: A fleet of eight Dutch East Indiamen, sailing from Batavia to Holland, stopped at the Cape of Good Hope. While they were anchored, a storm arose and all eight ships sank near the mouth of the Salt River in Table Bay with a total loss of over 2 million guilders in Oriental treasures and spices. They were the *Inpenrode* (650 tons/660.5 tonnes), commanded by Captain Dirk Elsberg; the *Flora* (850 tons/864 tonnes), commanded by Captain Gerrit Pik (only six of her crew of 140 men were saved); the *Paddenburg* (850 tons/864 tonnes), commanded by Captain Arie van Veurden; the *Buis* (600 tons/610 tonnes), commanded by Captain Hendrik Orsel; the *Duinbeek* (800 tons/813 tonnes), commanded by Captain Jan van Thiel; the *Goudriaan* (630 tons/640 tonnes), commanded by Captain Jurriaan Zeeman; the *Papenburg* (650 tons/660.5 tonnes), commanded by Captain Jan van Heemstede; and the *Westerwijk* (850 tons/864 tonnes), commanded by Captain Wouter Bos. Salvage at the time yielded only some masts and rigging.

1738: The Dutch East Indiaman *Rodenrijs* (650 tons/660.5 tonnes), commanded by Captain Jan van Heemstede and coming from Batavia to Holland with a cargo valued at 340,000 guilders, was wrecked in Table Bay. Only six men drowned, although all the cargo was lost.

1740: The Dutch East Indiaman *Vis* (650 tons/660.5 tonnes), commanded by Captain Jan Sikkes and en route from Holland to Batavia, was struck by a freak wind and sank as she entered Table Bay. Contemporary salvors recovered about 40,000 of the 330,000 guilders in gold and silver specie aboard the ship. The salvage operation halted after sharks killed two divers.

1747: The Dutch East Indiaman *Reigersdaal* (850 tons/863.5 tonnes, 48 cannons), commanded by Captain Johannes Band and sailing between Holland and Batavia with 250,000 guilders, was wrecked on a reef 4 miles (6.5 kilometers) south of the entrance to Saldanha Bay and all 297 souls aboard perished. A contemporary salvage attempt produced only spars, rigging, and cordage. Divers located her in 1979 and recovered over 20,000 silver coins and other artifacts.

1755: The British East Indiaman *Doddington*, commanded by Captain James Sampson, wrecked on Bird Island near Algoa Bay and quickly went to pieces. Only 23 of the 270 people on board survived. She carried 4 tons (4.064 tonnes) of gold and silver specie, some of which salvors recovered in recent times.

1756: The Dutch East Indiaman *Schuilenburg* (300 tons/305 tonnes), commanded by Captain Jan Tobias Toon, sailed in a fleet of 43 ships from Holland for Batavia. On board she carried 320,000 guilders in silver specie and four chests with 2,500 gold ducats each. The report of an inquiry, held after the ship wrecked on the coast between False Bay and Table Bay, revealed that many private merchants carried huge amounts of unregistered gold and silver on this voyage, "as is the norm on all voyages to the Indies."

1756: An unidentified French slave ship, while on a voyage from Guinea to Mauritius Island, wrecked north of Blomberg Strand in Table Bay, but no one died. She was carrying over 300 slaves and a large amount of gold dust, gold nuggets and ivory tusks.

1773: The Dutch East Indiaman *Jonge Thomas* (1,150 tons/1,168.5 tonnes), commanded by Captain Brend de la Main (or Maire), was sailing between Holland and Batavia with 460,000 guilders in gold and silver specie, including eight chests with 20,000 gold ducats from the Utrecht Mint. A sudden storm caused her to capsize and quickly sink Table Bay shortly after pulling up her anchors.

1775: The Dutch East Indiaman *Nieuw Rhoon* (1,150 tons/1,168.5 tonnes, sixty cannons), commanded by Captain Jakob Koelders and sailing from Sri Lanka to Holland with a cargo valued at 430,000 guilders, sought safe haven from a storm in Table Bay and struck a reef (today Whale Rock) near Robben Island and sank.

1776: The French East Indiaman *La Ceres* was sailing from Pondicherry, India, France's principal trading base on the Coromandel Coast, to France with a cargo valued at 378,000 livres, and sank during a gale in Table Bay.

1780: The Dutch East Indiaman *Mentor* (1,150 tons/1,168.5 tonnes, 44 cannons), commanded by Captain Johan de Korte and returning to Holland with 150,000 guilders in Oriental treasures, was lost off Cape Agulhas after striking a reef in a heavy storm.

1782: The Dutch East Indiaman *Vrouwe Katharina Johanna* (900 tons/914.5 tonnes), commanded by Captain Jacob Meyer and sailing between Batavia and Holland with a cargo of over 150,000 guilders, stopped at Table Bay for fresh water and to drop off the sick. She then set sail, but some hours later returned with a serious leak and sank there before repairs could be made.

1782: One of the world's most famous treasure wrecks and the richest British sailing ship ever lost was the East Indiaman *Grosvenor*. She was a frigate of 729 tons (741 tonnes) mounting 26 guns, sailing

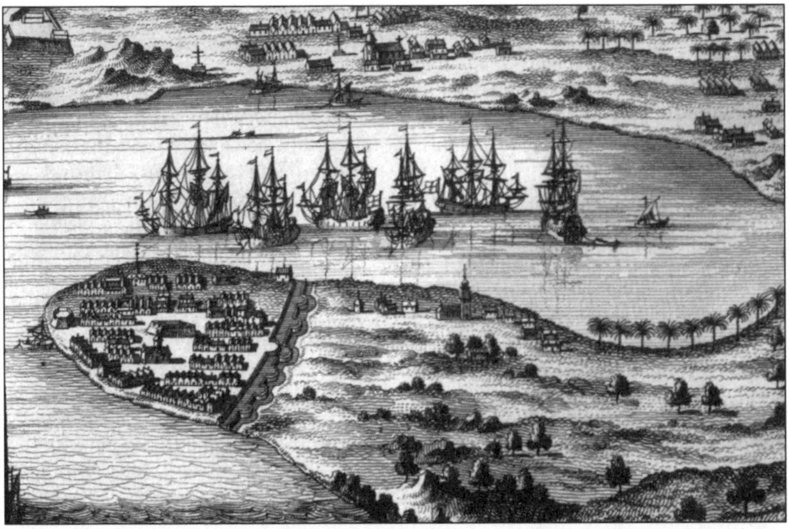

Fleet of Dutch East Indiamen in Saldanha Bay, waiting for good weather before attempting to sail around the dreaded Cape of Good Hope.

from India for England. Among the treasures crammed into her hold were the jewel-encrusted gold peacock throne of India, 720 large gold ingots, 2.6 million gold "Pagoda" coins, and 19 chests of diamonds, emeralds, rubies and sapphires. Due to an error in navigation, the ship wrecked on the deserted South African coast near Point St. Lucia, 700 miles (1126.5 kilometers) northeast of Cape Town. The loss of life was staggering. Most people drowned, and natives massacred all but a few of those who made it to shore. This outstanding shipwreck has been the focus of numerous expeditions, but the area's treacherous waters have foiled most of them.

1783: The Danish East Indiaman *Nicobar*, commanded by Captain Andreas Christij and sailing from Copenhagen to Bengal, with "a great amount of treasure," stopped at False Bay because so many of people had died in an epidemic during the voyage. Shortly after setting sail, she wrecked in a gale and most of those aboard perished. In 1987 divers discovered the wreck site and brought up a large amount of Swedish copper plate money (*kopperplatmynt*).

1784: The Dutch East Indiaman *Hoop* (800 tons/813 tonnes), commanded by Captain Sijbrand Sax and sailing between Batavia and Holland with over 120,000 guilders in cargo, was lost in a violent storm off the Cape of Good Hope. All of her crew and passengers were lost with the cargo.

1785: The Dutch East Indiaman *Stralen* (880 tons/813 tonnes), commanded by Captain Willen de Wijn and sailing between Batavia and India and Holland with over 900,000 guilders in cargo, including more than 350,000 pieces of Chinese porcelain, was totally lost in a storm while anchored at Table Bay. Three unsuccessful salvage attempts found nothing. Later it was discovered that the captain and two other officers were smuggling back two chests of diamonds and other precious stones, which were also lost.

1785: The Dutch East Indiaman *Amstel* (1,150 tons/1,168.5 tonnes, 48 cannons), commanded by Captain Gottlieb Mulder and sailing from China to Holland with 803,000 guilders in Oriental treasures and other cargo, was totally lost off Cape Aqulhas and only six of her crew survived.

1787: The Dutch East Indiaman *Avenhorn* (880 tons/894 tonnes), commanded by Captain A. Arend Thobiasz and sailing between Batavia and Holland with 109,000 guilders in cargo, was lost 6 miles (10 kilometers) west of the Cape of Good Hope.

1788: The Dutch East Indiaman *Maria* (900 tons/914.5 tonnes), commanded by Captain A. Arend Thobiasz and carrying a cargo from Batavia and Ceylon to Holland valued at 255,000 guilders, ran aground and went to pieces in Plettenberg Bay near the Cape of Good Hope.

1789: The Dutch East Indiaman *Drietal Handelaar*s (502 tons/510 tonnes), commanded by Captain Kornelis de Vries and sailing between Batavia and Holland with 260,000 guilders in cargo, was totally lost just east of the Cape of Good Hope.

1790: The Danish East Indiaman *Erfprins van Augustenburg* (570 tons/579 tonnes), sailing between Copenhagen and Japan with a large amount of treasure, was wrecked in Table Bay during a gale. All the people were saved, as well as 36 chests of coins.

1791: The Dutch East Indiaman *Middleburg* (1,150 tons/1,168.5 tonnes), commanded by Captain Jan Van Gennep with 650,000 guilders in Oriental treasures, was burned in Saldanha Bay, off Hoedjies Point, by the crew to prevent the British from capturing her. Some of her cargo had been salvaged from the wreck of a Portuguese East Indiaman *Nossa Senhor de Bonfim e Sancta Maria*, lost in the Mozambique Channel. Divers found the site in 1969 and recovered more than 20,000 pieces of porcelain, over 300 pounds (136 kilograms) of jade artifacts, and almost 1 ton (1.01 tonne) of carved ivory, but there is still a great deal left.

1796: The Swedish East Indiaman *Gothenburg*, commanded by Captain Carl Trutiger and sailing from Sweden to India with 96 chests of gold and silver specie, wrecked at Green Point near the Cape of Good Hope.

1799: The Danish warship *Oldenburg* (64 cannons), sailing from Copenhagen to Japan, was wrecked in Table Bay. Everyone survived, but the 12 chests of gold and silver coins listed on the manifest were lost.

1799: The British warship *Sceptre* (64 cannons), commanded by Captain Valentine Edwards and sailing in a convoy to India with over £200,000 sterling in treasure, stopped at Table Bay due to bad weather and while there was totally lost. Only 128 of 290 people on board survived. A small portion of her treasure was recovered soon after the disaster.

1805: The French frigate of war *L'Atalante*, commanded by Captain Gaudin, was totally lost in Table Bay during a gale. Only one man drowned, but ten chests of gold coins were never recovered.

1813: The British merchantman *William Pitt* (572 tons/581 tonnes), commanded by Captain Butler and sailing between Batavia and England with a cargo valued at over £300,000 sterling, was totally lost several leagues east of Algoa Bay with a total loss of lives and cargo. Several contemporary attempts failed to find any trace of the ship except for timbers on a beach.

1817: The French warship *L'Alouette*, commanded by Captain Claude Rigodet and sailing between France and Reunion Island with "a large amount of gold and silver coinage," plus silverware, weapons and wine, was wrecked during a heavy fog on Albatross Rock off Olifantsbos Point.

1831: The British East Indiaman *Duke of Northumberland* (608 tons/618 tonnes), commanded by Captain G. Wood and sailing from Madras to London with "a cargo of great value," wrecked near Cape Agulhas, at a place now named Northumberland Point.

1844: The British East Indiaman *St. Mungo* (355 tons/361 tonnes), commanded by Captain Lamond and sailing from India to England with a cargo valued at £341,000 sterling, wrecked during a storm on some rocks off Cape Agullas and only a few of the people on board were saved.

1852: The British East Indiaman *Birkenhead* (1,400 tons/1,422 tonnes), commanded by Captain R. Salmond, was a troop-carrying ship with large amount of gold specie aboard when she sank off Danger Point on a reef now called Birkenhead Rock. It was one of South Africa's worst maritime disasters, claiming 445 lives. She has been partially salvaged in recent years.

(Above) Chinese blue-and-white porcelain, dating around 1575, was recovered from a wreck just east of the Cape of Good Hope.

(Right) One of over 100,000 Dutch silver ducatoon coins recovered by Charles Shapiro from a seventeenth-century Dutch wreck in Table Bay.

(Below) Various kinds of treasure off a late seventeenth-century Dutch East Indiaman off Rodriquez Island.

(*Above*) Model of the French East Indiaman *St.Géran*, lost on a reef off Mauritius Island in 1744 and located and excavated in recent years.

(*Right*) Henry Holmes holding a large silver serving spoon with a cannon ball attached to it, with hundreds of lead musket and pistol balls, which he found on a wreck off Mauritius Island.

(*Below*) While spear fishing on a reef off Mauritius Island, Marx recovered these coins and other objects from an unidentified French wreck.

Chapter 23

Indian Ocean's Richest Shipwrecks

The Indian Ocean is vast, stretching from Antarctica to southern Asia and from eastern Africa to southeast Australia. It covers 28 million square miles (72,514,400 square kilometers), some areas of which have yet to be thoroughly explored. Since the dawn of human history the Indian Ocean has been used for trade. As early as 3000 B.C. the Babylonians had regular seaborne commerce with India, and by 2500 B.C. the Egyptians had sail-driven merchantmen over 100 feet (30.5 meters) long voyaging all along the east coast of Africa. The Old Testament records that *ca.* 950 B.C. King Solomon of Israel contracted Phoenicians, the best mariners at the time, to build a fleet of ships in the Gulf of Aquaba on the Red Sea to sail to gold-producing Ophir, believed to be modern Yemen in Saudi Arabia. They took copper to trade and returned with "the fine gold of Ophir," silver, apes, ivory and peacocks.

As early as 100 B.C. Romans sailed the Indian Ocean from the Red Sea to India. Recent archaeological evidence suggests that they reached Vietnam two centuries later. In the second century A.D. *The Periplus of the Erythraean Sea* appeared. Written by a Romanized Greek, it is a combination handbook for merchants detailing the best areas for trade and a navigational pilot book covering the Red Sea, east Africa, and as far as India. The importance of trade in antiquity is evidenced in the ninth chapter:

> From Malao (Berbera) it is two courses to the mart of Moundou, where ships anchor more safely by an island lying very close to the land. The imports to this are as aforesaid [Chapter 8 mentions iron, gold, silver, drinking cups, etc.], and from it likewise are exported the same goods [Chapter 8 mentions myrrh, douaka, makeir and slaves], and fragrant gum called *mokrotou*. The inhabitants who trade here are more stubborn.

The first European to open a sea route to China was a Greek merchant named Alexander, veteran of the Red Sea–India route. In A.D. 120 he rounded the southern tip of India and sailed across the Bay of Bengal to Malacca, Malaysia. After trading there, he sailed around the southern tip of Malaysia and cruised the Gulf of Siam, heading northward to reach the present-day frontier between North Vietnam and China.

The earliest geographers believed the Indian Ocean to be an immense lake connected to China by land. Only after 1488, when the Portuguese explorer Bartolomeu Dias sailed from Lisbon down the west coast of Africa and rounded the Cape of Good Hope and reported an ocean beyond it, did cartographers change their charts to show an ocean.

As in many other chapters of history, no documentation exists to show when Arab mariners began long-distance trading voyages to the west coast of Africa for gold, ivory and slaves. The earliest evidence comes from recently discovered remains of an Arab trading vessel from *ca.* 300 A.D. found off Zanzibar Island. Once European East Indian companies began trade with the Orient, Indian Ocean maritime traffic increased a great deal.

From 1405 to 1433 China enjoyed a brief period of unparalleled maritime exploration when Admiral Zheng He (also known as Cheng Ho) sailed to various parts of the Indian Ocean, South Pacific, Persian Gulf and distant Africa. His nine-masted flagship was 400 feet (122 meters) long, massive compared to Columbus' *Santa María*. Zheng He's ships were well designed with watertight

The crew of the British East Indiaman *Abergavenny* being rescued as the ship sinks.

bulkheads for storing drinking water and supplies, which helped keep a ship afloat if breached. His exterior rudders could be raised to reduce a ship's draft in shallow waters. Zheng He made seven voyages around the Indian Ocean, traveling over 30,000 nautical miles and visited thirty lands, several of them on the east coast of Africa. He died in 1433 at age 62 and was buried at sea. Three years later China issued an imperial ban on the construction of oceangoing ships and for the next five centuries, Chinese mariners did no more exploring.

In November 1497 Vasco da Gama rounded the Cape of Good Hope and sailed north along the coast in hopes of finding the legendary Monomotapa gold mines. In December he passed the farthest point reached by Bartolomeu Dias a few years before. Proceeding north, he came to a large protected bay he named Natal (now Durban). Everywhere he sought information about the Monomotapa mine, but learned nothing. For some reason he didn't stop at Sofala, for centuries a port of call for Arab traders, where he might have learned the sea route to India.

Still further to the north da Gama discovered Mozambique where the inhabitants first thought his ships were those of Arab traders, who had been coming since the eighth century to obtain gold, ivory and slaves. The Muslim ships were quite different from those of the Portuguese. Instead of canvas, they used matted palm leaves for sails and leather thongs rather than nails lashed the timbers to the ship's ribs. Several Muslim ships were in port loaded with gold, precious stones and spices. Through interpreters, da Gama got the loan of one of their pilots so he could lead them to India. With the Muslim pilot showing the way, da Gama crossed the Indian Ocean and reached Calcutta in May 1498. Before long, ships of many nations were following this route.

One of Portugal's most important Indian Ocean possessions was the small island of Hormuz (Ormuz), strategically located at the entrance to the Persian Gulf. Long before the Portuguese captured the island (they took it briefly in 1507, then ruled from 1520 until the mid-seventeenth century), Hormuz profited greatly as the entrepôt for all trade between India and Persia. Gold coins, called xerafim, were minted at Hormuz as early as 1350 and circulated throughout the Indian Ocean and the Orient. The Portuguese established a fort and small fleet of warships and by 1520 ruled over an expanded area of the Persian Gulf from which they obtained all sorts of spices and drugs, silks and tapestries, horses from Persia, as well as vast amounts of pearls from Bahrein Island.

1502: When one of Vasco de Gama's ships discovered the Almirante Islands, southwest of the main Seychelles group and east of Tanzania, they found survivors from a Muslim ship that had wrecked there several years before "with a large amount of gold, ivory and pearls," while sailing from "Arabia" to Mozambique.

1505: The Portuguese East Indiaman the *Lionarda*, commanded by Captain Vasco Gomes, sailing from Goa for Lisbon with a cargo valued at 465,000 crusadoes, was wrecked off Mombasa, Kenya, which became a Portuguese base in 1529.

1505: The Portuguese ship *São João*, commanded by Captain Francisco da Naia and sailing between Lisbon and India with "a large amount of treasure," wrecked on an uncharted reef, then named Baixos de Judia and subsequently the Baixos (or Bassas) da India. Only two men were rescued by another ship in the convoy.

1506: The Portuguese ship *Judia,* returning from Goa to Lisbon "with a valuable cargo," was wrecked on the Bassas da India. Another ship in the convoy rescued 14 of over 300 men aboard.

1506: The fleet of Captain Tristan da Cunha was sailing from Lisbon to Goa. Two unidentified Portuguese East Indiamen, carrying " many chests of gold and silver," were wrecked on the west coast of Madagascar Island. Other ships in the fleet rescued only a few survivors.

1507: Three unidentified Portuguese ships sailing between Lisbon and India with large amounts of treasure on board ran aground during the night while rounding the southern tip of Madagascar Island and were total losses. By daylight other ships rescued a small number of people.

1509: The Portuguese ship *São Vicente* (600 tons/610 tonnes), commanded by Captain Francisco de São and sailing between Goa and Lisbon with a valuable cargo, wrecked on the Shoals of Padua. Other ships in the convoy saved nothing but some of her people. The *Santa Clara,* commanded by Captain Rodrigo Rebelo, which was sailing with the *São Vicente,* was totally lost on a reef to the south of Padua Shoals.

1511: The Portuguese East Indiaman *São Sebastao,* also known as *Sebastão Velha* (880 tons/894 tonnes), sailing between Lisbon and Goa, with 540,000 crusadoes of treasure, was fleeing from pirates when she struck a reef at the mouth of the Red Sea and sank.

1512: The Portuguese East Indiamen, the *São Cristovão* and the *San Antonio,* sailing from Lisbon to Malacca, and carrying over 600,000 crusadoes in gold and silver, were lost on the São Lazaro Shoals, located about 200 miles (322 kilometers) north of Madagascar. About fifty survivors in long boats reached Mombasa, Kenya.

1516: Two Portuguese East Indiamen—the *Santa Maria de Serra,* commanded by Captain João Martin de Silviera, and the *Nossa Senhora de Piedade,* commanded by Captain Gueira de Montoyo Castelhano—sailing between Lisbon and Malacca with a total of 540,000 crusadoes in treasure, wrecked on the São Lazaro Shoals. Other ships in the fleet rescued 87 of the men.

1520: The Portuguese East Indiaman *Santo Antonio de Chyllas,* in a fleet commanded by Captain Pero de Silva and with 740,000 crusadoes in gold and silver, sailed from Lisbon with a stop at Mozambique Island, then headed for Goa, but wrecked on a reef on the south coast of present-day Yemen, then called the Baixo de Santo Antonio.

1522: The Portuguese East Indiaman *São Jorge,* commanded by Captain Garcia Coutinho and sailing from Lisbon to Hormuz, with "a vast amount of gold and silver," put into the port of Muscat in present-day Oman to obtain water and while there, a storm arose and the ship lost her anchors and wrecked on a reef.

1525: The Portuguese East Indiaman *Santo Corpo* (1,200 tons/1,219 tonnes), the flagship of the armada of Filipe de Castro, carrying over half a million crusadoes in treasure and sailing between Lisbon and Hormuz, wrecked at Ras al Haad, Oman, and only a few souls were saved by other ships.

1525: The Portuguese East Indiaman *São João* (900 tons/914.5 tonnes), commanded by Captain Filipe de Brito and sailing from Lisbon to Goa with a "large amount of treasure" on board, wrecked at Cape Rocalgate on the Yemen Coast in the Gulf of Aden.

1527: The Portuguese East Indiaman *São Sebastão,* commanded by Captain Pero Mascarenhas, in the armada of Vasco da Gama and carrying 317,000 crusadoes in treasure, wrecked on the west side of Madagascar Island in a storm. Only three men of the 675 aboard the ship were rescued.

1527: The Portuguese East Indiaman *Nossa Senhora da Conceição,* commanded by Captain Alexio de Abreu and sailing in the armada of Captain Manuel de Lacerda, from Lisbon to India with "a large amount of treasure on board," was wrecked along with two other unidentified armada ships on the west coast of Madagascar Island. Survivors from all three ships reached shore. Some of them survived a year and were rescued.

1528: The Portuguese East Indiaman *Flor da Rosa* (890 tons/904 tonnes), commanded by Captain Antonio de Abreu and sailing from

Lisbon to India with "a large amount of gold and silver on board," suffered heavy damage in a storm off the Cape of Good Hope and then anchored off the southwest shore of Madagascar. She put out six anchors when another storm came up, but all the anchor lines parted and she wrecked on the coast. Other ships in the armada rescued some of her people.

1528: The Portuguese East Indiaman *São Vicente* (850 tons/864 tonnes), commanded by Captain Afonso Vaz Azambujo and sailing between Lisbon and India with 450,000 crusadoes in treasure, was totally lost on the reefs surrounding João da Nova Island and only some of her crew were rescued.

1529: Three unidentified French privateering vessels from the port of Dieppe, France, spent several months capturing and plundering dozens of Muslim vessels in the Indian Ocean. During their return voyage, all three wrecked while trying to round the southern tip of Madagascar. The French vessels had Portuguese navigators on board who knew the waters of the Indian Ocean.

1530: The Portuguese East Indiaman *Santa Maria* (1,400 tons/1,422.5 tonnes), commanded by Captain Diogo da Fonseca and sailing between Lisbon and Hormuz with 340,000 crusadoes in gold and silver specie, was wrecked on Socotra Island, south of the Arabian Peninsula. When an unidentified ship was sent to pick up the survivors, it too struck a reef and sank with very few survivors.

1530: The Portuguese East Indiaman *Santa Maria de Ajuda*, also called the *Nossa Senhora D'Ajuda*, commanded by Captain Duarte da Fonseca and sailing from Lisbon to Goa, with 540,000 crusadoes in treasure, made a stop at Madagascar to find survivors of the ship of Captain Manuel de Lacerda, which had been lost there three years before. While searching for survivors along the west coast of this island, this ship also wrecked.

1540: The Portuguese East Indiaman *Esperança* (700 tons/711 tonnes), commanded by Captain Pero Lopes de Sousa and with cargo valued at 444,000 crusadoes, was returning from India to Lisbon. Separated from its armada during a storm, she wrecked on the east side of Madagascar. There were no survivors.

1541: The Portuguese East Indiaman *Santiago*, commanded by Captain Cristovão de Mendonça, in the armada of Captain Martin

Afonso de Sousa and sailing from Lisbon for Hormuz with 450,000 crusadoes in treasure on board, wrecked at Dabul on the Makran Coast of Iran, in the Gulf of Oman and only a few people were saved. The ship had copper ingots as ballast instead of stones.

1544: The Portuguese East Indiaman *Santa Catalina* (1,450 tons/1,473 tonnes, 42 cannons), commanded by Captain Lopo de Azevedo and coming from Lisbon with 119 chests of gold and silver specie, was wrecked on the northwest part of Madagascar.

1547: The Portuguese East Indiaman *Santa Cruz,* commanded by Captain Bernardo Nasci and carrying over 1 million crusadoes in gold and silver, first fought off pirates in the Mozambique Channel and later wrecked on Socotra Island. The Portuguese had settled there in 1507, but were forced to leave in 1511 because of repeated pirate attacks.

1548: The Portuguese East Indiaman *São Filipe,* commanded by Captain João Figueira de Barros and sailing from Lisbon to Goa with gold and silver specie valued at 440,000 crusadoes, was lost on the southernmost of the Comoro Islands and only a few of her people were saved.

1549: The Portuguese East Indiaman *Salvador,* also known as the *Burgaleza* (1,200 tons/1,219 tonnes, 34 cannons), commanded by Captain João Figueira de Barros and sailing between Lisbon and India with gold and silver specie valued at 440,000 crusadoes, was wrecked on one of the Chago Islands. Seven men were rescued four years later by a passing ship that spotted their signal fire.

1555: The Portuguese East Indiaman *Nossa Senhora da Conceição* (1,900 tons/1,930.5 tonnes, 68 bronze cannons), sailing from Lisbon to India with 3.4 million crusadoes in treasure, was lost on the shoals of Pero dos Banhos Reef near the Chago Islands in the middle of the Indian Ocean. The island of Pero Banos was described in 1555 as being only 300 yards (274 meters) in diameter.

1558: The Portuguese East Indiaman *Conceição,* commanded by Captain Francisco Nobre and sailing from Lisbon to Cochin, with 754,000 crusadoes in gold and silver, was wrecked on the Pero dos Banhos Reef. The document describing this ship loss states that in 1555 another Portuguese East Indiaman, the *Santa Maria da Barca,* was also lost on this same reef.

1559: The Portuguese East Indiaman *Águia* (1,400 tons/1,422.5 tonnes), commanded by Captain Paio de Noronha and carrying over 1 million crusadoes in treasure from Lisbon to India, was wrecked on the northern tip of Madagascar. Of the 1,137 people aboard the ship, only 87 were picked up by another ship in the fleet.

1559: The Portuguese East Indiaman *Santa Maria de Barca*, carrying over 3 million crusadoes in cargo, including three chests of diamonds, was lost off the southeast coast of Madagascar on a return voyage to Lisbon. Two Muslim vessels appeared and rescued many of the people in the water, and then began beheading everyone. A few Portuguese jumped overboard and swam ashore to tell the tale to the British, who rescued them.

1560: The Portuguese East Indiaman *Águia*, commanded by Captain João Rodriques Salema de Carvalho, and sailing from Lisbon to Goa with 340,000 crusadoes in treasure, spent the winter at Mozambique Island. Then while continuing on to Goa, she wrecked in a storm off Mombasa, where she was headed to seek shelter.

1561: An unidentified Muslim ship, coming from Achen on the northern tip of Sumatra, Indonesia, carrying over 200,000 crusadoes in treasure captured from a Portuguese ship off Malacca, was en route to deliver the treasure to the sultan of a Red Sea port. Two Portuguese warships intercepted and sank her off Qishn, Iran.

1566: Six Spanish warships under the command of Captain Ferdinand de Monroy, sailed from Manila with the intention of attacking Moorish shipping. They came upon a Moorish fleet in the Cardu Channel in the Maldive Islands, sailing between Java and Mecca. During the battle, the "largest and richest" of the Moorish ships was sunk, along with the Spanish *Almiranta*, the *Santissima Trinidad*.

1570: The Portuguese East Indiaman *Santa Maria de Beléem* (2,200 tons/2,235 tonnes), commanded by Captain Pedro Leitao de Gamboa, carried 1,400 soldiers to Goa and Cochin, plus arms and munitions. On her return voyage from Goa to Lisbon with a cargo valued at 570,000 crusadoes, she sank near Hormuz during a storm. About 200 of the 772 people aboard reached a small deserted island and were rescued two years later.

1573: Two Portuguese East Indiamen—the *Reis Magno* (1,200 tons/1,219 tonnes) and the *São Francisco* (1,600 tons/1,626 tonnes)—

both sailing from India to Lisbon with a total of 1.1 million crusadoes in cargo, disappeared during a storm off the southern end of Madagascar. Three expeditions failed to find any traces of the ships or survivors.

1575: The Portuguese East Indiaman *São Francisco,* commanded by Captain Duarte Melo and sailing for Lisbon from Malacca and Goa, with a cargo valued at 460,000 crusadoes, stopped at Madagascar to find survivors from the above two ships, but while sailing along the shore, she struck upon a reef and was lost.

1577: Two Portuguese East Indiamen—the *São João,* commanded by Captain Miguel de Arnide, and the *São Pedro* (900 tons/914.5 tonnes), commanded by Captain Manuel de Medeiros—both sailing between Lisbon and India with "a large amounts of treasure," wrecked on the Pero dos Banhos Shoals. Some survivors from the *São Pedro* got ashore. They fashioned a small boat from wood from the wreck and reached Cochin after great hardships.

1582: The Portuguese East Indiaman *São Luis* (890 tons/904 tonnes, 38 cannons), commanded by Captain Luis Caldeira and sailing from Lisbon for India with 444,000 crusadoes in gold and silver, wrecked on a reef off the northern end of Madagascar. Salvors were able to raise only several of her bronze cannons.

1582: The Portuguese East Indiaman *Reis Magos* (1,750 tons/1,778 tonnes), commanded by Captain Manuel de Miranda, sailed from Cochin with a cargo valued at 850,000 crusadoes and was wrecked in a storm on Lakshadweep Island off the southwest coast of India. Most of her people made it ashore, but her cargo was a total loss.

1583: The Portuguese East Indiaman *Nossa Senhora da Reliquias* (1,350 tons/1,371.5 tonnes, 56 cannons), commanded by Captain Juan de Gama Brito and sailing between Malacca and Goa with 422,000 crusadoes in cargo, was wrecked in a storm on Little Nicobar Island in the Andaman Sea. Most of the people got on shore. A raft built from wreckage eventually reached the coast of India with a few survivors. A rescue vessel was dispatched for the other survivors, but they were never found. It was feared they had been killed and eaten by the natives.

1584: The Portuguese East Indiaman *Boa Viagem* (1,800 tons/1,829 tonnes), commanded by Captain Lourenço Soares de Melo, sailed

Drawing showing the Portuguese East Indiaman *São Paulo*, lost in 1567 with a cargo of unknown value, on the João de Nova Reef.

from Lisbon for India with a stop in Persia (Iran) to deliver the new Portuguese ambassador to the court of the king of Persia. She carried 640,000 crusadoes in treasure, and was wrecked on the coast of Basra, Iraq. Only a few people survived.

1588: The Portuguese East Indiaman *São Salvador* (1,400 tons/1,422.5 tonnes), commanded by Captain Miguel de Abreu and sailing from India for Lisbon with a cargo valued at 430,000 crusadoes, developed a bad leak and was forced to seek safety in the port of Hormuz, where it sank. Most of her people and some of her cargo were saved.

1589: The Portuguese East Indiaman *São Antonio* (1,100 tons/1,118 tonnes, 44 cannons), commanded by Captain João da Cunha and sailing from Lisbon to India with 380,000 crusadoes in treasure, was wrecked on one of the Chagos Islands. A ship sailing with the *Antonio* rescued 54 survivors.

1591: The Portuguese East Indiaman *São Bartolomeu* (1,400 tons/1,422.5 tonnes, forty cannons), commanded by Captain Simão Vaz Velho, and carrying a large amount of gold and silver specie, was lost about 2 leagues off the northern tip of Madagascar Island while heading for Mozambique Island.

1591: The Portuguese East Indiaman *São Bernardo* (1,450 tons/1,473 tonnes, 46 cannons), commanded by Captain Simãao Vaz Telo and

Spanish pieces of eight recovered from the Portuguese East Indiaman *Santiago*, lost in 1595 on the Baixo de India.

sailing between India and Lisbon with a cargo valued at 350,000 crusadoes, was wrecked on Peros das Banhos Shoals.

1591: The English made their first voyage to the Indian Ocean, an area until this time totally controlled by the Portuguese. A fleet of English warships penetrated this forbidden area, and during a six-month period attacked and destroyed 38 Portuguese East Indiamen, eleven of which went to the bottom with all hands on board. According to royal officials of the king of Spain, who was also king of Portugal at this time, the cost in lives exceeded 10,000 and the cost in treasure and other cargo was over 35 million crusadoes. Unfortunately, the pertinent documentation on the names of the ships and where they were lost is not available; most likely the documents were destroyed in the Great Earthquake of Lisbon in 1755.

1593: The Portuguese East Indiaman *Bom Jesus* (2,000 tons/2,032 tonnes), sailing between Lisbon and India and carrying over 2.5 million crusadoes in treasure, wrecked on the Cargados Carajos Reef chain. The *São Bartholomeu*, which was sailing with her, disappeared at the same time, probably lost on the same reef. The reef chain, today called Cargados Carajos Shoals and Saint Brandon, lies north of Mauritius, and fishermen report sightings of many cannons and anchors from numerous old wrecks. In 1981 a group of South African treasure hunters discovered an unidentified British merchantman on a reef and recovered over 2,000 gold and silver pocket watches and other interesting artifacts, which indicates the ship was sailing between England and India or the Orient. From photographs of the watches, I can date the wreck around 1780 to 1820.

1595: The Portuguese East Indiaman *São Bartolomeu* (1,650 tons/1,676.5 tonnes), commanded by Captain Lopo de Pina de Azevedo and sailing between Lisbon and Macau (formerly Macao) with 238,000 crusadoes in treasure, was wrecked on the Bassas da India Reef and slipped off into deep water. There were no survivors.

1597: The Portuguese East Indiaman *Nossa Senhora da Vitoria* (1,300 tons/1,321 tonnes, 44 cannons), commanded by Captain João Rodriquez Correia and sailing from India to Lisbon with a cargo "of great value," was lost 3 leagues north of Mogadishu, Somalia, in 2 degrees north latitude. A ship sent to find survivors found nothing but some of her timbers on a beach.

1601: The Portuguese East Indiaman *Santo Antonio,* commanded by Captain Manuel Pais and sailing from Lisbon to India with 900,000 crusadoes in silver specie, was wrecked on the south side of Socotra Island, which lies south of Saudi Arabia.

1602: The French warship *Corbin* was lost sailing between France and India with 78 large chests of silver and gold coins. She struck on a reef and went down in deep water near Felidu Atoll in the Maldives Islands.

1606: One of the earliest Dutch East Indiaman losses was the ship *Westfriesland* (700 tons/711 tonnes), commanded by Captain Willem Jansz van Amsterdam and sailing between Bantam, Indonesia, and Holland with a large cargo of gold, precious stones, pearls, and spices of unknown value. She was lost on the southern part of Madagascar.

1607: The Portuguese East Indiaman *Nossa Senhora de Betancor* (1,500 tons/1,524 tonnes), commanded by Captain Bras Teles de Menezes and sailing from Lisbon to India and Malacca with " a large amount of gold and silver," was wrecked on the southwest side of Madagascar and only a few people were saved.

1607: The Portuguese East Indiaman *San Martinho* (2,200 tons/2,235 tonnes, 68 bronze cannons) was sailing between Goa and Malacca, Malaysia, with 850,000 crusadoes in silver and gold specie lost off Manaar, Sri Lanka. Most of the survivors who got ashore were captured by local pirates and massacred.

1608: The Portuguese East Indiaman *São Bartolomeu* (1, 450 tons/1,473 tonnes, 38 cannons), commanded by Captain Lopo de Almeida and coming from Lisbon to Sri Lanka with 366,000 crusadoes in treasure, was wrecked near Colombo and only some people were saved.

1608: The Portuguese East Indiaman *Nossa Senhora da Consolação,* commanded by Captain Diogo de Sousa and sailing between India and Lisbon with a cargo valued at 570,000 crusadoes, burned and sank off the northern tip of Madagascar. Seventy-seven survivors made it ashore and were rescued two months later.

1610: The Dutch East Indiaman *Eendracht* (240 tons/244 tonnes), commanded by Captain Adriaan Kornelis Haai, sailed from Holland with a large amount of gold and silver. She first stopped at Mauritius for ebony wood and then headed for the Moluccas. She caught fire and was run aground in the Bay of Antongel on the northeast part of Madagascar Island. She blew up before any of the treasure or other cargo could be saved.

1614: The Portuguese East Indiaman *Santo Antonio* (1,800 tons/1,829 tonnes), sailing from Lisbon to Malacca with 670,000 crusadoes of treasure, was wrecked on Socotra Island, located south of the Arabian Peninsula.

1614: The Portuguese East Indiaman *São Boaventura* (1,200 tons/1,219 tonnes), commanded by Captain Luis Ferreira Furtado de Mendonça and sailing from Goa to Lisbon with a cargo valued at 430,000 crusadoes, excluding one chest of diamonds and three chests of precious stones (these were always appraised in Lisbon), sank on the high seas within sight of Rodriquez Island. Some of her crew were able to reach the island and were rescued four years later. This small island is located 400 miles (644 kilometers) east of Mauritius Island.

1615: According to a well-known legend, the Dutch East Indiaman *Banda* was carrying 5 million guilders in gold coins and precious stones. The fact is that these ships mainly carried gold *to*, not *from*, the Orient unless it was in the form of jewelry. She may have carried precious stones, since the quickest route to riches in those days was to smuggle back precious stones, which were easy to conceal on a ship. In fact, the *Banda* (800 tons/813 tonnes), was the flagship in the fleet of Admiral Pieter Both and one of four Dutch East Indiamen lost in 1615 while returning to Holland from Batavia. The total value of the ships' cargoes was valued at only 1,335,000 guilders, much of it in the form of more than 300,000 pieces of Ming Dynasty blue-and-white porcelain, which the Dutch called *kraakware*. All four ships wrecked in a storm on the southwest side Mauritius Island and most of the survivors got ashore and were picked up a few days later by another Dutch ship. Contemporary salvage went on for four years and all but the porcelain and many iron cannons were removed from the ships. In recent years all four wreck sites were damaged by stupid salvors who used explosives and destroyed the remaining porcelain in their quest for gold and silver. I surveyed all four sites in 1979 for the Mauritius government, and all that remained were dozens of large iron cannons and millions of porcelain shards embedded in the reef.

1616: The Portuguese East Indiaman *São Juliao* (44 cannons), commanded by Captain Sebastão Peres, was sailing between Lisbon and India with 492,000 crusadoes in treasure. The Dutch pursued her once she passed the Cape of Good Hope. Unable to enter port at Mozambique because of a Dutch blockade, she continued north and was lost on one of the Comoro Islands. The Portuguese burned their ship and all 600 people got ashore and were eventually rescued. The India-built teak ship was 25 years old when she sank.

1619: The Portuguese East Indiaman *Nossa Senhora do Populo* (1,700 tons/1,727 tonnes), commanded by Captain Rui Freire de Andrade, was carrying soldiers, munitions, supplies, and over 1 million crusadoes in gold and silver specie to several Portuguese forts then under attack by Muslims, but wrecked on Qeshm Island in the Straits of Hormuz off the southern coast of Iran. While under attack, the ship was set on fire and blew up with a major loss of life and treasure.

1619: The Portuguese East Indiaman *São Pedro* (1,700 tons/1,727 tonnes, 64 cannons), in the armada of General Rui Freire de Andrade, who was carrying 600 soldiers, munitions, and arms for the Portuguese garrison at Hormuz, plus 389,000 crusadoes in treasure, was then to continue on to Malacca. While in port at Hormuz, her crew burned the ship when it was evident she would be captured during an attack by British warships.

1619: The Portuguese East Indiaman *São Martinho* (1,200 tons/1,219 tonnes), commanded by Captain Gonçalo da Silveira and sailing from Lisbon to Malacca with 434,000 crusadoes in treasure, was damaged in a terrible storm off South Africa. Unable to enter Mozambique because of Dutch ships cruising there, she made for Hormuz, near present-day Bandar Abbas, and wrecked there.

1621: The Portuguese East Indiaman *São Carlos* (1,200 tons/1,219 tonnes, 34 cannons), the flagship in an armada of 18 ships commanded by the Viceroy Afonso de Noronha, was carrying a large amount of gold and silver. Dutch warships attacked the armada after it left Mozambique. This ship was badly damaged in the encounter and was run aground on Baixo Mongical, a large reef to the east of Mozambique. Other ships in the armada saved the viceroy and most of the crew.

1621: The Portuguese warship *Todos os Santos,* commanded by Captain Fernão da Costa and sailing from Lisbon to Malacca with 365,000 crusadoes in treasure, was also taking soldiers and supplies to the garrison in Hormuz, which was under siege by the British. She was sunk by cannon fire from British ships as she attempted to enter this port.

1621: The Danes joined the Dutch and British in forming the East India Companies in 1617 to challenge Portugal's claim to the East Indies. When their first fleet had successfully obtained very valuable cargoes in the Orient and was in Tricomalee (on the north east coast of Sri Lanka) preparing to return to Copenhagen, a fleet of Portuguese warships surprised and captured one of the merchantmen. Another sank near the entrance of the port while it was attempting to escape.

1621: The British joined forces with Persia to attack the Portuguese, who had a large fort on Hormuz Island off the south coast of Iran. After capturing the fort, they attacked and burned five large Portuguese East Indiamen—the *São Pedro, São Antonio, Todos los Santos, São Matinho* and the *Nossa Senhora de Vitoria*—with combined cargoes valued at 3.44 million crusadoes. They had been sailing from India for Lisbon when bad weather forced them to stop at Hormuz Island.

1621: The Portuguese East Indiaman *São Bento* was lost during a battle with the Dutch in the port of Mozambique. She was sailing between Lisbon and Goa, India, with a large amount of gold and silver specie and bullion. Using grappling hooks, the local garrison of Portuguese soldiers recovered three bronze cannons before she disappeared beneath the muddy sea-floor.

1623: The Portuguese East Indiaman *São Braz,* commanded by Captain Cosme Cassão de Brito and sailing from Lisbon to Malacca and Macau with 444,000 crusadoes in gold and silver, wrecked on Baixo de Pederias, about midway between the coast of Mozambique and Goa. The name may be different today.

1623: The Portuguese East Indiaman *Nossa Senhora da Guia* (1,600 tons/1,626 tonnes), commanded by Captain Manuel Pessoa de Carvalho and sailing between Lisbon and Macau with 460,000 crusadoes in treasure, was wrecked on Jabal Zuqar Island near the entrance to the Red Sea. Many of her people were rescued.

1624: The Dutch East Indiaman *Arend* (400 tons/406.5 tonnes), commanded by Captain Meindert Egbertsz and sailing between Holland and Batavia with 560,000 guilders in gold and silver, was totally destroyed in a storm on the northern side of Mauritius Island. Dutch salvors sent to the wreck site found nothing of value.

1625: The Portuguese East Indiaman *São Simão* (1,400 tons/1,422.5 tonnes), commanded by Captain Antonio Moreira and sailing from Lisbon to Goa with 434,000 crusadoes in treasure, was lost on Europa Island in the Mozambique Channel and many people were saved.

1625: The Dutch East Indiaman *Gouda* (800 tons/813 tonnes), commanded by Captain Jan Willemsz Dijk and sailing between Batavia and Holland with a cargo valued at 253,027 guilders, was lost in a storm off the southern end of Réunion Island.

1628: The Portuguese East Indiaman *Santiago* (1,200 tons/1,219 tonnes, 36 cannons), commanded by Captain Francisco de Sousa de Castro and sailing from Lisbon to Macau with "a large amount of gold and silver," wrecked on Baixos de João de Nova, northeast of Madagascar. Some of her people were saved.

1628: The Dutch East Indiaman *Haring,* sailing from Holland to Batavia with 180,000 guilders in silver specie, was lost entering

Arakan, Burma, on the Bay of Bengal. Some of her silver was recovered at the time.

1630: The Dutch East Indiaman *Dubbele Arend* (360 tons/366 tonnes), commanded by Captain Jan Dirk Klein and sailing between Holland and Batavia with 320,000 guilders of treasure, was lost during a storm on the southeast corner of Mauritius Island while trying to find a safe port.

1634: A large Persian merchantman with "a huge amount of treasure on board" sought refuge from pursuing pirates under the guns of the fort on Hormuz Island. The pirates continued their attack, setting the Persian ship on fire. It exploded, killing all but seven of the 340 men on board. Many of the officers on this ship were Danes and Dutchmen.

1635: The English privateering ship *Samaritan* was lost during a storm after capturing six rich Mogul ships off India with vast treasures. She allegedly carried over £3 million sterling in gold, silver, pearls and precious stones, all plundered from two rich Moorish ships. The British sent two vessels to find the wreck, each carrying a diving bell and several divers. Instead, they found the remains of a Portuguese ship deeply buried in the sand in 7 fathoms of water off Grande Comoro Island and recovered six bronze cannons and an anchor, but no treasure.

1638: An unidentified Portuguese East Indiaman, sailing between Malacca and Goa with a cargo valued in excess of 2 million crusadoes, was totally lost trying to round the northern tip of the northernmost island in the Andaman Islands. Survivors reached shore only to be eaten by the natives. Two survived and were eventually rescued. They recounted that some of the natives wore various items of European apparel, no doubt taken from earlier shipwreck victims.

1639: The Dutch East Indiaman *Koning David* (200 tons/203 tonnes), commanded by Captain Jan Taaikaas, sailed from Holland for Batavia (Jakarta) on a special voyage to take 460,000 guilders in silver specie to merchants. These merchants had come from Holland two years earlier on a ship that went down with the money they brought to purchase Oriental products and spices. The *David* wrecked in a storm and was totally lost near Ambovombe on the southeast tip of Madagascar. Some of her crew were saved, but none of the silver.

1640: The Dutch East Indiaman *Rarop* (200 tons/203 tonnes), sailing between Holland and Batavia with 320,000 guilders in silver specie, wrecked on a reef between Colombo and Negombo, Sri Lanka. Colombo, first occupied by the Portuguese in 1534, fell to the Dutch in 1656 and then to the British in 1796. Modern-day sports divers accidentally found this wreck site and recovered an undisclosed number of silver coins.

1642: The Dutch East Indiaman *Haan* (480 tons/488 tonnes) was sailing from Holland to Batavia with 330,000 guilders in gold and silver. While working her way down the coast of West Africa, she was blown across the Atlantic to the coast of Brazil where she fought off two attacks by Portuguese warships. She crossed the Atlantic again, stopping at the Cape of Good Hope for provisions and water. There she took aboard 123,000 guilders in Dutch coinage, which had been left there by a Dutch ship that was unable to continue to her destination of Batavia. Continuing toward Batavia, the Haan was attacked near Mozambique by several Muslin ships, but beat them off with heavy losses. Her luck ran out and she was totally lost off Negombo, 20 miles (32 kilometers) north of Col-ombo, Sri Lanka.

1643: The British East Indiaman *Henry Bonaventure* (1,200 tons/1,219 tonnes), sailing from London for India with £367,000 sterling in gold and silver specie, wrecked on the southern tip of Madagascar. The following year three of her crew were rescued by another British ship.

1644: The Portuguese warship *São Nicolas*, carrying 378 chests of treasure and a great deal of arms and munitions from Lisbon to Macau, wrecked in a storm near Toamasina on the east side of Madagascar. Only 44 survivors were picked up by another ship.

1647: The Portuguese East Indiaman *Santo Milagre* (1,250 tons/1,270 tonnes, 36 cannons), commanded by Captain Manuel Jorge Greco, was sailing from Lisbon to Goa with 283 chests of gold and silver. After a stop at Mozambique, it wrecked on Geyser Reef, located midway between the Comoro and Madagascar Islands. Other ships in the armada rescued some people.

1647: The Dutch East Indiaman *Popkensburg* (260 tons/264 tonnes), sailing between Holland and Batavia with 240,000 guilders in treasure, was blown off course in storms and wrecked near Pedro Point on the northern tip of Sri Lanka. Only the crew were saved.

1647: The Portuguese East Indiaman *Santo Milagre* (1,300 tons/1,321 tonnes, 32 cannons), sailing between Lisbon and Malacca and Macau with 480,000 crusadoes in gold and silver, was wrecked on the northernmost of the Maldive Islands, south of the Eight Degree Channel. One hundred thirty-nine people from the ship reached this deserted island and were rescued some months later.

1649: The Portuguese East Indiaman *Nossa Senhora do Bom Sucesso* (1,600 tons/1,626 tonnes), sailing from Lisbon to India with 670,000 crusadoes in treasure, was lost on the coast at Ponta da Barra Falsa, Madagascar, and only a few of her people were saved.

1650: The Portuguese East Indiaman *São Francisco* (1,850 tons/1,880 tonnes, 38 cannons), commanded by Captain Luis Dultze Corte Real and sailing between Hormuz and Lisbon with a cargo of "immense value," wrecked on a reef near Aden, Yemen, and only the captain and two others were saved.

1653: The Dutch East Indiaman *Morgenster* (360 tons/366 tonnes), carrying 285,000 guilders in gold and silver from Holland to Batavia, for some unknown reason sailed up the Gulf of Oman and into the Persian Gulf where she was lost near Kangan Point. There were no survivors and no mention of any treasure recovered. The Dutch learned of this loss many years later from British merchants. It is suspected that local pearl divers recovered some of the treasure from this wreck.

1653: The Dutch East Indiaman *Oranje*, of either 700 or 1,200 tons (711 or 1,219 tonnes; reports differ), sailing between Holland and Batavia with an unknown amount of gold and silver aboard, was lost in the Gulf of Masirah, Oman. Only a few men got ashore and were rescued some years later by another Dutch ship.

1653: The Dutch East Indiaman *Robijn* (480 tons/488 tonnes), sailing between Holland and Batavia with 378,000 guilders in gold and silver, was wrecked on Jaziart Masirah Island in the Arabian Sea while searching for the *Oranje* and *Morgenster*, which had been separated from her in a storm. Only a few of her people were saved.

1654: The British East Indiaman *Endeavour* was lost in a storm off Sind, Pakistan, while sailing from England to India with £780,000 sterling in silver specie. Only one man of 382 aboard survived the disaster.

1658: The Dutch East Indiaman *Molen*, commanded by Captain Jacob Stevensz Molenwerf and sailing between Holland and Batavia, carried 340,000 guilders in treasure. For some reason she first stopped at St. Helena Island in the South Atlantic, where ships normally called only on homeward-bound voyages. She was lost in the vicinity of Galle, Sri Lanka, and some of her survivors found refuge there.

1658: The British East Indiaman *Persia Merchant*, commanded by Captain Roger Middleton, was lost near Ingramrudco Island in the Maldives Islands, carrying £670,000 sterling in gold and silver specie. Less than fifty of the 440 souls aboard survived. In the 1980s a European group searched in vain for several years for this wreck, spending half a million U.S. dollars. They may not have been serious because they didn't use a magnetometer and searched visually.

1659: The Dutch East Indiaman *Avondster* (360 tons/366 tonnes), commanded by Captain Sander Gerritsz van Os and sailing between Batavia and Holland with a cargo valued 222,980 guilders, had to turn back to Batavia because of leaks. She departed again, but the ship was leaking badly, so she tried to enter the port of Gallee, Sri Lanka, and wrecked in a storm only 3 leagues from port.

1660: The British East Indiaman *Smyrna Merchant* was lost on João de Nova Island while sailing between England and India. She carried £175,000 sterling in silver specie and bullion and about a quarter of this treasure was taken off by survivors rescued by another ship in the convoy. Reefs surround this island, which was uninhabited, except for occasional fishermen, and over the centuries many richly laden homeward-bound ships have met their doom.

1661: The Dutch East Indiaman *Weesp* (560 tons/569 tonnes), sailing between Siam and India with 9 tons (9.144 tonnes) of gold ingots, was lost near Japara Island in the Andaman island group, in the eastern part of the Bay of Bengal. According to documents, locals ate all survivors.

1661: Dutch East Indiaman *Hercules* (540 tons/549 tonnes), sailing between Holland and Batavia with 470,000 guilders in treasure, suffered severe damage in gales off South Africa. Unable to reach Batavia, she headed for Galle, Sri Lanka, but was wrecked 4 leagues to the north of the port there.

1661: The Dutch East Indiaman *Wapen Van Holland* (920 tons/935 tonnes), commanded by Captain Maaten Doedesz and sailing between Batavia and Holland with 520,566 guilders in spices and Oriental treasures (excluding value of the porcelain), was wrecked on Rodriquez Island. Its existence was reported by various mariners, but not put on most charts and it was difficult to relocate again after some of the sightings.

1662: Three Dutch East Indiamen—the *Gekroonde* (1,200 tons/1,219 tonnes), commanded by Captain Frederik Pool; the *Prins Willem* (1,200 tons/1,219 tonnes), commanded by Captain Adriaan van Leene; and another unidentified ship of 700 tons (711 tonnes)—were sailing together from Batavia to Holland with over 1.35 million guilders in cargoes. Storms drove them far to the south of their intended route and all three were lost on some uncharted islands in 25 to 26 degrees south latitude, to the southeast of Madagascar. A Dutch ship found a small boat with just two men from one of the wrecks about two months after the disaster. The two survivors had resorted to cannibalism to stay alive. Originally there were 12 in the boat and ten were eaten. Finding the site is problematical. Even if the survivors gave the correct latitude, the island may have disappeared under the sea. There are no charted islands in these latitudes within thousands of miles of this position.

1662: The Dutch East Indiaman *Arnhem* (1,000 tons/1,016 tonnes), commanded by Captain Pieter Anthonisz and sailing between Batavia and Holland with a cargo of 1.2 million guilders in Oriental treasures and spices, was lost on Brandao Island in the Cargados Carajos Reef chain.

1663: The Dutch East Indiaman *Emmeloord,* commanded by Captain Frans Hendriksz van Stralen and sailing between Holland and Batavia with 327,000 guilders in gold and silver, wrecked on Damman Island, opposite Bahrain in the Persian Gulf. Some of the crew were rescued and later ransomed.

1663: The Dutch East Indiaman *Dolfijn* (520 tons/528 tonnes), sailing between Holland and Batavia with a large consignment of gold and silver, was first forced into Plymouth, England, due to bad weather and then continued for Batavia. She was totally lost near Galle, Sri Lanka, where the Dutch had built a fort in 1643 and the survivors sought refuge there.

1666: The Dutch East Indiaman *Vlissengen* (400 tons/406.5 tonnes), commanded by Captain Reinier Reiniersz and sailing between Holland and Batavia, carrying "a large amount of silver," was lost in the Bay of Galle, Sri Lanka.

1669: The Dutch East Indiaman *Landman* (474 tons/482 tonnes, thirty cannons), was sailing from Holland to Batavia with 457,000 guilders of treasure. As the ship entered Galle, Sri Lanka, she caught fire and sank.

1670: In 1674 a French warship found 132 survivors on Mahe, one of the Seychelles Islands, who had been aboard "a very rich" Portuguese East Indiaman that sank in 1670 while sailing between Goa and Lisbon.

1671: The Dutch East Indiaman *Zwarte Leeuw* (300 tons/305 tonnes), sailing from Holland to Batavia with 370,000 guilders in gold and silver, first stopped to pick up the survivors from the *Wille Leeuw,* on the Bengal coast, and then headed for Batavia. She sank near Batticaloa, Sri Lanka, with very few survivors.

1674: The Portuguese East Indiaman *Trinidade* (1,840 tons/1,869.5 tonnes, 56 bronze cannons), commanded by Captain João Vieira and sailing between Lisbon and Goa, India, with 2.3 million crusadoes in gold and silver bullion and specie, was totally lost in the Kuris Muria Islands off the east side of Oman.

1674: A brief news item in a Dutch newspaper mentioned that a very rich Dutch East Indiaman on its voyage to Batavia was lost on Male Island in the Maldives Islands chain. No name was given.

1674: An unidentified French East Indiaman, en route to Colombo, Sri Lanka, suffered grave damages during storms off the Cape of Good Hope and lost two of her masts. She then sank off Galle, Sri Lanka. No amount of treasure on her is given, but a letter states her loss "was a serious financial loss" to the French East India Company.

1674: The Portuguese East Indiaman *Santa Clara* (2,400 tons/2,438.5 tonnes, 66 bronze cannons), commanded by Captain Martin Flores de Alves and sailing between Lisbon and Macau, then to Japan, carrying gold and silver valued at 1.3 million crusadoes, was destroyed in a storm on the shore of Camorta in the Nicobar chain of islands, which are located south of the Andaman Islands. A Portuguese vessel rescued three survivors of this wreck 12 years later.

1674: An unidentified British East Indiaman, commanded by Captain James Thurman and sailing between London and Calcutta with "a large amount of silver specie on board," was wrecked on the southernmost reef of the Chago Island Archipelago.

1677: The Portuguese East Indiaman *Nossa Senhora de Belém* (1,400 tons/1,422.5 tonnes, 42 cannons), commanded by Captain Gonçalo Pereira and sailing from Lisbon to Goa with an unknown amount of treasure, was badly damaged in a storm off the Cape of Good Hope and wrecked near Ambovombe, Madagascar.

1678: The Portuguese East Indiaman *Nossa Senhora de Belém* (1,900 tons/1,930.5 tonnes, 64 cannons), sailing between Macau and Goa and then to Lisbon, with 1.3 million crusadoes in Oriental treasures, was totally lost on the southernmost of the Andaman Islands. A Dutch ship rescued several survivors who spent three weeks in a small boat; natives massacred and ate others who went ashore.

1680: The Dutch East Indiaman *Ceylon* (776 tons/788.5 tonnes, fifty cannons), sailing between Holland and Batavia with an unknown amount of treasure, was wrecked on one the southern islands in the Maldive group and only some people were saved.

1681: The French East Indiaman *Soleil d'Orient* (1,000 tons/1,016 tonnes), one of the richest French East Indiamen ever lost, has been much sought after. On board were emissaries from the king of Siam who were bringing literally tons of precious gifts to King Louis XIV. They included large amounts of diamonds and rubies and hundreds of objects fashioned from gold. She also carried Oriental goods valued at over 400,000 livres. She hit a reef near Fort Dauphin on the southeast corner of Madagascar and went down in minutes, carrying over 5 million livres in treasure. Robert Stenuit mounted two unsuccessful expeditions to find this wreck.

1684: The British East Indiaman *Merchants Delight*, commanded by Captain Edward São and sailing from England to India with £237,000 sterling in treasure, wrecked off Maceiria Island, located about 15 miles (24 kilometers) off the coast of Oman in the Arabian Sea. Arabs rescued some of the people on board and took them to Muscat, along with some of the treasure they had salvaged.

1689: The Portuguese East Indiaman *Concepção* (1,850 tons/1,880 tonnes, 62 bronze cannons), commanded by Captain Martin de Figeras, was sailing from Goa to Lisbon with over 1 million crusadoes in Oriental objects of gold, silver, jade, ivory, sandalwood and ebony. In a bad gale it ran onto Baixos da São Anton reef, about 300 miles (483 kilometers) northeast of the northern tip of Madagascar. Only 47 of the more than 600 people aboard managed to get to a nearby small deserted island. Six years later, a passing ship spotted a signal fire on the island and sent a boat to investigate. They found only three men alive; the others had died or been eaten by their shipmates. Several other East Indiamen were lost in this area, including a very rich French ship in 1745.

1689: The Dutch East Indiaman *Waveren* (488 tons/496 tonnes), commanded by Captain Reiner de Groot and coming from Holland to Batavia with 333,000 guilders in gold and silver, was wrecked in a storm off the southernmost Andaman Island. Sixty-four men were rescued by another ship in the fleet.

1690: The Dutch East Indiaman *Grote Visserij* (638 tons/648 tonnes, 48 cannons), sailing from Holland with 418,000 guilders in treasure and heading to Batavia, was badly damaged by a gale off South Africa and totally lost at Klippenpunt about 15 miles (24 kilometers) west of Cape St. Francis, Madagascar Island.

1694: The Portuguese East Indiaman *Nossa Senhora de San Juan* (1,600 tons/1,626 tonnes), commanded by Captain Antonio da Silva and carrying 250,000 crusadoes in gold and silver to ransom Portuguese who survived a shipwreck on the coast of Burma several years before, was lost on Negrais Island off Cape Negrais on the south coast of Burma.

1700: The Dutch East Indiaman *Boor* (192 tons/195 tonnes) was sailing between Batavia and Cape Town, with a cargo of unknown value. The ship disappeared and nothing more was heard of her until 22 years later when another Dutch ship stopped at Cocos Island, now Keeling Island, situated 12 degrees south latitude and 97 degrees east longitude, about 580 miles (933 kilometers) southwest of Java. This deserted island appeared on no contemporary charts or sailing direction books. Originally there were 127 survivors who subsisted on coconuts, crabs and marine life. However, all but 29 died over the years.

1701: The Dutch East Indiaman *Zanloper* (244 tons/248 tonnes), commanded by Captain Kornelis van de Kriek and carrying two chests of gold bullion and 34 chests of silver specie, was sailing between Holland and Sri Lanka when she was totally lost near Triconomalee on the Bay of Bengal, about 110 miles (177 kilometers) southeast of Jaffa. Only her people were saved.

1701: The British East Indiaman *De Grave* (700 tons/711 tonnes, 52 cannons), commanded by Captain William Young and sailing from India to England with a cargo valued at over £320,000, sterling was wrecked on the east coast of Madagascar several leagues south of Toamasina. Before the survivors reached the French Fort Dauphin, islanders killed all but one man and a boy. Two years later, after great hardship, these two were rescued by a passing British ship.

1708: Two Dutch East Indiamen—the *Concordia* (900 tons/914.5 tonnes), commanded by Captain Joris Vis and carrying a cargo valued at 302,000 guilders, and the *Zuiderburg* (618 tons/628 tonnes), commanded by Captain Jan Likkert, with a cargo valued at 205,000 guilders—were sailing together between Batavia and Holland when they wrecked at night on the reefs of Tromelin Island, 280 miles (451 kilometers) northeast of the northern tip of Madagascar.

1709: The Dutch East Indiaman *Kromstrijn* (678 tons/689 tonnes), commanded by Captain Dirk van der Meer and sailing between Holland and Batavia with 470,000 guilders in treasure, was lost on the south side of Great Nicobar Islands. Natives ate all the survivors. Parts of her hull were spotted on the beach by a passing Dutch ship soon afterward. They sent a boat ashore to find any survivors, but were attacked and had to retreat.

1710: Two Dutch East Indiamen—the *Zandhorst* (520 tons/528 tonnes) with a cargo valued at 570,000 guilders, and the *Korssloot* (630 tons/640 tonnes), commanded by Captain Jakob Visser and with a cargo valued at 470,000 guilders—were sailing together from Sri Lanka to Holland when, due to faulty navigation, they wrecked on Agalega Island, east northeast of the northern tip of Madagascar. Over 200 survivors from both wrecks were rescued 17 months later by a passing Dutch ship that spotted their signal fires.

1710: The Dutch East Indiaman *Huiste Nieuwburg* (618 tons/628 tonnes), commanded by Captain Jan Kooster and sailing between

Holland and Sri Lanka, capsized and sank shortly after leaving the port of Galle. She was carrying 2.5 tons (2.540 tonnes) of gold ingots and 45 chests of silver specie.

1711: The Dutch East Indiaman *Sloten* (610 tons/620 tonnes), coming from Batavia with 220,000 guilders in cargo, wrecked in a storm on the east side of Mayotte Islands in the Comoro Island group but most of her people made it ashore and were rescued ten months later by an English ship.

1712: The British East Indiaman *Blenheim,* sailing from England for India with a cargo of 120 chests of silver and gold coins, was lost near Al Basrah, Iraq.

1716: The Dutch East Indiaman *Oude Zupe* (600 tons/610 tonnes), commanded by Captain Gerrit Verburg and sailing from Sri Lanka to Holland, with a cargo valued at 177,000 guilders, put into Mauritius for repairs after surviving a bad storm and wrecked just north of Port Louis.

1721: Dutch East Indiaman *Gamron* (848 tons/862 tonnes), commanded by Captain Daniel van Krimpen and sailing from Holland to Batavia "with a large amount of treasure," caught fire and was run aground between Matara and Dondra Head, Sri Lanka, where she exploded with a total loss of life and treasure.

1721: The Dutch East Indiaman *Bleijenburg* (1,100 tons/1,118 tonnes), commanded by Captain Jan Lindeboom and with a cargo valued at 450,000 guilders, wrecked on Aldabra Island, located 270 miles (434.5 kilometers) north of Madagascar. In 1511 a Portuguese explorer's vessel was also lost on this island, but little is known about the event.

1721: The Dutch East Indiaman *Raadhuis Van Middleburg* (890 tons/904 tonnes), commanded by Captain Jakob Delincourt and sailing between Batavia and Holland with a cargo valued at 320,000 guilders, wrecked on one of the Cargados Carajos Islands. Seventy-six survivors managed to reach Mauritius Island.

1721: The French pirate Olivier La Vasseur, also called "La Buse," attacked two Portuguese East Indiamen off the Seychelles Islands, capturing one. The other unidentified ship of sixty cannons "with a huge amount of treasure on board," as well as the archbishop of Goa and the Ccount of Ericeira, who was to be the new viceroy of India, sank near Praslin Island in the Seychelles Islands. Some of the people were able to reach shore.

1722: The Dutch East Indiaman *Rijnestein* (608 tons/618 tonnes), commanded by Captain Pieter Bitter and sailing between Batavia and Holland with a cargo valued at 242,314 guilders, was totally lost on Tromelin Island in a storm.

1722: The Dutch East Indiaman *Samson* (800 tons/813 tonnes), commanded by Captain Kornelis van Reet, with a cargo valued 369,000 guilders, wrecked in 26 degrees and 15 minutes south latitude southeast of Rodriquez Island, where no islands exist today. Sailing separately that year, another Dutch East Indiaman *Amstelveen* (1,150 tons/1,168.5 tonnes), commanded by Captain Theunis de Haan and with a cargo valued at 454,000 guilders, was lost on this same island. Survivors from both wrecks were picked up some months later.

1722: The Dutch East Indiaman *Huis Te Foreest* (600 tons/610 tonnes), commanded by Captain Pieter Rus, was lost on east side of Mauritius Island, coming from Batavia en route to Holland with a huge amount of Chinese porcelain and 23 chests of objects made of gold, silver, ivory and jade, plus two chests of precious stones.

1724: The Dutch East Indiaman *Fortuin* (800 tons/813 tonnes, 44 cannons), commanded by Captain Jan Kole, and sailing between Holland and Batavia with a stop at Cape Town, was carrying 475,000 guilders in gold and silver bullion and specie. She was lost on the first island south of Male Island in the Maldive Islands. Once ashore, some of the survivors found survivors from a French East Indiaman that had been lost near there six years before.

1725: The Dutch East Indiaman *Agatha* (600 tons/610 tonnes), commanded by Captain Wouter Brand and sailing from Batavia to Holland with a cargo valued at 188,000 guilders, allegedly wrecked on an island in 31 degrees south latitude. The nearest island to this position is Amsterdam Island , but its position is 39 degrees of south latitude and almost 500 miles (805 kilometers) further to the southeast. To make matters even more confusing, two other Dutch East Indiamen—the *Valkanisse* (1,150 tons/1,168.5 tonnes), commanded by Captain Abraham Bustijn and with a cargo valued at 193,000 guil-

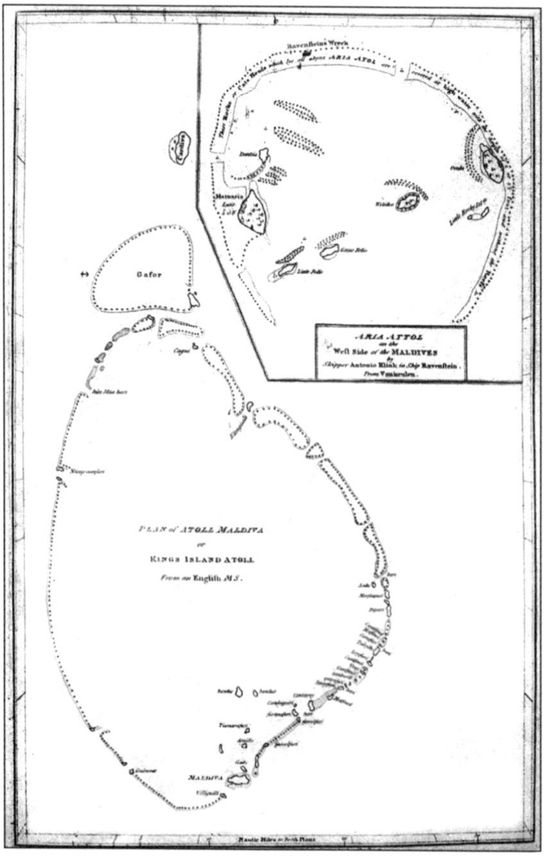

Chart showing the exact location of the wreck of the Dutch East Indiaman *Ravenstein*, lost in 1726 on Aria Atoll in the Maldives Islands.

ders, and the *Theodora* (600 tons/610 tonnes), commanded by Captain Pieter Belaart and with a cargo valued at 256,000 guilders—were lost the following year on this same island. In 1728 a Dutch ship that was searching for six other missing ships, which had sailed from Batavia for Holland in 1727 and disappeared, picked up survivors from all three wrecks.

1726: The Dutch East Indiaman *Ravenstein* (800 tons/813 tonnes), commanded by Captain Anthonie Klink and sailing between Holland and Batavia with 300,000 guilders in silver and gold specie, was lost on the northernmost of the Maldive Island chain.

1726: The Dutch East Indiaman *Risdan* (520 tons/528 tonnes), commanded by Captain Kornelis Dam and sailing with "a large amount of gold and silver" between Holland and Batavia, was blown off course by a storm and totally lost on Kadam Island in the Merqui Archipelago, Thailand.

1727: The Dutch East Indiaman *Velserbeek* (650 tons/660.5 tonnes, 42 cannons), commanded by Captain Kornelis Kerkhoven, was sailing between Padang, Sumatra, and Bengal, India, with 34 chests of gold bullion, when she was lost in a storm at night near Little Nicobar Island. A nearby ship saved some of the people aboard.

1731: The Dutch East Indiaman *Knapenburg* (900 tons/914.5 tonnes), commanded by Captain Pieter Tinnekins, was sailing between Holland and Japan with 670,000 guilders in treasure. After stopping at Sri Lanka, she headed for Japan, but was lost on Camorta in the Nicobar Island group.

1734: The Dutch East Indiaman *Groet* (850 tons/864 tonnes), commanded by Captain Dirk Mulder and sailing between Batavia and Holland with a cargo valued at 325,000 guilders, wrecked on the east side of Rodriquez Island and when survivors got ashore, they found other survivors from a French East Indiaman.

1735: The Dutch East Indiaman *Barbwestein* (1,100 tons/1,118 tonnes, 56 cannons), commanded by Captain Jan van Est and sailing between Holland and Japan with over 400,000 guilders in gold and silver, was lost in a nocturnal storm 3 leagues east of the port of Galle, Sri Lanka. There were very few survivors.

1738: The Dutch East Indiaman *Krooswijk* (600 tons/610 tonnes), sailing from Bengal to Holland with a cargo valued at 192,000 guilders, was totally lost on La Dique in the Seychelles Islands.

1739: Two Dutch East Indiamen, sailing together from Sri Lanka to Holland—the *Van Alsem* (650 tons/660.5 tonnes), with a cargo valued at 126,000 guilders, and the *Landskroon* (850 tons/864 tonnes, 48 cannons), with a cargo valued at 159,000 guilders—were lost in a storm on the southeast reefs of Diego Garcia, one of the Chago Islands.

1739: Four Dutch East Indiamen were sailing together from Batavia to Holland—the *Kerkzicht* (650 tons/660.5 tonnes), commanded by Captain Huyg Kuyper, with a cargo valued at 117,000 guilders; the *Klarabeek* (705 tons/716 tonnes), commanded by Captain Adriaan Cats, with a cargo valued at 258,000 guilders; the *Sint*

Laurens (850 tons/864 tonnes), commanded by Captain Pieter van Hoorn, with a cargo valued at 258,000 guilders; and the *Kasteel Van Tilburg* (850 tons/864 tonnes), commanded by Captain Jurriaan Wolbergen, with a cargo valued at 166,000 guilders. All four were wrecked on the east side of Praslin in the Seychelles Islands. Most of the people were saved and a small portion of the cargo as well.

1739: The Dutch East Indiaman *Veneburg* (650 tons/660.5 tonnes), sailing between Batavia and Holland with a cargo valued at 116,000 guilders, was lost on the southeast side of Madagascar. Most the people on board were rescued by another ship, but none of her treasure was saved.

1743: The Dutch East Indiaman *Ridderkerk* (500 tons/508 tonnes, 32 cannons), commanded by Captain Jan Licent and sailing between Holland and Batavia with "a substantial amount of gold and silver," was lost at Conati, Iran, on the Persian Gulf. The name must have changed over the years. I can't find it on any maps or charts.

1746: The Dutch East Indiaman *Nieuwland* (850 tons/864 tonnes), commanded by Captain Jan de São and sailing between Batavia and Holland with a cargo valued at 210,000 guilders, plus four chests of precious stones and two of pearls, was totally lost on Baixos da India reef in the Mozambique Channel.

1747: The British East Indiaman *Heathcote*, sailing from London to Iran with 6 tons (7 tonnes) of silver specie, was lost near Al Mukha in Straits of Bab al Mandab, Yemen.

1747: Three Dutch East Indiamen, sailing together from Batavia for Holland—the *Domberg* (850 tons/864 tonnes), commanded by Captain Leendert Bonekamp, with a cargo valued at 213,000 guilders; the *Vrijheid* (650 tons/660.5 tonnes), commanded by Captain Kornelis Mangelaar, with a cargo valued at 124,000 guilders; and the *Rooswijk* (1,150 tons/1,168.5 tonnes), commanded by Captain Paulus Lindenberg, with a cargo valued at 417,000 guilders—were lost on João da Nova Island where so many other ships have met their doom over the years.

1751: The Dutch East Indiaman *Hogersmilde* (850 tons/864 tonnes, 46 cannons), commanded by Captain Herman Laurier and sailing from Surat to Batavia with a cargo valued at 378,000 guilders, was lost in a bad storm near Lanta Island off the west coast of Thailand.

1753: The Dutch East Indiaman *Rotterdam* (850 tons/864 tonnes), was sailing between Holland and Batavia with 250,000 guilders in cash. Fleeing from a pirate attack, the captain ran her aground near the southern tip of Madagascar and set her on fire to keep the treasure from the pirates. All survivors, except for two African slaves, were massacred.

1756: The Dutch merchant ship *Zwemmer* (90 tons/91.5 tonnes), carrying seven chests of gold specie to Colombo, Sri Lanka, was totally lost trying to enter the port. Salvage attempts failed to recover any of the gold. Small ships such as this one were stationed for long periods in Batavia and carried on trade all over the India Ocean.

1756: The Dutch East Indiaman *Elswoud* (850 tons/864 tonnes, 54 cannon; on four previous voyages to the Orient, it had been named the *Eendracht*), commanded by Captain Dirk Stijve and sailing from Holland to Sri Lanka with 340,000 guilders in treasure, was wrecked between Galle and Matara, Sri Lanka.

1756: The Dutch East Indiaman *Persijnenburg* (880 tons/894 tonnes), commanded by Captain Pieter Arendse and sailing from Batavia for Holland with a cargo valued at 229,000 guilders, plus the value of the porcelain being used as ballast, was totally lost on one of the Cargados Carajos Islands. Ironically, the ship was taking nine prisoners from Batavia to Cape Town to be used as slaves there, and the only survivors were three of these men.

1760: The French pirate vessel *Le Dom Royal,* had captured a number of rich prizes and one slave ship, and all of the plunder and slaves were aboard this ship when it wrecked in a storm off Mahe, one of the Seychelles Islands. Some of the pirates and slaves survived. The pirates were rescued by another pirate vessel and the slaves were later picked up by a vessel sent from Mauritius Island.

1762: The Dutch East Indiaman *Marienbos* (1,150 tons/1,168.5 tonnes; on four previous voyages to the Orient, it was named *Lekkerland*), was commanded by Captain Nicolaas Piertersz and carried 467,000 guilders in treasure. She sailed from Texel and ran aground on the Southern Haaks and had to go back into port for repairs. Once again sailing for Batavia, she was attacked by pirates off Madagascar, but escaped, only to be totally lost in a heavy storm near Colombo, Sri Lanka. The people on board consisted of 183 seamen,

107 soldiers, and eleven passengers. Only two seamen survived the disaster.

1762: The Dutch East Indiaman *Sparenrijk* (850 tons/864 tonnes, 48 cannons), commanded by Captain Andries Lint and sailing between Holland and Batavia with 463,000 guilders in gold and silver, headed to Goa to attack Portuguese shipping, but was lost in a heavy storm near Galle, Sri Lanka.

1762: The Dutch East Indiaman *Rhoon* (1,150 tons/1,168.5 tonnes), commanded by Captain Jan Bernard Schaper and sailing between Holland and Sri Lanka with 435,000 guilders in gold and silver, first had a mutiny off Madagascar because the supply of beer on board became undrinkable. The mutiny was quelled and all 24 of the mutineers flung overboard. Then, in a heavy storm, the ship was totally lost near the mouth of the Kaku River located between Colombo and Galle, Sri Lanka.

1763: The Dutch East Indiaman *Amstelveen* (1,150 tons/1,168.5 tonnes, 56 cannons), commanded by Captain Nicolaas Piertersz and sailing between Holland and Batavia, with 430,000 guilders in gold and silver, first stopped in the Cape Verde Islands for some unknown reason and then again at the Cape of Good Hope to deliver and pick up mail. Blown off course in gales, she wrecked at Mocha on the south coast of Yemen.

1763: The Dutch East Indiaman *Visvliet* (880 tons/894 tonnes), with a cargo valued at 825,000 guilders (one of the richest in those days), was sailing between Bengal and Holland when she was totally lost on Male in Maldives Islands.

1763: The Dutch East Indiaman *Bronstee* (600 tons/610 tonnes), with a cargo valued at 314,000 guilders and sailing from Batavia to the Cape of Good Hope and then to Holland, was lost trying to round the southern tip of Mauritius Island. Most of the people were saved, but none of the cargo.

1764: The Dutch East Indiaman *Radermacher* (1,150 tons/1,168.5 tonnes), commanded by Captain Jan de la Noove and sailing from Batavia for Holland with a cargo valued at 278,000 guilders, excluding nine chests of precious stones and a large amount of gold church plate that another Dutch ship plundered off a Portuguese ship, was totally lost on the reefs of Baixos da India. Several ships that witnessed the disaster were unable to rescue any survivors because the seas were too high.

1764: The Dutch East Indiaman *Amelisweert* (1,150 tons/1,168.5 tonnes, 58 cannons), commanded by Captain George Christiaan Honsdorp and sailing between Holland and Surat, Sri Lanka, with "a large treasure" on board, headed for the Chago Islands where two sodomizers were to be marooned as punishment. As they approached the Chago Archipelago, a gale struck and the ship was lost on a reef. Only a few of the crew were saved.

1768: Dutch East Indiaman *Rotterdam* was wrecked on the southern part of Mauritius Island and about half of her cargo of 380,000 guilders in gold and silver, along with 130 men, were saved. She had sailed from Holland for Batavia in 1765, but was badly damaged by squalls and had to stay at Cape Town for almost a year while repairs were made. More than half of her crew deserted during this time and soldiers had to be forced to serve as sailors for the voyage to Batavia.

1768: An unidentified Dutch East Indiaman, returning from Batavia to Holland "with a very valuable cargo," was wrecked close to Colombo, Sri Lanka, and only some of her crew were saved.

1770: The Dutch East Indiaman *Vrouwe Maria Jakoba* (880 tons/894 tonnes), commanded by Captain Klaas Ariensz and sailing from Batavia with a cargo worth 212,000 guilders, was totally lost in a storm on Réunion Island.

1770: Two Dutch East Indiamen sailing together from Bengal to Holland—the *Enkhuizen* (880 tons/894 tonnes), commanded by Captain Johan Sigismund Hoeve, with cargo worth 617,000 guilders, and the *Vaillant* (880 tons/894 tonnes), commanded by Captain Thomas van Wagtendonk, with cargo valued at 607,000 guilders—were lost trying to round the southern tip of Madagascar. Only 63 people from both ships reached shore and were eventually rescued.

1771: The richest Dutch shipwreck ever recorded in this area was that of the Dutch East Indiaman *Verelst* (1,300 tons/1,321 tonnes). While sailing between Batavia and Holland, she was dashed to pieces on a barrier reef off the modern fishing village of Grand Gaube, Mauritius Island. In addition to a cargo valued in excess of 2 million guilders, she carried 740 pounds (336 kilograms) of diamonds in 17 iron-bound chests. The governor of Batavia described one of the diamonds as being "the size of a man's fist." If true, this makes it the largest diamond ever discovered. The *Verelst* had more diamonds than any other wreck in the world and may have contained the richest cargo of any shipwreck in the Indian Ocean. Several years later an unidentified French East Indiaman was lost on this same reef and only nine people survived .

1773: The Dutch East Indiaman *Duinenburg* (1,100 tons/1,118 tonnes), commanded by Captain Pieter Thomasz and sailing from Batavia to Holland with a cargo valued at 114,000 guilders, was lost on the reefs. of Baixos da India.

1773: The Dutch East Indiaman *Vrouwe Margaretha Maria* (880 tons/894 tonnes), commanded by Captain George Steendekker, "with a very valuable cargo," sailing first from Batavia to Bengal and then to Holland, was lost on Middle Andaman Island.

1774: The British East Indiaman *Huntington,* sailing back to England, was lost between Saddle and Anjouan Islands in the Comoro group with over 400,000 pieces of Chinese porcelain and three chests of jewels and precious stones. Portuguese from Mozambique sent a salvage vessel to find and salvage this wreck, and although they spotted wood from the wreck on a beach, they couldn't find the wreck. Most likely the wreck was in another area, and the timbers had drifted to the beach, driven by wind and current.

1775: The British East Indiaman *Middleton* (1,750 tons/1,778 tonnes), commanded by Captain Attenbrough and sailing from India to England with a cargo valued at £345,000 sterling, wrecked a league south of Muscat in a storm. The following day a very rich Moorish merchantman, carrying 600,000 gold rupee coins, was wrecked with a total loss of life in the same storm 2 leagues south of Muscat, Oman.

1776: The Dutch East Indiaman *Geinswens* (1,100 tons/1,118 tonnes), commanded by Captain Michiel Hendrik Kerke, sailed from Holland for Sri Lanka with 540,000 guilders in silver specie. She left Texel with 350 people, but onboard deaths and desertions at Table Bay, South Africa, reduced the number to 211 when the ship was lost off Galle Point, Sri Lanka. Only nine survived.

1779: The Dutch East Indiaman *Zeeploeg* (1,150 tons/1,168.5 tonnes), commanded by Captain Jan Stil and sailing from China to Cape Town, and then on to Holland with a cargo valued at 692,863 guilders, wrecked on the southernmost of the Maldives Islands and only a few of the people aboard were saved.

1781: The Dutch East Indiaman *Indiaan* (1,150 tons/1,168.5 tonnes), commanded by Captain Gerrit Opdal and sailing between Cape Town and Mauritius Island with 128 chests of gold and silver specie, was totally lost on the southwest side of Madagascar.

1783: The Dutch East Indiaman *Botland* (1,150 tons/1,168.5 tonnes), commanded by Captain Jakob Johnson and sailing between Holland and Calcutta with "a large amount of gold and silver," stopped at Colombo, Sri Lanka, because of bad weather. Shortly after anchoring lightning struck, blowing up the ship with a total loss of life and treasure.

1784: Two Dutch East Indiamen—the *Overduin* (1,150 tons/1,168.5 tonnes, 58 cannons), commanded by Captain Christiaan Meyer, with 123,000 guilders of cargo, and the *Bredenhof*, (850 tons/864 tonnes, 38 cannons), commanded by Captain Pieter van der Weert and sailing between Batavia and Cape Town with 100,000 guilders of cargo—were wrecked near Ambovombe, Madagascar.

1784: The Dutch East Indiaman *Harmonie* (1,150 tons/1,168.5 tonnes), commanded by Captain Kornelis Philippus Hoek and sailing from Batavia to Cape Town with 130,000 guilders of cargo, was totally lost on the reefs of Baixos da India.

1785: The Dutch East Indiaman *Zeeduin* (1,150 tons/1,168.5 tonnes, 64 cannons), commanded by Captain Jan Frederik Zegert and sailing between Batavia and Holland with a stop at Cape Town, with a cargo worth 550,000 guilders, was totally lost in a gale on the southeast coast of Madagascar.

1786: The Dutch East Indiaman *Vrede en Vrijheid* (760 tons/772 tonnes, 44 cannons), commanded by Captain Dirk Huizing and sailing between Batavia and Cape Town with 110,000 guilders of cargo, was lost on Diego Garcia Island in the Chago Archipelago. A ship sailing with her saw the disaster and sent word to Batavia that some people had gotten ashore on a small deserted island. When a rescue vessel arrived four months later, they found 34 people from the *Vrede en Vrijheid*, and 17 Portuguese from a Portuguese East Indiaman that had wrecked there six years before.

1789: The Dutch East Indiaman *Rotterdams Welvaren* (880 tons/894 tonnes), commanded by Captain Willem Jakob Kudde and sailing from Batavia to Cape Town and then on to Holland, with "a large valuable cargo," was wrecked on a small island off the north end of Madagascar. To offset desertions during the voyage, 26 Chinese slaves were aboard serving as seamen.

1790: The Dutch East Indiaman *Slot ter Hoge* (1,150 tons/1,168.5 tonnes, 58 cannons), commanded by Captain David Hartig and sailing between Batavia and Cape Town with a cargo valued at 236,000 guilders, excluding Chinese porcelain, was wrecked off the east side of Mauritius Island. The manifest does not list two chests of precious stones and one of pearls that private merchants were bringing back.

1792: The British East Indiaman *Winterton*, heading for India, was lost north of St. Augustin Bay on Madagascar. She was carrying over 8 tons (8.128 tonnes) of silver specie, a small amount of which was salvaged soon afterwards. This wreck has been the object of several unsuccessful treasure hunts by South African groups. In 2001 treasure hunters from Durban declared they had discovered the wreck, but there has been no word from them since.

1792: The Dutch East Indiaman *Gouverneur Falck* (1,150 tons/1,168.5 tonnes, sixty Ccannons), commanded by Captain Jan Anthonie Lubben and sailing with 229,000 guilders of cargo between Batavia and Cape Town, was totally lost on Aldabra Island, located north of Madagascar. A vessel sent to rescue survivors from the wreck also found 98 Frenchmen who had wrecked there three years before.

1792: The Dutch East Indiaman *Barbestein* (1,150 tons/1,168.5 tonnes), commanded by Captain Johan Koenraad Knot and sailing between Batavia and Cape Town and then on to Holland with a cargo valued at 249,000 guilders, was wrecked on the east side of Madagascar, near Manakara, and most of the crew and passengers were rescued.

1801: The French pirate ship *Parachi* (44 cannons) was attacked by two British warships and, in a sinking condition, was run aground on Europa Island in the Mozambique Channel. She was reported to have a "large amount of plunder" captured from several rich Muslim ships.

1802: The British East Indiaman *Cabalva* (1,200 tons/1,219 tonnes), commanded by Captain James Dalrymple and carrying a varied cargo, including 21 tons (21.337 tonnes) of Spanish silver specie, wrecked near the southern end of Cargados Carajos Reef. Two British East India Company ships sent to salvage the wreck recovered a small part of the cargo, but none of the silver coins. In 1987 sports divers from Mauritius discovered the wreck and picked up over 200 gold pocket watches and several hundred Spanish pieces of eight.

1806: The British East Indiaman *Blenheim,* jointly commanded by Sir Thomas Trouridge and Admiral Austin Bissel, coming from England to India with "a very large amount of gold and silver," wrecked on an uncharted reef now named Blenheim Reef, south of the Chago Islands in the center of the Indian Ocean. All 590 souls aboard perished. A ship that was sailing with her, the *Java* (32 guns), commanded by Captain George Pigot and carrying "a substantial amount of treasure," attempted to pick up survivors. She also wrecked and was lost on the same reef with a total loss of life. Two other ships in the convoy continued on to India.

1843: The British East Indiaman *Ceylon,* commanded by Captain Moresby, and sailing from London to Bombay and Calcutta with treasure valued at £337,000 sterling, was wrecked on Cheraman Reef in the Lakshadweep Islands chain located south of India. Most of the crew reached a nearby deserted island and the captain saved two chests containing 5,000 gold coins and two others with silver plate.

1860: The British merchantman *Malabar* was lost at Point de Galle, Sri Lanka, carrying £300,000 sterling in silver specie. Two attempts failed to recover the silver.

CHAPTER 24

INDIA'S RICHEST SHIPWRECKS

India's maritime history began long before that of most other nations. Seafarers from the highly developed Harappan culture along the Indus River in present-day Pakistan made long ocean voyages with hundred-oared ships as early as 2500 B.C. Two centuries later, Indians constructed the first tidal dock for cleaning the bottom of vessels and repairing them. The first known pilot book, the Rig Veda, was written around 2000 B.C. in India and gave sailing directions and pertinent information for the entire Indian Ocean and most of the Far East.

The influence of the sea on the subcontinent increased with time. In 325 B.C. Alexander the Great conquered the northern part of India. He built a harbor at Patala where the Indus River enters the Arabian Sea, and his army returned to Mesopotamia in ships built in this port. Even before Alexander, the Indians had a flourishing trade with Greece and Rome. Pliny, the Roman historian, tells of obtaining precious stones, perfumes, sandalwood, spices and indigo from India in exchange for gold.

Starting in the fifth century A.D. the Hindus of India conquered Burma, Malaya, Sumatra and Java where they established trading posts to take advantage of the region's riches. Records show that in the years from 844 to 884 they obtained an annual average of 8 tons (8.128 tonnes) of gold from Sumatra alone. Imagine how many of the gold-laden ships were lost over the centuries.

The French used Ponticherry as their main port in India.

In 1292 Marco Polo described Indian ships built of fir timbers and sheathed with wood (teak) that protected the bottom from marine borers. Another fourteenth-century account notes that Indian ships were capable of carrying as many as 750 people, plus crew, which gives us a fair idea of both their shipbuilding skills and the ability of their seaman to sail such large vessels. Centuries later the British and Portuguese built most of their East Indiamen in Indian shipyards.

In 1497, nine years after Bartolomeu Dias reported discovery of the Indian Ocean, the Portuguese king appointed Vasco da Gama to lead an expedition to find a sea route to India. Da Gama reached Calcutta on the Malabar Coast in May 1498. Hostile natives and Arab traders, who wanted no competition, prevented him from establishing a colony, but he saw how incredibly rich the place was and took a precious cargo of spices back to Lisbon. Less than six months later, Pedro Alvaro Cabral sailed from Lisbon for India with a fleet of 13 well-armed ships and a large amount of trading goods. Off the coast of West Africa he was blown so far to the west that he accidentally discovered Brazil. Off the Cape of Good Hope four ships sank in a gale. Ironically, Bartolomeu Dias, who had discovered the cape, naming it the "Cape of Storms," commanded one of the lost ships. This time the Portuguese were better armed and at Calcutta they destroyed many Muslim ships and seized their cargoes. Cabral established a trading base there, but after he

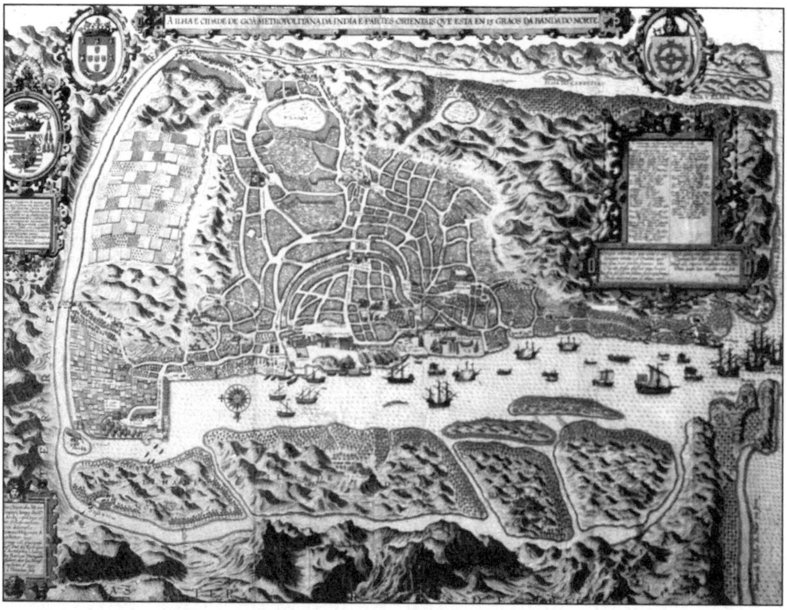

The rich spice port of Goa, India, where the majority of the Portuguese East Indiamen made a stop on their voyages to the Orient.

left for Portugal, Arab traders massacred all the Portuguese who had stayed. In July 1501 Cabral thrilled Lisbon with the imported Indian spices, porcelain, incense, aromatic woods, pearls, diamonds and rubies.

When news of the massacre reached Lisbon, the king dispatched da Gama to Calcutta with a large fleet. Afonso de Albuquerque, a brilliant military man, sailed with him to command the land forces. After bombarding the town from the sea, Albuquerque's men landed and vengefully slaughtered several thousand inhabitants. Sailing down the coast, the Portuguese set up trading stations at Goa and Cochin. The British took Calcutta in 1690 and it became one of their main trading bases in the Orient.

Goa, on the Malabar Coast, was the capital of Portuguese India from 1510 until it was annexed by India in 1962. The Dutch, Portugal's commercial and religious rivals, blockaded Goa throughout the seventeenth century. It became the main ship-building port for all the Portuguese East India ships. The capacity of a carrack was

Afonso de Albuquerque was the man most responsible for Portugal's conquest of India.

four times greater than that of the largest treasure fleet galleon. Constructed of Indian teak, which was far superior to the pine and oak used in Spanish ships, some of them lasted over fifty years. Portuguese ships returning from India and the Orient rarely used stones for ballast because the great quantities of Chinese porcelain they carried provided enough weight to stabilize the ships. Goa was the main Portuguese source not only for spices, but also for other valuable items such as gems and pearls. From 1600 to 1730, when diamonds were discovered in Brazil, more diamonds were shipped from this port than all of the rest of the world combined.

Cochin, also on the Malabar Coast, had been a center for spice trading for 1,500 years before the Portuguese established a factory there in 1502. The Malabar pepper traders demanded payment in gold, so the Portuguese established mints in Goa and Cochin to make gold coins called *São Tomes*. The British captured Cochin in 1635 and the Dutch took it in 1663.

Bombay had been ruled by various Hindu and Muslim dynasties since the beginning of the Christian era. The Portuguese took control in 1534, and in 1668 the British East India Company took over. In 1708 Bombay became the center of British authority in India. By the end of the seventeenth century, all of the European East Indian companies had trading factories all around the coast of India.

1510: The Portuguese merchantman *São Joáo* (600 tons/610 tonnes), commanded by Captain Fernão Peres de Andrate and coming from Lisbon to Goa with "a large amount of treasure," wrecked on the Bar of Goa, India, and all of her people, cannons and some of her treasure were saved.

1512: An unidentified Portuguese warship, which had been a part of the fleet of Afonso de Albuquerque, was sailing from Malacca, Malaysia, to Goa with "a great deal of plunder," which the Portuguese had captured in Malacca and other ports in the India Ocean, and wrecked several leagues south of Cochin with a total loss of life and treasure.

1514: The Portuguese East Indiaman *São Julian*, also called the *Santa Maria da Serra* (1,800 tons/1,829 tonnes), commanded by Captain Alonso Soares and sailing between Lisbon and Goa with 560,000 crusadoes in treasure, wrecked on a reef near Goa and about half of her treasure was saved.

1515: The Portuguese East Indiaman *Flor da Rosa* (660 tons/670.5 tonnes), commanded by Captain Diogo Fernandes da Beja and sailing from Malacca to Lisbon with a cargo valued at 870,000 crusadoes, was attempting to enter the port of Goa in a storm and wrecked, quickly breaking to pieces.

1520: An armada, commanded by Captain Juan Fernandez da Beja, entered the port of Diu on India's northwest coast and captured 14 Moorish ships. The Portuguese amassed over 2 million crusadoes in plunder, most of which was stored on board the flagship *Santa Maria da Serra*. During the night, a fire broke out and the ship blew up with a total loss of life and treasure

1522: The Portuguese East Indiaman *Nazaré* (900 tons/914.5 tonnes), commanded by Captain Pedro da Silva and sailing between Lisbon and Goa with 560,000 crusadoes in treasure on board, was anchored off Goa waiting to be unloaded when a sudden storm sprang up and the ship capsized and sank with very few survivors.

1528: The Portuguese East Indiaman *São Sebastao*, also named the *Biscainha*, commanded by Captain João de Freitas, was sailing from Goa to Lisbon with a cargo valued at over 500,000 crusadoes. She was a 14-year veteran on the Portugal–India route and was in poor condition. Her captain failed to convince the viceroy of India that it was too dangerous to sail the ship back to Lisbon, and an hour after leaving Goa, the ship burst apart and sank with a total loss of life and cargo.

1531: The Portuguese East Indiaman *Santa Maria da Esperança,* also called the *Boa Esperança,* commanded by Captain Manuel de Macedo and coming from Lisbon to India with 650,000 crusadoes in gold and silver, wrecked in a storm at Cape Comorin, on the southern extremity of India. Only some of her people were saved. Among them were two women who had disguised themselves as seamen.

1542: The Portuguese East Indiaman *Santiago* (700 tons/711 tonnes), commanded by Captain Martim Afonso de Sousa and sailing from Malacca to Lisbon with a cargo worth over 400,000 crusadoes, was wrecked near Baçaim (Bassein) about 43.5 miles (70 kilometers) from Bombay on the Arabian Sea. Only a few lives were lost.

1547: The Portuguese East Indiaman *São Boaventura,* commanded by Captain Pedro da Sousa, and carrying 960,000 crusadoes in treasure and the new viceroy of India with all of his personal possessions, arrived at Goa from Lisbon. Soon after the viceroy disembarked, a storm arose and the ship sank with all her treasure.

1549: The Portuguese East Indiaman *Flor do Mar* (1,650 tons/1,676.5 tonnes), commanded by Captain Diogo de Noronha, in the armada of Captain Afonso de Noronha and sailing from Lisbon to India with 673,000 crusadoes in gold and silver, was wrecked at the mouth of the Mazagao River, 38 leagues from Goa. Many survived and were later rescued.

1553: The Portuguese East Indiaman *Santa Cruz,* also known as the *Zambuco* (1,200 tons/1,216.5 tonnes), commanded by Captain Antonio Moniz Barreto and carrying 550,000 crusadoes in gold and silver bullion and specie, spent six months repairing damage from a storm off South Africa, then headed for India, but was wrecked near the mouth of the Ceitapor River, 30 leagues south of Goa. Seventy men were saved.

1554: The Portuguese East Indiaman *São Bonaventura* (1,600 tons/1,626 tonnes), commanded by the new viceroy of India, Dom Pedro de Mascarenhas and sailing from Lisbon to Goa with treasure valued at 780,000 crusadoes, sank on the bar of Goa soon after arriving and none of her treasure was saved. The viceroy reported to the king that he lost personal treasure valued at 65,000 crusadoes.

1563: The Portuguese East Indiaman *São Filipe* (1,750 tons/1,778 tonnes), commanded by Captain Vasco Lourenço de Barbuda, in the armada of Captain Jorge de Sousa, was half loaded with cargo valued at 870,000 crusadoes, when a waterspout destroyed the ship off Goa. There were no survivors.

1564: The Portuguese East Indiaman *Nosssa Senhora da Ajuda* (1,650 tons/1,676.5 tonnes), commanded by Captain João de Meneses and sailing from Lisbon to India with 389,000 crusadoes in treasure, wrecked on Baixo de Chilao near Cochin. Only a few people were saved.

1575: The Portuguese East Indiaman *Reliquias* (1,400 tons/1,422.5 tonnes), commanded by Captain Francisco Cavalleiro, ran aground on the bar at the port of Cochin as she was leaving with a cargo of "great value." A storm came up as the cargo was being unloaded and the ship went to pieces. Most of her cargo was lost.

1593: The Portuguese East Indiaman *São Cristoval* (1,250 tons/1,270 tonnes, 36 cannons), commanded by Captain Antonio Teixeira de Macedo and arriving from Lisbon with 278,000 crusadoes, was wrecked and quickly broke up on the bar of Goa. Only a few people were saved.

1596: The Portuguese East Indiaman *Nossa Senhora de Belen*, also known as the *Madre de Deus de Guadelupe* (1,600 tons/1,626 tonnes, 34 cannons), commanded by Captain Luis da Gama and preparing to sail for Lisbon with a "very valuable amount of cargo," caught fire in Cochin and was totally consumed.

1598: Local fishermen call a wreck near Cochin "the Portuguese bank" because their nets have been picking up gold and silver coins on this site for years. It is known that numerous Portuguese ships were lost here throughout the Colonial Period, but the only one with treasure was the *Nossa Senhora de Guadalupe*, lost in 1598, which when she burned while at anchor with over 1 million crusadoes in treasure aboard. She had been sailing between Goa and Lisbon and stopped off Cochin to deliver mail.

1600: The Portuguese East Indiaman *São Joáo* (900 tons/914.5 tonnes), commanded by Captain Gonçalo Roiz Caldeira and sailing between Hormuz and Goa with "a very valuable cargo," was attacked by the Dutch. The ship caught fire and sank 2 leagues seaward of Goa with a total loss of life and cargo.

1606: The Portuguese East Indiaman *São Andres* (1,650 tons 1,676.5 tonnes, 38 cannons), commanded by Captain Luis de Brito de Melo, was arriving from Lisbon with 548,000 crusadoes of treasure when she was attacked by four Dutch ships and sunk by cannon fire on the Bar of Goa.

1608: The Portuguese East Indiaman *Santo André* (2,300 tons/2,337 tonnes), sailing between Lisbon and Goa with 1.1 million crusadoes aboard, sank on the Bar of Goa while entering port. Many other ships have been lost on this bar. Several expeditions to find wrecks here failed, mainly because they lie in very deep silt and mud and there is no underwater visibility.

1608: The Portuguese East Indiaman *Nossa Senhora do Loreto,* commanded by Captain Jeronimo Teles and sailing between Lisbon and Goa with treasure valued at 430,000 crusadoes, was attacked by a Dutch ship as it was entering the port of Goa. She was totally destroyed by fire and most aboard died.

1610: The Portuguese East Indiaman *Santo Antonio* (1,900 tons/1,930.5 tonnes), commanded by Captain Diogo de Sousa de Menezes and returning from China to Goa and then Lisbon, was lost near Cape Cormorim in Kerala state. Her cargo was described as "being one of the richest ever seen."

1615: The Portuguese East Indiaman *Nossa Senhora da Nazaré* (1,200 tons/1,219 tonnes), commanded by Captain Luis Massene, and two unidentified ships were sailing between Lisbon and Goa. The *Nazaré* carried 960,000 crusadoes in gold and silver bullion and specie. A large English warship attacked the Portuguese ships as they entered the port of Goa, and all three were sunk.

1615: The viceroy of India sent a squadron of warships under the command of Captain Henrique de Sousa to attack the port of Calcutta. The Portuguese sank 12 Moorish ships in the port, including a huge ship owned by the Moorish emperor of India, which had just taken on "a colossal treasure" and was preparing to sail to Mecca and other ports in the Red Sea.

1615: The Dutch East Indiaman *Nassau* (300 tons/305 tonnes), commanded by Captain Jan Piertersz and sailing between Holland and the Moluccas with 230,000 guilders in gold and silver specie, tried to enter the Andragiri River in a storm and was totally lost. The river is on the Coromandel Coast in southeastern India, but its name may have changed over the years.

1616: The Dutch East Indiaman *Lleine Aeolus* (240 tons/244 tonnes), commanded by Captain Pieter Kornelisz and sailing between Holland and the Moluccas with an unknown amount of gold and silver specie, was totally lost at the mouth of the Tapti River on the Coromandel Coast of India.

1616: The Portuguese East Indiaman *Nossa Senhora da Boa Nova* (2,000 tons/2,032 tonnes, 58 cannons), sailing from Goa for Lisbon with a cargo of unknown value, was wrecked leaving port on the bar of Goa. All of her people and some of her cargo were saved.

1617: The Dutch East Indiaman *Middleburg* (800 tons/813 tonnes), commanded by Captain Maarten Reiniersz and sailing between Holland and Batavia with a large consignment of gold and silver bullion and specie, was totally lost near the port of Surat in the Gulf of Cambay in northwestern India. Surat, north of Bombay (now Mumbai), was India's chief port during the sixteenth, seventeenth, and eighteenth centuries.

1625: The Portuguese East Indiaman *Misericordia,* carrying 475,000 crusadoes in gold and silver specie, was lost near Bombay. During the same storm another Portuguese East Indiaman, the *Sancto Antonio,* was also lost at the same time and nearby. She was also carrying gold and silver specie of unknown value.

1628: The Dutch East Indiaman *Leeuwin* (400 tons/406.5 tonnes and 34 cannons), commanded by Captain Jan Willemsz and sailing between Holland and Pulicat, a port the Dutch used about 12 miles (20 kilometers) north of Madras, carrying 340,000 guilders in gold and silver specie and bullion, was wrecked near the entrance of the port of Cochin.

1638: The Dutch East Indiaman *Gravenhage* (300 tons/305 tonnes), sailing between Holland and Batavia with "a large amount of silver bullion and specie" aboard, made a stop at Goa to attack Portuguese ships there and was totally destroyed in a battle. All Dutch ships had orders to attack any enemy shipping. This took precedence over trading. On the other hand, the Portuguese were under strict orders never to fight enemy ships unless they were attacked.

1638: The Dutch East Indiaman *Vlissingen* (350 tons/356 tonnes), commanded by Captain Huibrecht Huibrechtsz and sailing between Holland and Batavia with 270,000 guilders in treasure, was attacking Portuguese shipping off Goa. The crew set fire to their ship when they realized they would be captured.

1638: The British East Indiaman *Comfort,* commanded by Captain Clarke, carried "forty-seven chests of Spanish coinage." Off Calcutta she was attacked and boarded by swarms of pirates from several Moorish vessels. They shut the Comfort's crew below decks. The English lit a long fuse and crawled out the lower gunports. The ship exploded, reportedly killing as many as 1,400 pirates. Another pirate vessel picked up the English survivors and later ransomed them back to the British.

1643: The Dutch East Indiaman *Amboina,* sailing between Batavia and Surat with 245 chests of gold and silver, wrecked on the Coromandel Coast about 100 miles (161 kilometers) north of Madras and only some of her people were saved. Two other unidentified Dutch ships sank in the same area during the storm that wrecked the Amboina.

1644: The Dutch East Indiaman *Terschelling* (800 tons/813 tonnes), sailing from Holland to Pulicat, India, to purchase spices, had 120,000 guilders in silver specie aboard. She encountered several Portuguese ships off Negapatnam, where the Portuguese established a base in 1599. In the battle she was blown up and sank with a total loss of life and treasure. Negapatnam is on the Coromandel Coast 160 miles (257.5 kilometers) south of Madras.

1653: The Dutch East Indiaman *Overschie* (360 tons/366 tonnes), sailing between Holland and Batavia with 267,000 guilders in gold and silver, wrecked on the Coromandel Coast near Pondicherry. The crew and one chest of gold coins were saved.

1653: The Dutch East Indiaman *Wapen Van Batavia* (340 tons/345.5 tonnes), sailing between Holland and Batavia with 340,000 guilders in treasure, was attacked by Malabar pirates and tried to seek safety in the nearby Cochin. However, after realizing that they couldn't make port before being captured, the Dutch blew up their ship.

1653: The British East Indiaman *Bonito,* carrying £220,000 sterling in treasure, was caught in a typhoon in the port of Madras and lost. The same typhoon sank an unidentified Dutch East Indiaman, carrying 200,000 Indian gold rupee coins, off Cuddalotre on the Coromandel Coast.

1654: The Dutch East Indiaman *Reiger* (560 tons/569 tonnes, 34 cannons), commanded by Captain Jan Hoogzaad and sailing between Holland and Batavia, made a stop at Pulicat to drop off mail. While in the port, she caught on fire and blew up. All of her crew perished and 290,000 guilders in treasure were lost.

1654: Portuguese East Indiaman *Santa Helena* (1,650 tons/1,676.5 tonnes, 38 cannons), commanded by Captain Manuel de Piana da Cunha and sailing from Lisbon to India with 329,000 crusadoes in gold and silver specie, was wrecked on the Bar of Goa. Only some of her people were saved.

1658: The Portuguese East Indiaman *São Tomé* (1,250 tons/1,270 tonnes), was commanded by Captain Francisco Gomes da Silva. While leaving Goa for Lisbon with a cargo valued at 754,000 crusadoes, she was attacked by the Dutch and burned and sunk by her crew when it was evident she would be captured.

1658: The Portuguese East Indiaman *Santa Maria de Anzic* (1,600 tons/1,626 tonnes, 44 cannons), commanded by Captain João Rodriquez Viegas was sailing from Goa to Lisbon "with a very valuable cargo." The armada with this ship tried to leave the port three times, but each time had to return because a squadron of Dutch ships waited off shore to intercept them. On the fourth attempt, the armada gave battle to the Dutch, and this ship was set on fire and sunk to evade capture by the Dutch.

1660: The Portuguese East Indiaman *Bom Jesus de São Domingo* (1,900 tons/1,930.5 tonnes, 46 cannons), commanded by Captain Pantaleao, was sailing from Goa to Lisbon with a cargo valued at 439,000 crusadoes. Soon after crossing the bar of Goa, she was attacked by a Dutch ship. Her crew burned and sank her to keep her from capture.

1661: The Dutch East Indiaman *Terschelling* (520 tons/528 tonnes), was lost in the Bay of Bengal in a gale. She was on her way to Batavia with over 300,000 guilders in treasure. Only 34 survivors were eventually rescued and taken to Batavia.

1666: The Dutch East Indiaman *Hasselt* (365 tons/371 tonnes), commanded by Captain Jokob Hendriksz Moker and sailing between Batavia and Arakan with "a large amount of gold and silver," was wrecked while trying to enter Arakan.

1668: The Dutch East Indiaman *Ooievaar* (627 tons/637 tonnes), commanded by Captain Adriaan Huibertsz and carrying 186 chests of silver specie from Holland to Batavia, was lost in the Ganges delta and only her crew was saved.

1670: The Dutch East Indiaman *Polanen* (670 tons/681 tonnes) was sailing between Holland and Sri Lanka with 345,000 guilders in treasure, and had to put into the port of Tuticorin, India, for repairs after a storm. While entering the port, she wrecked and quickly went to pieces in high seas. This port had been in the hands of the Portuguese since 1540 until it was taken by the Dutch in 1658 and held by them until the British acquired it in 1825.

1670: The Dutch East Indiaman *Witte Leeuw* (360 tons/366 tonnes), carrying 367,000 guilders in treasure, was lost sailing between Holland and Batavia near Palmyras Point in the Bay of Bengal. All of her crew was saved, but they recovered only a small portion of the treasure.

1671: The Dutch East Indiaman *Buienskerke* (510 tons/518 tonnes), commanded by Captain Adriaan Schenkel, who died during the voyage, sailed from Holland for Batavia with 400,000 guilders in treasure. She was lost on the Isle of Galle on the Bengal Coast. Prior to wrecking, a mutiny broke out on the ship. It was quelled and the mutineers were thrown into the sea. Punishment on Dutch ships was very severe.

1672: The Dutch East Indiaman *Loosduiden* (340 tons/345.5 tonnes), sailing from Holland to Batavia with 167,000 guilders in silver specie, was totally lost near the Ganges Delta.

1673: The Dutch East Indiaman *Westwoud* (212 tons/215.5 tonnes), sailing between Holland and Batavia with 212 chests of silver bullion and specie, was totally lost near Tekkali in the Bengal Gulf.

1674: The Dutch East Indiaman *Osdorp* (448 tons/455 tonnes), commanded by Captain Pieter Dirksz Haan and sailing between Holland and Batavia with a cargo valued at 487,000 guilders, was wrecked at Baleswar near the Mouth of the Ganges River.

1674: The Dutch East Indiaman *Brak,* sailing between Holland and Batavia, with 220 chests of silver specie and bullion, was blown far off course in a gale and wrecked at the mouth of the Hooghly River in the Ganges Delta. A few survivors eventually reached Batavia.

1678: The Dutch East Indiaman *Kleine David* (100 tons/101.5 tonnes), commanded by Captain Kornelis Fransz and sailing from Holland to Pulicat to purchase spices, with 160,000 guilders in gold and silver specie on board, caught fire on the Coromandel Coast and was lost close to Pulicat, where the Dutch had a fort since 1610, their main base on the east coast of India.

1682: The Dutch East Indiaman *Wapen Van Veere* (627 tons/637 tonnes), commanded by Captain Jan Bartelsz and sailing from Batavia to Surat with 435,000 guilders in treasure, wrecked entering the port of Tuticorin to escape pursuing pirate vessels.

1688: The Dutch East Indiaman *Naaldwijk* (332 tons/337 tonnes, 28 cannons), commanded by Captain Jan Zeeman, was sailing between Holland and China via Calcutta with 16 chests of gold bullion and specie, plus a large amount of lead bars. While trying to enter the port of Calcutta in bad weather, she wrecked near Sundarban Beach and only two of the crew survived.

1693: The Dutch East Indiaman *Borsenburg* (320 tons/325 tonnes), commanded by Captain Joost van der Tocht and carrying 640,000 guilders in treasure, sailed from Holland to Batavia and then on to Surat, in the Gulf of Cambay, about 150 miles (241 kilometers) north of Bombay. It wrecked there and the crew saved about half of its treasure.

1693: A Muslim armada of eight ships, six with forty to sixty cannons, and two with twenty to 25 cannons, blockaded

Goa. A Lisbon-bound Portuguese East Indiaman *Nossa Senhora da Conceição,* also called the *Sol Dourado,* was carrying a cargo worth 490,000 crusadoes. She attempted to get through the blockade, but in a fierce battle, she was blown up by the enemy and sank near the bar of Goa.

1700: The Dutch East Indiaman *Soldaat* (288 tons/293 tonnes), commanded by Captain Conelis Jansz, was sailing between Holland and Surat with 245,000 guilders in treasure to pick up survivors from a ship lost in that area, before heading for Batavia. When attempting to enter Surat at night, the ship was wrecked. All the people aboard were saved, as well as about 50,000 guilders of treasure.

1704: A fleet of Dutch and Muslim ships captured several rich Portuguese East Indiamen off Surat and then attacked the city. Because of faulty navigation, two of the Muslim warships, one of seventy cannons and the other of fifty cannons, were wrecked, carrying "large amounts of treasure."

1712: The Dutch East Indiaman *Zierikzee* (400 tons/406.5 tonnes), commanded by Captain Anthonis Jansz and sailing between Holland and Batavia with 289,000 guilders in gold and silver bullion and specie, made the customary stop at Goa to attack Portuguese shipping. During a battle, she was wrecked and blown up by her crew to prevent the cargo from falling into the hands of the Portuguese, who were infuriated by this action and beheaded all of the Dutch survivors.

1718: The Dutch East Indiaman *Brug* (600 tons/610 tonnes, 34 cannons), commanded by Captain Pieter de Boer and sailing from Batavia to Calcutta and other ports with 379,000 guilders in treasure on board, was totally lost in a storm and quickly went to pieces at the mouth of the Ganges River. Only six men were saved.

1724: The Danish East Indiaman *St. Charles,* sailing between Copenhagen and India with 400,000 florins in gold and silver, was lost in a storm at the mouth of the Ganges River. Most of the people and some of the treasure was saved.

1729: The Dutch East Indiaman *Samaritaan* (600 tons/610 tonnes, 44 cannons), commanded by Captain Willem Sempel and sailing from Holland for Batavia with 300,000 guilders in gold and silver, was blown off course by storms and wrecked on one of the Lakshadweep

Islands off the Malabar Coast. Six survivors got ashore with a chest of gold specie and were rescued several months later, but two died going back to Batavia.

1730: The Dutch East Indiaman *Johanna* (550 tons/559 tonnes), commanded by Captain Hendrik van Beek and sailing with a "large amount of treasure" between Holland and Batavia with a stop at Calcutta, was totally lost on the Ganges River.

1737: Three British East Indiamen—the *Newcastle*, commanded by Captain John Crabb; the *Decker*, commanded by Captain Williamson; and the *Devonshire*, commanded by Captain Prince—were wrecked during a monsoon on the Rogue River in the Bay of Bengal. Another unidentified British East Indiaman sank off the mouth of this river.

1745: The Dutch East Indiaman *Ruyven* (650 tons/660.5 tonnes, 48 cannons), commanded by Captain Christiaan de Jong, sailed from Goeree-Overflakkee Island in the Netherlands for Batavia with 16 chests of precious stones and two chests of pearls. She was forced to put into the Ganges River because of bad weather and there she was totally lost.

1748: The Dutch East Indiaman *Nieuw Walcheren* (850 tons/864 tonnes, 56 cannons), commanded by Captain Jakob Hogermolen, first stopped at Table Bay (Cape Town) to drop mail and obtain fresh water and victuals, and then continued on to Batavia with 289,000 guilders in gold and silver, but she was diverted to Surat by a small vessel sent out from Batavia to pick up survivors from a Dutch wreck. Lightning struck the ship as the anchor was being pulled up for departure from Surat, and she blew up with a total loss of life and treasure.

1751: The Dutch East Indiaman *Hogersmilde* (850 tons/864 tonnes, 56 cannons), commanded by Captain Herman Laurier and sailing between Surat and Batavia with "a great fortune" in precious stones and pearls, was lost on one of the Lakshadweep Islands off the southwest coast of India.

1753: The Dutch East Indiaman *Voorburg* (880 tons/894 tonnes, 52 cannons), commanded by Captain Klaas van den Hoed and sailing between Holland and Batavia with 430,000 guilders in silver, was attacked three times by pirates. She fought them off each time and then headed for Calcutta for repairs. Off Paradip in the Bay of Bengal, she was lost in a storm.

1753: The Dutch East Indiaman *Bredenhof* (850 tons/864 tonnes), commanded by Captain Jan Neilson and sailing from Holland to Sri Lanka with 315,000 guilders in gold and silver, wrecked in a storm on a small island, part of the group known as Adam's Bridge between India and Sri Lanka with the Gulf of Mannar on the south side and the Palk Strait on the north side. Most of her people, but none of the treasure, was saved.

1754: The Dutch East Indiaman *Wimmenum* (1,150 tons/1,168.5 tonnes), commanded by Captain Johan Louis Philippi and sailing between Holland and Japan, with 300,000 guilders in cash, was attacked by pirates off the Malabar Coast, just south of Cochin and blew up with a total loss of life and treasure.

1756: The Dutch East Indiaman *Bloemendaal* (1,150 tons/1,168.5 tonnes, 62 cannons), commanded by Captain Hilde Hendricksz Hoek and sailing between Holland and Batavia with 215,629 in cash, plus 26 chests of gold and silver bullion, was forced to seek safety at Surat and sank trying to enter the port.

1761: During a typhoon that struck the east coast of India, the French East Indiaman *Duc d'Aquitaine* and two British East Indiamen, the *Duke* and *Sunderland*, with "huge treasures on board," were lost in the port of Pondicherry on India's southeastern coast. Several miles south of this port three other British East Indiamen—the *Protector, Newcastle* and *Queenborough*—were wrecked. The value in treasure and cargo on the five English ships exceeded £1.6 million pounds sterling.

1762: The Dutch East Indiaman *Getrouwigheid* (850 tons/864 tonnes, 46 cannons), commanded by Captain August Heyenburg and with 490.000 guilders in treasure, was sailing from Holland to Batavia. En route she headed for Goa to attack Portuguese shipping in the open roadstead, but was lost in a bad storm a league off the port of Goa. The Portuguese captured some of her crew.

1766: The British East Indiaman *Falmouth* (980 tons/996 tonnes), sailing between England and Calcutta with £178,000 sterling in Spanish silver specie, wrecked during a monsoon near the mouth of the Ganges River. All the silver was lost, but 160 of the 360 people on board survived. Five years later, the British East Indiaman *Duke of Albany*, carrying £340,000 sterling in treasure from England to

Calcutta, is thought to have sunk in the same spot after striking the *Falmouth*'s wreckage.

1768: The Dutch East Indiaman *Vrouwe Petronella* (880 tons/894 tonnes, 58 cannons), commanded by Captain Steven Booms and sailing between Holland and Batavia with "a large amount of treasure on board," was attacked and severely damaged by Muslim pirates. Heading to Calcutta for repairs, she wrecked at night near the mouth of the Ganges River. Her navigator survived and was later convicted of faulty navigation and hanged.

1777: The British East Indiaman Marquis of *Rockingham* (758 tons/770 tonnes), carrying "a large amount of treasure," struck a rock near the coast 10 leagues south of Madras (now known as Chennai) and sank in deep water with a total loss of life.

1780: The Dutch East Indiaman *Jonge Hellingman* (850 tons/864 tonnes), commanded by Captain Lukas Aams and sailing between Holland and Batavia with a stop in Calcutta, carried 383,000 guilders in treasure. She was lost on sand banks off Bengal. All of her people were saved, as well as some of her treasure.

1786: The Dutch East Indiaman *Patriot* (1,150 tons/1,168.5 tonnes), commanded by Captain Adriaan Frederik van de Graaf and sailing between Holland and Japan with over 400,000 guilders of treasure on board, wrecked off Madura in southern India. A ship sailing with them rescued 22 people.

1802: The British East Indiaman *Isabella*, sailing from England to Bombay with £423,000 sterling in gold and silver specie, was wrecked during a storm while trying to enter Bombay, but most of the people aboard were rescued.

1811: The British East Indiaman *Marquis of Wellesley* (990 tons/1,006 tonnes), sailing from China to England with a cargo valued at over £1 million sterling, sank 2 leagues off Bombay while trying to enter this port during a monsoon.

Some of the hundreds of Roman and Greek amphorae recovered by Marx in the 1970s off the coast of Syria, Lebanon, and Israel.

(Above) These British gold coins were recovered from a wreck near Bombay.

(Right) Four Portuguese gold coins found on a Dutch warship off Banda Island, most likely plunder from a Portuguese ship.

(Below) European East Indiamen obtained vast amounts of diamonds and other precious stones in many Indian ports.

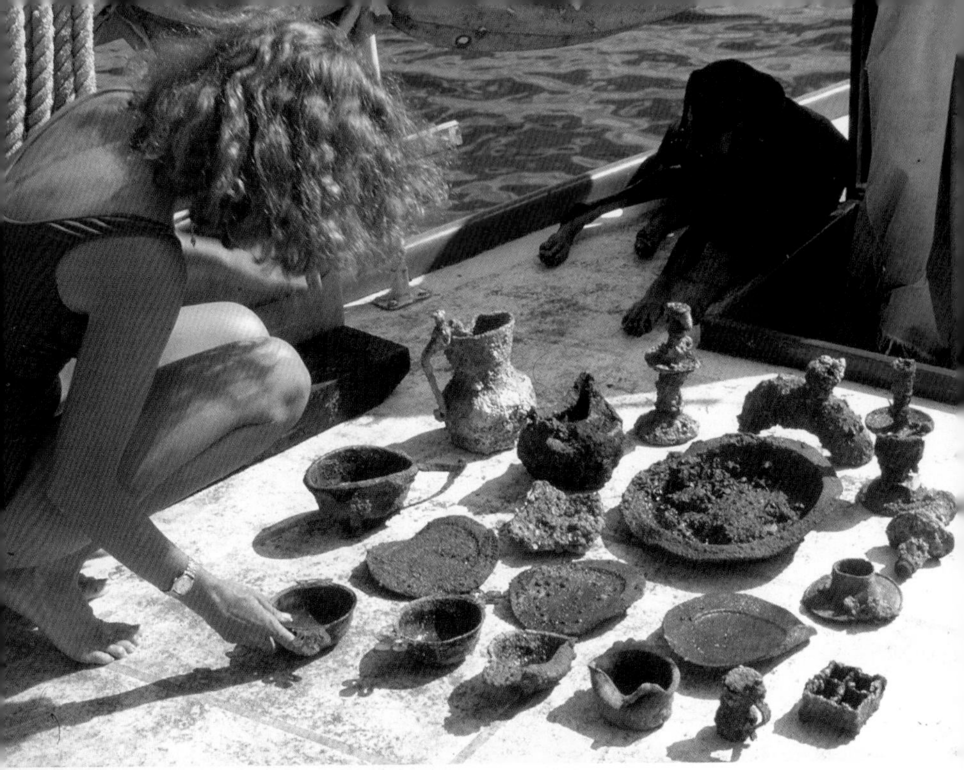

(Above) Jenifer Marx examines pewter and silverware recovered from the Dutch warship *Utrecht*, lost in 1648 off Brazil.

(Left) Most Dutch cannons and other ship's fittings have the VOC marking on them, which indicates they were property of the Dutch East India Company.

(Below) Gold objects made by Indonesian artisans in the sixteenth century and found on an Achenese pirate vessel off Banda Achen on Sumatra Island.

Chapter 25

Indonesia's Richest Shipwrecks

In 1492 when Spain expelled all Jews, many moved to Amsterdam and the Dutch economy quickened. The infusion of Jewish merchants and capital soon made Holland a thriving mercantile nation. Prior to Spain's takeover of Portugal in 1580, the Dutch had been content to act as middlemen in Far East commerce. However, when Spain closed this door to them, they had to go directly to the source for Oriental luxuries that had become necessities in prospering sixteenth-century Europe. At first, they sought a northeast passage around Russia. When this was unsuccessful, they sought to establish a route via the Straits of Magellan, but found this far too hazardous and expensive. Between 1598 and 1601, explorer Oliver van der Noort became the first Dutchman to circumnavigate the globe. Subsequently, the Dutch followed in the wake of the Portuguese via the Cape of Good Hope.

A syndicate of Amsterdam businessmen backed the first Dutch fleet to the Orient. Three of the four ships sent out were lost on the homeward voyage, and the enterprise was a financial disaster. However, in July 1599 the second fleet of Dutch East Indiamen returned to Holland from the Orient with an enormous amount of spices and other products. An anonymous contemporary wrote: "For as long as Holland has been Holland, there have never arrived ships as richly laden as these." For days church bells all over Amsterdam rang in jubilation.

Seventeenth-century Batavia, the principal base in the Orient for the Dutch East Indiamen.

So many Dutch companies became involved in the lucrative commerce that the governing States-General brought them together, forming the Dutch East India Company, which received its charter in 1602. The Dutch made the Javanese city of Batavia (Jakarta) in Indonesia, their main base in the Far East and the capital of the Dutch East Indies. By the mid-seventeenth century, over 200 large ships were annually engaged in the Dutch East Indies trade. In 1669, at the peak of its power, the Dutch company had forty warships, 150 merchant ships and 10,000 soldiers based in Batavia alone.

During the course of the sixty-year war between Spain and Holland (1605–1665), the company stripped Portugal (which was united with Spain from 1580 to 1640) of all its East Indian possessions. The Dutch took Amboina (Ambon) in 1605 and other islands in the Moluccas, India, Ceylon and Formosa. In various Malaysian ports the Dutch traded with the Chinese for silks, porcelains and objects made of gold, silver, jade and ivory, some of which they re-exported to Japan and traded for lacquer work, silver and copper. From Ceylon they obtained rubies and garnets, cinnamon and manufactured objects made of precious metals and ivory. India provided them with enormous amounts of gemstones, ivory, cotton cloth and rice. Business was very profitable. Between 1602 and 1696, annual company dividends were never less than 12 percent and sometimes as high as 63 percent.

The roadstead of seventeenth-century Batavia with Dutch East Indiamen at anchor.

1509: A squadron of Portuguese warships, commanded by Admiral Diogo Lopes de Sequeira, was sent from India to search for enemy shipping in the Straits of Malacca. They approached two Achenese merchant ships entering the port of Pedir and two others at the port of Pacem on the northwest coast of Sumatra. The Achenese set their ships on fire to keep the Portuguese from sacking them. Captive Achenese said all four ships carried large amounts of gold, Chinese porcelain, and "other valuable goods."

1511: Despite banner headlines that periodically proclaim a new shipwreck discovery as that of "the richest ever lost," the richest ship ever lost anywhere was the Portuguese warship *Flor do Mar*. It was the flagship of a fleet commanded by Admiral Afonso de Albuquerque, who spent ten years sacking 28 lands bordering the Indian Ocean. The *Flor* was loaded with accumulated plunder when it was lost in 1511 on a reef in the Straits of Malacca off the northeast coast of Sumatra. Among the riches that sank with her were 80 tons (81.28 tonnes) of gold figurines of Buddha, animals, birds and other objects, and more than 200 chests of

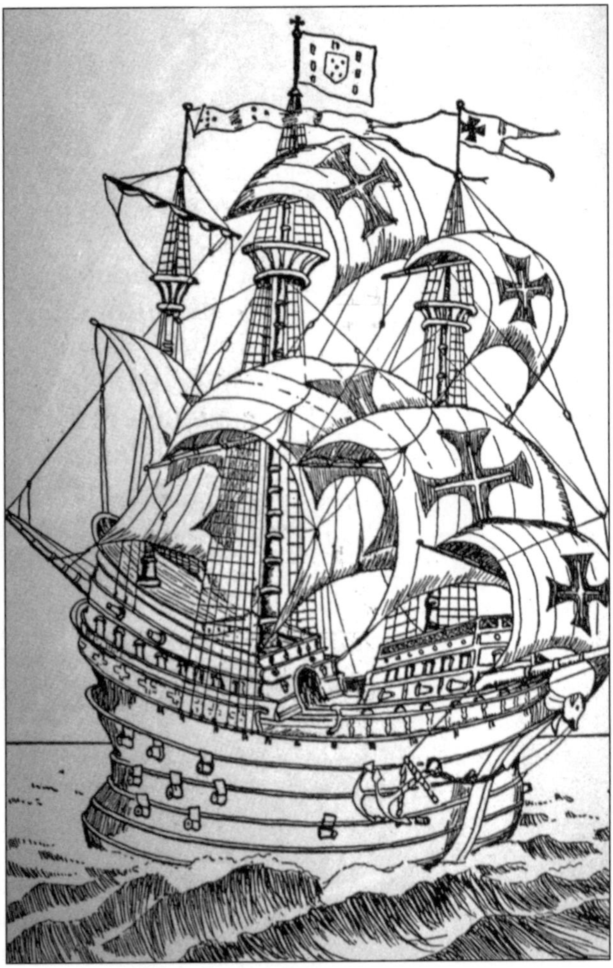

Drawing of the *Flor do Mar*, the flagship of Afonso de Albuquerque, which was lost on a reef off Sumatra Island in 1511, while carrying the greatest treasure ever lost at sea.

precious stones and pearls. While working for the Indonesian government, I discovered this wreck in 1990 and brought up over $1 million worth of fantastic items of treasure and other artifacts. Unfortunately, the project was terminated after a week because of protests from many nations that claimed ownership of the treasure on the wreck. A decision on ownership of the wreck and her treasures is pending in the International Court of Justice in The Hague.

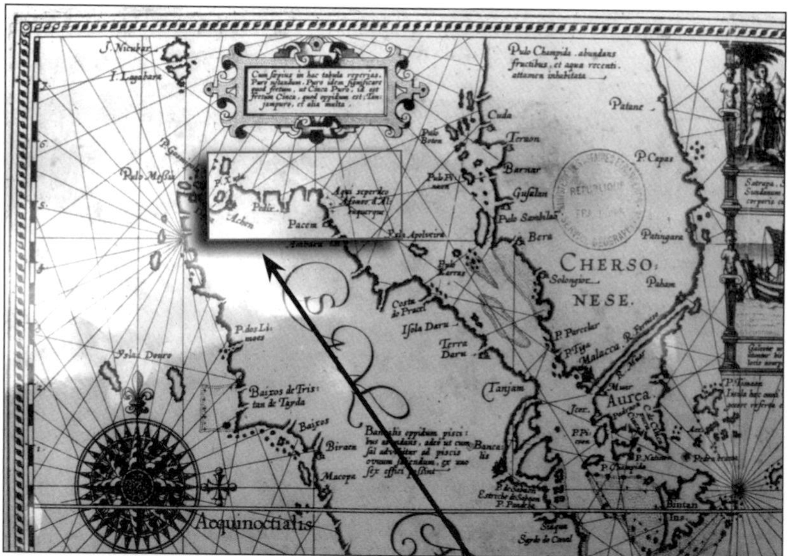

This chart, discovered by author Marx in 1960, helped him pinpoint the location of the *Flor do Mar*. It states *(see blowup at right):* "Aqui seperdeo Afonso d'Albuquerque", which means "Here was lost Afonso d'Albuquerque" (the admiral of the fleet).

Near northern end of Sumatra Island on this chart it has a "Diamond Point", which also aided Marx in discovering the *Flor do Mar*. (See the blowup above). Contemporary writings stated that diamonds from the shipwreck washed ashore at this location after storms.

Divers from Marx's team recovering treasures on the wreck of the *Flor do Mar.*

1527: The Portuguese East Indiaman *Espíritu Santo*, commanded by Captain Francisco de Melo, set sail from Banda Aceh at the northern tip of Sumatra and the westernmost point of Indonesia with a large amount of treasure, which was described in letters as being "more gold than has ever been seen at one time before." This gold may have been salvaged from the 1511 wreck of the *Flor do Mar*, which was lost just down the coast, but this is only conjecture. An hour after setting sail, a storm struck and the ship sank. Seven of the 247 Portuguese aboard, plus many slaves, survived.

1561: The Portuguese East Indiaman *São Paulo* was officially sailing from Lisbon to Goa. For some reason she went far off course and wrecked at Barus, on Sumatra's west coast, about 30 miles (48 kilometers) south of Banda Aceh. Her cargo was valued at over 2.2 million crusadoes in gold and silver bullion and specie. Some 550 souls went down with her.

1563: The Portuguese East Indiaman *São Paulo* (1,200 tons/1,219 tonnes), commanded by Captain Rui de Melo da Camera, was sailing between Lisbon and Malacca with over 800,000 crusadoes in gold and silver. A storm forced her to Brazil and after making repairs, she set off for the Indian Ocean. While attempting to enter the Straits of Malacca, she wrecked during a storm on a reef about a half league from the northern end of Sabang Island (also named We' Island), near the northern end of Sumatra. Some of the people reached the island on rafts from the ship's wreckage and eventually got to Malacca.

1565: The Portuguese East Indiaman *São Sebastião* (800 tons/813 tonnes, 32 cannons), commanded by Captain Pedro Lopes Rebelo and sailing between Lisbon and Malacca with 330,000 crusadoes in treasure, was attacked and sunk by Banda Aceh pirates a few leagues south of Banda Aceh. Pirates massacred the few men who managed to reach shore.

1569: The Portuguese East Indiaman *Nossa Senhora de Loreta* (1,200 tons/1,219 tonnes), commanded by Captain Juan de Mello and sailing between Goa and China with 698,000 crusadoes and a cargo of lead, was lost on Subi Island in the South China Sea north of Borneo. Only 47 of the 600 people aboard survived the disaster.

1594: The Portuguese merchantman *Santissima Trinidade* (750 tons/762 tonnes), commanded by Captain Francisco de Sa and sailing from Goa to Macao with 342,000 crusadoes in treasure, was pursued by Achenese pirates soon after entering the Straits of Malacca. During the chase, the ship wrecked on a reef about a league northwest of the port of Banda Aceh on the northern tip of Sumatra. The survivors were later ransomed in Malacca.

1603: The Dutch East Indiaman *Enkhuizen* (300 tons/305 tonnes), commanded by Captain Klaas Thijsz Collet and sailing from Holland to the Moluccas with silver and gold specie to purchase spices, wrecked at Halmahera Island (Jailolo Gilolo) in the Moluccas.

1608: Two Dutch East Indiamen—the *China* (420 tons/427 tonnes), commanded by Captain Kornelis Maartensz, and the *Walcheren* (700 tons/711 tonnes), commanded by Captain Arend Maartensz—sailed from Holland for the Moluccas with "a large amount of treasure." They first stopped at Goa, but bad weather forced them away before they could fight any of the Portuguese ships anchored there. After arriving at Ternate, they both sank in a typhoon.

1613: The Dutch East Indiaman *Brak* (100 tons/101.5 tonnes), commanded by Captain Jakob Ijsbrandsz and sailing from Holland to the Moluccas with 167,000 guilders in gold and silver, ran aground and quickly went to pieces in the port of Makassar on Sulawesi Island (formerly Celebes).

1617: The Dutch East Indiaman *Grote Aeolus* (300 tons/305 tonnes), commanded by Captain Bouwe Bouwesz and coming from Holland with 239,000 guilders in silver specie, was lost in the port of Makian on Tidore Island in the Moluccas. Only a few of her cannons were recovered.

1617: The Portuguese East Indiaman *Nossa Senhora de Belém* commanded by Captain Pereira de Sande and sailing from Malacca to the Moluccas with 165,000 crusadoes to purchase spices, was lost near the Buru Islands in the Ceram Sea and only some of the people on her were saved.

1619: The Dutch East Indiaman *Hoorn* (700 tons/711 tonnes), commanded by Captain Willem Ijsbrand Bontekoe and coming from Holland with 157,450 guilders in gold and silver, plus more treasure belonging to some merchants, stopped at Fogo Island for provisions. While there, she caught fire and blew up. The fire occurred when a crewman, sent below to get brandy, dropped a candle, causing the brandy to ignite. Fogo is 80 miles (129 kilometers) west of Sumatra in 5 degrees south latitude.

1619: The Dutch East Indiaman *Zeelandia,* also known as the *Nieuw Zealand* (800 tons/813 tonnes, 58 cannons), commanded by Captain Jan van Meldert and sailing from Holland to Batavia with 245,000 guilder in gold and silver specie, was wrecked on the west coast of Sumatra near Langsa. Contemporary native divers recovered several chests of silver coins. The salvage effort was halted when a shark killed a diver.

1620: The Dutch East Indiaman *Zuider Eendracht* (620 tons/630 tonnes), sailing between Holland and the Moluccas with 220,000 guilders in gold and silver, had just anchored off Bantam in the Moluccas when a storm came up and she capsized and sank.

1620: The Dutch East Indiaman *Goede Fortuin* (700 tons/711 tonnes, 46 cannons), commanded by Captain Jan Gijsbertsz Bonneter and sailing from Holland to Batavia with 287,000 guilders in gold and silver, was lost near Socatara on the south side of Java Island. Only some of the people were saved.

1622: The Dutch East Indiaman *Eendracht*, sailing between Holland and Batavia, was lost on the west side of Ambon Island (also Amboina and Ambonia), carrying 320,000 guilders in treasures.

1623: The British East Indiaman *Sun*, commanded by Sir Thomas Dale, along with four other East Indiamen, was on one of the earliest English voyages to the Far East. Since she was the flagship of the squadron, we can assume she carried all or at least most of the £890,000 sterling in silver specie to purchase silks, spices and porcelain. She wrecked on Engano Island near Batam Island, just south of Singapore.

1624: An unidentified Japanese merchantman, sailing from Nagasaki to Batavia to purchase cannon and other weapons from the Dutch and carrying a large amount of gold ingots, was totally lost on Baween Island off the north coast of Java.

1625: The Dutch East Indiaman *Griffioen* (320 tons/325 tonnes), commanded by Captain Pieter Hendriksz and sailing from Goerre to Batavia with 278,000 guilders in treasure, was chased by pirates and deliberately run aground and set on fire by her crew, off one of the Sula Islands in the Molucca Sea.

1627: The Dutch East Indiaman *Bantam* (800 tons/813 tonnes), commanded by Captain Douwe Anthonisz, sailed from Holland with 320,000 guilders in treasure. After arriving in Batavia, she caught fire and capsized.

1629: The Dutch East Indiaman *Goulden Leeuw* (550 tons/559 tonnes), sailing between Holland and Batavia with 340,000 guilders in treasure, was intercepted by Portuguese warships in the Sunda Straits. She was blown up and sank during the battle.

1630: The Dutch East Indiaman *Kameel* (500 tons/508 tonnes), commanded by Captain Reiner Saecq and sailing between Holland and Batavia, with 263,000 guilders in treasure, caught fire soon after arriving off Batavia and sank near Boompjes Island.

1630: Two Dutch East Indiamen—the *Oostzanen* (450 tons/457 tonnes) and the *Walcheren* (550 tons/559 tonnes)—coming from Holland to Batavia with unknown amounts of treasure, exploded and sank in a battle with three Portuguese warships off Jambi on Sumatra. The Portuguese killed all of the survivors.

1632: The Dutch East Indiaman *Nijmwegan* (550 tons/559 tonnes, 34 cannons), commanded by Captain Dirk Adamsz and sailing from Batavia for Holland with 224,000 guilders in Oriental treasure on board, was lost on Borkumer Reef only a few hours out of Batavia.

1633: The Dutch East Indiaman *Schiedam* (360 tons/366 tonnes, 32 cannons), sailing from Holland to the Coromandel Coast and then on to Batavia and carrying 127 chests of gold and silver specie, wrecked on Boompjes Island as she approached Batavia. Only the people were saved.

1633: The Dutch East Indiaman *Delftshaven* (400 tons/406.5 tonnes), sailing between Holland and Batavia with 380,000 guilders in silver, "burst because of carelessness" shortly after anchoring off Batavia. She probably struck a rock or reef.

1634: The Dutch East Indiaman *Gouden Leeuw*, sailing from Batavia to Banda Island to buy spices with 137,500 guilders in treasure, wrecked on the north side of Borneo while fleeing from pirates.

1634: The Dutch East Indiaman *Breedam* (200 tons/203 tonnes), commanded by Captain Michiel Vis and sailing between Batavia and Japan with 124 chests of gold and silver specie, was lost soon after leaving port on Duizend Island. Only some of her crew were saved.

1637: The Dutch East Indiaman *Noordwijk* (300 tons/305 tonnes), sailing with 74 chests of silver specie from Batavia to Japan, was wrecked near the Patrapa River on Sumatra. Coins from this wreck are occasionally found on the beach after bad storms.

1637: The Dutch East Indiaman *Prins Willem* (500 tons/508 tonnes), commanded by Captain Laurens Kornelis Verbeek and sailing from Batavia to Holland, was wrecked at Varkenseiland in the Sunda Straits, The value of her cargo was 314,000 guilders, and only part of her porcelain cargo was recovered at the time of loss.

1642: The Dutch East Indiaman *Maan* (200 tons/203 tonnes, 22 cannons), sailing from Batavia to the Moluccas with "many chests of gold and silver specie," was wrecked in a storm on Solor Island, west of the Lomblen Islands in the Straits of Sunda. Only the people were saved.

1642: The Dutch East Indiaman *Hollandia* (700 tons/711 tonnes), sailing from Batavia to China with 348,000 guilders in gold and silver, was wrecked on Lombok Island, one of the Sunda Islands, east of Bali. Salvors recovered none of her treasure.

1643: The Dutch East Indiaman *Otter* (200 tons/203 tonnes), sailing between Batavia and China with 530,000 guilders of treasure, wrecked on a reef near Boetoeng, off the southeast coast of Sulawesi Island. Salvors were able to recover only four of her bronze cannons.

1643: The Dutch East Indiaman *Maastricht* (600 tons/610 tonnes), sailing from the Malabar Coast to Batavia with a cargo valued at 445,000 guilders, was chased by pirates and wrecked near Banda Aceh on the northern tip of Sumatra. The pirates massacred survivors, except for a few merchants who were later ransomed.

1646: The Dutch East Indiaman *Frederik Hendrik* (1,100 tons/1,118 tonnes, 64 cannons), commanded by Captain Michiel Vis and sailing between Batavia and Japan with 367,000 guilders in gold and silver, was wrecked on a reef in the Bangka Straits. A ship sailing with her rescued 63 survivors.

1647: The Dutch East Indiaman *Valkenburg* (200 tons/203 tonnes), sailing between Batavia and Taiwan with 212,000 guilders in treasure, was wrecked on rocks and then went down in deeper water east of Bangka Island between Sumatra and Borneo.

1650: The Dutch East Indiaman *Zaandijk,* sailing between Holland and Batavia, with 178,000 guilders in gold aboard, was lost on a reef south of Sulawesi (Celebes). Three salvage attempts failed to recover any of the gold.

1650: The Dutch East Indiaman *Bergen Op Zoon* (300 tons/305 tonnes), commanded by Captain David Dingemans and sailing between Batavia and China with "a vast amount of treasure," was lost on a reef south of Sulawesi Island. Two salvage attempts recovered only three anchors and some rigging.

1650: The Dutch East Indiaman *Tiger* (1,000 tons/1,016 tonnes), sailing between Batavia and Japan, was carrying 24 tons (24.38 tonnes) of silver ingots and two chests of gold coins. While fleeing from pirates, she wrecked on a reef on Butung Island, south of the Sulawesi Islands.

1651: The Dutch East Indiaman *Luipaard* (320 tons/325 tonnes), sailing between Batavia and Japan with 324,000 guilders in gold and silver, blew up and was totally lost on a reef south of the Sulawesi Islands as she fled from Chinese pirates.

1651: The Dutch East Indiaman *Zutphen* (550 tons/559 tonnes), sailing from Holland to Batavia with 387,000 guilders in gold and silver bullion and specie, was attacked by pirates off the northern coast of Java and wrecked on Vlaamse Bank. The ship was then set on fire to keep it from the pirates, who massacred most of the survivors. Several Dutch ships witnessed the attack, but light winds made it impossible for them to help the stricken ship.

1654: The Dutch East Indiaman *Goude Hoop,* commanded by Captain Simon Turver and sailing between Holland and Batavia with "a large amount of gold and silver," was pursued by pirates and wrecked near Novo Tello on Amboina (Ambon) Island in the Moluccas.

1656: The Dutch East Indiaman *Wachter,* sailing from Holland to Batavia with 284,000 guilders in gold and silver, was wrecked at Palembang, Sumatra, where she had gone for repairs after a bad storm. Local divers working for the Dutch recovered about half of her treasure.

1658: The Dutch East Indiaman *Windhond,* also called the *Witte Windhond* (360 tons/366 tonnes), sailed from Holland to Batavia with 221,000 guilders. She wrecked while trying to anchor off this port in a storm and was lost on Boompjes Island. Only a few men were saved.

1660: The Portuguese East Indiaman *São Mateo,* sailing between Borneo and Goa, and carrying a cargo valued over 450,000 crusadoes, was lost in Udjung Harbor on Sulawesi Island. All her crew was massacred except for the captain who was later ransomed.

1660: Two large unidentified Portuguese warships were lost in a battle with Dutch ships off Sulawesi Island. One blew up and sank and the other sank from cannon holes below the waterline. Combined, they carried over 700,000 crusadoes in treasure. Over 500 Portuguese lost their lives.

1661: The Dutch East Indiaman *Haas* (200 tons/203 tonnes), commanded by Captain Joris Jansz Zomer and sailing between Batavia and Japan with 231 chests of gold and silver, was wrecked on the reefs of Roti Island near Timor.

1664: The Dutch East Indiaman *Leeuwin* (400 tons/406.5 tonnes), sailing from Batavia to China with over 300,000 guilders in treasure, wrecked at Makassar on Sulawesi Island and only some people were saved.

1665: The Dutch East Indiaman *Parkiet,* commanded by Captain Ijsbrant van Banke and sailing between Sri Lanka and Batavia with nine chests of precious stones and other cargo, was wrecked at Bimelepatnam on the southern end of Sumatra and only some of the crew was saved.

1665: The Dutch East Indiaman *Nachtegaal,* commanded by Captain Fijaart Niendertsz Bakker and sailing from Holland to Batavia with 342 chests of silver specie and bullion, was wrecked off Ceram Island in the Moluccas. Salvors recovered only part of the rigging.

1666: The Dutch East Indiaman *Rijnland* (795 tons/808 tonnes), commanded by Captain Wilke Wybertsz and coming from Holland with over 300,000 guilders in treasure and other cargo, caught fire off Batavia and blew up, causing several other smaller ships anchored nearby to explode and sink when gunpowder ignited.

1668: The Dutch East Indiaman *Purmerland* (218 tons/221.5 tonnes), sailing between Batavia and Japan with 233,000 guilders in treasure, stopped at Makassar on Sulawesi Island for repairs, and while there her gun powder room caught fire and the whole ship exploded.

1668: The Dutch ship *Geit,* was sent to Makassar to salvage a wreck. Divers brought up over 100,000 guilders in silver specie. As the ship prepared to depart for Batavia, a lightning strike caused the ship to explode with a total loss of life and treasure.

1668: The Dutch East Indiaman *Zierijzee* (400 tons/406.5 tonnes), commanded by Captain Jut Jakobsz Buis and sailing between Holland and Batavia "with a very valuable cargo," sank off the port of Makassar on Sulawesi Island when struck by a freak wind gust.

1670: The Dutch East Indiaman *Nieuwenden* (210 tons/213 tonnes), sailing between Holland and Batavia with 328,000 guilders in treasure, wrecked on a reef between Bima and Makassar on Sulawesi Island.

1670: The Dutch East Indiaman *Kaneelboom* (300 tons/305 tonnes), sailing between Bengal and Batavia with 289 chests of silver specie, was wrecked near Banda Aceh on the northern end of Sumatra.

1671: The Dutch East Indiaman *Schermer* (636 tons/646 tonnes), commanded by Captain Hans Swart and sailing between Batavia and Holland with 476,000 guilders in Oriental treasures (which included silks, spices and porcelain), was wrecked on Bangka Island in the Bangka Straits. Only some of her people were saved.

1672: An unidentified Portuguese East Indiaman, sailing from Macao to China with 340,000 crusadoes in gold and silver, was wreck on Bunguran Island in the Natuna Island group in the South China Sea north of the northwest tip of Borneo.

1672: The Dutch East Indiaman *Waterhoen* (193 tons/196 tonnes), commanded by Captain Pierter Willemsz, sailed from Holland in a fleet for Batavia, carrying 437,000 guilders in silver and gold. Off Mozambique Island the Dutch attacked Portuguese ships, and the *Waterhoen* was damaged. While sailing to Batavia alone, she wrecked at Ambon Island in the Moluccas.

1674: The Dutch East Indiaman *Gouden Leeuw* (330 tons/335 tonnes), was sailing from Holland to Batavia with 433,000 guilders in gold and silver bullion and specie. The ship lost its rudder when it hit a submerged wreck near one of the Tiger Islands off Batavia. When a storm arose she dropped anchors, but was driven on an island. Most of the people and some of the treasure were saved.

1677: The Dutch East Indiaman *Uitdam* (448 tons/455 tonnes), commanded by Captain Michiel Kornelisz and sailing between Batavia and Japan with 328,000 guilders in gold and silver bullion and specie, was wrecked on Fortuin Island near Sumatra.

1677: The Dutch East Indiaman *Sticht Van Utrecht* (990 tons/1,006 tonnes), commanded by Captain Karsten Piertersz and sailing from Holland to Batavia in 1676, had an interesting voyage. In the English Channel she beat off an attack by Turkish pirates in war galleys. Near Mozambique, during an attack from three Portuguese ships, she lost her mizzenmast, but managed to escape. Off Krakatoa Island she was attacked again by two Chinese pirate vessels and sank one of them before escaping. She wrecked returning from Japan on a reef off

Batavia. Her cargo was saved and port officials ordered the ship to be stripped and burned. After the fact, it became known that Dutch merchants who had made the voyage to Japan had concealed a large amount of gold and silver objects beneath the ballast, which was lost when the ship burned.

1681: The Dutch East Indiaman *Den Briel* (766 tons/788.5 tonnes, 48 cannons), commanded by Captain Theunis Andriesz and sailing from Holland to Batavia with a stop in Galle, Sri Lanka, carrying 273,000 guilders in gold and silver, was wrecked on a reef in the Moluccas called Arrakan Reef and only a few of the people were saved by another ship in the fleet.

1682: The Dutch East Indiaman *Gooiland* (468 tons/475.5 tonnes), commanded by Captain Balthus Groen and sailing between Batavia and China, with 430,000 guilders in silver, sank in a storm off Palembang on Sumatra.

1682: The Dutch East Indiaman *Huis Te Velsen* (750 tons/762 tonnes), sailing between Batavia and China with a stop in the Moluccas and carrying " a large amount of treasure," was totally lost on Ternate Island in the Moluccas.

1683: The Dutch East Indiaman *Huis Te Noordwijk* (506 tons/514 tonnes), commanded by Captain Kornelis Jansz de Zeeuw and sailing between Holland and Batavia with 356,000 guilders in gold and silver, wrecked on Damar Island, one of the Saraswati Islands in the Moluccas. Salvors were unsuccessful in recovering any of the treasure.

1684: The Dutch salvage vessel *Bode* (96 tons/97.5 tonnes), commanded by Captain Adriaan Roelofsz van Asperen, was sailing to Batavia after successfully salvaging an unidentified Portuguese East Indiaman lost near Banda Aceh on the northern part of Sumatra. Four divers drowned during the three-month salvage operation, which used diving bells. They recovered over 780,000 guilders in Portuguese gold and silver specie, plus valuable objects of unknown value. The *Bode* wrecked during a storm near the Pulau Seribu (Thousand Islands) in the bay as she approached the anchorage off Batavia.

1684: The Dutch East Indiaman *Huis Te Kleef* (564 tons/573 tonnes), commanded by Captain Gerrit Albertsz Schellinger, wrecked near the Pulau Seribu and was a total loss. The value of her cargo was in excess of 478,000 guilders. She had sailed from Batavia to Burma, then Surat, then Galle, Sri Lanka, and finally Palembang on Sumatra, purchasing various kinds of Oriental treasures. At Palembang she picked up 95 survivors from another Dutch East Indiaman wrecked off Medan, Sumatra.

1685: The Dutch East Indiaman *Aadenburg* (482 tons/490 tonnes, 36 cannons), commanded by Captain Jan Jansz Bitter and sailing from Batavia to China with "a large amount of gold and silver bullion and specie," sank after hitting a reef off Buton Island (also known as Boetoeng), off the southeast side of Sulawesi Island.

1686: The Dutch East Indiaman *Prins Willem Hendrik* (1,094 tons/1111.5 tonnes), commanded by Captain Adriaan van Kreuningen and sailing between Batavia and Thailand with 570,000 guilders in gold and silver, was totally lost on Bangka Island in the Gaspar Strait. Only a few people were saved.

1690: The Dutch East Indiaman *Zijpe* (488 tons/496 tonnes, 38 cannons), commanded by Captain Jan Modderman, was coming from Holland to Batavia. with stops at Cape Town and Surat, carrying 643,000 guilders in gold and silver specie. She was in the process of anchoring off Batavia when lightning struck the ship and blew up with a total loss of lives and treasure.

1696: The Dutch East Indiaman *Hendrik Maurits* (1,195 tons/1,214 tonnes, 62 cannons), sailing between Batavia and China, with "a large amount of treasure," was wrecked on Ternate Island in the Moluccas. Some of those saved were captured by Chinese pirates and taken away for ransom.

1697: The Dutch East Indiaman *Bronstede* (253 tons/257 tonnes), commanded by Captain Jakob Barendsz Sonbeek and sailing between Batavia and China "with a large amount of treasure on board," sprang a bad leak soon after leaving port. The captain tried to get into Semarang on Java's north coast, but the ship struck a reef and went to pieces in rough weather.

1697: The Dutch East Indiaman *Huis Te Zilverstein* (1,017 tons/1,033 tonnes, 58 cannons), commanded by Captain Hans Beurens and sailing between Batavia and China with 444,000 guilders in treasure, wrecked entering Makassar on Sulawesi Island during a storm.

1698: The Dutch East Indiaman *Honselaardijk* (722 tons/733.5 tonnes), commanded by Captain Kornelis Ole and preparing for a voyage to Bengal and China, with some treasure already loaded, sank in a bad storm while at anchor at Batavia. Very few people were saved.

1702: The Dutch East Indiaman *Schellag* (290 tons/295 tonnes), commanded by Captain Jakob de la Palma, had just arrived in Batavia with a valuable cargo coming from Japan and sank in the roads of Batavia. There were some survivors.

1703: The Dutch East Indiaman *Moerkapelle* (685 tons/696 tonnes), commanded by Captain Willem de Haze, who died during the voyage, sailed from China for Batavia with "a very valuable cargo." She wrecked on the shoals off Palembang, Sumatra.

1709: TheDutch East Indiaman *Kattendijk* (759 tons/771 tonnes), commanded by Captain Kornelis de Gueus and sailing from Batavia for Thailand with 221,000 guilders in gold and silver, was wrecked on Bangka Island in the Sunda Straits.

1711: The Dutch East Indiaman *Theeboom* (526 tons/534.5 tonnes), commanded by Captain Tobias Uilenberg and sailing from Batavia to China with 431,000 guilders in gold and silver, was totally lost on the south side of Banda Island in the Moluccas.

1714: The Dutch East Indiaman *Heilbot* (100 tons/101.5 tonnes), sailing between Ambon and Batavia with 150,000 in silver specie recovered from an unidentified Dutch East Indiaman lost near Ambon several years earlier, wrecked on Sepanjang Island, one of the Kangean archipelago off the east end of Java in the Bali Sea.

1718: The Dutch East Indiaman *Donkervliet* (794 tons/807 tonnes, 46 cannons), commanded by Captain Dionys van Vlierden and sailing from Batavia to China with 476,000 guilders in gold and silver on board, stopped at Makassar on Sulawesi Island. Two hours after leaving this port, she struck a reef and sank. Several boats from the island rescued 137 people who said that sharks had eaten many others.

1726: The Dutch East Indiaman *Aagtekerke* (850 tons/864 tonnes), commanded by Captain Jan Witboom and sailing between Holland and Batavia with 460,000 guilders in treasure, was wrecked on We'

Island, located near Banda Aceh on Sumatra's northern tip where the Strait of Malacca meets the Indian Ocean.

1728: The Dutch East Indiaman *Ouwerkerk* (658 tons/669 tonnes, 44 cannons), commanded by Captain Jan de Vos and sailing between Batavia and Japan with "a large amount of gold and silver," wrecked shortly after leaving port near Japara on the north coast of Java.

1730: The Dutch East Indiaman *Noordbeek* (858 tons/872 tonnes, 46 cannons), commanded by Captain Herman Brand and sailing from Batavia to Japan with 412,000 guilders in gold and silver, was wrecked near Ternate in the Moluccas.

1735: The Dutch East Indiaman *Wendela* (600 tons/610 tonnes, 34 cannons), commanded by Captain Pieter Visser and sailing between Batavia and Holland with a cargo valued at 467,000 guilders, excluding the value of 37,000 pieces of Chinese porcelain, wrecked on Sipura, one of the Mentawai Islands off the west coast of Sumatra.

1737: The Dutch East Indiaman *Susanna* (600 tons/610 tonnes, 32 cannons), commanded by Captain Pieter Kronenburg and sailing between Batavia and Japan with 563,000 guilders in gold and silver, wrecked in a storm at Rembang on the north coast of Java.

1740: The Dutch East Indiaman *Spiering* (810 tons/823 tonnes, 44 cannons), commanded by Captain Johannes Verklocken and carrying Spanish silver pieces of eight worth 145,000 guilders aboard, was en route from Batavia to Japan when she sank at Watubela Island near the Banda Islands, in the Moluccas

1740: The Dutch East Indiaman *Valkenisse* (1,150 tons/1,168.5 tonnes, 62 cannons), commanded by Captain Elias Moeninx and sailing between Batavia and China with 444,000 guilders in gold and silver bullion and specie, was wrecked near Bantam Island in the Moluccas. Two salvage attempts recovered none of her treasure because she broke up and shifting sands quickly covered the remains.

1741: The Dutch East Indiaman *Steenhoven* (850 tons/864 tonnes, 44 cannons), commanded by Captain Simon Muller and sailing from Batavia to Japan with 442,000 guilders in gold and silver, was wrecked near Banda Island in the Moluccas.

1746: The Dutch East Indiaman *Hofwegan* (650 tons/660.5 tonnes), commanded by Captain Jan de Wit and coming from China to Batavia, exploded and was a total loss soon after reaching the Roads of Batavia. Her cargo was estimated at 450,000 guilders.

1746: The Dutch East Indiaman *Nieuw Vijvervreugd* (1,150 tons/1,168.5 tonnes, sixty cannons), commanded by Captain Adriaan van Dorp and coming from China with a cargo valued at 640,000 guilders, exploded shortly after arriving in the Roads of Batavia.

1748: The Dutch East Indiaman *Leeuwerik* (650 tons/660.5 tonnes), commanded by Captain Adriaan Laurens and sailing from Batavia to Japan with 450,000 guilders in gold and silver, wrecked at Makassar on Sulawesi Island while fleeing from pirates.

1748: The Dutch East Indiaman *Maarsseveen* (850 tons/864 tonnes), commanded by Captain Arnold de la Forcade, was lost east of Sulawesi. She blew up after a fire broke out. There is no documentary mention of what she carried, but she was coming from China and must have had valuable cargo.

1752: The Dutch East Indiaman *Schakenbos* (850 tons/864 tonnes), commanded by Captain Dirk Klein and sailing from Batavia to China with 450,000 guilders in gold and silver, was wrecked on a small island in the Manipa Strait in the Moluccas.

1752: The Dutch East Indiaman *Geldermalsen*, sailing between Batavia and Holland, was lost off Bintan Island in the Straits of Malacca. The majority of her cargo consisted of 343 tons (348.5 tonnes) of tea and 239,000 pieces of Chinese porcelain (used as ballast), over 400 pounds (181.5 kilograms) of gold ingots, and six chests of diamonds. In 1985 Max de Rham and Michael Hatcher discovered the wreck at a depth of 130 feet (40 meters). They recovered over 110,000 pieces of porcelain, all of the gold, and numerous artifacts. The rest of the porcelain and the chests of diamonds are still on the wreck.

1761: The Dutch East Indiaman *Kleverskerke* (850 tons/864 tonnes, 46 cannons), commanded by Captain Willem 't Hoen and sailing from Japan to Batavia, with a cargo valued at 470,000 guilders, stopped at Makassar on Sulawesi Island and, soon after leaving, was wrecked in a storm on a reef.

1764: The Dutch East Indiaman *Zeelelie* (600 tons/610 tonnes), commanded by Captain Jakob la Mote and sailing between Batavia and Japan with 440,000 guilders in treasure, was to make a stop at Banda Island in the Moluccas, but wrecked when the ship was several hours from Banda.

1765: The Dutch East Indiaman *Oosterbeek* (1,100 tons/1,118 tonnes), commanded by Captain Jan Zarcharias Nauwman and sailing between Batavia and China with 470,000 guilders in treasure on board, was wrecked on the coast of East Java on one of the Lesser Sunda Islands.

1765: The Dutch East Indiaman *Pijlswaart* (880 tons/894 tonnes, 44 cannons), commanded by Captain Hans Eggers and returning to Batavia from China with a cargo valued at 670,000 guilders, caught fire when lightning struck the ship, which exploded only an hour away from the Roads of Batavia.

1766: The Dutch East Indiaman *Giessenburg* (1,150 tons/1,168.5 tonnes, 66 cannons), commanded by Captain Thijs Fierman and sailing from Batavia for China with 780,000 guilders in treasure, wrecked at Weter Island, one of the Barat Daya Islands in the Banda Sea. Only some people were saved.

1769: The Dutch East Indiaman *Herog Van Brunswijk* (1,150 tons/1,168.5 tonnes, 66 cannons), commanded by Captain Jan Schellinger and sailing between Batavia and Japan with "a large treasure on board," wrecked between Navekarre and Kalpitaya in the Sulawesi Sea.

1784: The Dutch East Indiaman *Europa* (1,200 tons/1,219 tonnes), commanded by Captain Pieter Kardon and sailing between Batavia and China with 314 boxes of silver specie, struck upon an unmarked rock off Indramajore on the north coast of Java Island and quickly sank with a total loss of life and treasure.

1789: The Dutch East Indiaman *Jonge Frank* (592 tons/601.5 tonnes), commanded by Captain Jakob Veer and sailing from Holland to Batavia with 390,000 guilders in treasure, stopped at Cape Town and picked up part of the cargo of the homeward-bound ship *Maria*, which had wrecked there the previous year. Shortly after arriving in the Roads of Batavia, she sank during a storm.

1789: The British East Indiaman *Vansittart* (unusual for a British ship to have a Dutch name) was sailing between England and China, carrying over 100 tons (102 tonnes) of silver bullion and specie, when she struck a reef off the east side of Bangka Island and went down in deep water. Contemporary salvors, using grappling hooks, recovered only a few chests of silver and she has been an elusive target for treasure hunters in recent years.

1795: The Dutch East Indiaman *Herog Van Brubnswijk* (1,150 tons/1,168.5 tonnes, 58 cannons), commanded by Captain Jan Olhof, had just anchored in the roads of Batavia, coming from China with a cargo valued at 770,000 guilders, when she sank in a storm with great loss of life and all of her cargo.

1795: The British East Indiaman *Resistance* (44 cannons), commanded by Captain Edward Packenham and sailing between Batavia and England with a cargo valued at £195,000 sterling, caught fire in the Straits of Bangka. To save as many lives as possible, the ship was run aground on the east side of Bangka Island, where she blew up, killing all but four of the 300 men on board.

1796: The Dutch East Indiaman *Draak* (1,150 tons/1,168.5 tonnes), commanded by Captain Anthonie van Rijn, having just arrived from China "with a very valuable cargo," was anchored in the roads of Batavia when lightning struck and she burned and sank.

1797: The British East Indiaman *Ocean*, carrying "a large amount of gold and silver specie," wrecked on Paternosters Reef, named by the Portuguese who many years before lost a rich ship there. It is located north of Kalatoa Island in 7 degrees and 19 minutes of south latitude. Natives killed some of the survivors; others suffered dreadfully in long boats before reaching Ambon in the Moluccas 500 miles (805 kilometers) away.

1806: The Dutch East Indiaman *Schrikverwekker* (68 guns), commanded by Captain Hendrik Alexander Ruysch, had 450 people on board and 450,000 guilders in gold and silver specie. She was wrecked on Agnieteneilanden Reef in the Pulau Seribu Islands northwest of the roads of Batavia. Only two people drowned, but when salvage vessels came to recover her treasure, the wreck site could not be found.

Facing page treasures:

(Top left) Dutch delftware pitcher, early 17th century, recovered from Dutch merchantman lost off of Vietnam.

(Top right) Religious gold jewel-studded crown recovered from an unidentified Portuguese shipwreck (17th century) off Malacca, Malaysia.

(Center left) Large Chinese blue and white porcelain jug with military motif which sold in a Christies auction in 2005 for $27.8 million, recovered from the *Flor do Mar.*

(Lower) Some of the thousands of jade figurines recovered from the *Flor do Mar.* Remember that jade comes in all colors including white, black, and green as you see in this photo.

COROA-PRATA-
SEC. XVII
PROV. N.S.AJ

(Right) Four 12-inch high jade figurines of female musicians dating from early Han period. Recovered from a wreck site in the Philippines.

(Below) Portuguese document with a drawing of each ship in a fleet sailing between Lisbon and the Orient in 1500.

Chapter 26

Far East's Richest Shipwrecks

After capturing Calcutta in 1501, Portuguese Admiral Afonso de Albuquerque returned to Lisbon where he outfitted a large fleet of 22 ships. He selected the 700-ton (711-tonne) *Flor do Mar* as his flagship. This famous ship served as his home in the Indies for the next eight years as he conquered 28 countries, starting with Mozambique on the southeast coast of Africa and systematically working his way up the coast with his Portuguese army, pillaging every port they visited. Once they had stripped coastal towns, they moved on to settlements along the Red Sea and from there struck across to India, Burma and Siam, all of which fell to the Portuguese sword. The conquerors amassed a staggering amount of treasure in gold specie, marvelously wrought gold objects such as statues of Buddha, silver objects, jewelry, gems, pearls and even beautiful girls.

In 1509, while Albuquerque was still in the Red Sea, he dispatched one of his ships under the command of Diego Lopes de Sequeira to Malacca on the Malay Peninsula to reconnoiter. Malacca was celebrated as the emporium of the East, one of the richest cities in the world. It was the Singapore of the period, its harbor filled with ships from as far away as Japan, China, Arabia, India and Africa. From elephants to Ming Dynasty porcelain, every type of luxury and exotic merchandise was available. Gold was so abundant that traders exchanged gold coins by weight rather than by count. Duarte Barbosa, one of the Portuguese who came with

The narrow, dangerous Straits of Malacca, located between Sumatra Island and the south coast of Malaysia, has accounted for the loss of many ships over the years.

Sequeira, wrote: "Many of the Malay nobles and merchants were so rich that they possessed 6,000 pounds of gold and upwards and precious stones were as plentiful as raindrops."

When Sequeira and his unruly followers arrived at Malacca, the sultan and his subjects initially offered them hospitality. The Portuguese were permitted to establish a trading factory and things went well for a time, but when the sultan realized that their visit was the prelude to an invasion of his city, he imprisoned them and seized their ship. Sequeira managed to smuggle out a letter telling Albuquerque of Malacca's wealth and of his imprisonment. Albuquerque quickly prepared for an attack on Malacca.

Upon reaching Malacca in July 1511 with 18 ships and 1,000 soldiers, he demanded the immediate release of his countrymen and restoration of their property and ship. The sultan insisted that the Portuguese sign a treaty of peace. Albuquerque refused. A few days later, he burned several rich merchant vessels and threatened to burn others if his men were not released. He promised to leave if Sequeira and his men were freed. The sultan took him at his word and released the prisoners, a decision he was to bitterly regret.

Albuquerque broke his promise to depart and attacked against overwhelming odds. Roughly a third of Malacca's population of 100,000 was of fighting age and a battle raged for twelve days. Thousands of Malays were slaughtered, even after they surrendered. The sultan, his royal court and the surviving inhabitants fled to the hills and eventually took refuge on the other side of

The port of Malacca, which was the Singapore of its day, after the Dutch took it from the Portuguese in 1644.

the peninsula at Johor. Malacca remained a Portuguese possession until the Dutch captured it in 1641.

Albuquerque gave his men three days' license to plunder the deserted city. The spoils they took stagger the imagination. From the sultan's palace alone they took over sixty tons (61 tonnes) of gold, valued at over 15 million crusadoes, in the form of buddhas, animals, birds, plus the sultan's throne and gilded furniture, tons of gold coins and ingots, precious stones and pearls. They took three times this amount in gold and silver from warehouses, merchants' homes, and from ships in the harbor. They looted over 200 chests of diamonds, rubies, emeralds, sapphires and other precious stones and took the sultan's 2,000 bronze cannons that had failed to protect the city.

By the end of December, satisfied that the fledging colony was on its feet, Albuquerque loaded all of the plunder on four ships, leaving the others to defend the port. Almost all of the gold and precious stones were crammed aboard his flagship, the *Flor do Mar*. The ships set sail for Lisbon. Two days later, they were struck by a fierce storm. Two of the extremely overloaded ships sank with a total loss of lives and treasure. Several hours later, the *Flor do Mar*, with 400 souls on board and the greatest treasure ever carried on a single ship, struck a reef off the northeastern tip of Sumatra near the entrance to the Straits of Malacca. Five of the ship's officers managed to reach one of the remaining ships, the *Trinidad*. Instead of sending small boats from the *Trinidad* to rescue those on his flagship, a callous Albuquerque set sail for India. Soon after, the *Flor do Mar* broke up and sank in deeper water. Only three men reached shore by swimming. After reaching India, Albuquerque wrote to the king: "We have lost the richest treasure on the earth."

The Portuguese were not content with cornering the world's spice market through Goa and Cochin. The main source of spices was the Spice Islands, in the Indonesian archipelago, primarily the Moluccas. After capturing Malacca, Albuquerque sent out an expedition to conquer the Spice Islands. They reached Banda Island where the ships took on a fine cargo of cloves and then sailed back to Lisbon. Soon after Portuguese expeditions seized the two main Spice Islands of Ternate and Timor as well other islands in the Indonesian archipelago and held them until the Dutch expelled them in the early seventeenth century.

Malacca quickly became the richest, most important Portuguese possession in the Orient and arguably the most important trading center in the world. In 1557 the Portuguese established a settlement and trading base at Macau (formerly Macao) near present-day Hong Kong. Macau was an advantageous location for trade with Japan and China. The first contact Japan had with the West was a Portuguese ship that had been blown off its course to China about 1542. Subsequently, the renowned Portuguese Black Ships made annual trading voyages to Nagasaki, Japan, and Canton, China. They were under constant attack by the Dutch sailing out of Batavia (Jakarta) and by pirates, especially the Sumatran Achenese.

Information about the Portuguese in the Orient is thin. There is almost no original documentation. On November 1, 1755, the Great Earthquake of Lisbon destroyed over two-thirds of the city, killing over 15,000 people. Among the thousands of buildings laid to waste were the Casa do India and several other archives, which collapsed and then burned. The royal treasury, "which was filled with gold and precious stones, more than all of the other rulers of Europe combined possessed," toppled into the Tagus River and nothing was ever recovered from it.

1513: Four large unidentified Portuguese merchantmen—each loaded and preparing to depart from Malacca with valuable cargoes of Oriental treasures—were attacked by a fleet of over 100 Javanese pirate galleys. The Portuguese claimed to have sunk all of the pirate vessels—no doubt a gross exaggeration—and one of the Portuguese ships with a cargo valued at over 1 million crusadoes was burned and sunk off the port of Malacca.

1523: An unidentified Muslim ship, sailing from India to Palembang on Sumatra Island with "a large fortune" in precious stones, pearls and gold jewelry, was totally lost on Langkawi Island off the northwest coast of Malaysia. The Portuguese in Malacca sent two small boats to conduct salvage operations, but no treasure was found.

1534: Four unidentified Portuguese East Indiamen were preparing to set sail from Malacca for Goa, India, with over 4 million crusadoes, when a fleet of over 100 Sumatran pirate ships attacked them in port. The Portuguese burned their own ships and fled ashore. None of the treasure was ever recovered.

1555: An unidentified Portuguese East Indiaman, sailing between Goa and China and carrying 598,000 crusadoes in gold and silver, sank between the coasts of Malaysia and the Andaman Islands in the Andaman Sea.

1558: The Portuguese East Indiaman *Nossa Senhora de Belém* (800 tons/813 tonnes, forty cannons), commanded by Captain Leonel de Sousa and sailing between Nagasaki, Japan, and Macau with a cargo valued at 1.7 million crusadoes, wrecked on the south side of Hainan Island, China. One of the 64 survivors was the famous poet Luis de Camões, the greatest figure in Portuguese literature. The Chinese ransomed him and the other survivors for 10 tons (10.16 tonnes) of lead ingots, a commodity much in demand in China.

1567: The Spanish merchantman *San Luis y San Carlos* (980 tons/996 tonnes), commanded by Captain Roman de Gusman and sailing from Macau to Manila with a cargo consisting of porcelain and works of art crafted of gold, silver, ivory and jade and valued at 890,000 pesos, was totally lost on the Parcel Islands in the South China Sea, about 130 miles (209 kilometers) south of Hainan Island. Today, China's claim to this island group is disputed by six other nations.

The rich Portuguese port of Malacca under attack by Achenese pirates in 1567. This was a common occurrence every few years. At times the pirates had over 300 vessels in their fleets.

1568: The Portuguese East Indiaman *São João*, commanded by Captain Simão Ferriera and sailing between Malacca and China with over 2 million crusadoes in gold and silver bullion and specie, was lost when currents and poor visibility sent her onto rocks off the south side of Parcel Island in the South China Sea. Pirates salvaged some small amount of her treasure after killing most of the survivors and holding the rest for ransom.

1572: In 1557 the Portuguese established a major trading base on Macau, an island off present-day Hong Kong. Soon after, they began trading with xenophobic Japan. Each year the Japanese emperor permitted the Portuguese to send one to three large ships from Macau to Nagasaki, carrying European goods the Japanese needed, such as silver, gold, lead and copper. For these the Japanese traded porcelain, silks and exotic objects made of gold, silver, jade and ivory. They also carried goods between Japan and China, whose emperor had forbidden direct trade with Japan. They called these Portuguese ships "Black Ships" because their hulls were black with a coat with tar. The first loss of a Black Ship was the *Nossa Senhora da Rosario* (1,200 tons/1,219 tonnes, 44 cannons), commanded by Captain Antonio Manoel de Vilhana and carrying gold and silver valued at 673,000 crusadoes. She was caught in a typhoon and sank within a league of Amakasa Island, to the west of Kyushu Island. There were only two survivors.

1582: The Portuguese East Indiaman *São Mateus*, commanded by Captain João Casado da Silva and coming from Sumatra with over 4 tons (4.06 tonnes) of gold and other valuable cargo, arrived in Malacca as a fleet of Achenese pirates appeared and attacked the ship. To keep her out of the hands of the pirates, the captain set her on fire and she blew up, scattering gold coins like rain drops all over the area. Only a few of her crew escaped in a small boat; the others perished in the explosion.

1583: The Portuguese East Indiaman *Nossa Senhora de la Guia*, sailing between Goa, India, and Macau with 1.3 million crusadoes in treasure on board, was driven into Malacca by Sumatran pirates. The Portuguese set her on fire when it appeared the pirates would board. She blew up and was a total loss.

1583: The Portuguese merchantman *Nossa Senhora do Se* (800 tons/813 tonnes), commanded by Captain Simão Ferreira and sailing between Macau and Malacca with a cargo valued at over 1 million crusadoes, was wrecked in a bad storm on some rocks near the mouth of the Johore River, Malaysia, where the city of Johore Baru stands, close to the north coast of Singapore Islands. Contemporary salvors were able to recover only nine of her bronze cannons and several chests of Chinese porcelain.

1586: The Portuguese East Indiaman *Nossa Senhora da Madre* (2,200 tons/2,235 tonnes), commanded by Captain Manuel Henriques de Andrade and sailing from Goa, India, to China with 1.7 million crusadoes in treasure, was totally lost at Kojei Island, located south of Pusan, Korea. Some of the crew survived, only to be imprisoned and later ransomed.

1586: The Spanish Manila galleon *San Felipe* (2,300 tons/2,337 tonnes), commanded by Captain Juan Hurtado and sailing between Manila and Acapulco, Mexico, with a cargo valued at 3.4 million pesos in Oriental treasures, was lost near Tosa Point on Kyushu Island, Japan. There was a great loss of life and the only things salvaged were bales of silks and spices that floated free from the wreck.

1587: The Spanish Manila galleon *San Martín* (1,300 tons/1,321 tonnes), commanded by Captain Lope de Palacios, sailed from Acapulco to Manila and after unloading 1.65 million pesos in gold and silver, headed to Macau to trade with 478,000 pesos in gold and silver. She wrecked about a half league from Macau while attempting to enter the port. None of the treasure was salvaged.

1595: A fleet of four Spanish merchantmen, commanded by Luis de las Merinbas, sailed from Manila to trade in Cambodia and China. One, the *San Francisco Xavier* (860 tons/874 tonnes), commanded by Captain Ferdinand de los Rios and carrying 450,000 pesos in gold and silver, struck some rocks off Gaolan Island, east of Macau, and slipped off into deep water. Another of the ships saved a few men. Everything else was lost.

1595: The Spanish Manila galleon *San Felipe* (1,400 tons/1,422.5 tonnes, 46 cannons), commanded by Captain Hernando de Bunaventura and sailing between Manila and Acapulco with a cargo of treasures valued at 2.34 million pesos, was caught in a typhoon and wrecked on the coast of Susaki in Tosa Bay, on the south side of Shikoku Island. The emperor of Japan, who claimed all shipwrecks, employed divers who recovered a small part of the cargo of gold, silver, and ivory objects. An unknown number of people survived, including 16 Jesuit and Franciscan missionaries, who were crucified at the emperor's orders.

1598: Three unidentified Manila galleons sailed from Manila with a large amount of gold and silver to use for trading in Cambodia. The two largest wrecked with a total loss of life and treasure during a typhoon near Canton, China.

1598: Portuguese in Macau chartered an unidentified Chinese junk for a voyage to Japan. On the return, she foundered 2 leagues off Dongshan Island, east of Shantou in the Taiwan Straits. She sank with over 400,000 pesos in Japanese silver ingots, earmarked for trade with China.

1600: The Dutch East Indiaman *De Liefde* (340 tons/345.5 tonnes), commanded by Captain Jacob Jansz Quaeckernaeck and carrying "a significant amount of treasure," was destroyed in a typhoon and sank in deep water at the entrance to Tokyo Bay (then called Edo Bay). The cargo was lost, but few people died.

This painting shows the Chinese port of Canton in the nineteenth century with the *godowns* (warehouses) of many foreign nations. It was the first port opened to foreign traders in 1673.

1601: Three Portuguese Black Ships sailed from Macau to trade in China and one of them the *São Bento* (1,200 tons/1,219 tonnes), carrying 29 tons (29.5 tonnes) of silver ingots, wrecked near the mouth of the Tang River in China's Kwangtung province. Only a few of the people were saved.

1602: In a diplomatic exchange, the Spanish in Manila sent extravagant gifts to the Japanese emperor, and he sent a ship with an ambassador carrying precious gifts for the king of Spain. During a typhoon the Japanese ship wrecked on the northern tip of Taiwan and only two men were saved.

1604: An unidentified Portuguese East Indiaman, (2,000 tons/2,032 tonnes), sailing from Macau to the Philippines with a cargo valued at 500,000 crusadoes, was fleeing from Chinese pirates when it wrecked on the Spratly Islands, located about halfway between Vietnam and Borneo in the South China Sea.

1604: The Portuguese East Indiaman *Nossa Senhora das Merces* (800 tons/813 tonnes, 44 cannons), commanded by Captain Manuel de Barreto Rolim, was sailing between Lisbon and Macau with 380,000 crusadoes in gold and silver bullion and specie. Two Dutch ships attacked when she stopped at Malacca. The *Merces* was burned, sinking with a total loss of life. A Dutch warship also sank.

1606: Two Dutch East Indiamen—the *Middleburg* (600 tons/610 tonnes), commanded by Captain Simon Lambrechtsz Mau, and the *Nassau* (320 tons/325 tonnes), commanded by Captain Abraham Mathijsz—both with unknown amounts of treasure aboard were sailing between Holland and Johore off the east coast of Malaysia. They attacked several Portuguese ships anchored at Malacca. Several days later they ran into a fleet of seven Portuguese warships off Cape Rochado, Malaysia, and during a battle both caught fire and exploded with almost total loss of life. Nearby, the Portuguese sank another Dutch ship, the *Amsterdam*. Several days later, when the Portuguese warships were anchored off Malacca, a Dutch fleet of warships attacked and sank the *São Simão* and captured the *Santa Cruz*. Seeing that they were out-gunned, the Portuguese then set fire to the five remaining galleons and destroyed them. All seven of these Portuguese warships were carrying large amounts of treasure.

1607: The Spanish merchantman *Trinidad* (1,200 tons/1,219 tonnes, 36 cannons), commanded by Captain Juan Carlos de Zaragosa and sailing between Macau and Manila with a cargo of Oriental products, including a great amount of Chinese and Japanese porcelain, valued at 760,000 pesos, was totally wrecked in a typhoon on the south side of Hainan Island in the South China Sea.

1607: The largest Portuguese ship lost to this date was the *Nossa Senhora de Conceição* (2,300 tons/2,337 tonnes). As she was setting sail from Malacca, heading for Goa, with a cargo worth in excess of 2 million crusadoes, a fleet of Dutch ships appeared, and she went down in a battle within sight of the port.

1607: The Portuguese East Indiaman *Nossa Senhora de Concepção* (1,800 tons/1,829 tonnes, 66 cannons), commanded by Captain Duarte de Guerra and sailing between Goa, and China with 1.33 million crusadoes in gold and silver, was totally lost on a small deserted island off the southeast coast of Malaysia near present-day Mersing.

1609: Three Manila galleons left Manila for Acapulco. They weathered three typhoons, the last of which caused the *San Francisco Xavier* (1,400 tons/1,422.5 tonnes), to lose her rudder. She wrecked at Motoyoshi on the east coast of Honshu Island, Japan. About half of the people aboard survived, including the ex-governor of Manila, and they were well treated by order of the emperor of Japan.

1610: The Portuguese East Indiaman *Madre de Deus*, also called the *Nossa Senhora da Graça* (1,800 tons/1,829 tonnes), commanded by Captain Andre Pessoa and carrying 1,254,000 crusadoes in gold and silver, anchored in the port of Nagasaki where it had permission from the Japanese to trade. When a force of 1,000 Samurai soldiers attacked, the captain blew up his own ship and it sank in 200 feet (61 meters) of water with all 379 hands. Contemporary Japanese salvors recovered a few chests of silver and crates of silk. In the 1920s Japanese commercial divers recovered three of the wreck's bronze cannons, an astrolabe and other artifacts, but none of the treasure, which lies buried under harbor mud.

1611: The Portuguese East Indiaman *Bon Jesus* (2,200 tons/2,235 tonnes), sailing from Macau to Nagasaki, Japan, carrying 780,000 crusadoes in gold and silver, plus other goods, was lost on the Fujian Coast of Japan.

1613: The Dutch East Indiaman *Rode Leeuw* (400 tons/406.5 tonnes), commanded by Captain Volkert Thijsz, after capturing over 800,000 pesos in gold and silver from a Manila galleon near Manila, was heading to Batavia when a typhoon blew her off course and she wrecked near Japan's Osaka Bay.

1614: The Dutch East Indiaman *Oranje* (700 tons/711 tonnes), commanded by Captain Willem Jansz and coming from Holland to the Moluccas with 238,000 guilders in gold and silver, was lost on Aur Island off the east coast of Malaysia in the South China Sea.

1616: The Manila galleon *Santissima Trinidad* (950 tons/965 tonnes), commanded by Admiral Rodrigo de Triana, set sail from Manila for Acapulco with 760 souls aboard and a cargo valued at over 3 million pesos. At the time she was considered the richest galleon ever to sail from the Philippines. Contrary winds forced her to take a more northerly course than usual, and when the ship was in sight of Cape Satano on the Osumi Strait, Japan's southern extremity, a typhoon struck. The ship was flung upon the rocks of this headland and quickly went to pieces with a total loss of treasure. Local inhabitants massacred about eighty people who got ashore.

1618: The Dutch warship *Jakarta* (34 cannons), entered the port of Macau to attack six Portuguese merchantmen that had just returned with treasures from Japan. They expected little resistance from the Portuguese; however, instead of cutting their anchors and running, the vessels surrounded the *Jakarta* and were about to capture it when her captain had her blown up and she sank with "a considerable amount of treasure aboard."

1620: The British East Indiaman *Unicorn*, sailing from Java to Japan with "a significant amount of silver specie," was wrecked on the east side of Tioman Island in the South China Sea off the east coast of Malaysia. Another document states she sank on the coast of China.

1620: The Portuguese East Indiaman *Conceição* (1,800 tons/1,829 tonnes), commanded by Captain Filipe da Cruz Silveira and sailing between Lisbon and Malacca with 860,000 crusadoes in treasure, was wrecked on a small island off Malacca.

1623: The Dutch East Indiaman *Muiden* (160 tons/162.5 tonnes), sailing from Holland to Batavia, was blown off course by a typhoon and lost off Kolongsoe Island near Xiamen, China, with 340,000 guilders in silver specie and tin ingots.

1623: The Dutch East Indiaman *Valk* (120 tons/122 tonnes), sailing between Holland and Batavia with an unknown amount of treasure, was struck by a typhoon, then chased by pirates and wrecked off the west side of Taiwan.

1625: An unidentified Dutch East Indiaman, coming from Batavia with treasure in excess of 450,000 guilders, was wrecked in a typhoon several leagues east of Nagasaki. Only some of the people were saved.

1625: The Dutch East Indiaman *Risdan* was lost off coast of Johor, Malaysia, at a site now called "Elephant Rock," commemorating her cargo of elephant tusks. Some of the ivory and several tons of lead ingots were salvaged in recent times. Unknown to the modern-day salvors, she also carried 135,000 guilders in silver specie and bullion, which are still on the wreck.

1627: An unidentified Portuguese East Indiaman (a Black Ship) of around 2,000 tons (2,032 tonnes), sailing between Macau and Nagasaki, with over 1 million crusadoes in treasure and a large amount of lead and tin ingots, was lost soon after reaching Nagasaki.

1627: The Dutch East Indiaman *Ouderkerk* (100 tons/102 tonnes), sailing between Batavia and Japan with 340,000 guilders in treasure, sank off Amoy in Fukien province, China, in a battle with the Portuguese.

1627: The Dutch East Indiaman *Domberg*, commanded by Captain Jasper Klaas and sailing between Holland and Japan with an unknown amount of treasure, was chased by pirates and burned in the Chincjeu River, China.

1627: An unidentified Portuguese East Indiaman, coming from Japan with a cargo valued at 780,000 crusadoes, had just anchored off Malacca when a fleet of Sumatran pirate vessels attacked. The Portuguese set fire to their ship, to prevent her from falling into the hands of the pirates. Unfortunately, only a small number of the men on the ship were able to get ashore before she blew up.

1627: The Dutch East Indiaman *Zierikzee* (800 tons/813 tonnes), commanded by Captain Mathijs Albertsz Balk and sailing from Batavia to the Cape of Good Hope with a cargo valued at 349,000 guilders, was totally lost at Rayong Island in the bight of Bangkok.

1628: The Dutch East Indiaman *Alkamaar* (600 tons/610 tonnes), sailing between Holland and Batavia with "a large amount of treasure," was lost near Arakan, Burma, in the Bay of Bengal and only 17 of the people aboard were saved.

1630: The Dutch East Indiaman *Haan* (150 tons/152.5 tonnes), sailing between Batavia and Japan with "a considerable amount of gold and silver specie," was lost near Fuzhour in the Straits of Taiwan.

1631: The Dutch East Indiaman *Witte Beer* (300 tons/305 tonnes), sailing between Batavia and Japan with 247,000 guilders in gold and silver, plus other cargo, was lost near Hirado Island off the northwest coast of the province of Kyushu, Japan. The survivors were massacred.

1631: The Dutch East Indiaman *Beverwijk* (160 tons/162.5 tonnes), commanded by Captain Marten Hendriksz and sailing between Batavia and Japan with "a large amount of gold and silver," wrecked on the south side of Hainan Island in the South China Sea. Most of those aboard were saved and ransomed.

1633: The Dutch East Indiaman *Brouwershaven* (200 tons/203 tonnes), commanded by Captain Willem Jakobsz and sailing with 36 chests of silver coins from Batavia to Taiwan, was chased by pirates, run ashore, and burned on the east side of Taiwan.

1633: An unidentified large Portuguese East Indiaman (Black Ship), carrying 650,000 crusadoes of treasure from Macau, wrecked with a total loss of life and treasure near the tip of the Osumi Peninsula located east of Nagasaki.

1634: The Dutch merchantman *Kleine Erasmus* (240 tons/244 tonnes), sailing from Batavia to Japan with 432,000 guilders of treasure, was totally lost near Miyazaki on Kyushu Island, Japan.

1634: The Dutch East Indiaman *Walcheren* (550 tons/559 tonnes), sailing from Batavia to Borneo with "a large amount of silver specie," struck on a reef off the northwest coast of Borneo, near Kota Kinabalu, Indonesia.

1635: The Dutch East Indiaman *Grotebroek* (240 tons/244 tonnes), sailing between Batavia and Japan with 220,000 guilders in treasure, was wrecked near Tarpia, Vietnam, in the Gulf of Thailand. Survivors saved only three chests of silver specie.

1635: The Portuguese East Indiaman (Black Ship) *Nossa Senhora do Carmo* (2,200 tons/2,235 tonnes, 68 cannons), commanded by Captain Antonio Pedro Dias and sailing from Macau to Nagasaki with 1.23 million crusadoes in treasure and other products, wrecked on Shimokoshiki Island in the South China Sea, about 75 miles (121 kilometers) south of Nagasaki.

1636: The Dutch East Indiaman *Keizerin* (200 tons/203 tonnes), with 280,000 guilders of treasure, was blown far off course in a typhoon. After first seeking safety on Taiwan, she was totally lost in a second typhoon in the Bay of Padaran on the west coast of Cambodia.

1636: The Dutch East Indiaman *Wieringen* sailed from Holland for Pulicat, India. Off Malacca she was attacked by several Portuguese ships and exploded with a total loss of life and treasure.

1637: The Dutch East Indiaman *Zwaan* (200 tons/203 tonnes), commanded by Captain Adriaan Waaghals and sailing with cargo valued at 293,000 guilders from Batavia to Martaban, Burma, was attacked by pirates off Martaban and burned by her crew to prevent capture.

1637: The Dutch East Indiaman *Ter Veede* (350 tons/356 tonnes), sailing between Batavia and Japan with 327,000 guilders in treasure, was lost on the Pescadore Islands in the Taiwan Straits between China and Taiwan.

1637: The Portuguese East Indiaman (Black Ship) *São Julião* (1,850 tons/1,880 tonnes), commanded by Captain Braz de Albuquerque and sailing from Nagasaki to Macau, was badly damaged in a typhoon and wrecked on the west side of Taiwan with a cargo valued at 1,655,000 crusadoes. Some of the people, but none of the treasure, were saved.

1639: The Dutch East Indiaman *Zon* (200 tons/203 tonnes), sailing between Batavia and Japan with 133 chests of gold and silver, was chased by pirates in the Straits of Taiwan and lost on the Pescadore Islands.

1639: The Dutch East Indiaman *Aemlia* (600 tons/610 tonnes), commanded by Captain Joost Salters and sailing between Batavia and Japan, stopped at Taiwan where the Dutch had built a fort and set up a trading factory. She wrecked while being chased by pirates near Taipei on the northern end of Taiwan.

1643: The Dutch warship *Franeker,* sailing between Batavia and Galle, Sri Lanka, engaged in a battle with the Portuguese off Malacca. Before she went down, the Portuguese removed some of the 178 chests of silver specie she carried. All of the crew were beheaded.

1643: The Dutch East Indiaman *Hert,* also called the *Vliegende Hert* (200 tons/203 tonnes), sailing between Batavia and Japan with 320,000 guilders in gold and silver, plus other cargo, was wrecked on the Pescadore Islands in the Straits of Taiwan.

1645: The Portuguese East Indiaman *São Tomé* (a Black Ship, 1,700 tons/1,727 tonnes), commanded by Captain Estavao de Miranda and coming from Macau with "a large treasure" and a group of 24 Jesuit priests, wrecked on Tanega Island in the Osumi Strait, south of Japan's Kyushu Island.

1647: The Dutch East Indiaman *Jonker* (200 tons/203 tonnes), carrying 16 tons (16.25 tonnes) of silver bullion and other treasure, was lost near Guangzhou, China. About a half of the treasure was salvaged, according to documents.

1647: An unidentified Portuguese merchantman of Antonio Soares Vivas, operating out of Macau, was sunk in a typhoon hear the coast of Johor Baru, Malaysia. She was carrying over 450,000 crusadoes in silver bullion.

1650: The Dutch East Indiaman *Witte Duig* (380 tons/387 tonnes), sailing between Batavia and Japan with 375,000 guilders in treasure, was wrecked near Shantou on the southeast coast of China.

1650: The Dutch East Indiaman *Potvis* (300 tons/305 tonnes), sailing between Batavia and China with 145 chests of gold and silver specie, was totally lost on the coast midway between Hong Kong and Shantou, China. Many of the survivors were ransomed.

1652: The Dutch East Indiaman *Koe* (360 tons/366 tonnes), sailing from Batavia to China with 224,000 guilders in treasure, was totally lost on Shangchuan Island, located between Hong Kong and China's Hainan Island.

1652: The Dutch East Indiaman *Delft* (670 tons/681 tonnes), commanded by Captain Kornelis Piertersz Roggeven and sailing between Goeree-Overflakee, Netherlands, and Japan with 564,000 guilders in treasure, wrecked in a storm while trying to round the southern tip of Taiwan. Two nearby Dutch ships were too focused on battling the storm to pick up survivors.

1652: The Dutch East Indiaman *Diamant* (1,100 tons/1,118 tonnes, 66 cannons), sailing between Holland and Batavia with 482,000 guilders in treasure, wrecked on an island then called Schouwen, off the north coast of New Guinea. Many people survived, only to be eaten by the natives. Seven people survived two weeks in a long boat to reach the south coast of Java.

1653: The Dutch East Indiaman *Zwarte Vos,* commanded by Captain Theunis Eissen, and sailing between Batavia and Japan with "a considerable amount of gold and silver" on board, was lost near the mouth of the Cambodia River, probably a branch of the Cambodia's Mekong River.

1653: The Dutch East Indiaman *Delfshaven* (300 tons/305 tonnes, thirty cannons), commanded by Captain Kornelis Kornelisz van Houten and sailing between Batavia and Japan with "a large amount of gold and silver on board," was wrecked on Maja Island off the Kapuas River in the western end of Borneo (now Kalimantan Barat, Indonesia).

1653: The Dutch East Indiaman *Sperwer* (540 tons/549 tonnes), sailing between Taiwan and Japan with 320,000 guilders in silver specie, was totally lost on Dayo Island, north of Fuzhou, China, while fleeing from pirates.

1653: The Dutch East Indiaman *Smient* (400 tons/406.5 tonnes), commanded by Captain Thijs Krab and sailing between Batavia and Taiwan with 290,.000 guilders of treasure, was wrecked on Pratas Reef in the South China Sea, located about 185 miles (298 kilometers) south of Shantou on the southeast coast of China and east of Dongsha Island in the South China Sea. The reef is called "Pratas" or silver because a Portuguese ship carrying many tons of silver ingots sank there in the early sixteenth century. Many other ships were lost there as well.

1654: The Dutch East Indiaman *Lam Witte,* sailing between Batavia and Japan with 354,000 guilders in gold and silver, hit a reef off the north coast of Taiwan and only a few souls were saved. The *Vrede* (800 tons/874 tonnes and 64 cannons), commanded by Captain Elbert Kornelis and carrying 432,000 guilders in treasure while sailing to Japan, wrecked on the same reef about a half-mile (.80 kilometer) east of the *Lam Witte.*

1655: The Dutch East Indiaman *Vleermuis Gulden,* sailing between Batavia and Japan with 475,000 guilders in gold and silver bullion and specie, was wrecked on the Pescadore Islands in the middle of the Straits of Taiwan between China and Taiwan. The ship wrecked on a reef then called Vuile Eiland after a Dutch ship lost there several years earlier.

1656: The Dutch East Indiaman *Maarssen,* sailing between Batavia and Japan with an unknown amount of treasure, stopped in Taiwan for repairs after a typhoon and sank there in another typhoon near present-day Taipei on Taiwan's southwest coast.

1656: An unidentified Portuguese East Indiaman (Black Ship), sailing from Macau to Japan with "a considerable treasure," sank in a typhoon near the northern tip of Taiwan. A Dutch ship encountered some survivors in a small boat.

1659: The Dutch East Indiaman *Trouw* (500 tons/508 tonnes, 38 cannons), sailing between Batavia and Japan with 340,000 guilders in gold and silver, wrecked during a storm off Hitoe, on Honshu Island, and only a few of those aboard were saved.

1660: The Dutch East Indiaman *Harp*, commanded by Captain Konwalles and sailing between Batavia and Japan with " a large amount of treasure," was wrecked off the center of the west coast of Taiwan. Half of the crew had died in an epidemic during the voyage out from Holland, and when she left Batavia on this last voyage, over half the crew were Indonesian natives and some Chinese slaves.

1661: The Dutch East Indiaman *Koudekerke* (200 tons/203 tonnes), sailing between Batavia and Japan with "a large treasure," was destroyed by Chinese pirates during a battle off the east coast of Taiwan.

1661: The Dutch East Indiaman *Urk*, sailing between Batavia and China with 440,000 guilders in silver and gold, was attacked and sunk by Chinese pirates off the east end of Hainan Island. All of the survivors were massacred except for two merchants who were ransomed.

1661: The Dutch warship *Kortenhoef* (216 tons/219.5 tonnes), commanded by Captain Luit Pieters, was on a voyage from Batavia to Japan with considerable treasure to ransom Dutchmen who were being held for ransom after a wreck. The ship had orders to deliver soldiers and supplies to Fort Zealand on Taiwan, which had been besieged by the Portuguese for several months. While off-loading soldiers and supplies, a storm arose and the ship was totally lost.

1661: The Dutch East Indiaman *Hector* (600 tons/610 tonnes), commanded by Captain Lukas Bouwersz van der Lek van Delfshaven and sailing between Batavia and Japan with 438,000 guilders in gold and silver, was attacked by Chinese pirates off Zhanjiang, north of Hainan Island in the South China Sea, and blew up and sank.

1661: The Dutch East Indiaman *Bloemendaal* (220 tons/223.5 tonnes), commanded by Captain Jan Kornelis Jol and sailing between Batavia and Burma with 287,000 guilders in treasure, struck a reef near the mouth of Burma's Pegu River, and sank.

1663: The Dutch East Indiaman *Graveland*, commanded by Captain Andries Piertersz and sailing from Nagasaki, with a cargo of Oriental treasures worth over half a million guilders and heading for Batavia, was totally lost in a typhoon in the Sea of Japan on one of the Oki Islands, north of Honshu.

1663: The Dutch East Indiaman *Vollenhoven*, commanded by Captain Bastiaan Jansz van Nieuwenden and sailing from Batavia to Japan "with a very rich cargo of gold and silver," wrecked on Mishima Island near Hiroshima. Natives beheaded most of the survivors.

1663: The Dutch East Indiaman *Ankeveen* (283 tons/287.5 tonnes), commanded by Captain Barend Joachimsz and sailing between Batavia and China with 349,000 guilders in gold and silver, wrecked near Wenzhou in the East China Sea.

1663: The Dutch East Indiaman *Peperbaal* (510 tons/518 tonnes), commanded by Captain Vincent Dirksz de Lange and sailing between Holland and Batavia with an unknown amount of treasure, was wrecked in the Mishima Islands near Hiroshima.

1663: The Dutch East Indiaman *Wapen Van Zealand*, with Vice-Admiral Willem Volgers and 479,000 guilders in gold and silver on board, was wrecked on a voyage from Batavia to China on the Parcel Islands in the South China Sea. Other ships in the convoy rescued some of the people.

1665: The Dutch East Indiaman *Rode Hert* (340 tons/345.5 tonnes, 34 cannons), sailing between Batavia and Japan with 329,999 guilders in silver specie, caught fire in the port of Decima, Japan, and was a total loss.

1667: The Dutch East Indiaman *Jonker*, sailing between Batavia and Japan with 345,000 guilders in treasure, was wrecked in the Hitachi Islands north of Honshu. About thirty survivors were picked up by local fishermen and executed.

1667: An unidentified Portuguese East Indiaman, one of the Black Ships, sailing from Macau with 1.2 million crusadoes in gold and silver bullion and specie, was totally lost in Japan's Fujian province, in the Taiwan Straits.

1670: The Dutch East Indiaman *Hoogkarspel* (212 tons/215.5 tonnes), commanded by Captain Meindert Roelofsz and sailing between the Gulf of Tonkin and China with "a large amount of gold and silver," was wrecked near the northwestern tip of Hainan Island in the South China Sea.

1670: The Dutch East Indiaman *Vredenburg*, was sailing between Batavia and Thailand with 37 chests of gold ingots and other cargo when struck by a bad storm and wrecked on Tioman Island in the South China Sea off the east coast of Malaysia. As survivors struggled to get ashore, a pirate vessel appeared close by. The Dutch set their ship on fire to keep the treasure from the pirates, who took revenge by massacring most of the crew. Some men got ashore, hid, and were later rescued.

1671: The Dutch East Indiaman *Zwarte Leeuw* (300 tons/305 tonnes, 24 cannons), sailing from Bengal to Batavia with a cargo worth over 250,000 guilders, was wrecked in a typhoon near Balikpapan on the southeast coast of Borneo. Natives ate some of the survivors who reached shore. Several others reached Surabaya on Java in a small boat.

1672: The Dutch East Indiaman *Wapen Van Goes* (671 tons/682 tonnes), sailing between Batavia and Japan with "a large amount of gold and silver," was wrecked in a storm off the east side of Taiwan.

1673: The Portuguese East Indiaman *Madre de Deus* (2,200 tons/2,032 tonnes), commanded by Captain Luis de Barrios and sailing between Macau and Nagasaki with 1.2 million crusadoes in gold and silver bullion and specie on board to buy Japanese goods, was scuttled by the Portuguese in Nagasaki's port when the Japanese seized it by for some unknown reason.

1673: An unidentified Dutch East Indiaman carrying 230,000 guilders in silver bullion and specie, sailing between Batavia and Japan, was totally lost near Oluan Point, the southern tip of Taiwan. Some of the people were saved.

1674: The Spanish merchantman *Nuestra Señora de Milagros* (780 tons/792.5 tonnes), commanded by Captain Juan Menedez de Ávila and sailing from Manila to China with 575,000 pesos in gold and silver bullion and specie, wrecked on the southern end of Japan's Shikoku Peninsula. One hundred-twelve people reached ashore, nine of whom were Jesuits who were executed. The other survivors were ransomed and made it back to Manila.

1679: The Spanish merchantman *San Tomás* (780 tons/792.5 tonnes), commanded by Captain Hernando Martínez and sailing from Manila to Macau with silver specie valued at 376,000 pesos, was totally lost after she was blown off course by a typhoon near Shantou in Guangzhou province, China, about 150 miles (241 kilometers) northeast of Hong Kong.

1681: An unidentified Dutch warship, anchoring in bad weather at Phu Quoc Island off the southwest coast of Cambodia, found over 100 Portuguese there who were survivors from a Portuguese East Indiaman, carrying over 1 million crusadoes in treasure that had been lost in the area four years earlier.

1684: The Dutch East Indiaman *Gele Beer* (412 tons/418.5 tonnes), commanded by Captain Herman Beets and sailing from Holland to Batavia with 453,000 guilders in gold and silver, was wrecked in a bad storm on Siberut Island, one of the Mentawai Islands off the west coast of Sumatra.

1690: The Dutch merchantman *Canton,* on a voyage from Batavia to China, with 675,000 guilders in gold and silver specie and bullion aboard, wrecked in the South China Sea on a small deserted island close to the southeast coast of Vietnam.

1697: The Dutch East Indiaman *Goudestein* (843 tons/856.5 tonnes), commanded by Captain Wijnands Bouwman and sailing from Batavia to Thailand with 453,000 guilders in treasure, was wrecked off Ligor (today Nakhon Si Thammarat) in the Gulf of Thailand.

1698: The Dutch East Indiaman *Spare* (603 tons/613 tonnes), commanded by Captain Klaas Voshol, while going from Japan to Batavia with a cargo valued at over 400,000 guilders, was lost at Tinggi Island off the present state of Johor, Malaysia, in the South China Sea.

1698: The Spanish merchantman *Nuestra Señora de Buen Viaje* (1,450 tons/1,473 tonnes), sailing from Manila to China and carrying 750,000 pesos in treasure, was lost in a typhoon near Xiamen in the Taiwan Straits.

1702: The Dutch East Indiaman *Bambeek* (845 tons/858.5 tonnes), commanded by Captain Evert Doedes and sailing from Batavia to Bengal with 378,000 guilders in gold and silver, was wrecked in a storm off Cape Rochado on the west coast of Malaysia. In 1995 sports divers found and raised seven bronze cannons believed to be from this wreck, at a depth of 20 fathoms.

1702: The Portuguese East Indiaman (Black Ship) *São Cristovao* (1,700 tons/1,727 tonnes), commanded by Captain João Rodriques de Castelo Blanco and sailing from Macau with 560,000 crusadoes in gold and silver to an unknown destination, was wrecked off the northwestern part of Taiwan. Only a few of the people were saved.

1702: The British East Indiaman *Speedwell,* sailing between Scotland and China, sought refuge from a storm off the port of Malacca. The Portuguese ashore, fearing an attack, opened cannon fire. While trying to flee, the *Speedwell* struck a reef. Some £220,000 sterling of her treasure were recovered by the Portuguese. All the survivors were beheaded.

1719: The Spanish merchantman *Nuestra Señora de Loreto* was sailing between Manila and Thailand with 575,000 pesos in gold and silver bullion when she was struck by a typhoon and wrecked near Nha Trang, Vietnam.

1719: The Dutch East Indiaman *Meeroog* (800 tons/813 tonnes, 44 cannons), commanded by Captain Pieter van Leent and sailing between Batavia and Japan with 455,000 guilders in gold and silver, was wrecked in a typhoon near Oluan Point, the southern tip of Taiwan. There were no survivors.

1719: Two Dutch East Indiamen, sailing from Batavia to Japan together, both wrecked. The *Slot Van Kapelle* (600 tons/610 tonnes), commanded by Captain Pieter van Heel and with 394,000 guilders in treasure aboard, wrecked off Shimkoshiki Island off the southern end of Kyushu, and only a few people were saved. The *Catherina* (800 tons/813 tonnes), commanded by Captain Lambert Bot and with 365,000 guilders in treasure, wrecked in Shibushi Bay on the southern tip of this island. A few men survived.

1724: The Dutch East Indiaman *Appollonia* (800 tons/813 tonnes, 48 cannons), commanded by Captain Gerbrand Mamus and sailing from Batavia to Japan with 567,000 guilders in gold and silver, was lost off Jiaojiang, China, in the East China Sea. A vessel sailing with the *Appolonia* picked up the only two survivors.

1726: The Dutch East Indiaman *Risdan* (520 tons/528 tonnes), commanded by Captain Kornelis Dam and sailing from Thailand to Batavia with a cargo valued at 433,000 guilders, was lost near Kuala Terengganu on the east coast of Malaysia in the South China Sea.

1727: The Dutch East Indiaman *Velserbeek* (650 tons/660.5 tonnes, 44 cannons), commanded by Captain Kornelis Kerkhoven and sailing between Padang on Sumatra and Bengal, India, with 322,000 guilders in silver specie, wrecked while fleeing from pirates several leagues north of Malacca in the Straits of Malacca. A small amount of her silver was recovered at the time.

1730: The Dutch East Indiaman *Meerhuizen* (600 tons/610 tonnes, 34 cannons), was commanded by Captain Leendert Danvers, who died during the voyage and was succeeded by Daniel Overbeek. She sailed from Coromandel to Batavia with 452,000 guilders in treasure and was wrecked on Langkawi Island in the Straits of Malacca.

1731: The Dutch East Indiaman *Knapenburg* (900 tons/914.5 tonnes), commanded by Captain Pieter Tinnekins and sailing from Batavia to Japan with "a large amount of gold and silver," was wrecked during a typhoon on Dongshan Island, China, between Shantou and Xiamen in the Straits of Taiwan. Chinese pirates killed most of the survivors, but a few reached land.

1735: The Dutch East Indiaman *Alblasserdam* (600 tons/610 tonnes), commanded by Captain Michiel Vonk and sailing between China and Batavia with a cargo valued at 650,000 guilders, was attacked off Taiwan by a fleet of pirate vessels. She escaped in a squall, then wrecked on one of the Parcel Islands with few survivors.

1745: An unidentified French East Indiaman was totally lost "with a substantial amount of treasure on board" on Sumei Island in the Gulf of Thailand. Portuguese salvors from Macau failed to find any of her treasure.

1748: The Dutch East Indiaman *Huis Te Persijn* (850 tons/864 tonnes, 44 cannons), commanded by Captain Dirk Bolk and sailing from Japan to Batavia with a cargo valued at 470,000 guilders, was wrecked on one of the Spratly Islands in the South China Sea, about midway between Borneo and Cambodia.

1754: The Spanish Manila galleon *Santa Anna,* sailing between Manila and Acapulco with a cargo valued in excess of $3.7 million pesos, was driven by a typhoon onto the shore in Japan's Bungo Strait. All the survivors were massacred.

1755: The Spanish merchantman *San Paulo,* commanded by Captain Esteben de Monserrat and coming from Manila with 430,000 pesos in gold and silver specie and heading to Macau, was totally lost on the Pratas reef in the South China Sea.

1759: The Dutch East Indiaman *Stadwijk* (1,150 tons/1,168.5 tonnes, 66 cannons), commanded by Captain Pieter de Rode and sailing between Batavia and Japan with 570,000 guilders in gold and silver, was totally lost on one of the Osuni Islands to the south of Japan's Kyushu Island. Japanese fishermen saved 77 people who were later massacred.

1761: The Swedish East Indiaman *Frederik Adolphus* was lost near Dongshe Qundao, China. She carried 345 boxes of silver bullion and specie, plus 45 tons (46 tonnes) of copper bars. Some of the cargo was salvaged at the time.

1766: The Dutch East Indiaman *Lindenhof* (1,150 tons/1,168.5 tonnes), commanded by Captain Hans Bruns, sailed from Holland to Batavia with 670,000 guilders in treasure on board. Upon arriving in Batavia, the treasure remained on the ship while water, provisions and replacements for 66 seamen, who died in an epidemic during the voyage between the Cape of Good Hope and Batavia, were taken on board. Then the ship set sail for China, but while passing the Spratly Islands, she was struck by lightning and exploded with a complete loss of life.

1768: The Dutch East Indiaman *Vredenhof* (1,150 tons/1,168.5 tonnes), commanded by Captain Aldert Aldertsz and sailing from Batavia to Japan with 470,000 guilders in treasure, was wrecked on Fukue, one of the Goto Islands, about 60 miles (97 kilometers) west of Nagasaki, which was her destination.

1776: The Dutch East Indiaman *Aschat* (1,150 tons/1,168.5 tonnes, 64 cannons), commanded by Captain Jan Paardekoper and sailing between Batavia and China "with a large amount of gold and silver on board," was wrecked near Nha Trang on the southeast coast of Vietnam.

1783: The Dutch East Indiaman *Herstelder* (600 tons/610 tonnes), commanded by Captain Frederik Godert Wever and sailing between Batavia and Thailand with "a large amount of gold and silver," wrecked on Sumei Island in the Gulf of Thailand while fleeing from pirates.

1784: The Dutch East Indiaman *Compagnies Welvaren* (1,150 tons/1,168.5 tonnes), commanded by Captain Christiaan Fredrik Winterheim and sailing between Batavia and Sri Lanka with 473,000 guilders in treasure, wrecked a league north of Cape Rachado (now Tanjong Tuan), which is north of Malacca.

1784: The Dutch East Indiaman *Dolfin* (1,150 tons/1,168.5 tonnes), commanded by Captain Axel Land and sailing between Holland and Batavia with 455,000 guilders in gold and silver, was attacked by pirates near Sumatra and headed for the safety of Dutch- controlled Malacca. Soon after anchoring there, a fire broke out and the ship blew up.

1784: The British merchantman *Premier* was lost on Panjang Island off the north coast of Borneo with over £450,000 sterling in gold and silver specie, some of which was salvaged at the time.

1785: An unidentified Spanish merchantman, sailing from Manila for Macau with 560,000 pesos in silver specie on board, was totally lost in a bad storm off Japan's Honshu Island, and all of the survivors were massacred, except for a few rich merchants who were ransomed.

1786: The Spanish merchantman *San Andrés* (1,200 tons/1,219 tonnes), commanded by Captain José Martín de Triana and sailing from Manila to Malacca, with 560,000 pesos in gold and silver specie, wrecked on the south side of Hainan Island in the South China Sea. There were 78 survivors, but none of the treasure was saved.

1788: The Dutch East Indiaman *Trompenburg* (1,150 tons/1,168.5 tonnes, 66 cannons), commanded by Captain Hendrik Elders and sailing between Batavia and Thailand with 370,000 guilders in gold and silver on board, was wrecked at Tioman Island, off the east coast of Malaysia in the South China Sea.

1788: The Dutch East Indiaman *Middlewijk* (880 tons/894 tonnes), commanded by Captain Kornelis de Klerk and sailing between

Batavia and China with 430,000 guilders of treasure, was wrecked on the southwest coast of Taiwan.

1789: The Dutch East Indiaman *Lam* (850 tons/864 tonnes), commanded by Captain Bartholomeus Veau and sailing from Batavia to Thailand with 360,000 guilders in treasure on board, was wrecked on the east Coast of Malaysia near Kuantan in the South China Sea. Only a few people were saved.

1789: The Dutch East Indiaman *Belviet* (880 tons/894 tonnes, 46 cannons), commanded by Captain Jan Montagne and sailing between Batavia and China with "a large amount of treasure," was wrecked during a typhoon on the east side of Taiwan and about half the crew of 229 men were saved.

1790: The Dutch East Indiaman *'T Loo* (1,150 tons/1,168.5 tonnes, 66 cannons), commanded by Captain Johan Pieen and sailing between Batavia and China with 550,000 guilders in gold and silver, sank during a typhoon between Hainan Island and the Parcel Islands. Another ship picked up 18 survivors in a small boat.

1790: The Dutch East Indiaman *Canton* (1,150 tons/1,168.5 tonnes), commanded by Captain Dirk Peek and sailing from Batavia to China with 570,000 guilders in treasure, was wrecked near Wenzhou, China, in the East China Sea. Locals recovered a part of her treasure.

1793: The Dutch East Indiaman *Batavier* (1,150 tons/1,168.5 tonnes, 66 cannons), commanded by Captain Pieter Volkwart and sailing from Batavia to China with 670,000 guilders in gold and silver, was wrecked on the east side of Malaysia near Kota Baru in the South China Sea. Most of the crew were saved.

1796: The British East Indiaman *Shah Munchah* (1,000 tons/1,016 tonnes), sailing between Canton, China, and Bombay, India, with a cargo valued at £255,000 sterling struck upon Pedro Branco Island in the Straits of Singapore and most of her crew survived. Today the Horsburgh Lighthouse is on this 450-foot-(137-meter) long rocky island.

1800: The British East Indiaman *Earl Talbot* (1,500 tons/1,524 tonnes), sailing between Bombay and Canton, China, with 112 tons (114 tonnes) of silver ingots, was totally lost during a gale on Pratas reef. Over 150 people drowned and no bullion was recovered.

1802: An unidentified Spanish merchantman, sailing between Manila and Canton, with 800,000 pesos in silver specie and bullion, wrecked in a storm at Brandon Bay near Hong Kong and only the people on board were saved. The British East Indiaman *Nautilus* (400 tons/406.5 tonnes), sailing between Calcutta and Canton with a large amount of treasure, was lost in the storm on nearby Iron Island near Hong Kong, and fewer than ten men were saved.

1802: The Spanish merchantman *Ferrotena* was lost in 1802 near Pedro Blanco Island in the Straits of Singapore, while sailing between Manila and Macau. She had 2.4 million pesos in silver and gold specie and bullion on board, about 40 percent of which was salvaged at time of loss.

1804: The Portuguese merchantman *St. Antonio* (500 tons/508 tonnes), while returning to her home port of Macau from Indochina with a cargo valued in excess of 330,000 crusadoes, wrecked on one of the Parcel Islands, and only a few of the crew reached safety on Hainan Island in a raft fashioned from wreck timbers.

1809: The British East Indiaman *True Briton* sank in the South China Sea off the east coast of Malaysia near Tioman Island, where some of the survivors reached shore. They reported that they had saved only one chest of gold specie from a large cargo of gold and silver specie.

1842: The British East Indiaman *Christina,* sailing between Macau and Bombay, was lost near the mouth of the Vietnam's Mekong River, with £450,000 sterling in silver specie, only a small amount of which was recovered.

1850: All the vessels in a fleet of Vietnamese pirate ships under the command of pirate leader Shan'ng Tsan, known to be carrying an immense treasure, sank in a tempest in the Gulf of Tonkin, with very few survivors.

1851: The British merchantman *Pasha* was lost off Formosa Point, Malaysia. She carried over $600,000 (1851 value) in gold bullion, plus several boxes of diamonds of unknown value. About half of the treasure was salvaged soon after the disaster.

1851: The British merchantman *Ardaseer*, sailing between China and India, went down close to Singapore with £132,000 sterling, about one-third of which was taken off ship before she sank.

1856: The British merchantman *Neptune*, carrying £243,000 sterling in gold and other cargo, was lost at Barat Menam, Malaysia, while in flight from pirates.

1861: The American merchantman *Bald Eagle*, sailing between Hong Kong and San Francisco with $100,000 in gold and silver specie, was lost near the southern tip of Vietnam, off Mui Ca Mau.

A conservator using a dental-like tool to recover artifacts from a coral-encrusted chest.

(Top) The Portuguese city of Macao produced enormous amounts of gold jewelry, which were carried back to Europe on East Indiamen and the Manila galleons going to Acapulco, Mexico. These objects were found on a sixteenth-century Portuguese wreck off Johor Baru, Malaysia.

(Center) Many East Indiamen carried different types of Oriental works of art, such as this seventh-century A.D. Tang Dynasty bronze horse, recovered from a sixteenth-century Portuguese wreck off Tioman Island in the South China Sea.

(Lower) Many of the ships lost in the Philippines struck on shallow reefs and then slid off into deep water. Marx used this ROV to locate the remains of several in depths up to 2,000 feet (610 meters).

Treasures of the Sea

(Top left) Exquisite Chinese multi-colored porcelain saucer recovered from the Manila galleon *Nuestra Señora de Buen Viaje*, lost in 1754 off Pago Bay on the east side of Guam Island. *(Top right)* Chinese blue-and-white porcelain plate recovered from the wreck of the Manila galleon *Nuestra Señora de Pilar y Zaragosa y Santiago*, lost in 1690 off the southwest tip of Guam Island. *(Center)* Coral-encrusted pewter pitcher recovered from the *Manila Galleon Santo Cristo de Burgos*, lost in 1726 off Ticao Island in the Straits of San Bernardino. *(Lower left)* One of a pair of 8-inch-long emerald earrings recovered from the 1656 *Maravallis* wreck off the Bahamas. They were sold at auction in New York for $8.5 million. *(Lower right)* Marx holds a coral-encrusted clump of about 500 coins, which sold at a recent auction for $25,000.

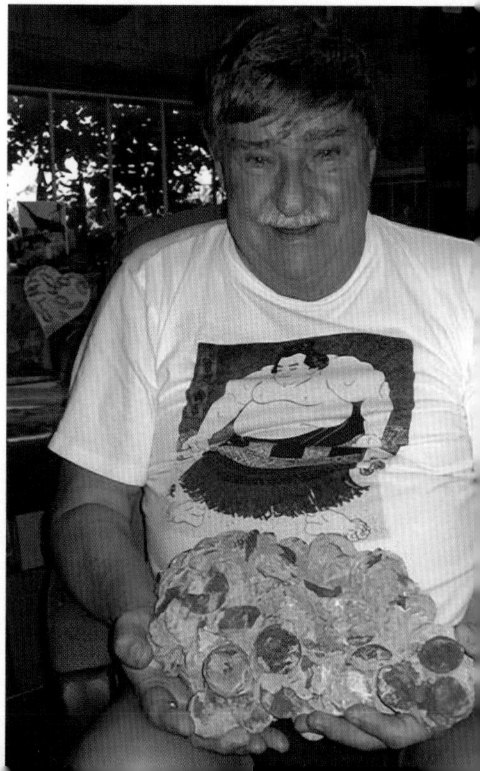

CHAPTER 27

THE PHILIPPINES' RICHEST SHIPWRECKS

Ferdinand Magellan, in 1520, was the first European to visit the Philippines, but the Spanish Crown made no effort to establish a colony there for almost half a century, even though the islands belonged to the half of the world designated as Spanish territory by Pope Alexander VI in the 1495 Treaty of Tordesillas. In 1564 Philip II decided that he wanted a share of the lucrative East Indian spice trade monopolized by Portugal. He sent an expedition led by Miguel Lopez de Legazpi to conquer the Philippines and establish a trading base. The plan to cut in on the spice trade fell through in the face of determined opposition from the Portuguese, who held sovereignty over most of the East Indies and were more powerful than the Spaniards in Eastern waters. Nevertheless, a flourishing traffic sprang up between the Philippines and Mexico. Manila, the clearinghouse for the treasures of the East, became a city of impressive size and splendor.

Beginning in 1565 a fleet of four to eight galleons, called the Manila galleons, sailed annually from Acapulco to Manila and back again. The Manila galleons averaged between 700 and 2,000 tons (711 and 2,032 tonnes) and were by far the largest ships used for Spanish commerce. The voyage from Acapulco to Manila was generally uneventful, lasting from eight to ten weeks with an occasional storm. The return crossing was another matter. It was one of the most difficult voyages in the world. The winds come from the east in the latitude of the Philippines, and galleons leaving Manila

The port of Manila around 1650. It was the main base of the Manila galleons in the Orient.

had to sail against them, making laborious progress northward until they sighted Japan in order to reach a belt of westerly winds. Typhoons were a frequent menace on this leg of the journey.

Once galleons entered the belt of westerly winds at 40 degrees north latitude, they sailed due east, braving icy weather and rough seas, until sighting what today is the coast of California. Once land was sighted, the worst of the voyage was over and the galleons worked their way down to Acapulco, hugging the coast all the way. The hazardous voyage took anywhere from four to eight months, depending on luck. Quite often it was bad luck, and a number of ships were lost on the Manila-to-Acapulco run with considerable loss of life. Three hundred to 600 men, inhumanely crowded together, sailed aboard each galleon. On an average crossing, more than 100 men perished from exposure, epidemics, scurvy, starvation or thirst. In 1656 all of the 450 men on one of two galleons making the voyage died in an epidemic. Two hundred men died on the other galleon. More than 230 of those great ships were lost in storms, wrecked on unmarked reefs and shoals, were destroyed by British or Dutch privateers, or went down due to negligent seamanship.

The gold and silver unloaded from the galleons in Manila were used to buy the varied products of the East. Spanish coinage spread throughout the Orient and remained legal tender there long after the Manila Galleon era ended. The Spanish government tried to slow the drain of silver and gold to China and other Asian countries by imposing harsh trade restrictions, but Europe's insatiable desire for exotic Oriental goods made it impossible to control.

A dazzling array of the Orient's luxurious products filled warehouses in Manila. Chinese silk was the item that Europeans coveted most, and the Manila galleons always returned to Acapulco laden with silk of many types, both plain and embroidered. The ships also transported amazing amounts of porcelain, fans, combs, exquisitely carved objects of ivory and sandalwood, bejeweled sword hilts of precious metals and a wide variety of exquisite jewelry. When Eastern trade soon expanded beyond China, the ships took on Persian rugs that came to Manila via India; spices from Java, Ceylon and the Moluccas; pearls from the Red Sea and a large variety of precious stones and diamonds from India, Burma, and Siam (now Thailand).

1574: The Manila galleon *Santa María de Begonia* (650 tons/660.5 tonnes), commanded by Captain Alonso Pérez de Triana and sailing from Acapulco to Manila with 1.7 million pesos in gold and silver, wrecked on the north side of Catanduanes Islands and all aboard perished.

1575: The Manila galleon *San Juanillo,* was lost off the east side of Catanduanes Island in the Straits of San Bernardino. She was coming from Acapulco carrying 875,000 pesos in gold bullion and silver specie and bullion. Only 45 of the 759 souls aboard survived.

1576: The Manila galleon *Espíritu Santo* (750 tons/762 tonnes), commanded by Captain Manuel de Villanueva and sailing from Acapulco to Manila with 1.87 million pesos in gold and silver bullion and specie, was caught in a typhoon as soon as it entered the Straits of San Bernardino and tried to find safety on the south coast of Cataduanes Island, where it wrecked 3 miles (5 kilometers) east of Virac with only a few lucky souls surviving. Soon after, a small chapel was built on the shore close to the disaster and a large cross was constructed inside the chapel from some of the ship's timbers. I found this wreck in 1986, but was unable to obtain a salvage permit from the Philippine government.

1590: The Manila galleon *Almiranta, San Felipe* (1,200 tons/1,219 tonnes), commanded by Captain Fernando de Castro and sailing between Acapulco and Manila with 1.7 million pesos in gold and silver, was hit by a typhoon in the Straits of San Bernardino and then wrecked on the north coast of Marinduque Island between the towns of Boac and Santa Cruz. Salvors were sent from Manila, but recovered only a small portion of the treasure—12 chests with 3,000 pieces of eight in each and some bales of clothing.

1598: The governor of the Philippines sent two large ships, the *Capitana* and *Almiranta,* to establish trade relationships in Cambodia and China. Each carried over half a million pesos in treasures. The *Almiranta* wrecked during a typhoon on Dalupiri Islands, one of the Babuyan Islands located off the northern tip of Luzon Island. The same typhoon inflicted grave damages on the *Capitana* and she wrecked near Pinghai, about 55 miles (88.5 kilometers) east of Macau where she was heading for repairs.

1599: An unidentified Manila galleon, coming from Acapulco with "a large amount of gold and silver" and heading for Manila, was totally lost on Catanduanes Islands in the Straits of San Bernardino in the eastern Philippines and only a few men survived.

1601: The Manila galleon *Santo Tomás* (1,300 tons/1,321 tonnes), commanded by Captain Juan Rodríquez de Ocuño and sailing between Acapulco and Manila with 2.65 million pesos in gold and silver, was caught in a squall in the Straits of San Bernardino and soon after wrecked near Bulan on the southern tip of Luzon Island. About half of those on board reached shore. Survivors carried some treasure off the ship. Contemporary salvors recovered only a small portion of the treasure. Two salvage attempts in the 1980s failed because the current in the wreck area runs over 3 knots, making diving impossible.

1608: Two Manila galleons—*San Ambrosia* and *San Telmo*—sailing together from Manila to Acapulco under the command of Captain-General Juan Tello Aguirre and with over 3 million pesos in Oriental treasures, were caught in a typhoon just before reaching the Straits of San Bernardino. The *San Ambrosia* hit the northern tip of tiny Capul Island and went off into about 250 feet (76 meters) of water. After learning that fishermen had been pulling up large amounts of porcelain just under Capul's lighthouse, I made an expedition there in 1988 to find the wreck, but strong currents prevented me from working. The *San Telmo* wrecked off the town of Catarman on the northern shore of Samar Island. General Felix Ramos (who later became Philippine president) took a team of navy divers to find the wreck, but, thwarted by the area's strong currents, they recovered very little.

1610: The Manila galleon *Santo Tomás,* coming from Acapulco with 2.5 million pesos in gold and silver bullion and specie on board, was lost near Catamban Bay on Catanduanes Island. Contemporary salvors recovered only around 220,000 pesos in silver specie. Sand quickly covered the wreck, so although its location was known, nothing more was recovered.

1617: The Dutch East Indiaman *Grote Aeolus* (320 tons/325 tonnes), commanded by Captain Job Kornelis and sailing from Holland to the Moluccas, with 330,000 guilders in gold and silver on board, detoured to Manila where she attacked a large Manila galleon. She caught fire during the battle and blew up with a total loss of life and treasure.

1617: Two Dutch East Indiamen—the *Grote Zon* (600 tons/610 tonnes), commanded by Captain Reiner Jansz, and the *Meeuwtje* (600 tons/610 tonnes), commanded by Captain Jan de Wit—sailing from Holland to the Moluccas with a total of 348,000 guilders in silver specie, first went to Manila, arriving two days after the loss of the *Grote Aeolus.* The two did not take the usual course to the Moluccas, but instead came via the Straits of Magellan in the fleet of Admiral Joris Spilbergen. Off Canate, near Callao, Peru, they had fought against eight Spanish warships, sinking two of them. Both were finally lost while fighting Spanish warships in Manila Bay. The *Grote Zon* was carrying booty estimated at 200,000 guilders that she captured from seven ships trading in the Philippines.

1617: The Dutch East Indiaman *Ter Veere* (700 tons/711 tonnes), commanded by Captain Willem Jakob van Arnemuiden, had also sailed with Spilbergen and arrived several days after the above battle in Manila Bay. The Spaniards, who were repairing their vessels from the previous engagement, came out and gave battle again and the *Ter Veere,* carrying 412,000 guilders in treasure to buy spices in the Moluccas, was on the verge of being captured, so the Dutch set her on fire and she blew up near the entrance to Manila Bay.

1618: A fleet of Dutch warships intercepted a fleet of Chinese merchant junks sailing from China to Manila laden with "enormous

Smaller Dutch warships attacking Manila galleons off Manila in 1618. They managed to sink three of the Spanish galleons.

riches" and captured about thirty of them. The Dutch then anchored off Playa Hondo, about 50 miles (80.5 tonnes) north of Manila Bay on the west coast of Luzon Island. When word of this event reached Manila, the Spaniards quickly armed a squadron of large ships and sent it after the Dutch. Finding them still at anchor at Playa Hondo, they attacked and sank three of the Dutch ships, including the flagship *New Sun of Holland,* which went down with over 1 million guilders in treasure and other cargo.

1619: The Manila galleon *Nuestra Señora de la Vida* (1,750 tons/1,778 tonnes), commanded by Captain José Martínez de Leiva and sailing from Acapulco to Manila with over 1.5 million pesos in gold and silver, was less than a half day's sail from Manila when, due to faulty navigation, she wrecked on a reef on the south side of Verde Island, opposite Mindoro Island. Soon afterward, divers recovered 743,000 pesos of her silver, and 27 bronze cannons, but none of the gold. They reported that the rest of the ship had slid off the reef into deep water. In 1985 Australia sports divers located part of this wreck on top of the reef and found an undisclosed amount of treasure. Asked by the National Museum of the Philippines to check out the site, I found that as much as 6 feet (2 meters) of live coral cover this portion of the wreck. We excavated a section of the ship's keel and keelson. We found many artifacts, but the only treasure was a gold ruby ring.

1620: Three Manila galleons departed Acapulco for Manila. The *San Nicolás* (1,350 tons/1,372 tonnes), commanded by Captain Juan de la Vega, and carrying about 1 million pesos in gold and silver, ran aground near Borongan on the southeast coast of Samar Island while fleeing from pirates. Most of those aboard got ashore. Later, about half of her treasure was salvaged. An unidentified smaller galleon wrecked on Palagpag Island off the east coast of Samar, and most of the unknown amount of treasure she carried was salvaged. The flagship of the fleet, the *Jesús María y San Joséf* (1,850 tons/1,880 tonnes), commanded by Captain Rodrigo de Triana, was attacked by the pirates who attacked the *San Nicolás* and sank near tiny San Bernardino Island in the Straits of San Bernardino with 2.6 million pesos on board.

1620: The Manila galleon *Santa Ana,* coming from Acapulco with 3.2 million pesos in gold and silver, was intercepted by the Dutch in the Straits of San Bernardino and hit by cannon fire. The captain ran her aground on the northern tip of Capul Island and the Dutch were able to get about 1 million pesos off her before she blew up. I searched for this wreck in 1987, but the current runs through this area at 5 knots, making it too difficult for diving or even the use of a remote-operated vehicle.

1620: The Manila galleon *Jesús María* was coming from Acapulco with 1.8 million pesos in gold and silver, sailing with the above *Santa Ana*. She was attacked at the same time and wrecked and capsized on tiny San Bernardino Island in the entrance of the San Bernardino Straits. The Spaniards set her on fire, but the Dutch got about half the treasure off before she also blew up and scattered over a wide area.

1631: The Manila galleon *Santa María Magdalena,* just loaded and ready to depart for Acapulco with a cargo valued at 2.1 million pesos in Oriental treasures, caught fire and blew up with a large loss of life and total loss of cargo at Cavite, near Manila.

1635: The Manila galleon *San Francisco Javier* (2,200 tons/2,235 tonnes), commanded by Captain-General Lorenzo de Ugalde and coming from Acapulco with over 3 million pesos in gold and silver, was dashed to pieces on the east side of Samar Island during a typhoon. Four ships sailing with her picked up some of her survivors. Three contemporary salvage attempts failed to recover any treasure from the site.

1640: The Dutch warship *Rijnburg* (200 tons/203 tonnes), sailing from Batavia (Jakarta) to Japan with 340,000 guilders in gold and silver, first went to the Philippines and sank in a battle with the Spaniards at Fortune Island, off Luzon Island.

1645: An unidentified Portuguese merchantman, coming from Macau with Oriental treasures worth over 500,000 cruzadoes and heading for Manila, was totally destroyed in a typhoon at Vigan, on the northern end of Luzon Island, and only a few people survived. The water was too deep for contemporary divers, but salvors recovered some chests of silks and porcelain with grappling hooks.

1646: The Manila galleon *San Luis,* arriving from Acapulco, with over 2 million pesos in gold and silver aboard, wrecked on the east coast of Cagayan. Some of the treasure was salvaged at the time.

1659: The Manila galleon *San Francísco Javier,* coming from Acapulco with 2.25 million pesos in gold and silver, was destroyed by a typhoon near the port of Borongan on Samar Island. Strong currents prevented any salvage at the time.

1669: The Dutch East Indiaman *Achilles* (550 tons/559 tonnes), sailing from Batavia to Japan with "a large amount of gold and silver," wrecked near Zamboanga on Mindanao Island and only a few of her crew were saved.

1674: The Manila galleon *San Ambrosio* (2,400 tons/2,438.5 tonnes), sailing between Acapulco and Manila with 3.56 million pesos in silver and gold specie and bullion, was lost during a typhoon off Sorsogon on the east coast of Luzon Island. Contemporary divers recovered about half of the treasure.

1694: The Manila galleon *San Diego,* arriving from Acapulco with over 3 million pesos in gold and silver bullion and specie, was driven onto a reef and sank during a typhoon at Nagugbu, near the entrance to Manila Bay. She slid off into deep water before salvors arrived and couldn't be salvaged.

1726: The largest and richest Manila galleon to sail up to this date was the *Santo Cristo de Burgos.* She left Manila for Acapulco with a cargo valued at 4.5 million pesos. Due to an approaching typhoon, she sought refuge in a bay on the north side of Ticao Island. She was totally destroyed by the storm and went down with great loss of life. I worked on this wreck in 1987 and recovered several thousand pieces of Chinese porcelain and some gold jewelry, but was driven away by Communist guerrillas (known as NPA).

Manila galleon being attacked by English warship, 1740 near the Philippines.

1729: The Spanish advice boat *Nuestra Señora de los Dolores* wrecked on the north coast of Mindanao while sailing from Acapulco to Manila. She was not authorized to carry any treasure when she left Acapulco, but in an inquiry it was discovered she had carried over 750,000 pesos in gold and silver contraband belonging to merchants in Manila. This was not unusual. Most ships carried contraband.

1735: The Manila galleon *Jesús, María y San Joseph,* coming from Acapulco with 2.3 million pesos in gold and silver specie and bullion, was lost in the Caliman group of islands located off Palawan Island. About 1.5 million pesos were salvaged at time of loss, but she still has plenty more.

1751: The Dutch East Indiaman *Zeelandia* (1,450 tons/1,473 tonnes), commanded by Captain Thomas Hardy and coming from Japan to Batavia with a cargo valued at 670,000 guilders, was pursued by pirates and wrecked on one of the Tawi-Tawi Islands in the Sulu Sea.

1756: The Dutch East Indiaman *Dieman* (850 tons/864 tonnes; named the *Kasteel Van Tilburg* on her voyage from Holland to Batavia in 1753), commanded by Captain Tobias Sielkens and sailing from Batavia to China with 760,000 guilders in treasure and other cargo, was lost near Quezon on the east side of Palawan Island in the Sulu Sea. The few people who survived were taken to Manila, and later ransomed.

1758: The Dutch East Indiaman *Drie Heuvelen* (850 tons/864 tonnes), commanded by Captain Gotlieb Silo and sailing from Batavia to Japan with 470,000 guilders in gold and silver, made a stop at Banda. She wrecked off Jolo Island in the Celebes Sea while fleeing from pirates, who massacred all survivors.

1758: The Dutch East Indiaman *Ouwerkerk* (540 tons/549 tonnes, 36 cannons), commanded by Captain Marinus de Jong and sailing between Batavia and Japan with 560,000 guilders in gold and silver, was caught in a typhoon in the Sulu Sea and wrecked on Basilan Island.

1782: The Dutch East Indiaman *Mercuur* (850 tons/864 tonnes), commanded by Captain Klaas Roem and sailing between Batavia and China with 670,000 guilders in gold and silver, sank near the Cagayan Islands in the Sulu Sea.

1797: The Manila galleon *San Andrées* was sailing from Acapulco to Manila with 2.35 million pesos in gold and silver. She went to pieces due to faulty navigation on Naranjos Shoals near Ticao Island in the Straits of San Bernardino. The current in this area is so strong that no salvage attempts could be made.

1841: The British East Indiaman *Sultana,* sailing from England to China with £480,000 sterling in treasure was lost near Cape Buliluyan, off the southern tip of Palawan Island.

Chart showing where the British East Indiaman *Royal Captain* was lost in 1773 off the south end of Palawan Island.

CHAPTER 28

AUSTRALIA & NEW ZEALAND'S RICHEST SHIPWRECKS

Until modern times there was very little shipping in the remote waters of Australia and New Zealand, and few of the ships that were lost carried significant amounts of treasure. Most inbound ships brought immigrants and general merchandise. There are no known shipwrecks in New Zealand that fit the criteria for inclusion in this book.

1619: The Dutch East Indiaman *Dordrecht* (800 tons/813 tonnes), commanded by Captain Reiner Jansz and sailing from Holland to Batavia with 320,000 guilders in gold and silver, was wrecked on the west coast of Australia in 32 degrees and 20 minutes south latitude.

1629: The Dutch East Indiaman *Batavia,* commanded by Captain Jakob la Mote and sailing from Holland to Batavia with 130,000 guilders, was lost on Morning Reef in the Houtman Abrolhos chain of islands off Western Australia. Many survivors reached a nearby deserted island where they engaged in cannibalism before some were rescued. In 1971 the *Batavia* was located and partially salvaged.

1656: The Dutch East Indiaman *Vergulde Draeck,* sailing from Holland to Batavia with 78,600 guilders (mostly in Spanish pieces of eight), wrecked north of Fremantle, Australia. Salvage was attempted at the time of disaster and again in the 1960s by local treasure hunters, but a large amount of silver coins remain.

1712: The Dutch East Indiaman *Zuytdorp,* also spelled *Zuiddorp* (1,152 tons/1,170.5 tonnes), commanded by Captain Marinus

Dutch ships exploring the southern coast of Australia in 1642.

Wijsvliet and coming from Holland to Batavia with 250,000 guilders in treasure, wrecked on the west coast of Australia, about 40 miles (64 kilometers) north of the Murchinson River. Some survivors got ashore and inscribed their names and that of the ship on a rock. The wreck was first located in 1927 and has been partially salvaged.

1727: The Dutch East Indiaman *Zeewyk,* en route to Batavia from Holland, wrecked on Half Moon Reef in the Houtman Abrolhos chain of islands due to faulty navigation. She carried over 315,000 guilders in gold and silver specie, none of which has been recovered, although the site was located in recent years. The treasure probably lies deeply buried under shifting sands.

Sometime before 1809: An unidentified Portuguese merchantman, sailing from Lisbon to Macao with "a large amount of treasure," was lost off Pointe Cloates. It was found and partially salvaged in 1978.

1811: The American merchantman *Rapid* was lost near Pointe Cloates with a general cargo and an unknown amount of treasure on board, some of which was salvaged at the time of loss.

1852: The British merchantman *Eglington,* with 65,000 British gold sovereigns coins on board, was lost on North Beach about 20 miles (32 kilometers) north of Fremantle, Australia.

Diver using a special saw to cut sections of the Dutch East Indiaman *Batavia*, lost in 1629 on the Abrolhos Reef.

Bellarmine jugs and Spanish silver coins recovered from the Dutch East Indiaman *Gilt Dragon*, lost in 1656.

Underwater archaeologist from the Western Australian Museum preparing to blow up a section of the reef containing artifacts from a Dutch East Indiaman.

CHAPTER 29

PACIFIC OCEAN'S RICHEST SHIPWRECKS

Throughout the Colonial Period there was very little maritime traffic in the Pacific Ocean, so there are virtually no treasure wrecks in this immense body of water. The most notable traffic was on the trans-pacific route the Manila galleons plied for 250 years (1565–1815) between the Philippines and Acapulco, Mexico. I have a positive location for only four of the 230 Manila galleons that were lost. American whaling ships used the Pacific as their hunting grounds, but none carried treasure. None of the ship losses in the past two centuries can be considered treasure ships.

1568: The first loss of a Manila galleon was the *San Pablo* (750 tons/762 tonnes), carrying "a very large amount of treasure, porcelain and other goods," sailing between Cebu, Philippines, and Acapulco. She wrecked on the north end of Guam during a typhoon and a small number of survivors were rescued seven years later when another Manila galleon visited the island.

1581: An unidentified Portuguese East Indiaman, sailing between Malacca and Manila with a cargo valued at 455,000 crusadoes, was driven into the Pacific Ocean by a typhoon and wrecked on one of the Caroline Islands. Seven survivors lived on the deserted island for 22 years before being rescued by a vessel from Guam.

1603: The Manila galleon *Santa Margarita*, sailing between Manila and Acapulco with over 3 million pesos in Oriental treasure, was severely damaged in a typhoon in the north Pacific. Her captain decided to seek refuge in the Marianna Islands, and the ship wrecked

Earthenware jars, called "olive jars," were used on all Spanish ships during the Colonial Period. This one, found on Guam, is believed to have been thrown overboard from one of Magellan's ships, which anchored in that area in 1520.

on Tinian Island (north of Guam). Salvors came from Manila and recovered about 500,000 pesos of her treasures.

1638: The Manila galleon *Nuestra Señora de la Concepción* sailed from Manila with 2.25 million pesos in Oriental goods. Hit by a typhoon, she sought refuge in the Marianna Islands and was lost on Saipan Island. Intensive salvage on the wreck site in the three years following the disaster recovered about half of the lost treasure. Modern-day treasure hunters in 1987 and 1988 brought up more. Much of her treasure is believed to have slipped off into very deep water.

1690: The Manila galleon *Nuestra Señora del Pilar* was sailing between Acapulco and Manila with 2.2 million pesos in gold and silver bullion and specie. She had stopped at Guam to deliver supplies for Jesuit missionaries living there and, while rounding the southern tip of the island, she struck a reef. About 300,000 pesos in silver specie were removed, but before the rest could be saved, she slipped off into deep water just west of tiny Cocos Island. In 1987 I located the area where the ship struck on the reef and found some silver coins and artifacts, but was unable to get permission to locate the main section of the wreck in deep water.

1754: The Manila galleon *Nuestra Señora del Buen Viaje* was sailing between Manila and Acapulco with a cargo of Oriental treasures valued at over 2 million pesos when she was caught in a typhoon. After losing all her masts and rudder, she drifted for three months at the mercy of wind and waves before wrecking on the east side of Guam. I located his wreck in 1988, but the bulk of her treasure lies in several thousand feet of water just offshore. The Guam government refused permission to excavate.

1775: The Manila galleon *Nuestra Senora de la Concepción* (2,200 tons/2,235 tonnes), commanded by Captain Francisco David and sailing between Acapulco and Manila with gold and silver bullion and specie valued at 3.35 million pesos, wrecked in a typhoon on the east side of Tinian Island and was a total loss. Of the 478 souls on board, only 43 survived. Salvors from Manila recovered about one-third of the treasure and reported that the remainder had fallen into water too deep for recovery.

pars.
Quiuira
Cicuie
Tiguex
dos hermanos
Los Bolcanes.

abriga
La farfana
Restinga de
ladrones.
Humunu vel ya
di buoni segni
Zamal
uinangan
ARCHIPELA
GO DIS

Selected Bibliography

Archibald, E.H.H. *The Wooden Fighting Ship.* London: Blandford Press, 1968.

Bassetts, D.K. *The Trade of the English East India Company in the Far East.* London: Royal Asiatic Society, 1960.

Bell, A.C., and A. Gray. *Voyage of Francis Pyrard of Laval to the East Indies, the Maldives, the Moluccas and Brazil,* 3 vols. London: Hakluyt Society, 1887–1890.

Boxer, Charles R. *The Tragic History of the Sea 1589–1622.* London: Cambridge University Press, 1957.

______. *The Golden Age of Brazil.* Berkeley: University of California Press, 1962.

______. *The Dutch Seaborne Empire: 1600–1800.* New York: Alfred A. Knopf, 1965.

______. *The Portuguese Seaborne Empire: 1415–1825.* New York: Alfred A. Knopf, 1969.

Bruce, J. *Annals of the East India Company.* London: Royal Asiatic Society, 1810.

Bruijn, J.R. *Dutch-Asiatic Shipping in the 17th and 18th Centuries,* 3 vols. The Hague: Martinus Nijhoff Company, 1987.

Burman, J.L. *Great Shipwrecks on the Coast of Southern Africa.* Cape Town: C. Struik Company, 1967.

______. *Strange Shipwrecks of the Southern Seas.* Cape Town: C. Struik Company, 1968.

Casson, Lionel. *The Ancient Mariners.* New York: Macmillan, 1959.

______. *Ships and Seamanship in the Ancient World.* Princeton: Princeton University Press, 1971.

Chaunu, Huguette, and Pierre Chaunu. *Seville et l'Atlantique (1504–1650)*, 9 vols. Paris: SEVPEN, 1955.

Couta, Diogo de. *Decadas da Asia: 1602–1788*, 14 vols.Lisbon: Arquivo do Tombo, 1778–1788.

Duffy, James. *Shipwrecks and Empire.* Cambridge: Harvard University Press, 1955.

Duro, Fernandez Cesares de. *Naufragios de la Armada Espanola.* Madrid: Museo Naval, 1880.

______. *La Armada Espanola*, 9 vols.Madrid: Museo Naval, 1895–1903.

Esquemeling, John. *The Buccaneers of America.* London: Peter Balaguer & Son, 1684.

Faria y Sousa, Manuel de. *Asia Portuguesa*, 3 vols. Lisbon: 1665–1675.

Fonseca, Quirino da. *Os Portugueses no Mar e das Naus.* Lisbon: Academia das Ciencias de Lisboa, 1926.

______. *Diarios da Navegacao da Carreira da India.* Lisbon: Academia das Ciencias de Lisboa, 1938.

Furnivall, J.S. *Netherlands Indies.* Cambridge: Harvard University, 1944.

Glamann, K. *Dutch Asiatic Trade.* Copenhagen: University of Copenhagen, 1954.

Guilmartin, John F., Jr. *Galleons and Galleys.* London: Cassell & Co., 2002.

Hall, D.G.E. *History of South East Asia.* London: University of London Press, 1964.

Haring, C.H. *Trade and Navigation between Spain and the Indies in the Time of the Hapsburgs.* Cambridge: Harvard University Press, 1918.

Klerck, E.S. de. *History of the Netherlands East Indies*, 2 vols. Rotterdam: W.L. & J. Brusse, 1938.

Konstam, Angus. *The History of Shipwrecks.* New York: The Lyon Press, 1999.

Lattimore, Owen, and Eleanor Lattimore. *Silks, Spices and Empire.* New York: Delacorte Press, 1968.

Leur, J.C. van. *Indonesian Trade and Society.* The Hague: W. van Hoeve, 1955.

Linschoten, J.H. *His Discours of Voyages into ye East and West Indies.* London: 1598.

Marx, Jenifer G. *The Magic of Gold.* New York: Doubleday, 1978.

______. *Pirates and Privateers of the Caribbean.* Malabar: R.E. Krieger Publishing Co., 1991.

Marx, Robert F. *Following Columbus.* New York: World Publishing Co., 1964.

______. *The Battle of the Spanish Armada, 1588.* New York: World Publishing Co., 1965.

______. *The Battle of Lepanto, 1571.* New York: World Publishing Co., 1966.

______. *Treasure Fleets of the Spanish Main.* New York: World Publishing Co., 1968.

______. *Shipwrecks of the Virgin Islands and Puerto Rico.* San Juan: University of Puerto Rico, 1970.

______. *Shipwrecks in Mexican Waters.* Mexico City: CEDAM, 1971.

______. *Shipwrecks of the Western Hemisphere.* New York: World Publishing Company, 1971.

______. *The Underwater Dig: Manual of Underwater Archaeology.* New York: David McKay Co., 1975.

______. *Shipwrecks in Florida Waters.* Chuluota: Mickler House Publishers, 1985.

______. *Sunken Treasure: How to Find It.* Garland, TX: Ram Publishing Co., 1990.

______. *In the Wake of Galleons.* Falstaff: Best Publishing Co., 2001.

Marx, Robert F., and Jenifer G. Marx. *In Quest of the Great White Gods*. New York:, Crown Publishing Co., 1992.

Menzies, Gavin. *1421: The Year China Discovered America.* New York: William Morrow Co., 2002.

Milburn, W. *Oriental Commerce; Containing a Geographical Description of the Principal Places in the East Indies*, 2 vols. London: Black, Parry & Co., 1813.

Mill, James. *The History of British India*, 6 vols.London: Baldwin, Cradock, and Joy, 1826.

Pares, R. *War and Trade in the West Indies.* Oxford: Oxford University Press, 1936.

Parry, J.H. *The Spanish Seaborne Empire.* New York: Alfred A. Knopf, 1966.

______. *Trade and Dominion of the European Overseas Empires.* London: Weidenfeld & Nicolson, 1971.

Perez-Mallaina, Pablo E. *La Armada del Mar del Sur.* Seville: University of Seville, 1987.

Peterson, Mendel. *History under the Sea.* Washington: Smithsonian Institution Press, 1965.

______. *The Funnel of Gold.* Boston: Little, Brown & Co., 1975.

Renier, G.J. *The Dutch Nation.* London: Allen & Unwin, 1944.

Schurtz, William L. *The Manila Galleon.* New York: E.P. Dutton, 1939.

Temple, R.C. *Travels of Peter Mundy in Europe and Asia: 1608–1667*, 5 vols. London: The Hakluyt Society, 1907.

Theal, George McCall. *The Beginning of South Africa History.* London: University of London, 1902.

Turner, Malcolm. *Shipwrecks & Salvage in South Africa: 1505 to the Present.* Cape Town: C. Struik Company, 1988.

Veita Linaje, Joseph de. *Norte de la Contratacion de las Indias Occidentales.* Seville: Iuan Francisco de Blas, 1671.